PRESIDENTIAL WAR POWER

PRESIDENTIAL WAR POWER

Second Edition, Revised

Louis Fisher

University Press of Kansas

Published by the University Press of Kansas (Lawrence, Kansas 66049), which
was organized by the Kansas Board of Regents and is operated and funded by
Emporia State University, Fort Hays State University, Kansas State University,
Pittsburg State University, the University of Kansas, and Wichita State University

Library of Congress Cataloging-in-Publication Data

Fisher, Louis.
    Presidential war power / Louis Fisher. — 2nd ed., rev.
        p.   cm.
    Includes bibliographical references and index.
    ISBN 0-7006-1332-3 (cloth : alk. paper) — ISBN 0-7006-1333-1 (pbk. : alk. paper)
    1. War and emergency powers—United States. 2. National security—Law and
legislation—United States. 3. United States—Foreign relations—Law and
legislation.   I. Title.
KF5060.F57 2004
342.73'062—dc20

                                                                              2004001962

British Library Cataloguing-in-Publication Data is available.

Printed in the United States of America

10 9 8 7 6 5 4 3

The paper used in this publication meets the minimum requirements of the
American National Standard for Permanence of Paper for Printed Library Materials
Z39.48–1984.

To the republican principle
that reserves war-making
to the legislature

CONTENTS

PREFACE

The first edition of this book was treated to a lead review in the *New York Times Book Review* on May 7, 1995. The reviewer, Theodore Draper, noted that ever since the Korean War, "Presidents have been violating the Constitution of the United States." He wrote that I had "taken on all of the Presidents and their lawyers who have contrived for almost half a century to offer excuses for autonomous Presidential war-making," and called my book "a hygienic effort to bring us back to the law."

Those same goals motivate this second edition. The last nine years have underscored the extent to which the power of war has shifted to the presidency, with little restraint by Congress or the courts and little comprehension by the general public of the damage done to constitutional values, representative government, and democracy. The contemporary definition of executive power—to send troops anywhere in the world whenever the President likes—would have astonished the framers of the Constitution. Their structure of government very deliberately rejected the British models that gave the executive exclusive control over foreign affairs and the war power. Instead, the framers vested in Congress explicit control over the initiation and authorization of war, power over foreign commerce, approval of treaties, confirmation of ambassadors, power of the purse, and other authorities over external affairs.

The trend of presidential war power since World War II—the last congressionally declared war—collides with the constitutional framework adopted by the founding fathers. The period after 1945 created a climate in which Presidents have regularly breached constitutional principles and democratic values. Under these pressures (and invitations), Presidents have routinely exercised war powers with little or no involvement by Congress.

The scope of presidential war powers climbed to such heights that Congress felt compelled to pass the War Powers Resolution in 1973. Later, in 1980 and 1991, it adopted new statutory procedures to tighten legislative controls over covert actions. The Iran-Contra affair of the Reagan administration was not an aberration. It was merely a recent example of newly fashioned theories of executive power operating without effective checks from Congress, the judiciary, or the public. Numerous lawsuits, brought by members of Congress, were routinely sidestepped by federal judges who declined to place limits on presidential power.

So great is the magnitude of executive power that President George H. W. Bush invaded Panama in 1989 without any involvement by Congress, and he threatened to take military action against Iraq in 1991 solely on the basis of resolutions adopted by the UN Security Council. Only at the eleventh hour did he obtain authority from Congress. The willingness of President Bush to use military force in 1991 without congressional authorization provoked a grave challenge to constitutional government.

President Bill Clinton used military force repeatedly without ever seeking authority from Congress, intervening in Iraq, Somalia, Haiti, Bosnia, Sudan, Afghanistan, and Yugoslavia. President George W. Bush came to Congress twice to seek legislative action on the Use of Force Act of 2001 and the Iraq Resolution of 2002. However, he later announced that he ordered the use of military force under what he considered his constitutional authority, not authority granted by Congress.

To find a comparable threat to constitutional government we have to go back to 1950, when President Truman, on his own authority, ordered troops to Korea. Truman, Bush I, Clinton, and Bush II claimed they could send American troops into large-scale combat without first receiving authorization from Congress, and in each case they justified their position largely on the basis of resolutions adopted by the UN Security Council. When Clinton was unable to obtain authority from the UN for his war against Yugoslavia, he turned to NATO for "authority." In all of these actions, Presidents appealed to international or regional institutions rather than to Congress.

What are the constitutional sources for presidential war power? At what point is prior authorization by Congress required? Why has Congress failed to protect its constitutional prerogatives over questions of war and peace? What role do the federal courts have in policing the limits of executive power? How do we keep presidential power consistent with the Constitution and the intent of the framers? Those questions, of fundamental interest to the liberties of American citizens, drive this book.

The entire manuscript of the first edition was read by David Gray Adler and Loch Johnson, who offered a number of helpful suggestions. I appreciate their close reading and the many contributions they have made to the study of war powers over a period of years. Colleagues who read specific chapters include David Ackerman, Richard Best, Ellen Collier, Robert Gerber, Robert Goldich, Nancy Kassop, Leonard W. Levy, Robert Spitzer, and Duane Tananbaum. I gained much from their insights. Over the years

I have kept in touch with other scholars, including John Hart Ely, Michael Glennon, Louis Henkin, Edward Keynes, Harold Hongju Koh, Jules Lobel, John Norton Moore, Richard Pious, Robert Turner, and John Yoo. They are not responsible for what I have written, but in many ways they have sharpened and deepened my understanding of the constitutional relationships between Congress and the President. I am delighted to publish once again with the University Press of Kansas, which has published and encouraged an outstanding list of books on constitutional aspects of the presidency. At each stage of production the staff members maintained a remarkable level of professionalism and competence. For the first and second editions I appreciate the careful copyediting by Leslee C. Anderson.

A number of my articles, professional papers, and congressional testimony prepared the way for the first edition. In particular, I want to single out the following: "Foreign Policy Powers of the President and Congress," 499 *The Annals* 148 (1988); "The Foundations of a Scandal [Iran-Contra]," 3 *Corruption and Reform* 157 (1988); "Congressional Access to Executive Branch Information: Lessons from the Iran-Contra Affair," 6 *Government Information Quarterly* 383 (1989); "How Tightly Can Congress Draw the Purse Strings?" 83 *American Journal of International Law* 758 (1989); "The Legitimacy of the Congressional National Security Role," in *The Constitution and National Security* (National Defense University, 1990); "War Powers: The Need for Collective Judgment," in *Divided Democracy: Cooperation and Conflict between the President and Congress,* ed. James A. Thurber (1991); "The Power of Commander in Chief," in *The Presidency and the Persian Gulf War,* ed. Marcia Lynn Whicker et al. (1993); "Historical Survey of the War Powers and the Use of Force," in *The U.S. Constitution and the Power to Go to War: Historical and Current Perspectives,* ed. Gary M. Stern and Morton H. Halperin (1994); Congressional Checks on Military Initiatives," 109 *Political Science Quarterly* 739 (1994–95); and "The Korean War: On What Legal Basis Did Truman Act?" 89 *American Journal of International Law* 21 (1995).

Publications since that time have prepared the way for the second edition: "Clinton's Not King—War Is for Congress," *National Law Journal,* June 19, 1995, pp. A21–22; "What Power to Send Troops?" *New York Times,* December 2, 1995, p. 21; "President Clinton as Commander in Chief," in *Rivals for Power: Presidential-Congressional Relations,* ed. James A. Thurber (1996); "The Bosnia Commitment," *Legal Times,* March 11, 1996, pp. 22–23; Presidential Independence and the Power of the Purse," 3 *U.C. Davis Journal of International Law and Policy* 107 (1997); "Sidestepping Congress: Presidents Acting under the UN and NATO," 47 *Case Western Reserve*

Law Review 1237 (1997); "The War Powers Resolution: Time to Say Good-bye (with David Gray Adler), 113 *Political Science Quarterly* 1 (1998); "Military Action against Iraq," 28 *Presidential Studies Quarterly* 793 (1998); "Without Restraint: Presidential Military Initiatives from Korea to Bosnia," in *The Domestic Sources of American Foreign Policy,* ed. Eugene R. Wittkopf and James M. McCormick (1999); "Congress Sleeps: War Powers after Vietnam," 5 *The Long-Term View* 118 (2000); "Unchecked Presidential Wars," 148 *University of Pennsylvania Law Review* 1637 (2000); "Litigating the War Power with *Campbell* v. *Clinton,*" 30 *Presidential Studies Quarterly* 564 (2000); "Congress Controls Decisions over War or Peace," *Human Events,* February 25, 2002, pp. 3, 17; "Clinton's Military Actions: No Rivals in Sight," in *Rivals for Power: Presidential-Congressional Relations,* ed. James A. Thurber (2002); "The Road to Iraq," *Legal Times,* September 2, 2002, pp. 34–35; "The War Power: No Checks, No Balance," in *Congress and the Politics of Foreign Policy,* ed. Colton C. Campbell et al. (2003); "Military Tribunals: A Sorry History," 33 *Presidential Studies Quarterly* 484 (2003); and "Deciding on War Against Iraq: Institutional Failures," 118 *Political Science Quarterly* 389 (2003).

I have testified on a number of these issues before congressional committees. On February 23, 1994, I appeared before the House Permanent Select Committee on Intelligence to discuss the constitutionality of covert spending. Executive-legislative powers regarding national security were at stake when I testified before the Senate Select Committee on Intelligence on February 4 and 11, 1998, and before the House Permanent Select Committee on Intelligence on May 20, 1998. On April 17, 2002, I testified on war powers before the Senate Committee on the Judiciary. I have spoken on the issue of war powers at West Point; the Naval Academy; the National Defense University, Ft. McNair, Washington, D.C.; the U.S. War College, Carlisle Barracks, Pa.; and the Center for National Security Law, Charlottesville, Va. In 1987, I served as the Research Director of the House Iran-Contra Committee and wrote major sections of the final report dealing with institutional and constitutional issues.

Over three decades with Congressional Research Service have given me the opportunity to work closely with members of Congress, their staff, and legislative committees. The views expressed in this book are personal, not institutional.

NOTE ON CITATIONS

All court citations refer to published volumes whenever available: *United States Reports* (U.S.) for Supreme Court decisions, *Federal Reporter* (F.2d) for appellate decisions, and *Federal Supplement* (F.Supp.) for district court decisions. For cases not yet published in *United States Reports,* citations are to the *Supreme Court Reporter* (S.Ct.). There are also citations to *Opinions of the Attorney General* (Op. Att'y Gen.) and to *Opinions of the Office of Legal Counsel* (Op. O.L.C.) in the Justice Department. Decisions that focus primarily on federal rules of civil and criminal procedure appear in *Federal Rules Decisions* (F.R.D.). Congressional legal sources are to the U.S. Statutes at Large (Stat.), the U.S. Code (U.S.C.), and United States Treaties and Other International Agreements (UST or TIAS). Several standard reference works are abbreviated as follows:

Elliot	Jonathan Elliot, ed., The Debates in the Several State Conventions, on the Adoption of the Federal Constitution, 5 vols. (Washington, D.C., 1836–1845)
Farrand	Max Farrand, ed., The Records of the Federal Convention of 1787, 4 vols. (New Haven, Conn.: Yale University Press, 1937)
FRUS	Foreign Relations of the United States, official documentary historical record, prepared by the Historian of the Department of State, beginning in 1863 (Washington, D.C.: Government Printing Office)
Journals of the Continental Congress	Journals of the Continental Congress, 1774–1789, 34 vols. (Washington, D.C.: Government Printing Office, 1904–1937)
Landmark Briefs	Landmark Briefs and Arguments of the Supreme Court of the United States: Congressional Law, ed. Phillip B. Kurland and Gerhard Casper (Bethesda, Md.: University Publications of America)
Richardson	James D. Richardson, ed., A Compilation of the Messages and Papers of the Presidents, 20 vols. (New York: Bureau of National Literature, 1897–1925)

Thorpe   Francis Newton Thorpe, ed., The Federal and State Con-
                    stitutions, Colonial Charters and Other Organic Law, 7
                    vols. (Washington, D.C.: Government Printing Office,
                    1909)

Weekly Comp.   Weekly Compilation of Presidential Documents, pub-
Pres. Doc.   lished each week by the Government Printing Office
                    since 1965

1

THE CONSTITUTIONAL FRAMEWORK

When the framers assembled in Philadelphia in 1787 to draft the Constitution, existing models of government in Europe placed the war power securely in the hands of the monarch. The framers broke decisively with that tradition. Drawing on lessons learned at home in the American colonies and the Continental Congress, they deliberately transferred the power to initiate war from the executive to the legislature. The framers, aspiring to achieve the ideal of republican government, drafted a Constitution "that allowed only Congress to loose the military forces of the United States on the other nations."[1] In their deliberations at the constitutional convention, the delegates held fast to the principle of collective judgment, shared power in foreign affairs, and "the cardinal tenet of republican ideology that the conjoined wisdom of many is superior to that of one."[2]

The British Models

The English Parliament gained the power of the purse in the 1660s to control the king. The power to initiate war, however, remained a monarchical prerogative. John Locke's *Second Treatise on Civil Government* (1690) spoke of three branches of government: legislative, executive, and "federative." The last consisted of "the power of war and peace, leagues and alliances, and all the transactions with all persons and communities without the commonwealth." The federative power (what we call foreign policy today) was "always almost united" with the executive. Separating the executive and federative powers, Locke warned, would invite "disorder and ruin."[3]

A similar model appeared in the *Commentaries* written by Sir William

---

1. Edwin B. Firmage, "War, Declaration of," in 4 Encyclopedia of the American Presidency 1573 (Leonard W. Levy and Louis Fisher, eds. 1994).
2. David Gray Adler, "Foreign Policy and the Separation of Powers: The Influence of the Judiciary," in Judging the Constitution: Critical Essays on Judicial Lawmaking 158 (Michael W. McCann and Gerald L. Houseman, eds. 1989).
3. John Locke, Second Treatise on Civil Government, §§ 146–48 (1690).

Blackstone, the great eighteenth-century jurist. He defined the king's prerogative as "those rights and capacities which the king enjoys alone."[4] Some of the prerogatives he considered *direct*—those that are "rooted in and spring from the king's political person," including the right to send and receive ambassadors and the power to make war or peace.[5] By vesting in the king the sole prerogative to make war, individuals entering society gave up the private right to make war: "It would, indeed, be extremely improper, that any number of subjects should have the power of binding the supreme magistrate, and putting him against his will in a state of war."[6]

Through the exercise of Blackstone's prerogative the king could make "a treaty with a foreign state, which shall irrevocably bind the nation."[7] The king could issue letters of marque and reprisal (authorizing private citizens to undertake military actions). As Blackstone noted, that prerogative was "nearly related to, and plainly derived from, that other of making war."[8] Blackstone considered the king "the generalissimo, or the first in military command," who had "the sole power of raising and regulating fleets and armies."[9] Whenever the king exercised his lawful prerogative he "is, and ought to be absolute; that is, so far absolute, that there is no legal authority that can either delay or resist him."[10]

These models of executive power were well known to the framers. They knew that their forebears in England had committed to the executive the power to go to war. However, when they declared their independence from England, they vested *all* executive powers in the Continental Congress. They did not provide for a separate executive or a separate judiciary. The ninth article of the first national constitution, the Articles of Confederation, provided: "The United States, in Congress assembled, shall have the sole and exclusive right and power of determining on peace and war." The single exception to that principle lay in the sixth article, which allowed states to engage in war if invaded by enemies or when threatened with invasion by Indian tribes.

The authority of the Continental Congress extended to both "perfect" and "imperfect" wars—to wars that were formally declared by Congress and those that were merely authorized. As the Federal Court of Appeals noted in 1782, a perfect war "destroys the national peace and tranquillity,

4. 2 William Blackstone, Commentaries on the Laws of England 238 (1803).
5. Id. at 239.
6. Id. at 257.
7. Id. at 251.
8. Id. at 258.
9. Id. at 262.
10. Id. at 250.

and lays the foundation of every possible act of hostility," whereas an imperfect war "does not entirely destroy the public tranquillity, but interrupts it only in some particulars, as in the case of reprisals."[11] The power over perfect and imperfect wars lay with the Continental Congress and would remain with the U.S. Congress. The Constitution drafted in 1787 and ratified the next year not only empowered Congress to declare war but authorized it to grant "Letters of Marque and Reprisal." Congressional control over perfect and imperfect wars was recognized by the Supreme Court in litigation growing out of the Quasi-War with France from 1798 to 1800 (see Chapter 2).

The states gave their governors broad power over the military, but that power was directed to actions of self-defense. For example, the New Hampshire Constitution of 1784 provided that the president of the state "shall have full power" to lead and conduct the military forces

> to encounter, expulse, repel, resist and pursue by force of arms, as well as by land, within and without the limits of the state; and also to kill[,] slay, destroy, if necessary, and conquer by all fitting ways, enterprize and means, all and every such person and persons as shall, at any time hereafter, in a hostile manner, attempt or enterprize the destruction, invasion, detriment, or annoyance of the state; and to use and exercise over the army and navy, and over the militia in actual service, the law-martial in time of war, invasion, and also in rebellion, declared by the legislature to exist.[12]

Clearly these executive powers were directed at defensive operations in response to invasion from the outside or rebellion from the inside. Similar authority was given to the governor of Massachusetts in the Constitution of 1780.[13] The value of having states engage in self-defense is reflected in the U.S. Constitution, which prohibits states from engaging in war "unless actually invaded, or in imminent Danger as will not admit of delay."[14]

Opposing Monarchical Powers

During their learned and careful debates at the Philadelphia convention, the framers vested in Congress many of Locke's federative powers and

11. Miller v. The Ship Resolution, 2 Dall. (2 U.S.) 19, 20 (1782).
12. 4 Thorpe 2463–64.
13. 3 Thorpe 1901.
14. U.S. Const., Art. I, sec. 10.

Blackstone's royal prerogatives. Given the governmental systems operating worldwide in 1787, with power concentrated in the executive, the scope of power granted to Congress is extraordinarily progressive and democratic. The power to go to war was not left to solitary action by a single executive, but to collective decision making through parliamentary deliberations. Joseph Story, who served on the Supreme Court from 1811 to 1845, wrote about the essential republican principle of vesting in the representative branch the decision to go to war:

> The power of declaring war is not only the highest sovereign prerogative; . . . it is in its own nature and effects so critical and calamitous, that it requires the utmost deliberation, and the successive review of all the councils of the nations. War, in its best estate, never fails to impose upon the people the most burthensome taxes, and personal sufferings. It is always injurious, and sometimes subversive of the great commercial, manufacturing, and agricultural interests. Nay, it always involves the prosperity, and not unfrequently the existence, of a nation. It is sometimes fatal to public liberty itself, by introducing a spirit of military glory, which is ready to follow, wherever a successful commander will lead; . . . It should therefore be difficult in a republic to declare war; but not to make peace. . . . The cooperation of all the branches of the legislative power ought, upon principle, to be required in this the highest act of legislation.[15]

On numerous occasions the delegates to the constitutional convention emphasized that the power of peace and war associated with monarchy would not be given to the President. On June 1, 1787, Charles Pinckney said he was for "a vigorous Executive but was afraid the Executive powers of ⟨the existing⟩ Congress might extend to peace & war &c which would render the Executive a Monarchy, of the worst kind, towit an elective one."[16] John Rutledge wanted the executive power placed in a single person, "tho' he was not for giving him the power of war and peace."[17] Roger Sherman considered "the Executive magistracy as nothing more than an institution for carrying the will of the Legislature into effect."[18] James Wilson also preferred a single executive but "did not consider the Prerog-

15. 3 Joseph Story, Commentaries on the Constitution of the United States 60–61 (1833).
16. 1 Farrand 64–65.
17. Id. at 65.
18. Id.

atives of the British Monarch as a proper guide in defining the Executive powers. Some of these prerogatives were of a Legislative nature. Among others that of war & peace &c."[19]

Edmund Randolph worried about executive power, calling it "the foetus of monarchy." The delegates to the Philadelphia convention, he said, had "no motive to be governed by the British Governmt. as our prototype." If the United States had no other choice he might adopt the British model, but "the fixt genius of the people of America required a different form of Government."[20] Wilson agreed that the British model "was inapplicable to the situation of this Country; the extent of which was so great, and the manners so republican, that nothing but a great confederated Republic would do for it."[21]

In a lengthy speech on June 18, Alexander Hamilton set forth his principles of government. Although later associated with vigorous and independent presidential power, he too jettisoned the British model of executive prerogatives in foreign affairs and the war power. Explaining that in his "private opinion he had no scruple in declaring . . . that the British Govt. was the best in the world,"[22] he nonetheless discarded the Blackstonian and Lockean models. He proposed that the President would have "with the advice and approbation of the Senate" the power of making treaties, the Senate would have the "sole power of declaring war," and the President would be authorized to have "the direction of war when authorized or begun."[23]

By the time the framers completed their labors, the President had been stripped of the sole power to make treaties. Instead he shared that power with the Senate. As late as August 6, with about a month remaining at the convention, the constitutional draft gave the Senate exclusive power to make treaties and to appoint ambassadors. Only in early September was it agreed to include the President in these decisions.[24]

In Federalist No. 75, Hamilton noted that the act of making treaties "will be found to partake more of the legislative than of the executive character, though it does not seem strictly to fall within the definition of either of them." Treaties required legislative action because they were contracts with foreign nations with "the force of law." Although it might be appropriate

19. Id. at 65–66.
20. Id. at 66.
21. Id.
22. Id. at 288.
23. Id. at 292.
24. 2 Farrand 155, 169, 183, 297–98, 392–93, 495.

in hereditary monarchies to vest the treaty-making power with the executive, "it would be utterly unsafe and improper to intrust that power to an elective magistrate of four years' duration." The history of mankind could not support transferring such power "to the sole disposal of a magistrate created and circumstanced as would be a President of the United States."

The framers rejected the British model for the appointment power, since the British monarch not only appointed officers but created the offices as well. The drafters at Philadelphia wanted to avoid that concentration of power, with its potential for abuse and corruption. They granted the President the right to send and receive ambassadors, but only after the Senate agreed to his nominations. He had no power to issue letters of marque and reprisal; that power was now vested exclusively in Congress. Although the President was made Commander in Chief, it was left to Congress to raise and regulate fleets and armies. The rejection of Locke and Blackstone was decisive.

The extent of this break with English precedents is set forth clearly in *The Federalist Papers*. In Federalist No. 69, Hamilton explained that the President has "concurrent power with a branch of the legislature in the formation of treaties," whereas the British king "is the *sole possessor* of the power of making treaties." The royal prerogative in foreign affairs was deliberately shared with Congress, he noted. Hamilton contrasted the distribution of war powers in England and in the American Constitution. The power of the king "extends to the *declaring* of war and to the *raising* and *regulating* of fleets and armies." Unlike the king of England, the President "will have only the occasional command of such part of the militia of the nation as by legislative provision may be called into the actual service of the Union." No such tether was attached to the king.

Associated War Powers

Through the granting of letters of marque and reprisal, sovereigns were able to authorize private citizens to wage war on other countries. By turning to citizens (or privateers), nations could quickly augment their armies and navies and respond more swiftly and with greater force to emergencies and threats. Privately owned vessels were authorized to prey on foreign vessels and take plunder, or "prizes." The phrase "letters of marque and reprisal" came to refer to any use of force short of a declared war.

Unlike Blackstone, who recognized that the king had the power to issue letters of marque and reprisal, the framers transferred that responsibility solely to Congress and associated it with the power to declare war. Congress is given the power "To declare war, grant letters of Marque and Reprisal, and make rules concerning Captures on Land and Water." Any initiation of war, whether by declaration or by marque and reprisal, was reserved to Congress. Thus, both general and limited wars were left to the decision of the representative branch. In 1793, Secretary of State Thomas Jefferson related marque and reprisal to the power to wage war. The making of a reprisal on a nation, he said, "is a very serious thing. . . . when reprisal follows, it is considered an act of war, & never yet failed to produce it in the case of a nation able to make war." If it became necessary to invoke this power, "Congress must be called on to take it; the right of reprisal being expressly lodged with them by the constitution, & not with the executive."[25] Jules Lobel concludes that the marque and reprisal clause "probably was intended to cover all reprisals or uses of force against other nations short of declared war."[26]

Seven clauses of the Constitution vest war powers in Congress. Clause 11 empowers Congress to declare war, grant letters of marque and reprisal, and make rules concerning captures on land and water. Clauses 12 and 13 empower Congress to raise and support armies and provide and maintain a navy. Clauses 14, 15, and 16 authorize Congress to make rules for the government and regulations of the land and naval forces, to call forth the militia, and to provide for the organizing, arming, and disciplining of the militia. At the top of the list stands clause 10, which empowers Congress "to define and punish Piracies and Felonies committed on the high Seas, and Offenses against the Law of Nations."

This cluster of powers broke with prevailing theories that placed war powers, foreign affairs, and judgments on the law of nations with the Executive. Blackstone, for example, regarded the law of nations as part of the king's power. The law of nations consisted of "mutual compacts, treaties, leagues, and agreements" between various countries.[27] It was the king's prerogative to make treaties, leagues, and alliances with foreign states.

At the Philadelphia convention, Madison emphasized the importance of drafting a constitution that would "prevent those violations of the law of

25. 6 The Writings of Thomas Jefferson 259 (Paul Leicester Ford, ed. 1892–1899).

26. Jules Lobel, "'Little Wars' and the Constitution," 50 U. Miami L. Rev. 61, 70 (1995). A rebuttal to Lobel is grounded almost solely on historical incidents without reference to constitutional values or legal principles. C. Kevin Marshall, "Putting Privateers in Their Place: The Applicability of the Marque and Reprisal Clause to Undeclared Wars," 64 U. Chi. L. Rev. 953 (1997).

27. 1 Blackstone's Commentaries 43.

nations & of Treaties which if not prevented must involve us in the calamities of foreign wars."[28] One of the early statutes passed by Congress was legislation in 1790, setting forth punishments for certain crimes against the United States. One provision established fines and imprisonment for any person who attempted to prosecute or bring legal action against an ambassador or other public minister from another country. Persons who took such actions were deemed "violators of the laws of nations" who "infract the law of nations."[29] An action against ambassadors and public ministers "tends to provoke the resentment of the sovereign whom the ambassador represents, and to bring upon the state the calamities of war.[30]

Finally, the Constitution vests in Congress the power to regulate foreign commerce, an area with a direct relationship to the war power. Commercial conflicts between nations were often a cause of war. In *Gibbons* v. *Ogden* (1824), Chief Justice John Marshall said of the commerce power that "it may be, and often is, used as an instrument of war."[31] Guided by history, the framers placed that power with Congress.

Repelling Sudden Attacks

The debates at the Philadelphia convention reveal that the framers were determined to circumscribe the President's authority to take unilateral military actions. The early draft empowered Congress to "make war." Charles Pinckney objected that legislative proceedings "were too slow" for the safety of the country in an emergency, since he expected Congress to meet but once a year. Madison and Elbridge Gerry moved to insert "declare" for "make," leaving to the President "the power to repel sudden attacks." Their motion carried on a vote of 7 to 2. After Rufus King explained that the word "make" would allow the President to conduct war, which was "an Executive function," Connecticut changed its vote and the final tally became 8 to 1.[32]

There was little doubt about the limited scope of the President's war power. The duty to repel sudden attacks represents an emergency measure that permits the President to take actions necessary to resist sudden attacks either against the mainland of the United States or against American

28. 1 Farrand 316.
29. 1 Stat. 117–18, §§ 25–28 (1790).
30. 1 James Kent, Commentaries on American Law 170 (1826).
31. 22 U.S. (9 Wheat.) 1, 190 (1824).
32. 2 Farrand 318–19.

troops abroad. The President never received a general power to deploy troops whenever and wherever he thought best, and the framers did not authorize him to take the country into full-scale war or to mount an offensive attack against another nation. John Bassett Moore, a noted scholar of international law, made this observation:

There can hardly be room for doubt that the framers of the constitution, when they vested in Congress the power to declare war, never imagined that they were leaving it to the executive to use the military and naval forces of the United States all over the world for the purpose of actually coercing other nations, occupying their territory, and killing their soldiers and citizens, all according to his own notions of the fitness of things, as long as he refrained from calling his action war or persisted in calling it peace.[33]

Reactions to the Madison-Gerry amendment reinforce the narrow grant of authority to the President. Pierce Butler wanted to give the President the power to make war, arguing that he "will have all the requisite qualities, and will not make war but when the Nation will support it." Roger Sherman objected: "The Executive shd. be able to repel and not to commence war."[34] Gerry said he "never expected to hear in a republic a motion to empower the Executive alone to declare war."[35] George Mason spoke "agst giving the power of war to the Executive, because not ⟨safely⟩ to be trusted with it; . . . He was for clogging rather than facilitating war."[36]

Similar statements were made at the state ratifying conventions. In Pennsylvania, James Wilson expressed the prevailing sentiment that the system of checks and balances "will not hurry us into war; it is calculated to guard against it. It will not be in the power of a single man, or a single body of men, to involve us in such distress; for the important power of declaring war is vested in the legislature at large."[37] In North Carolina, James Iredell compared the limited powers of the President with those of the British monarch. The king of Great Britain was not only the Commander in Chief "but has power, in time of war, to raise fleets and armies. He has also authority to declare war." By contrast, the President "has not the power of declaring war by his own authority, nor that of rais-

33. 5 The Collected Papers of John Bassett Moore 196 (1944).
34. 2 Farrand 318.
35. Id.
36. Id. at 319.
37. 2 Elliot 528.

ing fleets of armies. These powers are vested in other hands."[38] In South Carolina, Charles Pinckney assured his colleagues that the President's powers "did not permit him to declare war."[39]

The framers gave Congress the power to initiate war because they believed that Presidents, in their search for fame and personal glory, would have an appetite for war.[40] John Jay warned in Federalist No. 4 that "absolute monarchs will often make war when their nations are to get nothing by it, but for purposes and objects merely personal, such as a thirst for military glory, revenge for personal affronts, ambition, or private compacts to aggrandize or support their particular families or partisans. These and a variety of other motives, which affect only the mind of the sovereign, often lead him to engage in wars not sanctified by justice or the voice and interests of his people."

Many of these sentiments appear in the writings of Madison. In 1793, he called war "the true nurse of executive aggrandizement. . . . In war, the honours and emoluments of office are to be multiplied; and it is the executive patronage under which they are to be enjoyed. It is in war, finally, that laurels are to be gathered; and it is the executive brow they are to encircle. The strongest passions and most dangerous weaknesses of the human breast; ambition, avarice, vanity, the honourable or venial love of fame, are all in conspiracy against the desire and duty of peace."[41] Five years later, in a letter to Jefferson, Madison said that the Constitution "supposes, what the History of all Govts demonstrates, that the Ex. is the branch of power most interested in war, & most prone to it. It has accordingly with studied care, vested the question of war in the Legisl."[42]

Separating Purse and Sword

The idea of keeping the purse and the sword in distinct hands was a bedrock principle for the framers. They were familiar with the efforts of English kings to rely on extraparliamentary sources of revenue for their military expeditions and other activities, with some of the payments coming from foreign governments. Because of these transgressions, England

---

38. 4 Elliot 107.
39. Id. at 287.
40. William Michael Treanor, "Fame, the Founding, and the Power to Declare War," 82 Corn. L. Rev. 695 (1997).
41. 6 The Writings of James Madison 174 (Gaillard Hunt, ed. 1900–1910).
42. Id. at 312.

lurched into a civil war and Charles I lost both his office and his head.[43] The rise of democratic government is directly related to legislative control over all expenditures, including those for foreign and military affairs.

The U.S. Constitution attempted to avoid the British history of civil war and bloodshed by vesting the power of the purse squarely in Congress. Under Article I, Section 9, "No Money shall be drawn from the Treasury, but in Consequence of Appropriations made by Law." In Federalist No. 48, Madison explained that "the legislative department alone has access to the pockets of the people." In Article I, Section 8, Congress is empowered to lay and collect taxes, duties, imposts, and excises; to borrow money on the credit of the United States; and to coin money and regulate its value. This power of the purse, said Madison in Federalist No. 58, represents the "most compleat and effectual weapon with which any constitution can arm the immediate representatives of the people, for obtaining a redress of every grievance, and for carrying into effect every just and salutary measure."

The framers did more than place the power of the purse in Congress. They deliberately divided government by making the President the Commander in Chief while reserving to Congress the decision to finance military operations. Madison insisted on keeping the power of Commander in Chief at arm's length from the power to take the nation to war. To protect constitutional liberties, the latter had to be reserved to Congress:

> Those who are to *conduct a war* cannot in the nature of things, be proper or safe judges, whether *a war ought* to be *commenced, continued,* or *concluded.* They are barred from the latter functions by a great principle in free government, analogous to that which separates the sword from the purse, or the power of executing from the power of enacting laws.[44]

This understanding of the war power was widely held. Thomas Jefferson praised the transfer of the war power "from the executive to the Legislative body, from those who are to spend to those who are to pay."[45] At the Philadelphia convention, George Mason counseled that the "purse & the sword ought never to get into the same hands 〈whether Legislative or Executive.〉"[46]

The fact that Congress was given express power to declare war did not

43. Paul Einzig, The Control of the Purse 57–62, 100–106 (1959).
44. 6 The Writings of James Madison 148 (emphasis in original).
45. 5 The Writings of Thomas Jefferson 123.
46. 1 Farrand 139–40.

mean that the President could prevail in undeclared wars. Whether declared or undeclared, the decision to initiate war was left to Congress. The framers were well aware that nations approved war either by declaration or authorization. In Federalist No. 25, Hamilton acknowledged that the "ceremony of a formal denunciation of war has of late fallen into disuse."

Commander in Chief

The framers empowered the President to be Commander in Chief, but that title must be understood in the context of military responsibilities that Congress authorizes. The language in the Constitution reads: The President shall be Commander in Chief of the Army and Navy of the United States, and of the Militia of the several States, when called into the actual Service of the United States." Congress, not the President, does the calling. Article I gives to Congress the power to provide "for calling forth the Militia to execute the Laws of the Union, suppress Insurrections and repel invasions."

In *Federalist* No. 74, Hamilton explained part of the purpose for making the President Commander in Chief. The direction of war "most peculiarly demands those qualities which distinguish the exercise of power by a single head." The power of directing war and emphasizing the common strength "forms a usual and essential part in the definition of the executive authority." In Federalist No. 69, Hamilton offered a modest definition of commander-in-chief powers, claiming that the office "would amount to nothing more than the supreme command and direction of the military and naval forces, as first general and admiral of the Confederacy." He knew better than that. As Washington's aide during the Revolutionary War, Hamilton understood that "command and direction" are more than clerical tasks. They can be powerful forces in determining the scope and duration of war.

Designating the President as Commander in Chief represented an important technique for preserving civilian supremacy over the military. The person leading the armed forces would be the civilian President, not a military officer. One of the complaints included in the Declaration of Independence was that King George III had "affected to render the Military independent of and superior to the Civil Power." General Thomas Gage, British commander during the war of independence, issued orders to prevent his officers from interfering with the civil administration.[47]

47. Clarence E. Carter, "The Office of Commander in Chief: A Phase of Imperial Unity on the Eve of the Revolution," in The Era of the American Revolution 209–10 (Richard B. Morris, ed. 1971).

Attorney General Edward Bates later explained in 1861 that the President is Commander in Chief not because he is "skilled in the art of war and qualified to marshal a host in the field of battle." He is Commander in Chief for a different reason. Whatever soldier leads U.S. armies to victory against an enemy, "he is subject to the orders of the *civil magistrate,* and he and his army are always 'subordinate to the civil power.'"[48] In 1895, the Supreme Court noted that the purpose of the commander-in-chief clause "is evidently to vest in the President the supreme command over all the military forces,—such supreme and undivided command as would be necessary to the prosecution of a successful war."[49]

Scholars have long disagreed whether the term Commander in Chief merely confers a title or implies additional powers for the President. Justice Robert Jackson underscored the elusive nature of this power by remarking that the commander-in-chief clause implies "something more than an empty title. But just what authority goes with the name has plagued presidential advisers who would not waive or narrow it by non-assertion yet cannot say where it begins or ends."[50] He noted that the commander-in-chief clause is sometimes put forth "as support for any presidential action, internal or external, involving the use of force, the idea being that it vests power to do anything, anywhere, that can be done with the army or navy."[51] To this proposition he said that nothing would be "more sinister and alarming than that a President whose conduct of foreign affairs is so largely uncontrolled, and often even is unknown, can vastly enlarge his mastery over the internal affairs of the country by his own commitment of the Nation's armed forces to some foreign venture."[52]

Some studies would construe the commander-in-chief clause narrowly. Raoul Berger concluded: "How narrowly the function was conceived may be gathered from the fact that in appointing George Washington Commander-in-Chief, the Continental Congress made sure . . . that he was to be 'its creature . . . in every respect.'" Berger notes that instructions drafted by the continental Congress in 1775 told Washington "punctually to observe and follow such orders and directions, from time to time, as you shall receive from this, or a future Congress of the United Colonies, or committee of Congress."[53]

48. 10 Op. Att'y Gen. 74, 79 (1861) (emphasis in original).
49. United States v. Sweeny, 157 U.S. 281, 284 (1895).
50. Youngstown Co. v. Sawyer, 343 U.S. 579, 641 (1952).
51. Id. at 641–42.
52. Id. at 642.
53. Raoul Berger, Executive Privilege 62 (1974); 2 Journals of the Continental Congress 96 (1905).

Citing these precedents is misplaced for two reasons. First, they ignore the extensive delegations that the Continental Congress soon found necessary. For example, three days later the Congress gave these liberal instructions to General Washington: "whereas all particulars cannot be foreseen, nor positive instructions for such emergencies so before hand given but that many things must be left to your prudent and discreet management, as occurrences may arise upon the place, or from time to time fall out, you are therefore upon all such accidents or any occasions that may happen, to use your best circumspection."[54] Second, the precedents are drawn from the wrong period. The office of President in 1787 was created as a separate, coequal, and independent branch, unlike its status under the Continental Congress (a mere agent of Congress).

Scholarly Analysis

Scholars on the war power generally agree that the framers broke with available monarchical models and vested in Congress the exclusive power to initiate hostilities against foreign nations. Taylor Reveley, writing in 1981, concluded that if you asked a man in the state of nature to read the war-powers provisions in the Constitution and compare them to governmental practices after 1789, "he would marvel at how much Presidents have spun out of so little. On its face, the text tilts decisively toward Congress."[55] Charles Lofgren, in a 1986 study, wrote that the constitutional grants of power to Congress to declare war and to issue letters of marque and reprisal "likely convinced contemporaries even further that the new Congress would have nearly complete authority over the commencement of war."[56] The years following ratification of the Constitution reinforced the impression that Americans "originally understood Congress to have at least a coordinate, and probably the dominant, role in initiating all but the most obviously defensive wars, whether declared or not."[57]

In 1993, John Hart Ely wrote a major work on the record of Congress in the Vietnam War. He said that when academics try to divine the "original understanding" of the Constitution, the results can be "obscure to the point

---

54. 2 Journals of the Continental Congress 101 (1905).

55. W. Taylor Reveley III, War Powers of the President and Congress: Who Holds the Arrows and Olive Branches 29 (1981).

56. Charles A. Lofgren, "Government from Reflection and Choice": Constitutional Essays on War, Foreign Relations, and Federalism 36 (1986).

57. Id. at 38.

of inscrutability," but when the dispute narrows to the war power, all wars—big or little, declared or undeclared—"had to be legislatively authorized."[58] To David Gray Adler, the Constitution "makes Congress the sole and exclusive repository of the ultimate foreign relations power—the authority to initiate war."[59]

Looking to the Constitution's textual grants of the war-making power to the President, Michael Glennon found them "paltry in comparison with, and are subordinate to, its grants to Congress."[60] He could discover "no evidence that the Framers intended to confer upon the President any independent authority to commit the armed forces to combat, except in order to repel sudden attacks."[61] In a similar vein, Harold Koh noted that the first three articles of the Constitution "expressly divided foreign affairs powers among the three branches of government, with *Congress,* not the president, being granted the dominant role."[62] The framers "pointedly denied" the President other grants of power, such as the power to declare war, "thereby rejecting the English model of a king who possessed both the power to declare war and the authority to command troops."[63]

In contrast to these studies, John Yoo wrote a major article in 1996 arguing that the framers constructed a constitutional system that "encourage[d] presidential initiative in war."[64] He claims that the Constitution's provisions on the war power "did not break with the tradition of their English, state, and revolutionary predecessors, but instead followed in their footsteps."[65] He concludes that "the war power provisions of the Constitution are best understood as an adoption, rather than a rejection, of the traditional British approach to war powers."[66] That argument contradicts not only statements made at the Philadelphia convention and the state ratification debates but also the text of the Constitution.[67]

---

58. John Hart Ely, War and Responsibility: Constitutional Lessons of Vietnam and Its Aftermath 3 (1993).

59. David Gray Adler, "Courts, Constitution, and Foreign Affairs," in The Constitution and the Conduct of American Foreign Policy 19 (David Gray Adler and Larry N. George eds. 1996).

60. Michael J. Glennon, Constitutional Diplomacy 72 (1990).

61. Id. at 81.

62. Harold Hongju Koh, The National Security Constitution: Sharing Power after the Iran-Contra Affair 75 (1990) (emphasis in original).

63. Id. at 76.

64. John C. Yoo, "The Continuation of Politics by Other Means: The Original Understanding of War Powers," 84 Cal. L. Rev. 167, 174 (1996).

65. Id. at 197.

66. Id. at 242.

67. For closer analysis of Yoo's argument, see Louis Fisher, "Unchecked Presidential Wars," 148 U. Pa. L. Rev. 1637, 1658–68 (2000).

Over the next two centuries, a number of incidents were invoked by Presidents and their supporters to expand the President's potential for making war over the formal power of Congress for declaring war. In the nineteenth century, Presidents resorted to military force for the announced purpose of protecting American lives and property—actions that would be cited as a legal source for enlarging executive power. The concept of "defensive war" was stretched to justify presidential war-making throughout the world. Other developments in the twentieth century, including military security treaty provisions and the UN Charter, were used to inflate the President's war power beyond the intentions of the framers and beyond the control of Congress and the public.

2

PRECEDENTS FROM 1789 TO 1900

Presidential use of force during the first few decades after the Philadelphia convention conformed closely to the expectations of the framers. The decision to go to war or to mount offensive actions remained with Congress. Presidents accepted that principle for all wars: declared or undeclared. At first narrowly confined, the scope of presidential action gradually widened. Presidential movement of troops and vessels could provoke war, as in Mexico, and Presidents began to use force abroad to "protect American lives and property." Gradually the executive branch claimed for the President the power to initiate war and determine its magnitude and duration.

Indian Wars

The first exercise of the commander-in-chief clause involved actions by President Washington against certain Indian tribes, actions explicitly authorized by Congress. On September 29, 1789, Congress passed legislation "for the purpose of protecting the inhabitants of the frontiers of the United States from the hostile incursions of the Indians." To provide that protection, Congress authorized the President "to call into service from time to time, such part of the militia of the states respectively, as he may judge necessary for the purpose aforesaid."[1] In 1790 and again in 1791, Congress passed new authorizations to protect inhabitants in the frontiers.[2]

In response to the 1789 authorization, President Washington wrote to Governor Arthur St. Clair and gave him instructions to implement the statute. Washington's first preference was to arrange a cessation of hostilities and a peace treaty. If that could not be arranged, St. Clair was to call upon the nearest counties of Virginia and Pennsylvania for detachments of militia.[3] Two years later St. Clair's troops suffered a disastrous loss to the Indians. President Washington promptly notified Congress, promising a

---

1. 1 Stat. 96, sec. 5 (1789).
2. 1 Stat. 121, sec. 16 (1790); 1 Stat. 222 (1791).
3. 30 The Writings of George Washington 430 (John C. Fitzpatrick, ed. 1939).

further communication "of all such matters as shall be necessary to enable
the Legislature to judge of the future measures which it may be proper to
pursue."[4]

St. Clair's defeat triggered the first major congressional investigation. On
March 27, 1792, the House of Representatives considered a resolution to
request President Washington "to institute an inquiry into the causes of the
late defeat of the army under the command of Major General St. Clair."[5]
After debating the resolution, it was decided that the House, as "the grand
inquest of the nation," should conduct the inquiry and not the President.[6]
The resolution requesting the President to institute the inquiry was defeated, 35 to 21. Congress authorized the appointment of a committee to
inquire "into the causes of the failure of the late expedition under Major
General St. Clair; and that the said committee be empowered to call for
such persons, papers, and records, as may be necessary to assist their
inquiries."[7]

According to the account of Thomas Jefferson, President Washington
convened his Cabinet to determine the extent to which the House could
call for papers from the executive branch. The Cabinet considered and
agreed that the House "was an inquest, and therefore might institute
inquiries . . . [and] might call for papers generally." Moreover, the President
"ought to communicate such papers as the public good would permit, and
ought to refuse those, the disclosure of which would injure the public:
consequently were to exercise a discretion." Having laid the seeds of executive privilege, the Cabinet then decided that there was not a paper "which
might not be properly produced."[8] The congressional committee examined
papers furnished by the executive branch, listened to explanations from
department heads and other witnesses, and received a written statement
from General St. Clair.[9]

Throughout this period the executive branch understood that its military
operations against Indians were limited to defensive actions. In one message, President Washington referred to military operations "offensive or
defensive," but the full text of his message is designed to avoid any executive initiative in war-making and to limit military actions to defensive

4. Id. at 442.

5. Annals of Cong., 2d Cong., 1–2 Sess. 490 (1792).

6. Id. at 491.

7. Id. at 493.

8. 1 The Writings of Thomas Jefferson 303–5 (Albert Ellery Bergh, ed. 1903).

9. Annals of Cong., 2d Cong., 1–2 Sess. 601–2, 877, 895, 907, 1052–59, 1106–13, 1309–
17 (1792–1793).

measures.[10] Secretary of War Henry Knox wrote to Governor William Blount on October 9, 1792: "The Congress which possess the powers of declaring War will assemble on the 5th of next Month—Until their judgments shall be made known it seems essential to confine all your operations to defensive measures."[11] The following month Knox again wrote to Blount:

> All your letters have been submitted to the President of the United States. Whatever may be his impression relatively to the proper steps to be adopted, he does not conceive himself authorized to direct offensive operations against the Chickamaggas. If such measures are to be pursued they must result from the decisions of Congress who solely are vested with the powers of War.[12]

President Washington held consistently to this policy. Writing in 1793, he said that any offensive operations against the Creek Nation must await congressional action: "The Constitution vests the power of declaring war with Congress; therefore no offensive expedition of importance can be undertaken until after they have deliberated upon the subject, and authorized such a measure."[13]

In 1795, Knox informed Blount that President Washington had waited for the results of congressional deliberations on Indian policy, and that Congress had appropriated $50,000 for opening trade with the Indians and $130,000 for defensive protection of the frontiers. "All ideas of offensive operations," said Knox, "are therefore to be laid aside and all possible harmony cultivated with the Indian Tribes."[14] When Blount suggested that Congress might order an army to "humble, if not destroy the Creek Nation," Knox told him firmly that Congress was determined to avoid a direct or indirect war with the Creeks: "Congress alone are competent to decide upon an offensive war, and congress have not thought fit to authorize it."[15]

This sensitivity to congressional prerogatives is reflected in other executive documents during this early period. In a message of Congress on

10. 1 American State Papers: Indian Affairs 97 (1832).
11. 4 The Territorial Papers of the United States 195 (Clarence Edwin Carter, ed. 1936).
12. Id. at 220–21.
13. 33 The Writings of George Washington 73.
14. 4 The Territorial Papers of the United States 387.
15. Id. at 389. See also Francis Paul Prucha, The Sword of the Republic: The United States Army on the Frontier, 1783–1846, at 46–47 (1969), and Wiley Sword, President Washington's Indian War: The Struggle for the Old Northwest, 1790–1795 (1985).

November 16, 1818, President Monroe reviewed the military conflicts involving Indians in the Floridas. He described a number of battles, constituting self-defense, and why it was sometimes necessary to exceed boundaries while pursuing the enemy.[16] He also explained his instructions to Major-General Andrew Jackson to enter Florida in pursuit of the Seminoles without encroaching on the rights of Spain. On one occasion, however, Jackson found it necessary to seize Spanish posts with war materials to prevent their use by the Indians.[17] Monroe emphasized that in entering Florida "no idea was entertained of hostility to Spain." To preserve amicable relations between the United States and Spain, the posts were returned. Monroe recognized that the decision to go from peace to war belonged to Congress: "By ordering the restitution of the posts those relations are preserved. To a change of them the power of the Executive is deemed incompetent; it is vested in Congress only."[18]

As the years progressed, the distinction between defensive and offensive actions on Indian policy gradually blurred. The national government began using military force to drive Indians off their lands and into reservations, where they would be dependent upon the United States.[19] Presidential policies of restraint carried only so much weight in a country that was expanding in size and highly decentralized. State militias and citizen-soldiers acted with substantial autonomy, even to the extent of ignoring presidential proclamations on Indian Policy.[20]

President as "Sole Organ"

The President's function in communicating with other nations is sometimes interpreted as giving the President an upper hand in foreign affairs. From this alleged authority over foreign affairs are drawn additional powers that extend to presidential war-making. For example, Jefferson Powell states that the Constitution, "as Jefferson interpreted it, thus confirmed President Washington's view that foreign policy is an executive preroga-

16. 2 Richardson 610–11.
17. Id. at 611.
18. Id. at 612.
19. Francis Paul Prucha, The Great Father: The United States Government and the American Indians 534–61 (1984).
20. John K. Mahon, "Indian-United States Military Situation, 1775–1848," in 4 Handbook of North American Indians 150, 152 (William C. Sturtevant, ed. 1988).

tive."[21] If one accepts that the President has a prerogative over foreign affairs, it can next be argued that the President may initiate military operations to fulfill the foreign policy. Powell contends that the President possesses the "ability to warn of, or threaten, the use of military force" because that power "is an ordinary and essential element in the toolbox of that branch of government empowered to formulate and implement foreign policy."[22]

Yet Powell later acknowledges that Jefferson offered a more modest position: "except where the Constitution expressly provides otherwise, the conduct of foreign affairs is exclusively executive."[23] The source of this argument is a statement by Jefferson in 1790, when he served as Secretary of State:

> The transaction of business with foreign nations is Executive altogether. It belongs then to the head of that department, *except* as to such portions of it as are submitted to the Senate. *Exceptions* are to be construed strictly. The Constitution itself indeed has taken care to circumscribe this one within very strict limits: for it gives the *nomination* of the foreign Agent to the President, the *appointment* to him and the Senate jointly, the *commissioning* to the President.[24]

Advocates of presidential power love the line "The transaction of business with foreign nations is Executive altogether." There is something grandiose and sweeping about the language, or at least it appears that way. But those who champion presidential power make too much of Jefferson's sentence. As Powell explains, Jefferson was writing about a very narrow dispute concerning the Senate's role in the appointment of ambassadors and consuls. President Washington had asked Jefferson whether the Senate had a right to veto not only the person to be appointed but also the *grade* the President might want to use for the foreign mission. Jefferson concluded that if the Constitution intended to give the Senate a negative over the grade, "it would have said so in direct terms, and not left it to be effected by a sidewind."[25] In responding to this specific issue, Jefferson had no cause to address the larger role of Congress or the particular prerogatives of the House, such as the power to grant or withhold legislation and appro-

21. H. Jefferson Powell, The President's Authority over Foreign Affairs 45–46 (2002).
22. Id. at 119.
23. Id. at 60.
24. 16 The Papers of Thomas Jefferson 379 (Boyd, ed. 1961) (emphasis in original).
25. Id. at 380.

priations. He knew enough about those powers to persuade President Washington not to try to circumvent the House on a treaty with Algiers.[26]

Second, the passage speaks of "transactions," which means some form of communication between two parties. Read Jefferson's language as expansively as you like and it hardly gives the President primacy over foreign policy, much less a foothold to exercise military power unilaterally. At best it says that whenever Congress and the President have acted jointly to formulate foreign policy, it is the President who communicates, transmits, and explains that policy to other nations. Of course the President can initiate policies on his own, such as the Monroe Doctrine, but those statements of national policy survive only with congressional support or acquiescence. Presidential announcements on foreign policy can be revoked or modified at any time by Congress.

Advocates of independent presidential power over foreign affairs and the war power also cite a remark by John Marshall in 1800, when he served in the House of Representatives. In a debate over whether President John Adams should be impeached, Marshall said that the President "is the sole organ of the nation in its external relations and its sole representative with foreign nations."[27] The concept of the President as "sole organ" would later be popularized by the Supreme Court in the 1936 *Curtiss-Wright* case (see pp. 72–73). But Marshall never claimed a broad, independent power for the President or anything close to primacy in foreign affairs, much less in military initiatives. As will soon be noted, Marshall's performance as Chief Justice of the Supreme Court flatly eliminates that interpretation.

The Whiskey Rebellion

The Whiskey Rebellion of 1794 marks the first time a President called out the militia to suppress a domestic insurrection. In using troops, President Washington acted expressly on authority delegated to him by Congress. Legislation in 1792 provided that whenever the United States "shall be invaded, or be in imminent danger of invasion from any foreign nation or Indian tribe," the President may call forth the state militias to repel such invasions and to suppress insurrections.[28] The statute introduced a novel way of monitoring and checking presidential actions. Whenever the laws of the United States were opposed and their execution obstructed in any

---

26. Louis Fisher, The Politics of Executive Privilege 30–33 (2004).
27. Annals of Cong., 6th Cong. 613 (1800).
28. 1 Stat. 264, sec. 1 (1792).

state, "by combinations too powerful to be suppressed by the ordinary course of judicial proceedings, or by the powers vested in the marshals by this act," the President would have to be first notified of that fact by an Associate Justice of the Supreme Court or by a federal district judge. Only after such notice could the President call forth the militia of the state to suppress the insurrection.[29]

After Congress enacted a federal excise tax on distilled whiskey in 1791, farmers in western Pennsylvania resorted to violence to resist the revenue measure. There was fear that the rebellion would spread to other states. In a proclamation issued September 15, 1792, President Washington warned those who were resisting the law that it was his duty "to take care that the laws be faithfully executed" and directed all courts, magistrates, and officers to see that the laws were obeyed.[30] In 1794 he issued another proclamation, itemizing a long list of abuses against federal agents and stating that he had put into effect the procedures established by the militia statute of 1792. President Washington gave Justice James Wilson the evidence needed to verify the rebellion and received from Wilson a certification that ordinary legal means were insufficient to execute national law.[31] Washington called forth the militias of four states to put down the rebellion. District Judge Richard Peters joined Alexander Hamilton and District Attorney William Rawle in accompanying the troops. Hamilton and Rawle conducted hearings before Peters to identify the instigators, who were later tried in Philadelphia.[32]

Quasi-War with France

Much has been made of the President's authority to engage the country in undeclared wars, such as the "quasi-war" with France in 1798–1800. In a major legal defense of the Vietnam War, the State Department in 1966 remarked: "Since the Constitution was adopted there have been at least 125 instances in which the President has ordered the armed forces to take action or maintain positions abroad without obtaining prior congressional authorization, starting with the 'undeclared war' with France (1798–1800)."[33] Many of those "instances" will be analyzed in subsequent chapters, but the

29. Id., sec. 2.
30. 1 Richardson 116–17.
31. Id. at 150–52.
32. Homer Cummings and Carl McFarland, Federal Justice 43–45 (1937).
33. 54 Dep't of State Bull. 474, 484 (1966).

reference to war with France is clearly false. Congress debated the prospect of war openly and enacted a number of bills to put the country on a war footing.

President John Adams did not decide that he could, on his own authority, go to war against France. He asked Congress to prepare the country for war. While pledging to pursue negotiations toward a peaceful resolution, political conditions abroad compelled him to recommend to Congress "effectual measures of defense."[34] Congress carefully debated these bills, enacting several dozen to support military action by the President. A series of statutes granted supplemental funds for a naval armament, increased the number of ships, authorized another regiment of artillerists and engineers, reinforced the defense of ports and harbors, funded additional cannons, arms, and ammunition, empowered the President to raise a provisional army and seize French ships, and suspended commerce with France. Congress also terminated the 1778 treaty of amity and commerce with France.[35]

Although war was never formally declared, no one doubted that Congress had acted to authorize war. During the debates in 1798, Edward Livingston (D-N.Y.) considered the country "now in a state of war; and let no man flatter himself that the vote which has been given is not a declaration of war."[36] Attorney General Charles Lee, after taking into account the laws that Congress had passed, advised President Adams that "there exists not only an *actual* maritime war between France and the United States, but a maritime war *authorized* by both nations."[37] In a letter to Secretary of State John Marshall on September 4, 1800, Adams wondered whether it was necessary for him to ask Congress to make a general declaration of war against France. Congress had already, in Adams's judgment, "as well as in the opinion of the [Supreme Court] judges at Philadelphia, declared war within the meaning of the Constitution against that republic, under certain restrictions and limitations."[38]

Alexander Hamilton, always protective of executive authority, understood the limits of presidential power in the Quasi-War. Congress passed legislation on May 28, 1798, authorizing the President to seize armed French vessels.[39] He was asked what American ship commanders could do

34. 1 Richardson 226.
35. 1 Stat. 547–611 (1798).
36. 8 Annals of Congress 1519 (1798).
37. 1 Op. Att'y Gen. 84 (1798) (emphasis in original).
38. 9 The Works of John Adams 81 (Charles Francis Adams, ed. 1854).
39. 1 Stat. 561 (1798).

prior to the enactment of that bill. Hamilton was "not ready to say that [the President] has any other power than merely to employ" ships with authority "to *repel* force by *force* (but not to capture), and to repress hostilities within our waters including a marine league from our coasts." Any actions beyond those measures "must fall under the idea of *reprisals* & requires the sanction of that Department which is to declare or make war."[40]

By prompting several judicial decisions, the Quasi-War clarified the prerogatives of Congress over war and the deployment of military force. In 1800 and 1801 the Supreme Court recognized that Congress could authorize hostilities in two ways: either by a formal declaration of war or by statutes that authorized an undeclared war, as had been done against France. Military conflicts could be "limited," "partial," and "imperfect" without requiring Congress to make a formal declaration. In the first case, Justice Samuel Chase noted: "Congress is empowered to declare a general war, or congress may wage a limited war; limited in place, in objects, and in time. . . . congress has authorised hostilities on the high seas by certain persons in certain cases. There is no authority given to commit hostilities on land."[41] In the second case, Chief Justice John Marshall wrote for the Court: "The whole powers of war being, by the constitution of the United States, vested in congress, the acts of that body can alone be resorted to as our guides in this inquiry."[42]

Those cases do not imply that once Congress authorizes war, the President is at liberty to choose the time, location, and scope of military activities. In authorizing war, Congress may place limits on what Presidents may and may not do. Part of the legislation in the 1798–1800 period authorized the President to seize vessels sailing *to* French ports. President Adams exceeded the statute by issuing an order directing American ships to capture vessels sailing *to or from* French ports. Captain George Little followed Adams's order by seizing a Danish ship sailing from a French port. He was sued for damages, and the case came to the Supreme Court.

Chief Justice Marshall, writing for the Court, admitted that the case gave him much difficulty. He confessed that the "first bias" of his mind was very strongly in favor of the opinion that although the instructions from President Adams "could not give a right, they might yet excuse [a military officer] from damages." Initially, Marshall assumed an "implicit obedience, which military men usually pay to the orders of their superiors, which

---

40. 21 The Papers of Alexander Hamilton 461–62 (Harold C. Syrett, ed. 1974) (emphasis in original).

41. Bas v. Tingy, 4 U.S. 37, 43 (1800).

42. Talbot v. Seeman, 5 U.S. 1, 28 (1801).

indeed is indispensably necessary to every military system." To Marshall, that system of military hierarchy seemed to justify the actions of Captain Little, "who is placed by the laws of his country in a situation which in general requires that he should obey them." And yet on further reflection Marshall decided that Little could be sued for damages: "I have been convinced that I was mistaken, and I have receded from this first opinion. I acquiesce in that of my brethren, which is, that the instructions [by Adams] cannot change the nature of the transaction, or legalize an act which, without those instructions, would have been a plain trespass."[43]

In short, congressional policy announced in a statute necessarily prevails over inconsistent presidential orders and military actions. Presidential orders, even those issued as Commander in Chief, are subject to restrictions imposed by Congress.

In the case of Captain Little, Congress later decided that he should not have been liable for following a presidential order and in 1807 passed a private bill to reimburse him for the damages awarded against him.[44] The legislative history provides no reasons for the congressional action.[45] Congress may have concluded that federal law failed to adequately distinguish between lawful orders and unlawful orders. In 1789, Congress had directed military officers "to observe and obey the orders of the President of the United States."[46] Legislation in 1799 provided that any officer "who shall disobey the orders of his superior . . . on any pretense whatsoever" shall be subject to death or other punishment.[47] Not until 1800, after Captain Little had seized the vessel, did Congress clarify the duty of military officers. They were not to carry out any and all commands. Instead, they were specifically prohibited from executing "unlawful orders" issued by superior officers.[48]

Neutrality Act Prosecutions

During this period, federal courts decided a Neutrality Act case that also restricted presidential war power. President Washington issued his Proclamation of Neutrality in 1793 because he was concerned that military ini-

43. Little v. Barreme, 6 U.S. (2 Cr.) 169, 179 (1804).
44. 6 Stat. 63 (1807).
45. Annals of Cong., 9th Cong., 2d Sess., 230–31 (1806), 253, 260–61, 29, 30, 31, 32 (1807).
46. 1 Stat. 96, sec. 3 (1789).
47. 1 Stat. 711, sec. 24 (1799).
48. 2 Stat. 47 (1800) (Art. 14).

tiatives by private citizens might embroil the United States in the war between France and England.[49] Such private actions would undermine the constitutional powers of Congress. As Jefferson noted in private correspondence:

> . . . if one citizen has a right to go to war of his own authority, every citizen has the same. If every citizen has that right, then the nation (which is composed of all its citizens) has a right to go to war, by the authority of its individual citizen. But this is not true either on the general principles of society, or by our Constitution, which gives that power to Congress alone.[50]

Washington's proclamation raised a delicate issue: did it encroach upon the power of Congress to decide questions of war and peace? Washington asked his Cabinet whether he should call Congress back in special session to deal with this issue, but they advised against it.[51] His Secretary of the Treasury, Alexander Hamilton, responded to the legal attacks directed against the proclamation. Writing under the pseudonym "Pacificus," Hamilton argued that the management of foreign affairs was vested in the President, who is "the *organ* of intercourse between the nation and foreign nations [and] the *interpreter* of the national treaties."[52] To say the proclamation represented the enactment of new law was "entirely erroneous," Hamilton insisted. It only announced a fact and informed citizens of what previous laws required.[53] Hamilton's position was modest: the President could proclaim neutrality to keep the peace, waiting until Congress decided to change a condition of peace to a state of war.

In a series of essays signed "Helvidius," James Madison rebuked Hamilton for borrowing a theory of government based on British royal prerogatives. Under Hamilton's interpretation of executive power, Madison warned, "no citizen could any longer guess at the character of the government under which he lives."[54] Madison was particularly disturbed by Hamilton's view of presidential power:

49. 32 The Writings of George Washington 416 (letter to Secretary of the Treasury Alexander Hamilton, April 12, 1793).

50. 9 The Writings of Thomas Jefferson 189 (Bergh, ed.) (letter to Gouverneur Morris, August 16, 1793).

51. 32 The Writings of George Washington 420–21 n. 14.

52. 4 The Works of Alexander Hamilton 437 (Henry Cabot Lodge, ed. 1904) (emphasis in original).

53. Id. at 444.

54. 6 The Writings of James Madison 152 (Gaillard Hunt, ed. 1900–1910).

In no part of the constitution is more wisdom to be found, than in the clause which confides the question of war and peace to the legislature, and not to the executive department. . . . War is in fact the true nurse of executive aggrandizement. In war, a physical force is to be created; and it is the executive will, which is to direct it. In war, the public treasures are to be unlocked; and it is the executive hand which is to dispense them. In war, the honours and emoluments of office are to be multiplied; and it is the executive patronage under which they are to be enjoyed. It is in war, finally, that laurels are to be gathered; and it is the executive brow they are to encircle. . . .

Hence it has grown into an axiom that the executive is the department of power most distinguished by its propensity to war: hence it is the practice of all states, in proportion as they are free, to disarm this propensity of its influence.[55]

Washington's attempt at lawmaking contained a built-in check: enforcement of the proclamation needed statutory backing. When Gideon Henfield was prosecuted for violating the proclamation, he was acquitted because jurors rebelled against the idea of convicting someone for a crime established by a proclamation.[56] With no statute to cite, the government dropped other prosecutions.[57] After Congress returned in December, Washington told the two Houses that it rested with "the wisdom of Congress to correct, improve, or enforce" the policy his proclamation had established. It would be expedient "to extend the legal code" and the jurisdiction of federal courts in order to have effective enforcement, he added.[58]

In short, he needed law from the legislative branch. Congress responded by passing the Neutrality Act of 1794, giving the administration the firm legal footing it needed to prosecute violators. The Neutrality Act prohibited the exportation of any articles of war. Prohibited articles found on board a vessel would be forfeited, and if articles of war were exported to a foreign country, the vessel could be seized and the captain fined.[59] Congress also prohibited American citizens from accepting a commission to serve "a foreign prince or state in war by land or sea."[60] Nor could per-

55. Id. at 174.
56. Francis Wharton, State Trials of the United States during the Administrations of Washington and Adams 84–85, 88 (1849); Henfield's Case, 11 F. Cas. 1099 (C.C. Pa. 1793) (No. 6,360).
57. 2 John Marshall, The Life of George Washington 273 (1832).
58. Annals of Cong., 3d Cong., 1–2 Sess. 11 (1793).
59. 1 Stat. 369–70 (1794).
60. Id. at 381–82.

sons within the United States provide ships of war to be used by a foreign prince or state "to cruise or commit hostilities upon the subjects, citizens or property of another foreign prince or state with whom the United States are at peace."[61] Furthermore, persons within the territory or jurisdiction of the United States were prohibited from providing assistance to "any military expedition or enterprise to be carried on from thence against the territory or dominions of any foreign prince or state with whom the United States are at peace."[62]

Litigation tested Washington's neutrality policy. When French privateers seized vessels owned by citizens from England and other countries, those actions were challenged in American courts. However, federal district courts dismissed these cases for lack of jurisdiction, primarily because they were reluctant to decide, at their level, the novel legal issues that were presented. In 1794, the Supreme Court supplied some clarity to this area by holding that district courts had jurisdiction to hear these cases and that foreign nations had no authority to create courts within the jurisdiction of the United States to decide admiralty disputes.[63]

President Jefferson recognized the extreme danger of allowing private citizens to decide by themselves to deploy armed forces. In his fourth annual message he referred to complaints that persons residing within the United States had used armed merchant vessels in defiance of the laws of other countries: "That individuals should undertake to wage private war, independently of the authority of their country, can not be permitted in a well-ordered society."[64] The tendency, he said, was "to produce aggression on the laws and rights of other nations and to endanger the peace of our own."[65]

Numerous violations of the Neutrality Act came before the federal courts. In one of the significant cases defining the power of Congress to restrict presidential action, a circuit court in 1806 reviewed the indictment of Colonel William S. Smith for engaging in military actions against Spain. He claimed that his military enterprise "was begun, prepared, and set on foot with the knowledge and approbation of the executive department of our government."[66] The court repudiated his claim that a President or his assis-

61. Id. at 382, sec. 3.
62. Id. at 384, sec. 5.
63. Glass v. The Sloop Betsey, 3 U.S. (3 Dall.) 6 (1794). See also Findlay v. The William, 9 Fed. Cas. 57 (D. Pa. 1793) (No. 4,790); Moxon v. The Fanny, 17 Fed. Cas. 942 (D. Pa. 1793) (No. 9,895); Castello v. Bouteille, 5 Fed. Cas. 278 (D. S.C. 1794) (No. 2,504); and William R. Casto, The Supreme Court in the Early Republic 82–84 (1995).
64. 1 Richardson 358.
65. Id.
66. United States v. Smith, 27 Fed. Cas. 1192, 1229 (C.C.N.Y. 1806) (No. 16,342).

tants could somehow authorize military adventures that violated congressional policy. The court described the Neutrality Act as "declaratory of the
law of nations; and besides, every species of private and unauthorized hostilities is inconsistent with the principles of the social compact, and the
very nature, scope, and end of civil government."[67]

As to Smith's claim that he acted with the knowledge and approbation
of the executive branch, the court rejected the proposition that the Neutrality Act allowed executive officials to waive statutory provisions: "if a private individual, even with the knowledge and approbation of this high and
preeminent officer of our government [the President], should set on foot
such a military expedition, how can he expect to be exonerated from the
obligation of the law?" The court continued:

> Supposing then that every syllable of the affidavit is true, of what
> avail can it be on the present occasion? Of what use or benefit can it
> be to the defendant in a court of law? Does it speak by way of justi-
> fication? The President of the United States cannot control the statute,
> nor dispense with its execution, and still less can he authorize a per-
> son to do what the law forbids. If he could, it would render the exe-
> cution of the laws dependent on his will and pleasure; which is a
> doctrine that has not been set up, and will not meet with any sup-
> porters in our government. In this particular, the law is paramount.
> Who has dominion over it? None but the legislature; and even they
> are not without their limitation in our republic. Will it be pretended
> that the President could rightfully grant a dispensation and license to
> any of our citizens to carry on a war against a nation with whom the
> United States are at peace?[68]

The circuit court said that even if the President had known about the
expedition and approved of it, "it would not justify the defendant in a court
of law, nor discharge him from the binding force of the act of congress."
The court put the matter flatly: "Does [the President] possess the power of
making war? That power is exclusively vested in congress."[69] If a nation
invaded the United States, the President would have an obligation to resist
with force. But there was a "manifest distinction" between going to war
with a nation at peace and responding to an actual invasion: "In the for-

67. Id.
68. Id. at 1230.
69. Id.

mer case, it is the exclusive province of congress to change a state of peace into a state of war."[70]

The "Little Sarah" Incident

During the first year of Washington's neutrality policy, the French captured the British ship *Little Sarah* and brought it into the port of Philadelphia, where it was renamed *Petite Démocrate*, fitted with additional cannon, and made ready as a military vessel capable of privateering. With President Washington at Mount Vernon and not expected back to Philadelphia for several days, three members of his Cabinet met to decide what to do.

Secretary of the Treasury Hamilton and Secretary at War Knox wanted to establish a battery on Mud Island on the Delaware River, backed by a party of militia, to prevent the ship from reaching the Atlantic and engaging British vessels.[71] They were concerned that a failure to stop the vessel might be interpreted by the British as an act of war by the United States. The "*fitting out of privateers,* in our ports, by one of the belligerent powers, to cruise against any of the others is an unequivocal breach of neutrality."[72]

Secretary of State Jefferson disagreed. Any effort to stop the French ship by military means would lead to "bloody consequences."[73] The "actual commencement of hostilities, against a nation, for such this act may be, is an act of too serious consequence to our countrymen to be brought on their heads by subordinate officers, not chosen by them, nor cloathed with their confidence; and too presumptuous on the part of those officers, when the chief magistrate, into whose hands the citizens have committed their safety, is within eight and forty hours of his arrival here."[74] By the time Washington returned and could act, the ship had left the Delaware River and reached the Atlantic.

Jefferson Powell interprets this incident as a recognition of broad, independent presidential power to make war. He finds "an impressive unity of opinion among Washington, Jefferson, and Hamilton that the president could utilize his authority as commander-in-chief, at least to some extent, to execute his views of the obligations of the United States under the law of nations, without the need for express statutory or treaty-based authori-

---

70. Id.
71. 15 The Papers of Alexander Hamilton 70–71 (Syrett, ed. 1969).
72. Id. at 74 (emphasis in original).
73. 26 The Papers of Thomas Jefferson 449 (John Catanzariti, ed. 1995).
74. Id. at 450.

ty to do so."[75] To Powell, Jefferson thought it inappropriate for Cabinet officers to order the use of military force, "but he agreed with Hamilton and Knox that *the president,* as the constitutional officer responsible for the security of the Republic, could legitimately order 'the actual commencement' of military actions that might easily lead to all-out war."[76] The incident persuaded Powell that the President's "authority with respect to foreign affairs carried with it some power to take military action without congressional sanction in order to achieve the executive's goals."[77]

Those interpretations enlarge presidential power beyond anything that Washington or his advisers believed. First, "the obligations of the United States under the law of nations" are vested in Congress, not the President. Article II, Section 8, of the Constitution provides that among the enumerated powers of Congress is the power to "define and punish Piracies and Felonies committed on the high Seas, and Offences against the Law of Nations." Second, Washington was so unsure of his powers that when he returned he asked the Supreme Court for an advisory opinion on a range of questions dealing with the neutrality policy.[78] The Supreme Court declined to provide answers. Third, Hamilton, Knox, and Jefferson were not debating the President's power to *engage* in war. They were divided on how to *avoid* war. Hamilton and Knox thought that by preventing the ship from reaching the Atlantic they would avoid war with England. Jefferson thought that by withholding military action against the ship they would avoid war with France.

Jefferson offered this elliptical remark: "It appears to me the President wishes the Little Sarah had been stopped by military coercion, that is, by firing on her. Yet I do not believe he would have ordered himself had he been here, tho he would be glad we had ordered it."[79] Speculation as to what Washington did or did not believe cannot change the meaning of the Constitution, particularly in such a fundamental area as the war power.

Barbary Wars

From the precedents established by George Washington and John Adams, Thomas Jefferson was well aware when taking office in 1801 that the deci-

---

75. H. Jefferson Powell, The President's Authority over Foreign Affairs 54 (2002).
76. Id. at 58 (emphasis in original).
77. Id. at 61.
78. 33 The Writings of George Washington 15–19 (Fitzpatrick, ed. 1940).
79. 26 The Papers of Thomas Jefferson 499 (Catanzariti, ed. 1995).

sion to initiate military action lay with Congress. One of the problems he inherited was the odious U.S. practice of paying annual bribes ("tributes") to four states of North Africa: Morocco, Algiers, Tunis, and Tripoli. Regular payments were made so that they would not interfere with American merchantmen. A variety of local chieftains—with the titles of Beys, Deys, and Pashas—grew wealthy from this custom. Over a ten-year period, Washington and Adams paid nearly $10 million in tributes.[80]

In 1790, in his capacity as Secretary of State, Jefferson identified for Congress a variety of alternatives for dealing with the demands of the Barbary powers. The policy was to be established by Congress and implemented by the President:

> Upon the whole, it rests with Congress to decide between war, tribute, and ransom, as the means of re-establishing our Mediterranean commerce. If war, they will consider how far our own resources shall be called forth, and how far they will enable the Executive to engage, in the forms of the constitution, the co-operation of other Powers. If tribute or ransom, it will rest with them to limit and provide the amount; and with the Executive, observing the same constitutional forms, to make arrangements for employing it to the best advantage.[81]

On March 3, 1801, one day before Jefferson took office as President, Congress passed legislation to provide for a "naval peace establishment." Of the frigates to be retained and kept in constant service, six "shall be officered and manned as the President of the United States may direct."[82] On May 20, the State Department issued a directive to Captain Richard Dale of the U.S. Navy, calling attention to this statute. "Under this authority," Jefferson directed that a squadron be sent to the Mediterranean. In the event the Barbary powers declared war on the United States, the American vessels were ordered to "protect our commerce & chastise their insolence—by sinking, burning or destroying their ships & Vessels wherever you shall find them."[83] Having issued that order, based on congressional authority, Jefferson also wrote that it was up to Congress to decide what policy to pursue in the Mediterranean: "The real alternative before us is

80. Raymond Walters, Jr., Albert Gallatin: Jeffersonian Financier and Diplomat 150 (1957).

81. 1 American State Papers: Foreign Relations 105 (1832).

82. 2 Stat. 110, sec. 2 (1801).

83. 1 Naval Documents Relating to the United States Wars with the Barbary Powers 467 (1939).

whether to abandon the Mediterranean or to keep up a cruise in it, perhaps in rotation with other powers who would join us as soon as there is peace. But this Congress must decide."[84]

The Pasha of Tripoli, insisting on a larger tribute, declared war on the United States on May 14, 1801. On December 8, Jefferson informed Congress about the arrogant demands of the Pasha. Unless the United States paid tribute, the Pasha threatened to seize American ships and citizens. Jefferson told Congress that he had sent a small squadron of frigates to the Mediterranean to protect against the attack and then asked Congress for further guidance, stating he was "unauthorized by the Constitution, without the sanctions of Congress, to go beyond the line of defense." It was up to Congress to authorize "measures of offense also." Jefferson gave Congress all the documents and communications it needed so that the legislative branch, "in the exercise of this important function confided by the Constitution to the Legislature exclusively," could consider the situation and act in the manner it considered most appropriate.[85]

No doubt Jefferson's message to Congress omits many details of what happened militarily in the Mediterranean.[86] However, the key legal fact is that he went to Congress to seek statutory authority. He did not claim an independent and exclusive power to go to war. In 1805, when conflicts arose between the United States and Spain, he reported to Congress on the situation and spoke plainly about legal principles: "Congress alone is constitutionally invested with the power of changing our condition from peace to war."[87]

Alexander Hamilton, writing under the pseudonym "Lucius Crassus," issued a strong critique of Jefferson's message to Congress on military conflicts in the Mediterranean. Hamilton believed that Jefferson had defined the executive power too narrowly, deferring excessively to congressional prerogatives. Hamilton, always pushing the edge of executive power, argued that when a foreign nation declares war on the United States, the President may respond to that fact without waiting for congressional authority:

84. 8 The Writings of Thomas Jefferson 63–64 (Paul Leicester Ford, ed. 1897).

85. 1 Richardson 315. Earlier in the year, during Cabinet deliberations, Secretary of the Treasury Albert Gallatin argued that although the President "cannot put us in a state of war . . . if we be put into that state either by the decree of Congress or of the other nation, the command and direction of the public force then belongs to the Executive." The Complete Anas of Thomas Jefferson 213 (Franklin B. Sawvel, ed. 1903).

86. Abraham D. Sofaer, War, Foreign Affairs and Constitutional Power: The Origins 209–14 (1976); Montgomery N. Kosma, "Our First Real War," 2 Green Bag 2d 169 (Winter 1999).

87. Annals of Cong. 9th Cong., 1st Sess. 19 (1805).

The first thing in [the President's message], which excites our surprise, is the very extraordinary position, that though *Tripoli had declared war in form* against the United States, and had enforced it by actual hostility, yet that there was not power, for want of *the sanction of Congress,* to capture and detain her cruisers with their crews.

... [The Constitution] has only provided affirmatively, that, "The Congress shall have power to declare War;" the plain meaning of which is, that it is the peculiar and exclusive province of Congress, *when the nation is at peace* to change that state into a state of war; whether from calculations of policy, or from provocations, or injuries received: in other words, it belongs to Congress only, *to go to War.* But when a foreign nation declares, or openly and avowedly makes war upon the United States, they are then by the very fact *already at war,* and any declaration on the part of Congress is nugatory; it is at least unnecessary.[88]

Although Hamilton faulted Jefferson for reading his *defensive powers* too narrowly, Hamilton never advocated that the President had the constitutional authority to take the country from a state of peace to a state of war. Commitments of that nature required the President to come to Congress for authority. For example, nothing in Hamilton's broad reading of presidential authority would have allowed Clinton, in 1999, to go to war against Yugoslavia.

Recent studies by the Justice Department and statements made during congressional debate imply that Jefferson took military measures against the Barbary powers without seeking the approval or authority of Congress.[89] In fact, in at least ten statutes, Congress explicitly authorized military action by Presidents Jefferson and Madison. Congress passed legislation in 1802 to authorize the President to equip armed vessels to protect commerce and seamen in the Atlantic, the Mediterranean, and adjoining seas. The statute authorized American ships to seize vessels belonging to the Bey of Tripoli, with the captured property distributed to those who brought the vessels into port.[90] Additional legislation in 1804 gave explicit

---

88. 7 The Works of Alexander Hamilton 745–47 (John C. Hamilton, ed. 1851) (emphasis in original). Also reprinted at 25 The Papers of Alexander Hamilton 454–56 (Syrett ed., 1977).

89. 4A Op. O.L.C. 187 (1980); 140 Cong. Rec. 19809 (1994) (statement of Senator McCain, third column). The opinion by the Office of Legal Counsel was placed in the Congressional Record in 1993: 139 Cong. Rec. 25702–5 (1993).

90. 2 Stat. 129 (1802).

support for "warlike operations against the regency of Tripoli, or any other of the Barbary powers."[91] Duties on foreign goods were placed in a "Mediterranean Fund" to finance these operations.[92]

Jefferson often distinguished between defensive and offensive military operations, permitting presidential initiatives for the former but not the latter. In 1805, he notified Congress about a conflict with the Spanish along the eastern boundary of the Louisiana Territory (West Florida). After detailing the problem, he noted that only Congress had the constitutional authority to place the country at war. He therefore thought it "my duty to await their authority for using force in any degree which could be avoided."[93]

For purely defensive operations, Jefferson retained the right to act first and seek congressional approval later. After Congress had recessed in 1807, a British vessel fired on the American ship *Chesapeake*. Jefferson ordered military purchases for the emergency, reporting his action to Congress after it convened. "To have awaited a previous and special sanction by law," he said, "would have lost occasions which might not be retrieved."[94]

He later observed that fidelity to the written law is "doubtless *one* of the high duties of a good citizen, but it is not the *highest*." The laws of necessity, self-preservation, and "of saving our country when in danger" deserved a higher priority. He concluded: "To lose our country by a scrupulous adherence to written law, would be to lose the law itself, with life, liberty, property, and all those who are enjoying them with us; thus absurdly sacrificing the end of the means."[95] Jefferson was not opening the door to any and all presidential initiatives. He had something specific in mind: presidential actions in response to emergencies that threatened the survival of the nation, after which he would seek congressional approval. Future Presidents would attempt to justify U.S. military interventions in areas of the world (such as Grenada, Libya, Nicaragua, and Haiti) that posed no genuine threat to national security and without seeking the retroactive sanction of Congress.

Problems with the Barbary pirates persisted after Jefferson left office. The Dey of Algiers continued to make warfare against U.S. citizens trading

91. 2 Stat. 291 (1804).
92. Id. at 292, sec. 2; Annals of Cong., 8th Cong., 1st Sess. 1203, 1210–24 (1804). See also 2 Stat. 206 (1803); 2 Stat. 391 (1806); 2 Stat. 436 (1807); 2 Stat. 456 (1808); 2 Stat. 511 (1809); 2 Stat. 614 (1811); 2 Stat. 675 (1812); 2 Stat. 809 (1813).
93. 1 Richardson 377.
94. Id. at 416.
95. 5 The Writings of Thomas Jefferson 542 (H. A. Washington, ed. 1861) (emphasis in original).

in the Mediterranean and kept some in captivity. After the conclusion of the War of 1812 with England, Madison recommended to Congress in 1815 that it declare war on Algiers.[96] Instead of a declaration, Congress passed legislation "for the protection of the commerce of the United States against the Algerine cruisers." The first line of the statute read: "Whereas the Dey of Algiers, on the coast of Barbary, has commenced a predatory warfare against the United States." The legislative branch gave Madison authority to use armed vessels for the purpose of protecting the commerce of U.S. seamen on the Atlantic, the Mediterranean, and adjoining seas. U.S. vessels (both government and private) could "subdue, seize, and make prize of all vessels, goods and effects of or belonging to the Dey of Algiers."[97]

An American flotilla set sail for Algiers, where it captured two of the Dey's ships and forced him to stop the piracy, release all captives, and renounce the practice of annual tribute payments. Similar treaties were obtained from Tunis and Tripoli.[98] By the end of 1815, Madison could report to Congress on the successful termination of the war with Algiers.[99]

The War of 1812

After two decades of congressionally authorized military actions against Indians, France, and the Barbary pirates, Congress declared its first war in 1812. Much like President Adams had done in the Quasi-War with France, President Madison submitted a message to Congress on November 5, 1811, alerting it to a number of hostile and discriminatory actions by England that required Congress to prepare for war. Explaining the British measures that "trampl[ed] on rights which no independent nation can relinquish," Madison suggested that Congress "will feel the duty of putting the United States into an armor and an attitude demanded by the crisis, and corresponding with the national spirit and expectations."[100] Congress responded by passing legislation to raise additional military forces, organize a volunteer military corps, and augment the navy.[101]

Madison's message to Congress on June 1, 1812, identified a variety of "injuries and indignities": British impressment of American seamen, their

96. 2 Richardson 539.
97. 3 Stat. 230 (1815).
98. Robert Allen Rutland, The Presidency of James Madison 192–93 (1990).
99. 2 Richardson 547.
100. Id. at 479.
101. 2 Stat. 671, 676, 683, 685, 695, 699, 704 (1812).

violation of U.S. rights to neutral seas and the blockade of U.S. ports, England's refusal to revoke the Orders of Council (discriminatory economic measures against America), and its provocation of Indian raids against frontier settlements. Although these practices amounted to "a state of war against the United States," Madison left to Congress the issue of declaring war, "a solemn question which the Constitution wisely confides to the legislative department of the Government."[102]

The House Foreign Relations Committee acted quickly by advocating a declaration of war: "The mad ambition, the lust of power, and commercial avarice of Great Britain have left to neutral nations an alternative only between the base surrender of their rights, and a manly vindication of them."[103] On June 4 the House voted—79 to 49—to support the declaration of war. The Senate considered limiting the war to the high seas.[104] After a select committee reported the bill to declare war, a motion was made to return the bill to committee to merely authorize warships and privateers to make reprisals against Britain. That motion carried by a 17 to 13 vote.[105] When the modified bill was reported to the floor for final action, a motion to accept the committee's changes failed by a tie vote, 16 to 16.[106] Other attempts to limit the war to the high seas also failed.[107] Finally, on June 17, the Senate approved the declaration of war, 19 to 13. Both chambers debated in secret. The declaration of war, dated June 18, 1812, authorized the President to use "the whole land and naval force of the United States."[108]

"Mr. Madison's war" lasted 30 months, producing heavy losses along the Canadian front, a costly British embargo of the eastern seaboard, and the burning of Washington, D.C. (including the Capitol, the White House, and most of the executive department buildings). So severe were the economic conditions in the northeast that several states assembled at the Hartford Convention to discuss the merits of seceding from the Union. A peace treaty was ratified by the Senate after which Madison, on February 18, 1815, issued a proclamation of peace.

In prosecuting the War of 1812, President Madison called on the state militia pursuant to authority given him by Congress. A legal dispute reached

102. 2 Richardson 490.
103. Donald R. Hickey, The War of 1812, at 44 (1989).
104. Id. at 45.
105. Id. at 46; Annals of Cong., 12th Cong., 1st Sess. 266–67 (1812).
106. Annals of Cong., 12th Cong. 1st Sess. 270–71 (1812).
107. Hickey, The War of 1812, at 46.
108. 2 Stat. 755 (1812).

the Supreme Court in 1827. The Court said there could be no question of Congress passing legislation that gave the President the right to call up state militia to repel invasion from abroad or to suppress internal insurrections. The Court concluded that "the authority to decide whether the exigency has arisen, belongs exclusively to the president, and that his decision is conclusive upon all other persons."[109]

The Mexican War

The power of Commander in Chief is at its low point when there is no standing army because a President cannot deploy troops until Congress raises them. But when a standing army does exist, ready to move at the President's command, the balance of power can shift decisively. Such was the case with the Mexican War.

After Texas won its independence from Mexico in 1836, both Houses of Congress passed resolutions stating "that the independence of Texas ought to be acknowledged by the United States whenever satisfactory information should be received that it had in successful operation a civil government capable of performing the duties and fulfilling the obligations of an independent power." President Andrew Jackson hesitated to recognize the independence of Texas, fearing that such action could result in war with Mexico and invade the prerogatives of Congress. He advised Congress: "It will always be considered consistent with the spirit of the Constitution, and most safe, that [the power of recognition] should be exercised, when probably leading to war, with a previous understanding with that body by whom war can alone be declared, and by whom all the provisions for sustaining its perils must be furnished."[110]

In 1845, after almost a decade of negotiation, Texas was annexed to the United States. President Polk noted in his first annual message that year: "This accession to our territory has been a bloodless achievement. No arm of force has been raised to produce the result. The sword has had no part in the victory."[111] A year later, Polk would not hesitate to use military force to gain additional territory from Mexico—and to do so without Jackson's concern about the war prerogatives of Congress.

During the autumn of 1845, Polk relied on the diplomatic efforts of John Slidell "to purchase for a pecuniary consideration" Upper California and

109. Martin v. Mott, 25 U.S. (12 Wheat.) 19, 28 (1827).
110. 4 Richardson 1486.
111. 5 Richardson 2237.

New Mexico from Mexico.[112] Polk feared that Great Britain "had her eye" on California and "intended to possess it if she could." In asserting the Monroe Doctrine against foreign encroachment, Polk "had California & the fine bay of San Francisco as much in view as Oregon."[113] On February 13, 1846, he learned from a Spanish visitor that any government or administration in Mexico that agreed to sell Mexican territory to the United States would provoke "another revolution by which they would be overthrown. He said they must appear to be forced to agree to such a proposition." The visitor recommended that U.S. forces should be marched from Corpus Christi to the Del Norte and that a strong naval force should be assembled at Veracruz. Since it was "well known" that the Mexican government had no funds to pay the amounts due to U.S. citizens, when the Mexicans "saw a strong force ready to strike on their coasts and border, they would . . . feel their danger and agree to the boundary suggested."[114]

Polk related this story to his cabinet, adding that "it would be necessary to take strong measures towards Mexico before our difficulties with that Government could be settled." He proposed that Slidell be instructed to demand an early decision of the Mexican government, and that if the government refused to receive him or refused to pay the amounts due to American claimants without unreasonable delay, Slidell should board one of the U.S. war vessels at Veracruz. In that event Polk would send a "strong message" to Congress authorizing him to make another demand and if that were refused, "to confer authority on the Executive to take redress into our own hands by aggressive measures."[115] Secretary of State James Buchanan objected to this course of action but eventually produced some drafts for the instruction to Slidell.[116]

Polk delayed in sending the dispatch, and modifications were still being made on March 12.[117] On April 7, the President and his cabinet continued to debate what to do if Mexico refused to receive Slidell.[118] After Slidell was rejected the Polk administration hesitated again.[119] From April 18 to May 3, Polk discussed the Mexican problem with his cabinet on repeated occasions, promising to send a strong message to Congress, even to the

112. 1 The Diary of James K. Polk 34 (M. Quaife, ed. 1910).
113. Id. at 71.
114. Id. at 228–29.
115. Id. at 233–34.
116. Id. at 234–36.
117. Id. at 238–39, 287.
118. Id. at 319.
119. Id. at 325–26.

point of recommending a declaration of war for Mexico's failure to redress U.S. complaints.[120] On April 28 he directed Buchanan to prepare from the archives "a succinct history of these wrongs as a basis of a message to Congress, at his earliest convenience."[121]

Meanwhile, Polk had ordered General Zachary Taylor to occupy disputed territory along the Texas-Mexico border. On May 5, Polk and the cabinet talked about "the possibility of a collision between the American & Mexican forces."[122] On May 8, Slidell told Polk that only one course remained and that was "to take the redress of the wrongs and injuries which we had so long borne from Mexico into our own hands, and to act with promptness and energy." Polk agreed.[123] At the cabinet meeting on May 9, all concurred that if the Mexican forces committed any act of hostility on General Taylor's forces, Polk should immediately send a message to Congress recommending a declaration of war.[124] The cabinet adjourned about 2 P.M. Some four hours later it learned there had been a military clash between American and Mexican forces.[125]

Despite the legal uncertainties of the disputed land, Polk told Congress on May 11 that Mexico "has passed the boundary of the United States, has invaded our territory and shed American blood upon the American soil." He notified Congress that "war exists."[126] Senator John Calhoun tried to resist the stampede in Congress to rush blindly and mechanically toward a declaration of war, as though all other options had been removed by Polk:

> I agree . . . that the President has announced that there is war; but according to my interpretation, there is no war according to the sense of our Constitution. I distinguish between hostilities and war, and God forbid that, acting under the Constitution, we should ever confound one with the other. There may be invasion without war, and the President is authorized to repel invasion without war. But it is *our* sacred duty to make war, and it is for us to determine whether war shall be declared or not. If we have declared war, a state of war exists, and not till then.[127]

120. Id. at 337, 343, 354.
121. Id. at 363.
122. Id. at 379.
123. Id. at 382.
124. Id. at 384.
125. Id. at 386.
126. 5 Richardson 2292.
127. Cong. Globe, 29th Cong., 1st Sess. 784 (1846) (emphasis in original).

Other Senators echoed Calhoun's sentiments.[128] Senator John Middleton Clayton "condemned" the conduct of President Polk: "I do not see on what principle it can be shown that the President, without consulting Congress and obtaining its sanction for the procedure, has a right to send an army to take up a position, where, as it must have been foreseen, the inevitable consequence would be war."[129]

Similar points were made during debate in the House of Representatives. Rep. Isaac E. Holmes said legislators knew nothing more than that two armies had collided in disputed territory, "and I deny that war is absolutely, necessarily, the result of it."[130] Rep. Robert Rhett insisted that President Polk "has not made war; he does not recommend us to make war. Not a state of war exists, but a state of hostilities."[131] Yet those two legislators joined with others on May 11 to form a 174 to 14 majority in support of war against Mexico.[132] The Senate voted 40 to 2 in favor of war.[133] Congress declared war on May 13, recognizing that "a state of war exists."[134]

Polk offered some intriguing justifications for going to war. In part he pointed to "grievous wrongs perpetrated by Mexico upon our citizens throughout a long period of years" that remained unredressed.[135] As his critics in the Whig Party noted, England, France, Spain, Holland, Naples, and Denmark had all engaged in offenses against the United States without automatic resort to war.[136] Polk also said that Mexico "is too feeble a power to govern these Provinces, lying as they do at a distance of more than 1,000 miles from her capital."[137] He warned that a failure by the United States to relinquish Upper California would invite European nations to possess it, either by conquest or by purchase.

New Mexico, according to Polk, "has never been of any considerable value to Mexico."[138] Furthermore, Mexico was "too feeble" to prevent depredations by Indians against the inhabitants of New Mexico and other northern states of Mexico, and it "would be a blessing to all these northern States to have their citizens protected against them by the power of the

128. Id. (Senators Morehead and Archer).
129. Id. at 786.
130. Id. at 792.
131. Id. at 793.
132. Id. at 795.
133. Id. at 804.
134. 9 Stat. 9 (1846).
135. 5 Richardson 2291.
136. "The President's Message: The War," 5 The American Review: A Whig Journal 1, 10 (1847).
137. 5 Richardson 2389.
138. Id. at 2390.

United States."[139] Later, in submitting a treaty of peace to Congress (a treaty signed in 1848), Polk described the "valuable territories ceded by Mexico" but concluded that in the hands of Mexico they would have remained "almost unoccupied, and of little value to her or to any other nation, whilst as a part of our Union they will be productive of vast benefits of the United States, to the commercial world, and the general interests of mankind."[140] That line of argument would be used in subsequent decades by American Presidents to intervene in neighboring countries.

On May 13, the same day that Congress declared war, Buchanan prepared a dispatch to be sent to U.S. ministers in London, Paris, and other foreign courts, explaining that "our object was not to dismember Mexico or to make conquests" and that in going to war it was not the intention "to acquire either California or New Mexico or any other portion of the Mexican territory." Polk objected to this language, saying that it was "unnecessary and improper" to send such a statement. Although the United States had not gone to war for conquest, "it was clear that in making peace we would if practicable obtain California and such other portions of the Mexican territory as would be sufficient to indemnify our claimants on Mexico, and to defray the expenses of the war which that power by her long continued wrongs and injuries had forced us to wage." Polk told Buchanan that "it was well known that the Mexican Government had no other means of indemnifying us."[141]

Polk's action was censured by the House of Representatives in 1848 on the ground that the war had been "unnecessarily and unconstitutionally begun by the President of the United States."[142] This language was approved by a vote of 85 to 81. One of the members voting for the censure was Abraham Lincoln, who later wrote to a friend:

Allow the President to invade a neighboring nation, whenever *he* shall deem it necessary to repel invasion, and you allow him to do so, *whenever he may choose to say* he deems it necessary for such purpose—and you allow him to make war at pleasure. . . . This, our Convention understood to be the most oppressive of all Kingly oppressions; and they resolved to so frame the Constitution that *no one man* should hold the power of bringing the oppression upon us.[143]

---

139. Id. at 2390–91.
140. Id. at 2430.
141. 1 The Diary of James K. Polk 397.
142. Cong. Globe, 30th Cong., 1st Sess. 95 (1848).
143. 1 The Collected Works of Abraham Lincoln 451–52 (Roy Basler, ed. 1953) (emphasis in original).

During the war between the United States and Mexico, U.S. authorities acting under presidential orders conquered the port of Tampico. The Supreme Court offered this important limit on presidential power: "As commander-in-chief, he is authorized to direct the movements of the naval and military forces placed by law at his command, and to employ them in the manner he may deem most effectual to harass and conquer and subdue the enemy."[144] Notice the language: placed *by law* at his command. The power of Commander in Chief, necessarily broad, must adhere to the policy declared by Congress in law.

Bombarding Greytown

Although the Constitution does not expressly direct the President to protect American life and property in foreign countries, Presidents have sent U.S. forces abroad for that purpose on many occasions. They base such actions not on legislative authority but rather on inherent or implied executive responsibilities.

In 1854, an American ship was ordered to the Nicaraguan port of Greytown (now San Juan del Norte) to compel local authorities to make amends for an affront to an American diplomat. American firms in that area had also complained about property losses. When the commander of the American *Cyane* decided that the local authorities had failed to make appropriate amends, he proceeded to bombard the town from nine in the morning to mid-afternoon, pausing periodically to see whether town officials would yield. American forces subsequently went ashore to destroy by fire whatever remained of the town.[145] President Pierce, reporting this incident to Congress, described the commander's operation as a model of due process:

> [The commander] warned them by a public proclamation that if they did not give satisfaction within a time specified he would bombard the town. By this procedure he afforded them opportunity to provide for their personal safety. To those also who desired to avoid loss of property in the punishment about to be inflicted on the offending town he furnished the means of removing their effects to boats of his

144. Fleming v. Page, 50 U.S. (9 How.) 603, 615 (1850).
145. Milton Offutt, "The Protection of Citizens Abroad by the Armed Forces of the United States," Johns Hopkins University Studies in Historical and Political Science, ser. 44, no. 4 (1928), 32–34.

own ship and of a steamer which he procured and tendered to them for that purpose.[146]

A resident of Greytown sued for damages to his property, but in 1860 a federal circuit court upheld the commander's actions on the basis of the President's duty to protect lives and property in other countries. As the head of the executive branch, the President "is made the only legitimate organ of the general government, to open and carry on correspondence or negotiations with foreign nations, in matters concerning the interests of the country or its citizens." It is to the President that citizens abroad "must look for protection of person and of property." The court continued: "Now, as it respects the interposition of the executive abroad, for the protection of the lives or property of the citizen, the duty must, of necessity, rest in the discretion of the president. Acts of lawless violence, or of threatened violence to the citizens or his property, cannot be anticipated and provided for; and the protection, to be effectual or of any avail, may, not infrequently, require the most prompt and decided action."[147] In another case, in which a plaintiff attempted to recover property losses from the bombing of Greytown, the Court of Claims ruled that such questions were "international political questions" to be decided by the political departments.[148]

These court rulings did not attempt to explore the extent to which the President could destroy foreign property or commit acts of violence while protecting American interests. James Buchanan, American minister to the Court of St. James at the time of the Greytown bombardment, told the British government that he believed the American commander had acted without express authority and that his action would be disavowed by the American government. Instructed to the contrary by Secretary of State Marcy, Buchanan had to switch positions and defend the bombardment.[149]

After becoming President in 1857, Buchanan had an opportunity to express his own views about presidential power and the Greytown precedent. In a message to Congress on December 6, 1858, he stated that the executive branch "in its intercourse with foreign nations is limited to the employment of diplomacy alone. When this fails it can proceed no further." The President "can not legitimately resort to force without the direct

---

146. 6 Richardson 2816.
147. Durand v. Hollins, 8 Fed. Cas. (Cir. Ct. S.D.N.Y. 1860) (Case No. 4,186), p. 1123.
148. Perrin v. United States, 4 Ct. Cl. 534, 547 (1868).
149. Charles C. Tansill, "The President and the Initiation of Hostilities: The Precedents of the Mexican and Spanish-American Wars," reprinted in The President's War Powers: From the Federalists to Reagan 86 (Demetrios Caraley, ed. 1984).

authority of Congress, except in resisting and repelling hostile attacks."
Turning to the specific situation in Nicaragua, Buchanan said that the President would "have no authority to enter the territories of Nicaragua even
to prevent the destruction of the transit and protect the lives and property
of our own citizens on their passage."[150]

Buchanan reiterated the same principles in 1859. He told Congress that
the "executive governments" of Great Britain, France, and other countries,
"possessing the war-making power," could use military force to rectify outrages against the life and property of their subjects. "Not so the executive
government of the United States." If the President ordered a vessel of war
to any port to demand prompt redress of an outrage committed,

> the offending parties are well aware that in case of refusal the commander can do no more than remonstrate. He can resort to no hostile act. . . . The remedy for this state of things can only be supplied
> by Congress, since the Constitution has confided to that body alone
> the power to make war. Without the authority of Congress the Executive can not lawfully direct any force, however near it may be to the
> scene of difficulty, to enter the territory of Mexico, Nicaragua, or New
> Granada for the purpose of defending the persons and property of
> American citizens.[151]

A few years later, Congress had an opportunity to revisit the use of presidential power abroad in protecting lives and property. Legislation in 1868
(still in effect) promoted a more measured and pacific policy by directing
the President to demand from a foreign government the reason for depriving any American citizen of liberty. If it appeared wrongful and in violation of the rights of American citizenship, the President was to demand the
citizen's release. If the foreign government delayed or refused, the President could use such means "not amounting to acts of war" as he thought
necessary and proper to obtain the release.[152]

An early version of this bill gave the President the power to suspend commercial relations with a government that arrested and detained an American
citizen. Senator Charles Sumner rebelled against this grant of power: "Here

---

150. 7 Richardson 3047.
151. Id. at 3070.
152. 15 Stat. 223 (1868); 22 U.S.C. 1732 (2000). For a legislative history of this statute,
see Abner J. Mikva and Gerald L. Neuman, "The Hostage Crisis and the 'Hostage Act,'"
49 U. Chi. L. Rev. 292 (1982). Legislation in 1989 inserted "and not otherwise prohibited by law" after "acts of war." 103 Stat. 1900, sec. 9 (1989).

is a way to make war easy. To the President is given this alarming power. In Europe war proceeds from the sovereign; in England from the queen in council; in France from Louis Napoleon. This is according to the genius of monarchies. By the Constitution of our Republic it is Congress alone that can declare war. And yet by this bill One Man, in his discretion, may do little short of declaring war. He may hurl one of the bolts of war, and sever the commercial relations of two great Powers."[153] Another portion of the draft bill empowered the President—as an act of reprisal—to arrest and detain a citizen of a foreign country. Senator Oliver Morton objected to this provision because he was "not willing to place in the hands of the President of the United States the power to bring on war in any contingency."[154] The section on suspending commercial relations was eliminated on a vote of 30 to 7,[155] and the President's explicit power to retain foreigners as an act of reprisal was deleted also. In the end, the President was authorized to use such means "not amounting to acts of war."

The Civil War

Lincoln's vote in 1848 to censure Polk for "unnecessarily and unconstitutionally" beginning the Mexican War may appear to be hypocritical. During his own years as President he exercised military force without first obtaining authority from Congress. In April 1861, with Congress in recess, he issued proclamations calling forth the state militia, suspending the writ of habeas corpus, and placing a blockade on the rebellious states.

There are crucial differences between the actions of Polk and Lincoln. Polk's initiatives helped precipitate war with a foreign nation while Lincoln confronted a genuine internal emergency of civil war. Polk had some discretion over his actions; Lincoln was compelled to use force to put down an internal rebellion. Moreover, Lincoln had genuine doubts about the legality of his actions, particularly the suspension of the writ of habeas corpus, and openly requested statutory authority from Congress.

When Lincoln's blockade was upheld by the Supreme Court in 1863, Justice Robert Grier said that the President as Commander in Chief had no power to initiate war, but in the event of foreign invasion the President was not only authorized "but bound to resist force by force. He does not initiate the war, but is bound to accept the challenge without waiting for the

153. Cong. Globe, 40th Cong., 2d Sess. 4205 (1868).
154. Id. at 4235.
155. Id at 4330.

special legislative authority."[156] The President had no choice but to meet the crisis in the shape it presented itself "without waiting for Congress to baptize it with a name; and no name given to it by him or them could change the fact."[157]

Yet Grier carefully limited the President's power to defensive actions, noting that he "has no power to initiate or declare a war against either a foreign nation or a domestic State."[158] The executive branch took exactly the same position. During oral argument, Richard Henry Dana Jr., who was representing the President, acknowledged that Lincoln's actions had nothing to do with "the right *to initiate a war, as a voluntary act of sovereignty*. That is vested only in Congress."[159]

Unlike Truman, Bush I, and Clinton, Lincoln never claimed that he possessed full authority to act as he did. In fact, he admitted to exceeding the constitutional boundaries established for the President and thus needed the sanction of Congress. When Congress returned he explained that his actions, "whether strictly legal or not, were ventured upon under what appeared to be a popular demand and a public necessity, trusting then, as now, that Congress would readily ratify them."[160] Lincoln did not claim to act outside the Constitution. He acted under his powers and probably also those of Congress, believing that his actions (especially suspending the writ of habeas corpus) were not "beyond the constitutional competency of Congress."[161]

Lincoln therefore invoked each stage of the executive prerogative: acting in the absence of law and sometimes against it; explaining to the legislature what he had done, and why; and requesting the legislative body to authorize his actions. The superior lawmaking body was Congress, not the President. Congress debated this request at length, with members supporting the President on the explicit assumption that his acts were illegal.[162] Congress eventually passed legislation "approving, legalizing, and making valid all the acts, proclamations, and orders of the President, etc., as if they had been issued and done under the previous express authority and direction of the Congress of the United States."[163] Furthermore, Lincoln

---

156. The Prize Cases, 67 U.S. 635, 668 (1863).
157. Id. at 669.
158. Id at 668.
159. Id. at 660 (emphasis in original).
160. 7 Richardson 3225.
161. Id.
162. Cong. Globe, 37th Cong., 1st Sess. 393 (1861) (Senator Howe).
163. 12 Stat. 326 (1861).

based his actions partly on statutes enacted in 1795 and 1807, which authorized the President to use military force to suppress insurrections.[164]

Lincoln's proclamation emancipating the slaves proceeded through a number of drafts, at first relying on statutory authority but later invoking the power of Commander in Chief. The first draft, citing statutory authority, also noted that the proclamation was "a fit and necessary military measure" for ending slavery. He would, as Commander in Chief, declare on January 1, 1863, that all slaves in rebellious states "shall then, thence forward, and forever, be free."[165] A subsequent draft relied on the commander-in-chief clause while also "calling attention" to previous statutes on the subject of abolishing slavery.[166] The final Emancipation Proclamation made no mention of congressional statutes, grounding itself entirely on the President's power as Commander in Chief. At the conclusion of this document, Lincoln said he regarded the proclamation "sincerely to be an act of justice, warranted by the Constitution, upon military necessity."[167]

In one notable instance, Lincoln's exercise of war power collided with the judiciary. Lincoln's suspension of the writ of habeas corpus was opposed by Chief Justice Roger Taney, sitting as circuit judge. Taney ruled that since the President had no power under the Constitution to suspend the writ, the prisoner, John Merryman, should be set free. Merryman was suspected of being the captain of a secession troop and of having assisted in destroying railroads and bridges to prevent federal troops from reaching Washington, D.C. When Taney attempted to serve a paper at the prison to free Merryman, prison officials refused to let Taney's marshal carry out his duty. Avoiding a direct confrontation with Lincoln, which the judiciary could not afford, Taney merely noted:

> I have exercised all the power which the constitution and laws confer upon me, but that power has been resisted by a force too strong for me to overcome. . . . I shall, therefore, order all the proceedings in this case, with my opinion, to be filed and recorded in the circuit court of the United States for the district court of Maryland, and direct the clerk to transmit a copy, under seal, to the president of the United States. It will then remain for that high officer, in fulfillment of his constitutional obligation to "take care that the laws be faithfully exe-

164. The Prize Cases, 67 U.S. at 660, 668.
165. 5 The Collected Works of Abraham Lincoln 336–37 (Basler, ed. 1953).
166. Id. at 433–36.
167. 6 id. at 30.

cuted," to determine what measures he will take to cause the civil
process of the United States to be respected and enforced.[168]

Not until the war was over and Lincoln in his grave did the Court, in
1866, breathe some life into the privilege of the writ of habeas corpus. The
Court then held that military courts could not function in states where federal courts had been open and operating.[169] In response to this ruling,
Congress passed legislation to limit the Court's jurisdiction to hear cases
involving martial law and military trials. Although cases were already pending with regard to the conduct of U.S. officials during and immediately
after the war, Congress gave indemnity to all officials who implemented
presidential proclamations from March 4, 1861, to June 30, 1866, with respect
to martial law and military trials. The statute provided: "And no civil court
of the United States, or of any state, or of the District of Columbia, or of
any district or territory of the United States, shall have or take jurisdiction
of, or in any manner reverse any of the proceedings had or acts done as
aforesaid."[170]

Lincoln's military actions during the Civil War were reviewed by the
Joint Committee on the Conduct of the War. Triggered initially by the dis-
asters of Bull Run and other defeats, members of Congress introduced legislation to create a committee to investigate military operations.[171] Committee members were criticized for some of their procedures and operations,
but "they brought speed and energy into the conduct of the war; . . . fer-
reted out abuses and put their fingers down heavily upon governmental
inefficiency; . . . [and] labored, for a time at least, to preserve a balance and
effect a cooperation between the legislative and executive departments."[172]
The committee also strengthened Lincoln's hand against the eventual removal
of General George B. McClellan, prepared the groundwork for abolishing
slavery, uncovered corruption and inefficiency, and served as a "splendid
propaganda agency" in furthering the war effort.[173]

A recent study credits the committee with helping "bolster the resolve to
continue the war" but faults it for lacking military expertise and "refus[ing]

168. Ex parte Merryman, 17 Fed. Case No. 9,487 (1861), 153.
169. Ex parte Milligan, 71 U.S. (4 Wall.) 2 (1866).
170. 14 Stat. 432, 433 (1867).
171. Cong. Globe, 37th Cong., 2d Sess. 16–17, 29–32, 40 (1861).
172. William Whatley Pierson Jr., "The Committee on the Conduct of the Civil War,"
23 Am. Hist. Rev. 550, 575–76 (1918).
173. Hans L. Trefousse, "The Joint Committee on the Conduct of the War," 10 Civil
War Hist. 5, 7–9 (1964).

to defer to the experts."[174] The same could be said of Lincoln, who either regretted when he deferred to military experts (as with General Irvin McDowell's decision to attack the Confederates at Bull Run) or had to rein in military leaders whose actions were politically obtuse (General John C. Frémont's proclamation to shoot armed civilians and to free slaves of persons who aided the rebellion).[175] Both Lincoln and Secretary of War Edwin M. Stanton shared a "distrust of professional military men," and Lincoln came to have great doubts "about the value of military expertise."[176] At later times, as with the Vietnam War, it was more appropriate to fault members of Congress who *deferred* to the experts.

Spanish-American War

Aside from Polk's initiatives in Mexico and Lincoln's emergency actions during the Civil War, the power of war in the nineteenth century remained basically in the hands of Congress. Presidents recognized the rule of legislative supremacy in matters of going to war. In a case decided by the Supreme Court in 1889, England had called upon the United States to supply naval forces in a military action against China. The Court made it clear that offensive operations had to be authorized by Congress, not the President: "As this proposition involved a participation in existing hostilities, the request could not be acceded to, and the Secretary of State in his communication to the English government explained that the warmaking power of the United States was not vested in the President but in Congress, and that he had no authority, therefore, to order aggressive hostilities to be undertaken."[177] Significantly, the Court spoke not merely of the congressional power to *declare* war but of a broader power: *war-making*. The decision to spill the nation's blood and treasure was left to Congress, not the President. The lack of a declaration of war could not be a pretext for the executive branch to use armed force against another nation. That fundamental decision lay with Congress.

Congress would declare war in 1898 for a third time in response to Cuban rebellions against Spanish rulers. American sentiment, strongly favor-

---

174. Bruce Tap, Over Lincoln's Shoulder: The Committee on the Conduct of the War 255, 259 (1998).

175. David Herbert Donald, Lincoln 306–7, 314–15 (1995).

176. Id. at 351, 357.

177. The Chinese Exclusion Case, 130 U.S. 581, 591 (1889).

ing the rebels, prepared the way for U.S. intervention. The insurrection had destroyed sugar and tobacco plantations, affecting the interests of a number of American exporters and investors. The United States supplied about half of Cuban imports, while almost 90 percent of Cuban exports went to the United States.

Congress passed a concurrent resolution in 1896 offering the "friendly offices" of the United States to Spain for the recognition of an independent Cuba.[178] Spain rejected the offer. Some members of Congress itched for war. An associate of President Cleveland was once present when a delegation from Congress arrived at the White House to announce: "We have about decided to declare war against Spain over the Cuban question. Conditions are intolerable." Cleveland responded bluntly: "There will be no war with Spain over Cuba while I am President." A member of Congress protested that the Constitution gave Congress the right to declare war, but Cleveland countered by saying that the Constitution also made him Commander in Chief and "I will not mobilize the army." Cleveland said that the United States could buy Cuba from Spain for $100 million, whereas a war "will cost vastly more than that and will entail another long list of pensioners. It would be an outrage to declare war."[179] This standoff raises the intriguing possibility that a President, presented with a declaration of war from Congress, could veto it on the ground that intelligence obtained from diplomatic sources demonstrated that war was unnecessary. In such situations, one would assume that this information would be shared with Congress and derail efforts to declare war.

William McKinley entered the White House in March 1897 and devoted much of that year to passing the Dingley Tariff Act. However, in a message to Congress at the end of that year, McKinley's focus had begun to shift: "The most important problem with which this Government is now called upon to deal pertaining to its foreign relations concerns its duty toward Spain and the Cuban insurrection."[180]

On February 15, 1898, the American battleship *Maine* was destroyed while sitting in the Havana harbor. Two officers and 264 members of the crew died. McKinley ordered an investigation to determine the cause of the blast. In a message to Congress on April 11, he said that the destruction of the ship "was caused by an exterior explosion—that of a submarine

178. 28 Cong. Rec. 2256–57 (1896).
179. 2 Robert McElroy, Grover Cleveland 249–50 (1923).
180. 13 Richardson 6254.

mine."[181] By implication, Spain was responsible for the blast and the loss of American lives. Subsequent studies (released after the war) concluded that the explosion came from the *interior* of the ship.[182]

McKinley's message to Congress said that the right to intervene in Cuba "may be justified by the very serious injury to the commerce, trade, and business of our people and by the wanton destruction of property and devastation of the island."[183] Military intervention, however, was a matter for Congress to decide. He asked legislators "to authorize and empower the President to take measures to secure a full and final termination of hostilities between the Government of Spain and the people of Cuba.[184]

Congress passed a joint resolution on April 20 stating that the people of Cuba "are, and of right to be, free and independent" and that Spain should "at once relinquish its authority and government in the Island of Cuba and withdraw its land and naval forces from Cuba and Cuban waters." Congress empowered President McKinley "to use the entire land and naval forces of the United States, and to call into the actual service of the United States the militia of the several States, to such extent as may be necessary to carry these resolutions into effect."[185] The House majorities were large: 325 to 19 and 311 to 6.[186] The Senate was more divided, supporting the war 42 to 35.[187] On April 22, Congress increased the size of the military establishment to prepare for war.[188] Three days later Congress declared war, stating that war "has existed since the twenty-first day of April."[189]

The war lasted but a few months, and on August 12, Spain accepted an armistice. As a result of war, Cuba gained its independence and the United States acquired the Philippines, Puerto Rico, and Guam. The peace treaty, ratified on February 6, 1899, extended American territory to the Pacific, despite Congress's previous disclaimer of any intention to exercise control over Cuba, much less over other territories. U.S. aims in Cuba could most likely have been secured by diplomatic rather than by military means. Shortly after war had been declared, Senator John Coit Spooner wrote to a

---

181. Id. at 6290.
182. Lewis L. Gould, The Spanish-American War and President McKinley 35 (1982).
183. 13 Richardson 6289.
184. Id. at 6292.
185. 30 Stat. 738–39 (1898).
186. 31 Cong. Rec. 3820–21, 4063–64 (1898).
187. Id. at 4040.
188. 30 Stat. 361–63.
189. Id. at 364.

friend that "possibly the President could have worked out the business without war, but the current was too strong, the demagogues too numerous, and the fall elections too near."[190]

In a speech delivered in Boston in 1899, McKinley observed that the war power has a momentum of its own, often spiraling beyond the control of either Congress or the President: "What nation was ever able to write an accurate program of the war upon which it was entering, much less decree in advance the scope of its results? Congress can declare war, but a higher power decrees its bounds and fixes its relations and responsibilities. The President can direct the movements of soldiers on the field and fleets upon the sea, but he can not foresee the close of such movements or prescribe their limits."[191]

McKinley was too modest about his influence, suggesting that he was largely a pawn in world affairs. Once war broke out between the United States and Spain, it was McKinley who cabled Admiral Dewey: "Proceed at once to Philippine Islands. Commence operations at once, particularly against the Spanish fleet. You must capture vessels or destroy."[192] A war begun in Cuba and authorized by Congress quickly spread to the Far East because of a presidential decision. On April 20, Congress recognized the independence of Cuba and directed the President to use land and naval forces to carry this resolution into effect.[193] Two days later Congress increased the military establishment.[194] McKinley's cable to Dewey is dated April 24, one day before the declaration of war (stating that "war has existed since the twenty-first day of April").

After the peace treaty with Spain was ratified, rebels in the Philippines remained at war against the U.S. forces and were not subdued until 1906. Scattered hostilities continued as late as 1913.[195] The Senate held hearings in 1902 to examine charges of American atrocities against Filipinos, receiving testimony from American commanders who admitted to the burning and destruction of homes and shacks. When one Senator noted that the punishment fell "mainly upon the women and little children" and asked

190. Spooner to C. W. Porter, May 2, 1898; Spooner Papers, Container 135, page 224, Library of Congress.
191. Home Market Club Banquet, Boston, Mass., 1899, McKinley Papers, Library of Congress, 7–8.
192. 1 John D. Long, The New American Navy 181–82 (1903).
193. 30 Stat. 738 (1898).
194. Id. at 361–63.
195. R. Ernest Dupuy and William H. Baumer, The Little Wars of the United States 65–99 (1968).

whether such conduct by U.S. troops was within the ordinary rules of civilized warfare, an American general replied: "These people are not civilized."[196]

196. Hearings before the Senate Committee on the Philippines in Relation to Affairs in the Philippine Islands, 57th Cong., 1st Sess. 559 (1902); Richard E. Welch Jr., "American Atrocities in the Philippines: The Indictment and the Response," 43 Pac. Hist. Rev. 233 (1974).

3

AMERICA STEPS OUT: 1900–1945

By the time the nineteenth century closed, America's empire stretched far beyond the narrow confines of the eastern seaboard familiar to the founding fathers. To continental America was now added the Louisiana Purchase, the Floridas (East and West), Texas, territory from the Mexican War (California, Arizona, Nevada, New Mexico, and Utah), the Pacific northwest (Idaho, Oregon, and Washington), Alaska, and Hawaii. The war with Spain in 1898 extended the arm of America to Cuba and Puerto Rico in the Atlantic and to the Philippines and Guam in the Pacific.

President Theodore Roosevelt, in his fourth annual message in 1904, underscored America's long-term interest in its newly acquired empire. The people in the Philippines, he said, "are utterly incapable of existing in independence at all or of building up a civilization of their own."[1] The strategic value of this region was readily acknowledged. "I do not overlook the fact," said Roosevelt, "that in the development of our interests in the Pacific Ocean and along its coasts, the Philippines have played and will play an important part; and that our interests have been served in more than one way by the possession of the islands."[2]

In the early decades of the twentieth century, America intervened regularly in other countries to "protect lives and property." The two world wars (especially the second) shifted major international responsibilities to the United States. Because of mutual security treaties, including NATO and SEATO, the United States joined with other countries in collective security pacts. Despite legislative history to the contrary, executive officials would cite these treaties as an additional source of unilateral presidential authority. The United Nations Charter added to these expectations, triggering expansive (and erroneous) definitions of presidential power when operating under the umbrella of a UN operation.

1. 14 Richardson 6928.
2. Id.

56

Protecting Life and Property

On numerous occasions Presidents invoked the right to protect American lives and property abroad as justification for military intervention in foreign countries. Although "life and property" was the ostensible reason, these military adventures always served some larger purpose of American foreign policy. Presidents based military action not on legislative authority but on claims of inherent executive responsibilities. A prominent example from the nineteenth century was the U.S. bombardment of Greytown (see Chapter 2).

Military intervention is not automatically required to protect American lives. On December 9, 1891, President Benjamin Harrison reported to Congress about an incident in Valparaiso, Chile, that resulted in the death of two American seamen and the serious injury of several other Americans. Although the initial reply of the Secretary of Foreign Affairs of Chile's provisional government "was couched in an offensive tone," Harrison did not recommend the use of force. Instead, he told Congress that if Chile's subsequent response should be disappointing or delayed, "I will by a special message bring this matter again to the attention of Congress for such actions as may be necessary."[3] Any unilateral action contemplated by Harrison was to be nonmilitary: asking for a suitable apology and adequate reparation for the injury done to the United States[4] or terminating diplomatic relations with Chile.[5] The incident, as Harrison explained in messages to Congress, was favorably resolved without military force when Chile paid an indemnity to the families of the sailors killed or injured.[6]

Various studies have attempted to identify life-and-property actions. In 1928, Milton Offutt compiled a list of 76 instances between 1813 and 1927,[7] and in a 1945 study James Grafton Rogers collected 148 examples of U.S. military operations abroad. The latter list, however, includes many declared wars as well as actions taken by President Franklin D. Roosevelt before Pearl Harbor: the destroyers/bases agreement with Great Britain, the U.S. occupation of Greenland, and the armed convoy ordered by President Roosevelt.[8]

3. 12 Richardson 5621.
4. Id. at 5659.
5. Joyce Goldberg, The "Baltimore" Affair 103 (1986).
6. 12 Richardson 5662, 5747, 5750.
7. Milton Offutt, "The Protection of Citizens Abroad by the Armed Forces of the United States," Johns Hopkins University Studies in Historical and Political Science, ser. 44, no. 4 (1928).
8. James Grafton Rogers, World Policing and the Constitution (1945).

The twentieth century began with presidential use of force in China. In the spring of 1900, in the midst of the presidential campaign in the United States, an antiforeign group of Chinese revolutionists (called "the Boxers") demanded that foreigners be expelled from the country. Foreign legations in Peking were placed under siege and American lives were threatened. With Congress in recess, President McKinley hastily dispatched 5,000 U.S. troops from the Philippines as part of an international expeditionary force including Great Britain, Russia, Germany, France, and Japan. The *Philadelphia Times* called the action "an absolute declaration of war by the executive without the authority or knowledge of Congress, and it is without excuse because it is not a necessity."[9]

When Congress returned, McKinley described in detail the actions he had taken[10] and explained that his actions "involved no war against the Chinese nation."[11] Troops were used to rescue Americans from the imperiled legation, obtain redress from wrongs committed, secure the safety of American life and property, and prevent a spread of the disorders or their recurrence.[12]

A court case raised the question of whether the Boxer Uprising was a "war." Fred Hamilton, a U.S. serviceman charged with murder and found guilty by a military court, was tried and convicted under the 58th article of war, which requires that a general court-martial be assembled in "time of war." A circuit court in Kansas noted that Congress had increased the pay of military personnel fighting in China to the amount paid in "time of actual war." On the basis of that statutory action, including the occupation of Chinese territory by U.S. troops and the many military conflicts, there prevailed in China "a condition of war, within the spirit and intent" of the article of war.[13]

The customary justification for using American forces to protect life and property expanded in 1904 when President Theodore Roosevelt explained America's policy toward other nations in the Western Hemisphere. No nation, he said in his fourth annual message to Congress, need fear U.S. interference in its internal affairs—provided that it act with "reasonable efficiency and decency in social and political matters . . . [and] if it keeps order and pays its obligations." Yet if through mismanagement nations

9. Lewis L. Gould, The Presidency of William McKinley 221–22 (1980).
10. 13 Richardson 6417–25 (December 3, 1900).
11. Id. at 6423.
12. Id.
13. Hamilton v. M'Claughry, 136 Fed. 445, 451 (C.C. Kan. 1905).

failed to meet their foreign obligations, thereby inviting European nations to intervene in South America and the Caribbean to protect their interests, the United States would have to act first. "Chronic wrongdoing" he warned, "or an impotence which results in a general loosening of the ties of civilized society" might compel America to intervene.[14] The United States would interfere "only in the last resort" and "only if it became evident that their inability or unwillingness to do justice at home and abroad had violated the rights of the United States or had invited foreign aggression to the detriment of the entire body of American nations."[15]

This policy became known as the "Roosevelt Corollary" to the Monroe Doctrine. In a message to Congress on December 2, 1823, Monroe had warned European nations not to intervene in American waters: "We should consider any attempt on their part to extend their system to any portion of this hemisphere as dangerous to our peace and safety."[16] In announcing this policy, Monroe made no claim that he could use military power on his own authority to enforce it. Enforcement actions would depend on Congress.

On the basis of this policy of noninterference from other nations, Theodore Roosevelt now justified presidential power to intervene in this region. Troops would be sent abroad not to protect American lives and property but to promote American foreign policy. He had already given this new doctrine a trial run in 1903, responding to Colombia's refusal to ratify a treaty giving the United States a canal right-of-way in Panama (then a province of Colombia). In a draft message to Congress Roosevelt considered taking possession of the isthmus "without any further parley" with Colombia, but events made it unnecessary to deliver the message.[17] After encouraging a revolt by Panamanians, he dispatched U.S. warships to prevent Colombia from suppressing the insurrection.[18] For authority to intervene he cited the Treaty of New Granada of 1846, which he said guaranteed "free and open right of way or transit across the Isthmus of Panama."[19] The actual treaty language provided that the government of New Granada guaranteed to the United States that the right-of-way or transit across the

14. 14 Richardson 6923.

15. Id. at 6924.

16. 2 Richardson 787.

17. George E. Mowry, The Era of Theodore Roosevelt and the Birth of Modern America, 1900–1912, at 151 (1958).

18. Lewis L. Gould, The Presidency of Theodore Roosevelt 96–97 (1991).

19. 14 Richardson 6807. See also statement by Secretary of State Hay, reproduced in "The Panama Revolution," 27 Literary Digest 649 (1903).

isthmus "shall be open and free to the government and citizens of the United States."[20]

A treaty agreed to by a President and the Senate cannot be the basis for recognizing a unilateral power by the President to use military force, a result that would exclude the House of Representatives from its constitutionally assigned duties in the matters of war and peace. Nevertheless, Roosevelt promptly recognized Panama as an independent republic and used force to gain control of the canal zone. He justified his action by pointing to past revolutions, rebellions, insurrections, riots, and other outbreaks that had occurred in Panama: "In short, the experience of over half a century has shown Colombia to be utterly incapable of keeping order on the Isthmus. Only the active interference of the United States has enabled her to preserve so much as a semblance of sovereignty."[21] Roosevelt's logic is interesting: the United States had to intervene to protect another country's sovereignty.

After the new Republic of Panama offered to negotiate a treaty with the United States, Roosevelt submitted the treaty to the Senate, which ratified it in 1904. Roosevelt boasted: "I took the canal zone and let Congress debate, and while the debate goes on the canal does also."[22] His actions were so flagrant that the United States later agreed to make amends. The Thompson-Urrutia Treaty of 1922 gave Colombia special canal rights and a cash grant of $25 million to compensate, in effect, for Roosevelt's heavy-handed tactics. The original version of the treaty contained an expression of "sincere regret" for America's action in 1903,[23] but the final version merely said that the United States and Colombia were "desirous to remove all the misunderstandings growing out of the political events in Panama in November 1903."[24]

Roosevelt implemented his "corollary" when he intervened in the Dominican Republic to set up a fiscal protectorate. The Dominican Republic had built up more than $32 million in debts, primarily to European investors.[25] In 1904 Roosevelt began negotiating an agreement with the Dominican Republic, but Congress insisted that a presidential agreement would not be legally binding. A treaty would be required.[26] Opposition in

20. 9 Stat. 898 (1846).
21. 14 Richardson 6812.
22. Henry F. Pringle, Theodore Roosevelt 330 (1931).
23. Robert K. Murray, The Harding Era: Warren G. Harding and His Administration 340 (1969).
24. 42 Stat. 2122 (1922).
25. Gould, The Presidency of Theodore Roosevelt, at 175.
26. W. Stull Holt, Treaties Defeated by the Senate 214 (1933).

the Senate, coming primarily from Democrats, spelled defeat for his treaty. Early in 1905 an Italian cruiser sailed to the Dominican Republic to collect a debt. Roosevelt responded with military intervention and further negotiation, hoping that the Senate would approve the treaty when Congress returned in December. However, opponents in the Senate held firm, and the treaty was never brought to a vote.[27] Only after Roosevelt drafted a new treaty in 1907, taking into account the objections raised by legislators, did the Senate approve the pact.[28]

President William Howard Taft continued the Roosevelt Corollary by intervening twice in Nicaragua and once each in Honduras and Cuba.[29] Taft responded in part to pressure from American financial interests.[30] Although he used force against these smaller countries, in 1911 he defined his power as Commander in Chief narrowly when it came to intervening in Mexico to protect American lives and property. He told Congress that it was his duty as Commander in Chief to place troops "in sufficient number where, if Congress shall direct that they shall enter Mexico to save American lives and property, an effective movement may be promptly made." He "seriously doubt[ed]" if he had the power "under any circumstances" to intervene on Mexican soil to protect American lives or property. Even if he had such authority he "would not exercise it without express congressional approval."[31]

President Wilson's Forays

Self-determination and nonintervention ranked high among the guiding principles of President Woodrow Wilson, at least in theory. Yet those tenets were often subordinated to a crusading determination to export American constitutionalism to other countries. Taking the Greytown bombardment of 1854 as an acceptable precedent, he ordered American forces to occupy Veracruz in 1914. In a message to a joint session of Congress he said that Mexican officials, under the leadership of President Victoriano Huerta, had arrested several Americans. Although they were released with apologies

27. Id. 219–22.

28. Id. at 228; 35 Stat. 1880 (1907).

29. Offutt, "The Protection of Citizens Abroad by the Armed Forces of the United States," at 104, 107, 109, 111–13.

30. R. Ernest Dupuy and William H. Baumer, The Little Wars of the United States 158 (1968).

31. 15 Richardson 7659.

from the Mexican commander and an expression of regret from Huerta, Wilson was not satisfied. He wanted a formal salute of 21 guns to be given to U.S. naval vessels, a gesture Huerta declined to give. Other incidents convinced Wilson that Mexico had failed to show proper respect for America and that military action was necessary to preserve U.S. dignity and authority. He told Congress:

> No doubt I could do what is necessary in the circumstances to enforce respect for our Government without recourse to the congress, and yet not exceed my constitutional powers as President; but I do not wish to act in a manner possibly of so grave consequence except in close conference and co-operation with both the Senate and the House. I therefore come to ask your approval that I should use the armed forces of the United States.[32]

The House acted in one day to authorize the use of armed forces. The leader of the Republicans, James R. Mann, commented that if the reported incident had involved England, Germany, France, "or any other great power" there would be no clamor for a military response. But because Mexico "is weak, we think we have the moral right to declare practical war against her."[33] After perfunctory debate the House voted 337 to 37 for this language: "That the President of the United States is justified in the employment of armed forces of the United States to enforce the demands made upon Victoriano Huerta for unequivocable amends to the Government of the United States for affronts and indignities committed against this Government by Gen. Huerta and his representatives."[34]

When Senators had the effrontery to pause for one day to think about what they were doing, Wilson went ahead and ordered landing operations by the marines. The following day—just two days after his request—Congress completed action on the joint resolution justifying the President's use of force. The resolution was based entirely on "the facts presented by the President." Although authorizing the use of force, the joint resolution curiously "disclaims any hostility to the Mexican people or any purpose to make war upon Mexico."[35] After beginning with a trivial incident involving

32. 16 Richardson 7936.
33. 51 Cong. Rec. 6937 (1914).
34. Id. at 6957–58.
35. 38 Stat. 770 (1914). The Senate supported the joint resolution on April 21, 1914, by a vote of 72 to 13; 51 Cong. Rec. 7014 (1914).

U.S. seamen in Tampico, the dispute escalated to U.S. bombardment of Veracruz, American occupation of the town for seven months, and the downfall of Huerta.[36]

During the congressional debate, Senator George W. Norris deplored Wilson's demand for flag salutes by small countries: "This matter of saluting the flag is one of the relics that has come down to us through the ages; and a hundred years from now, when the world has advanced farther in civilization, this silly custom, this foolish rule, this international courtesy that has outlived its usefulness, will be forgotten and will be unknown, at least in practice."[37]

The following year Wilson intervened in Haiti to secure a government more acceptable to his administration. He confided to his Secretary of State, "I fear we have not the legal authority to do what we apparently ought to do."[38] Nevertheless, Wilson decided "there is nothing for it but to take the bull by the horns and restore order. A long programme . . . involves legislation and the cooperation of the Senate in treaty-making, and must therefore await the session of our Congress."[39] Unlike the Roosevelt Corollary, Wilson's action was not motivated by any threat of military intervention by European powers,[40] although there was some concern about German influence.[41] American troops remained in Haiti until 1934.

President Wilson's intervention in the Dominican Republic in 1916 resulted in a military occupation that lasted eight years.[42] There appeared to be little financial or commercial interest behind this intervention; a desire for markets or raw materials was not a principal motive.[43] There was some concern that European nations, especially Germany, might gain an unwanted foothold in the area, and the Wilson administration was determined to preserve a U.S. hegemony over the Caribbean region.[44] As an unintended consequence of this invasion, Rafael Trujillo participated in the U.S.–controlled Guardia Nacional and used that group as a unified military base to install himself as dictator for 31 years, from 1930 to his assassination in

36. Robert E. Quirk, An Affair of Honor: Woodrow Wilson and the Occupation of Veracruz (1962).

37. 51 Cong. Rec. 6999 (1914).

38. Arthur S. Link, Wilson: The Struggle for Neutrality 536 (1960).

39. Id.

40. Id. at 535.

41. Hans Schmidt, The United States Occupation of Haiti, 1915–1934, at 57–60 (1971).

42. Link, Wilson: The Struggle for Neutrality, at 543–49.

43. Id. at 549.

44. Bruce J. Calder, The Impact of Intervention: The Dominican Republic during the U.S. Occupation of 1916–24, xii (1984).

1961. He was able to consolidate power in part because the U.S. occupation had weakened the countervailing forces of the regional leaders.[45]

Also in 1916, in a variation of the life-and-property prerogative, Wilson ordered General John J. Pershing in "hot pursuit" of Pancho Villa. The expedition penetrated 350 miles into Mexico, lasted almost a year, and came close to outright war with Mexico.[46] The Senate considered several joint resolutions authorizing military action in Mexico, but no floor votes were taken.[47]

Intervention in Nicaragua

Intervention by the Reagan administration in Nicaragua, one prong of the Iran-Contra affair, was merely the latest of many U.S. incursions in that region. From 1909 to 1933, the United States was rarely out of Nicaragua, moving in repeatedly under the customary banner of protecting lives and property.

In 1909, President Taft sent in marines as part of a policy to undermine the presidency of Jose Santos Zelaya, leader of the Liberty Party. After U.S. forces sided with a rebellion sponsored by the Conservative Party, an unstable coalition of Liberals and Conservatives tried to govern, eventually giving way to Conservative control by 1911. In response to a Liberal revolt in 1912, Taft ordered U.S. troops to crush the rebellion. A legation guard of 100 American troops remained in Managua, helping to secure U.S. control of political and economic conditions in Nicaragua. The Taft administration exerted influence in the election of 1912 to obtain a Nicaraguan president to its liking,[48] and in the election of 1916 the Wilson administration actively supported the candidacy of General Emiliano Chamorro, who was elected.[49]

The U.S. Marines were not removed from Managua until August 4, 1925. Chamorro, who had been out of office, staged a coup d'etat and ousted President Carlos Solorzano. Under pressure from the United States and other Central American countries, Chamorro tried to name a successor but

45. Id. at xviii, 239.
46. Link, Wilson: The Struggle for Neutrality, at 233–34, 456, 467, 489–91; see also Arthur S. Link, Wilson: Confusion and Crises 196–208, 216–17 (1964).
47. 53 Cong. Rec. 1189–96, 9748–49 (1916).
48. Dana G. Munro, Intervention and Dollar Diplomacy in the Caribbean, 1900–1921, at 160–216 (1964).
49. Stuart H. Graham, Latin America and the United States 361 (1943).

Adolfo Diaz eventually became president. Diaz promptly appealed to the United States to aid him in the protection of the interests of Americans and other citizens. In response, President Calvin Coolidge sent war vessels to Nicaragua in 1926, citing the need to protect American lives and property.[50] He told Congress that U.S. military assistance was required because Mexico was supporting revolutionists in Nicaragua.[51]

This explanation, as well as other justifications for the intervention, provoked a skeptical response from Congress and major newspapers. In another effort to justify the use of American troops, the Coolidge administration released a memorandum suggesting that Mexico was trying to spread bolshevism in Nicaragua and Latin America. This account was discredited when Congress learned that the State Department had tried to conceal its role in disseminating this story in the newspapers.[52]

Senator John James Blaine (R-Wis.) led the charge to deny funds to the administration for its involvement in Nicaragua. His amendment read:

> *Provided,* That after December 25, 1928, none of the appropriations made in this act [naval appropriations] shall be used to pay any expenses incurred in connection with acts of hostility against a friendly foreign nation, or any belligerent intervention in the affairs of a foreign nation, or any intervention in the domestic affairs of any foreign nation, unless war has been declared by Congress or unless a state of war actually exists under recognized principles of international law.[53]

Although Blaine's amendment, as later modified, was defeated, the Senate debate on the President's power as Commander in Chief lasted day after day and signaled to the administration that its policy in Nicaragua faced an opposition that would only grow.[54] Finally, in 1932, Congress enacted this language in a naval appropriations bill: "No money appropriated in this Act shall be used to defray the expense of sending additional Marines to Nicaragua to supervise an election there."[55]

President Coolidge offered this reason for U.S. intervention: "We are not making war on Nicaragua any more than a policeman on the street is mak-

50. 68 Cong. Rec. 1324–25 (1927).
51. Id. at 1325.
52. Bryce Wood, The Making of the Good Neighbor Policy 17–20 (1961).
53. 69 Cong. Rec. 6684 (1928).
54. Id. at 7192.
55. 47 Stat. 439 (1932).

ing war on passersby."[56] Constitutional scholar Edward S. Corwin puzzled over this explanation: "In other words, our armed forces has just as much right to be on Nicaragua soil as a policeman has to appear on the streets of his home town."[57] U.S. troops were finally removed from Nicaragua in 1933.

The lengthy and costly interventions in Nicaragua and Haiti created so much dissent in America—within Congress, the executive branch, and the public—that the United States did not again intervene (openly) in the Caribbean or Central America until President Lyndon B. Johnson dispatched U.S. troops to the Dominican Republic in 1965. He feared that there would be a Communist takeover, although later he explained that "99 percent of our reason for going in there was to try to provide protection for these American lives and for the lives of other nationals."[58] In addition to this public intervention, the United States engaged in a number of covert operations during this period, including Guatemala in 1954 and Cuba in 1961 (see Chapter 10).

World War I

Upon the outbreak of the European war in 1914, President Wilson issued proclamations of neutrality.[59] To ensure the enforcement of those proclamations, he issued an order to prohibit "from transmitting or receiving for delivery messages of an unneutral nature, and from in any way rendering to any one of the belligerents any unneutral service, during the continuance of hostilities."[60] He later closed the Marconi Wireless Station at Siasconset, Massachusetts, because it had refused to comply with naval censorship regulations. Attorney General Thomas Gregory justified the action by stating that it was the President's right and duty, in the absence of any statutory restrictions, to close down or seize any plant "should he deem it necessary in securing obedience to his proclamation of neutrality."[61]

Wilson's policy of neutrality gave way gradually to a preference for England over Germany. Americans on the high seas were at risk after Germany announced that the waters around the British isles constituted a

---

56. Thomas A. Bailey, A Diplomatic History of the American People 678 (1969).
57. Edward S. Corwin, Total War and the Constitution 148 (1947).
58. Public Papers of the Presidents, 1965, II, at 616.
59. 16 Richardson 7969–77.
60. Id. at 7962.
61. 30 Op. Att'y Gen. 291, 293 (1914).

war zone and warned neutral ships to keep out of those waters. On May 1, 1915, the American tanker *Gulflight* was torpedoed, with the loss of two lives. A few days later another German torpedo sank the British steamer *Lusitania*. Of the 1,198 passengers who lost their lives, 124 were American. The *Lusitania* carried rifle cartridges, shrapnel, shell castings, and other war matériel.[62]

Wilson, assisted by Secretary of State William Jennings Bryan and counselor to the State Department Robert Lansing, drafted "notes" to be sent to Germany to articulate American policy on submarine warfare. Bryan believed that Germany had the right to prevent contraband from going to the Allies: "A ship carrying contraband should not rely upon passengers to protect her from attack—it would be like putting women and children in front of an army."[63] He also objected to the bias in American policy: "We unsparingly denounce the retaliatory methods employed by [Germany] without condemning the announced purpose of the allies to starve the non-combatants of Germany and without complaining of the conduct of Great Britain in relying on passengers, including men, women and children of the United States, to give immunity to vessels carrying munitions of war."[64] Nevertheless, Bryan acquiesced in Wilson's first note to Germany asking it to disavow the submarine attacks on neutral ships, to make reparation, and to prevent the recurrence of these incidents.[65]

Bryan urged Wilson to warn passengers against taking trips on vessels that carried contraband,[66] a position Wilson found "both weak and futile."[67] Lansing pressed for a harder line, insisting that citizens of neutral countries should be able to traverse the high seas—even in ships carrying armament—without fear of attack.[68] Preferring Lansing's position, Wilson drafted a second note that was more confrontational in tone.[69] Bryan tried to soften the language of the text.[70] When it became obvious that he had lost his battle within the administration and that he could not, in conscience, sign the second note, he resigned from office.[71]

Wilson took steps to prepare the nation for war. In an address delivered

62. 33 The Papers of Woodrow Wilson 135n (Arthur S. Link, ed. 1980).
63. Id. at 134–35.
64. Id. at 166.
65. Id. at 177.
66. Id. at 192.
67. Id. at 194.
68. Id. at 312–13.
69. Id. at 328–31.
70. Id. at 351–55.
71. Id. at 375–76.

to Congress on December 7, 1915, he recommended an increase in the size of the army, acceleration of shipbuilding, and strengthening of the merchant marine.[72] Nevertheless, his reelection campaign in 1916 relied heavily on a promise to keep America out of war. Wilson's renomination at the Democratic convention was accompanied by shouts of "He Kept Us Out of War." On the eve of the election, on October 31, 1916, he announced: "I am not expecting this country to get into war."[73]

When Germany refused to abandon its policy of unrestricted submarine warfare, Wilson broke diplomatic relations on February 3, 1917. On February 26, he asked Congress for authority to arm American merchant ships to protect them from German submarine attacks. In stepping from neutrality to armed neutrality, he offered a broad interpretation of his constitutional powers:

> I feel that I ought . . . to obtain from you full and immediate assurance of the authority which I may need at any moment to exercise. No doubt I already possess that authority without special warrant of law, by the plain implication of my constitutional duties and powers; but I prefer, in the present circumstances, not to act upon general implication. I wish to feel that the authority and the power of the Congress are behind me in whatever it may become necessary for me to do.[74]

The House passed the bill on March 1 by a vote of 403 to 13, but a number of Senators joined in a filibuster to block action on the proposal. Wilson denounced them as a "little group of wilful men, representing no opinion but their own."[75] After Congress adjourned without acting on Wilson's request, he proceeded to arm the vessels "for the sole purpose of defense." The administration's policy stipulated that no armed guard of any American merchant vessel "shall take any offensive action against any submarine of Germany or of any nation following the policy of Germany . . . unless the submarine is guilty of an unlawful act that jeopardizes the vessel, her passengers, or crew, or unless the submarine is submerged."[76]

It was Wilson, then, who made the crucial policy decision to move from

72. 16 Richardson 8106–10.
73. Harvey A. DeWeerd, President Wilson Fights His War: World War I and the American Intervention 21 (1968).
74. 16 Richardson 8211.
75. Id. at 8218.
76. 41 The Papers of Woodrow Wilson 395–96 (Link, ed. 1983).

neutrality to armed neutrality and finally to a state of war with Germany. In his history of World War I, Harvey A. DeWeerd said that of all the American pressures operating to bring the country into war in April 1917, "the greatest force was that of the President. His position, his opinions, his decisions, and his actions were decisive."[77] On April 2, 1917, Wilson called Congress into extraordinary session to review the continued use of German submarines against neutral vessels. Concluding that armed neutrality "now appears [to be] impracticable,"[78] he asked Congress to declare war on Germany, a step it took four days later. The Senate supported the declaration 82 to 6; the House vote was 373 to 50.[79]

The *Curtiss-Wright* Case

In recent decades, presidential power in foreign affairs has drawn much of its legal support from a badly reasoned, badly grounded decision issued by the Supreme Court in 1936. In *United States* v. *Curtiss-Wright Corp.*, the Court was asked to decide whether Congress had delegated too broadly when it empowered the President to declare an arms embargo in South America. The statute allowed the President to impose an arms embargo whenever he found that it "may contribute to the reestablishment of peace" between belligerents. Did this give the President too much discretion?

The previous year, in two cases, the Court had struck down the delegation of *domestic* power to the President.[80] All that was necessary in *Curtiss-Wright* was for the Court to announce that Congress could delegate more broadly in international affairs than in domestic affairs. The issue was never the existence of independent presidential power. The Court was asked whether *Congress,* in determining the extent of *its* power, could grant the President more discretion than would be permissible for domestic policy. Instead, the Court went far beyond the bounds of the case to find extraconstitutional powers for the President. Seldom has a court reached so far with so little evidence to support its conclusion.

The author of *Curtiss-Wright,* Justice George Sutherland, had been a Senator from Utah and a member of the Senate Foreign Relations Committee. The decision closely tracks the article "The Internal and External Pow-

77. DeWeerd, President Wilson Fights His War, at 7–8.
78. 16 Richardson 8227.
79. 55 Cong. Rec. 261, 412–13 (1917).
80. Panama Refining Co. v. Ryan, 293 U.S. 388 (1935); Schechter Corp. v. United States, 295 U.S. 495 (1935).

ers of the National Government" (printed as a Senate document in 1910) and his book, *Constitutional Power and World Affairs* (1919).[81] According to his biographer, Sutherland advocated "a vigorous diplomacy which strongly, even belligerently, called always for an assertion of American rights."[82]

There are many deficiencies in Sutherland's opinion. He insisted that foreign and domestic affairs are different "both in respect of their origin and their nature" because the powers of external sovereignty "passed from the Crown not to the colonies severally, but to the colonies in their collective and corporate capacity as the United States of America."[83] By transferring external or foreign affairs directly to the national government, and then linking foreign affairs to the executive, Sutherland supplied a powerful but deceptive argument for presidential power.

Sutherland's history is false. External sovereignty did not circumvent the colonies and the states and pass directly to an independent executive. In 1776, there was no President or separate executive branch. Only one branch of government functioned at the national level: the Continental Congress. It had to discharge all governmental duties, including legislative, executive, and judicial. Scholars, pointing out that the states in 1776 operated as sovereign entities and not as part of a collective body, have repudiated this part of Sutherland's opinion. The creation of a Continental Congress in 1776 did not disturb the sovereign power of the states to make treaties, borrow money, solicit arms, lay embargoes, collect tariff duties, and conduct separate military campaigns.[84] The Supreme Court has recognized that the American colonies, upon their separation from England, acquired certain elements of sovereignty.[85]

Even if the power of external sovereignty had somehow passed intact from the Crown to the "United States," the Constitution allocates that power both to Congress and the President. The President and the Senate share the treaty power. The President receives ambassadors from other countries, but U.S. ambassadors must be approved by the Senate. Congress has the power to declare war, to raise and support the military forces, to make rules for

---

81. S. Doc. No. 417, 61st Cong., 2d Sess. (1910).

82. Joel Francis Paschal, Mr. Justice Sutherland: A Man against the State 93 (1951).

83. 299 U.S. 304, 315–16 (1936).

84. Charles Lofgren, "*United States* v. *Curtiss-Wright Export Corporation*: An Historical Reassessment," 83 Yale L. J. 1 (1973); David M. Levitan, "The Foreign Relations Power: An Analysis of Mr. Justice Sutherland's Theory," 55 Yale L. J. 467 (1946); Claude H. Van Tyne, "Sovereignty in the American Revolution: An Historical Study," 12 Am. Hist. Rev. 529 (1907).

85. United States v. California, 332 U.S. 19, 31 (1947); Texas v. White, 74 U.S. 700, 725 (1869).

their regulation, to provide for the calling up of the militia to suppress insurrections and repel invasions, and to provide for the organization and disciplining of the militia. The Constitution also explicitly grants to Congress the power to lay and collect duties on foreign trade, to regulate commerce with foreign nations, and to establish a uniform rule of naturalization. Sutherland was also simplistic in drawing such a bright line between external and internal affairs and in assuming that the President's latitude was inordinately broad whenever he acted in foreign or international matters. The framers made no such distinctions and world events since 1936 have increased the overlap between foreign and domestic affairs.[86] In 1991 President Bush remarked: "I guess my bottom line . . . is you can't separate foreign policy from domestic."[87] Two years later President Clinton expressed a similar view: "There is no longer a clear division between what is foreign and what is domestic."[88]

Sutherland spoke strongly about the President's independent power to negotiate agreements with other countries: "He *makes* treaties with the advice and consent of the Senate; but he alone negotiates. Into the field of negotiation the Senate cannot intrude; and Congress itself is powerless to invade it."[89] But the power to negotiate is not the power to make foreign policy unilaterally. Edwin Borchard, a specialist in international law, said that the power discussed by Sutherland "does not give the President carte blanche to do anything he pleases in foreign affairs, for it is limited to 'negotiation and inquiry.'"[90]

Sutherland wrote eloquently about "this vast external realm, with its important, complicated, delicate and manifold problems." As a consequence, he said, legislation over the international field must often accord to the President "a degree of discretion and freedom from statutory restrictions which would not be admissible were domestic affairs alone involved."[91] He then went beyond this position (based on *statutory* grants of power) to argue for inherent presidential power. He claimed that the exercise of presidential power does not depend solely on an act of Congress because of the "very delicate, plenary and exclusive power of the President as the sole

---

86. Bayless Manning, "The Congress, the Executive and 'Intermestic' Affairs: Three Proposals," 55 Foreign Affairs 306 (1977).

87. Public Papers of the Presidents, 1991, II, at 1629.

88. Public Papers of the Presidents, 1993, I, at 2.

89. 299 U.S. at 319 (emphasis in original).

90. Edwin Borchard, "The Attorney General's Opinion on the Exchange of Destroyers for Naval Bases," 34 Am. J. Int'l L. 690, 691 (1940).

91. 299 U.S. at 319, 320.

organ of the federal government in the field of international relations."[92]
Sutherland searched for powers outside the Constitution.[93]

The magic term "sole organ" suggests that when it comes to foreign policy, the President is the exclusive policymaker. The language carries special weight because John Marshall used it in a speech in 1800 while serving in the House of Representatives. Given Marshall's elevation a year later
to become Chief Justice of the Supreme Court, Sutherland seemed to be
drawing from an impeccable, authoritative source, but Sutherland wrenched
Marshall's statement from context to imply a position Marshall never
advanced. At no time, either in 1800 or later, did Marshall suggest that the
President possessed unreviewable power to make foreign policy. Quite the
contrary.

During the debate in 1800, opponents of President John Adams argued
for his impeachment after he had agreed to turn over to England someone
charged with murder. Because the case was already pending in an
American court, some members of Congress recommended that Adams be
impeached for encroaching upon the judiciary and violating the doctrine
of separation of powers. At this point Marshall intervened to say that there
was no basis for impeachment. Adams, who was carrying out an extradition treaty entered into between England and the United States, had not
attempted to make national policy single-handedly. He was carrying out a
policy made jointly by the President and the Senate (for treaties). Only after
the policy had been formulated through the collective effort of the executive and legislative branches (by treaty or by statute) did the President
emerge as the "sole organ" in *implementing* national policy. It was here
that Marshall said that the President "is the sole organ of the nation in its
external relations and its sole representative with foreign nations."[94] The
President merely *announced* policy; he did not *make* it.

As Justice Robert Jackson later observed, the most that can be drawn
from *Curtiss-Wright* is the intimation that the President "might act in external affairs without congressional authority, but not that he might act contrary to an act of Congress."[95] Jackson noted that "much of the [Sutherland]
opinion is dictum"—comments extraneous to the issue before the Court.[96]
In 1981 a federal appellate court cautioned against placing undue reliance
on "certain dicta" in Sutherland's opinion: "To the extent that denominat-

92. Id. at 320.
93. Louis Henkin, Foreign Affairs and the Constitution 22 (1972).
94. Annals of Congress, 6th Cong., 613 (1800).
95. Youngstown Co. v. Sawyer, 343 U.S. 579, 636 n. 2 (1952).
96. Id.

ing the President as the 'sole organ' of the United States in international affairs constitutes a blanket endorsement of plenary Presidential power over any matter extending beyond the borders of this country, we reject that characterization."[97]

Even though Sutherland's opinion is filled with historical and conceptual inaccuracies, *Curtiss-Wright* became a popular citation for Court decisions (and academic commentary) upholding presidential power. The case is frequently cited to support not only broad delegations of legislative power to the President but also the existence of independent, implied, and inherent powers for the President.[98]

Legislative Constraints in the 1930s

By passing the Neutrality Acts of 1935, 1937, and 1939, Congress attempted to keep the United States out of foreign wars. Even though this legislation initially enjoyed the backing of the executive branch, the Neutrality Acts would later be cited as evidence that members of Congress lack the sophistication to participate effectively in issues of foreign policy and national security.

Although Congress would later receive the lion's share of criticism for the Neutrality Acts of the 1930s, executive officials also believed that this type of legislation would help insulate the United States from foreign wars. On January 11, 1933, President-elect Franklin D. Roosevelt said that he had "long been in favor of the use of embargoes on arms to belligerent nations, especially to nations which are guilty of making an attack on other nations . . . that is, against aggressor nations."[99] When the Chaco War in South America could not be resolved through negotiation, Roosevelt asked Congress in 1934 for authority to place an arms embargo on both belligerents and received that authority in a statute later upheld by the Supreme Court in *Curtiss-Wright*.[100]

97. American Intern. Group v. Islamic Republic of Iran, 657 F.2d 430, 438 n. 6 (D.C. Cir. 1981).

98. For broad-delegation arguments, see Ex parte Endo, 323 U.S. 283, 298 n. 21 (1944), Zemel v. Rusk, 381 U.S. 1, 17 (1965), and Goldwater v. Carter, 444 U.S. 996, 1000 n. 1 (1979). Inherent Powers are discussed in United States v. Pink, 315 U.S. 203, 229 (1942), Knauff v. Shaughnessy, 338 U.S. 537, 542 (1950), United States v. Mazurie, 419 U.S. 544, 566–67 (1975), and Dames & Moore v. Regan, 453 U.S. 654, 661 (1981).

99. Edwin Borchard, Neutrality for the United States 308 (1973).

100. Id. at 313–14; 48 Stat. 811 (1934); United States v. Curtiss-Wright, 299 U.S. 304 (1936).

A committee investigation by Senator Gerald P. Nye (R-N.Dak.) in 1934 popularized the theory that controls on the U.S. munitions industry would help keep the United States out of foreign wars. The Neutrality Act of 1935 provided for the prohibition of the export of arms, ammunition, and implements of war to belligerent countries. Under this legislation, "upon the outbreak or during the progress of war between, or among, two or more foreign states," the President would proclaim that fact and trigger the prohibition of war matériel to that region.[101] President Roosevelt signed the bill and called its purpose "wholly excellent" and "wholly good," cautioning that some "inflexible [embargo] provisions might drag us into war instead of keeping us out."[102] Some experts testified that the legislation created opportunities for presidential war-making.[103]

The outbreak of war in Spain in 1936 called attention to the fact that the neutrality legislation, confined to wars between nations, did not cover civil wars. Congress proceeded to pass separate legislation to prohibit the exportation of arms, ammunition, and implements of war from the United States to Spain.[104] In issuing a proclamation to comply with that statute, Roosevelt acknowledged that "the people of the United States and their representatives certainly were not prepared in 1937 to risk the slightest chance of becoming involved in a quarrel in Europe which had all the possibilities of developing into a general European conflict."[105]

Congress continued to pass other neutrality acts in 1937 and 1939. The 1937 statute carved out an exception for the Monroe Doctrine by providing that the neutrality policy "shall not apply to an American state or states, provided the American republic is not cooperating with a non-American state or state in such war."[106] The 1939 statute provided that either branch could find that a state of war existed in other countries. The President or Congress (acting by concurrent resolution) could declare the existence of war between foreign nations.[107]

Throughout 1939 Roosevelt criticized the embargo provisions of the Neutrality Acts and recommended their repeal, telling Congress that he now regretted signing the neutrality statutes in 1935 and 1937.[108] Although

101. 49 Stat. 1081 (1935).
102. 4 Public Papers and Addresses of Franklin D. Roosevelt 345–46 (1935 volume).
103. Borchard, Neutrality for the United States 327.
104. 50 Stat. 3 (1937).
105. 6 Public Papers and Addresses of Franklin D. Roosevelt 192 (1937 volume).
106. 50 Stat. 124, sec. 4 (1937).
107. 54 Stat. 4, sec. (1a) (1939).
108. 8 Public Papers and Addresses of Franklin D. Roosevelt 516 (1939 volume). See also 3–4, 154–55, 381–88, 395–97.

he objected to the use of arms embargoes and fought successfully for their removal from the 1939 bill, at the same time he announced: "Our acts must be guided by one single hard-headed thought—keeping America out of this war [in Europe]."[109]

Also during this period Congress considered a constitutional amendment proposed by Rep. Louis Ludlow (D-Ind.) to subject a declaration of war to a popular vote in a referendum. Except in the event of an invasion of the United States or its territorial possessions and attacks upon U.S. citizens residing in those areas, "the authority of Congress to declare war shall not become effective until confirmed by a majority of all votes cast thereon in a Nationwide referendum."[110] Sufficient signatures were collected to discharge the amendment from the House Committee on Rules, but in 1938 the House voted 209 to 188 against bringing the measure to the floor for further debate and consideration.[111]

World War II

Even more than Wilson, Franklin Delano Roosevelt led the country from a state of neutrality to one of war. On September 8, 1939, after Germany invaded Poland, Roosevelt proclaimed a state of limited emergency. In response to a Senate resolution, Attorney General Frank Murphy collected a list of statutes that became active upon the proclamation of a state of emergency or war. Murphy, without claiming to be presenting a complete list, referred to about 50 statutes granting powers that could be exercised by the President in time of national emergency or during a war in which the United States was neutral.[112]

The United States supplied war matériel to the Allies to help them in their struggle against Germany and Italy. In June 1940, when France requested additional assistance from the United States, Roosevelt expressed admiration for the "resplendent courage" of French armies resisting German invaders and pledged continuing assistance of airplanes, artillery, and munitions. But he cautioned: "I know that you will understand that these state-

109. Id. at 521.
110. 82 Cong. Rec. 250 (1937).
111. 83 Cong. Rec. 282–83 (1938). See also 82 Cong. Rec. 242–51, 1516–18 (1937); 83 Cong. Rec. 276–83 (1938); Buel W. Patch, "The Power to Declare War," 1 Editorial Research Reports 3–18, 398–99 (1938); and Donald R. Wolfensberger, Congress & the People: Deliberative Democracy on Trial 79–84 (2000).
112. Executive Powers under National Emergency, S. Doc. No. 133, 76th Cong., 2d Sess. (October 5, 1939).

ments carry with them no implication of military commitments. Only the Congress can make such commitments."[113] At a speech in Charlottesville, Va., that same month, he promised to "extend to the opponents of force the material resources of this nation."[114]

When France asked for some old U.S. destroyers to strengthen its naval forces in the Mediterranean, Roosevelt claimed he had no such authority: "Any exchange for American destroyers probably inacceptable because of enormous sea area which must be patrolled by us and would require Congressional action which might be very difficult to get. Our old destroyers cannot be sold as obsolete as is proved by fact. All of them are now in commission and in use or are in process of being commissioned for actual use."[115] Nevertheless, some members of Congress heard of rumors that "destroyers in our Navy were being transferred, or that negotiations were under way for the transfer of these naval vessels."[116] In response, Congress enacted a statute on June 28, 1940, seeking to prohibit such transfers unless the Chief of Naval Operations or the Chief of Staff of the Army "shall first certify that such material is not essential to the defense of the United States."[117]

Prime Minister Winston Churchill pressed Roosevelt for used destroyers. When Roosevelt presented the matter to his cabinet, White House aides suggested ways of transferring the vessels without obtaining authority from Congress. The administration enlisted the assistance of retired General Pershing, who urged that the United States give England and Canada "at least fifty of the over-age destroyers which are left from the days of the World War."[118] Wendell Wilkie, Republican candidate for the presidency in 1940, assured the administration that he would not make an issue of the transfer in the campaign.[119]

With the ground thus softened up, President Roosevelt announced on September 3 an agreement to exchange 50 "over-age" destroyers with Britain in return for the right to use bases on British islands in the Atlantic and the Caribbean.[120] Made solely by executive agreement, the destroyers/bases deal circumvented congressional control. Attorney General Robert Jackson defended the constitutionality of the agreement by claiming that the

113. 9 Public Papers and Addresses of Franklin D. Roosevelt 267 (1940 volume).
114. Id. at 264.
115. Charles Callan Tansill, Back Door to War: The Roosevelt Foreign Policy, 1933–41, at 591 (1952) (Roosevelt to Sumner Welles, June 1, 1940).
116. 86 Cong. Rec. 8775 (1940).
117. 54 Stat. 681, sec. 14 (1940).
118. New York Times, August 5, 1950, at 1.
119. Charles Callan Tansill, Back Door to War, at 597.
120. 9 Public Papers and Addresses of Franklin D. Roosevelt 391 (1940 volume).

President's function as Commander in Chief placed upon him a responsibility "to use all constitutional authority which he may possess to provide adequate bases and stations for the utilization of the naval and air weapons of the United States at their highest efficiency in our defense."[121] Jackson relied partly on Sutherland's opinion in *Curtiss-Wright*.[122]

Legal experts did not find Jackson's opinion convincing under either domestic law or international law.[123] Concluded one expert: "The destroyers have by now been transferred; but let no one say that it was accomplished 'legally.' The supplying of these vessels by the United States Government to a belligerent is a violation of our neutral status, a violation of our national law, and a violation of international law."[124] Edward S. Corwin also attacked Jackson's opinion, regarding the destroyer deal as an invasion of Congress's power to define for the United States the requirements of international law respecting neutrality and an invasion of Congress's constitutional power to declare war.[125]

Jackson himself, sitting later as Associate Justice of the Supreme Court, did not find all of his earlier writings on presidential power convincing either. In the Steel Seizure Case of 1952, attorneys for President Truman cited Jackson's arguments on several occasions.[126] Jackson merely noted: "While it is not surprising that counsel should grasp support from such unadjudicated claims of power, a judge cannot accept self-serving press statements of the attorney for one of the interested parties as authority in answering a constitutional question, even if the advocate was himself."[127]

Similar to Wilson's promise to the American people in 1916, Roosevelt pledged to keep the nation out of war. On October 23, 1940, in Philadelphia, he vigorously denied that his administration "wishes to lead this country to war." He repeated the Democratic Party platform: "We will not participate in foreign wars and we will not send our army, naval or air forces to fight in foreign lands outside of the Americas except in case of attack."[128] On

---

121. 39 Op. Att'y Gen. 484, 486 (1940).

122. Id. at 486–87.

123. Quincy Wright, "The Transfer of Destroyers to Great Britain," 34 Am. J. Int'l L. 680 (1940); Edwin Borchard, "The Attorney General's Opinion on the Exchange of Destroyers for Naval Bases," 34 Am. J. Int'l L. 690 (1934).

124. Herbert W. Briggs, "Neglected Aspects of the Destroyer Deal," 34 Am. J. Int'l L. 569, 587 (1940).

125. Edward S. Corwin, "Executive Authority Held Exceeded in Destroyer Deal," New York Times, October 13, 1940, sec. 4, at 6, 7.

126. 48 Landmark Briefs 705, 755–57, 920–22, 927–28 (1975).

127. Youngstown Co. v. Sawyer, 343 U.S. 579, 647 (1952).

128. 9 Public Papers and Addresses of Franklin D. Roosevelt 494, 495 (1940 volume).

October 30, in Boston, Roosevelt told the crowd: "I have said this before, but I shall say it again and again and again: 'Your boys are not going to be sent into any foreign wars.'"[129]

After his election, Roosevelt could be more open about giving military weapons to England. In a news conference on December 17, Roosevelt used a down-home argument to justify additional assistance to Great Britain. Instead of building ships and other weapons to be sold to England, he suggested that it might make more sense to let England use those materials rather than keep them in storage in America. In that way, defending England would defend America. Through such techniques he was trying to "eliminate the dollar sign." Roosevelt then gave his famous analogy:

> Well, let me give you an illustration: Suppose my neighbor's home catches fire, and I have a length of garden hose four or five hundred feet away. If he can take my garden hose and connect it up with his hydrant, I may help him to put out his fire. Now, what do I do? I don't say to him before that operation, "Neighbor, my garden hose cost me $15; you have to pay me $15 for it." What is the transaction that goes on? I don't want $15—I want my garden hose back after the fire is over.[130]

Asked whether this concept would require congressional approval, Roosevelt responded: "Oh, yes, this would require various types of legislation, in addition to appropriation."[131] On March 11, 1941, Congress passed the Lend-Lease Act, which authorized the President to manufacture any defense article and to "sell, transfer title to, exchange, lease, lend, or otherwise dispose of" the defense articles to any country whose defense he deemed vital to the defense of the United States.[132]

In an appeal to Congress on April 10, Roosevelt asked for legislation that would allow him to make use of foreign merchant vessels in American ports. About 80 foreign ships were lying idle in U.S. waters and another 150 vessels were idle in other ports of the Western Hemisphere. Roosevelt said that he lacked authority to use these ships.[133] Congress provided the necessary legislation.[134]

129. Id. at 517.
130. Id. at 607.
131. Id. at 610.
132. 55 Stat. 31 (1941).
133. 10 Public Papers and Addresses of Franklin D. Roosevelt 94 (1941 volume).
134. 55 Stat. 242 (1941).

On April 11, Roosevelt signed an agreement with Denmark that pledged America's defense of Greenland (a Danish possession) in return for the right to construct and operate defense installations on the island.[135] Also in April, he announced his decision to extend American naval patrols halfway across the Atlantic. The Navy would search for German submarines and report their presence to British commanders.[136]

On May 27, Roosevelt proclaimed the existence of an unlimited national emergency.[137] Within two weeks he had signed another agreement with Iceland to permit U.S. forces to land there in order to prevent Germany from occupying that island and using it as a naval or air base against the Western Hemisphere.[138] Still operating on the basis of independent executive power, Roosevelt seized the North American Aviation plant in Inglewood, California, on June 7 and followed that with the seizure of several other defense facilities.[139] On June 14, Roosevelt ordered the freezing of all remaining assets of Germany, Italy, and Axis-controlled countries.[140] Three months before Pearl Harbor, he issued his "shoot-on-sight" order to U.S. forces in defense waters, warning that German and Italian vessels would enter those areas at their own risk.[141]

Following Japan's attack on Pearl Harbor on December 7, 1941, Roosevelt asked Congress to declare war.[142] The Senate voted unanimously for the declaration, 82 to 0; the House vote was 388 to 1.[143] On December 11, Germany and Italy declared war on the United States. Congress promptly recognized a state of war with those nations.

In the autumn of 1942, President Roosevelt notified Congress that it had failed to enact two of his recommendations for inflation control. Now that four months had passed, the President told Congress that if it did not pass such legislation in the next month, authorizing him to stabilize the cost of living, he could be left with "an inescapable responsibility to the people of this country to see to it that the war effort is no longer imperiled by threat of economic chaos." In the event that Congress failed to act, "and act adequately, I shall accept the responsibility, and I will act."[144]

135. 10 Public Papers and Addresses of Franklin D. Roosevelt 96 (1941 volume).
136. Id. at 132–35.
137. Id. at 194.
138. Id. at 255.
139. Id. at 205.
140. Id. at 217.
141. Id. at 390–91.
142. Id. at 515.
143. 87 Cong. Rec. 9506, 9536–37 (1941).
144. 11 Public Papers and Addresses of Franklin D. Roosevelt 364 (1942 volume).

Congress provided the additional inflation controls only one day after his deadline.

In that same address to Congress, Roosevelt said that when the war was over, "the powers under which I act automatically revert to the people— to whom they belong."[145] Yet those powers did not revert to the people when the war was over; presidential powers are not surrendered so easily. President Harry Truman announced the end of the war in Europe on May 8, 1945, and on August 14 he announced the surrender of Japan. Nevertheless, in May 1946 he seized certain bituminous coal mines under authority of the War Labor Disputes Act, which empowered the President to take possession of any plant, mine, or facility as may be required for the "war effort." That authority remained in force until the President proclaimed the "termination of hostilities," a step Truman did not take until December 31, 1946, more than 16 months after Japan's surrender. By proclaiming that hostilities had terminated, Truman relinquished certain wartime powers but retained others that remained available during "a state of war" or a "state of emergency." Truman stressed that "a state of war still exists."[146]

The Supreme Court endorsed this consolidation of presidential power. The Housing and Rent Act of 1947 provided for an extension of wartime rent controls. In upholding this statute, the Court observed that the housing deficit, created by the demobilization of veterans and the reduction of residential construction during the war, had not yet been eliminated. The Court did concede that war in modern times affected the economy for years afterward and created a dangerous situation in which the war power "may not only swallow up all other powers of Congress but largely obliterate the Ninth and Tenth Amendments as well."[147]

In 1947 Congress terminated several "temporary" emergency war powers. Approximately 175 statutory provisions were involved, many dating back to World War I. Even with that action, 103 war or emergency statutes remained in effect.[148] On April 28, 1952, Truman finally signed a statement terminating the state of war with Japan and the national emergencies proclaimed by Roosevelt in 1939 and 1941. Although actual hostilities had lasted for fewer than four years, Roosevelt and Truman exercised emergency and war powers for more than twelve.

145. Id. at 365.
146. Public Papers of the Presidents, 1946, at 512–13.
147. Woods v. Miller, 333 U.S. 138, 146 (1948).
148. 61 Stat. 449 (1947); Public Papers of the Presidents, 1947, at 357.

4

THE UN CHARTER AND KOREA

In June 1950, President Truman ordered U.S. troops to Korea without first requesting congressional authority. For legal footing he cited resolutions passed by the UN Security Council, a beguiling but spurious source of authority. In 1990 the Bush administration tried the same tactic, using the Korean War as an acceptable precedent for taking offensive action against Iraq, again without seeking congressional approval. Like Truman, Bush claimed that Security Council resolutions were a sufficient base of authority. In Bosnia, too, President Clinton relied on UN resolutions and NATO agreements as sufficient authority to use military force without first seeking congressional approval. He cited a UN resolution as authority to invade Haiti.

UN machinery is not a legal substitute for congressional authority. If that were possible, the President and the Senate, through treaty action, could strip from the House of Representatives its constitutional role in deciding questions of war. Following the same logic, the President and the Senate, through a treaty process, could rely on the United Nations to determine trade and tariff matters, again bypassing the prerogatives of the House of Representatives. The history of the United Nations makes it very clear that all parties in the legislative and executive branches understood that the decision to use military force through the United Nations required prior approval from both Houses of Congress.

The League of Nations

The need for congressional approval for UN-sanctioned military actions is underscored by the history of the Versailles Treaty and the League of Nations. The Senate defeated the Versailles Treaty in 1919 and again in 1920, largely because a number of Senators insisted that any commitments of U.S. troops to a world body (the League of Nations) first had to be approved by Congress. On that issue and others, President Wilson refused to yield.

President Wilson submitted the treaty to the Senate on July 10, 1919, attaching to it the Covenant of the League of Nations. The Covenant pro-

vided for an assembly (giving each member nation an equal voice) and a
council (consisting of representatives from the United States, Great Britain,
France, Italy, Japan, and four other nations elected by the assembly).
Members pledged to submit to the League all disputes threatening war and
to use military and economic sanctions against nations that threatened war.
In an emotional address to the Senate, Wilson called the League of Nations
a "practical necessity" and "indeed indispensable." He said that statesmen
saw it as "the hope of the world. . . . Shall we or any other free people hesitate to accept this great duty? Dare we reject it and break the heart of the
world?"[1]

Senator Henry Cabot Lodge (R-Mass.) favored U.S. participation in the
League but proposed a number of "reservations" to protect American interests. The second of fourteen reservations concerned the congressional prerogative to decide questions of war:

> The United States assumes no obligation to preserve the territorial
> integrity or political independence of any other country or to inter-
> fere in controversies between nations—whether members of the
> league or not—under the provisions of Article 10, or to employ the
> military or naval forces of the United States under any article of the
> treaty for any purpose, unless in any particular case the Congress,
> which, under the Constitution, has the sole power to declare war or
> authorize the employment of the military or naval forces of the
> United States, shall by act or joint resolution so provide.[2]

Wilson opposed the Lodge reservations, claiming that they "cut out the
heart of this Covenant" and represented "nullification" of the treaty.[3] However, his principal advisers, including Secretary of State Robert Lansing,
Bernard Baruch, Herbert Hoover, and Colonel Edward Mandell House, all
urged Wilson to accept the reservations.[4] Personal spite caused Wilson to
dig in his heels. As the newspapers reported at the time, "The President
has strangled his own child."[5]

In fact, Wilson had no principled objection to the Lodge position on the

1. 17 Richardson 8735.
2. 58 Cong. Rec. 8777 (1919).
3. 63 The Papers of Woodrow Wilson 451 (Arthur S. Link, ed. 1990); 64 The Papers
of Woodrow Wilson 47, 51 (Link, ed. 1991).
4. Townsend Hoopes and Douglas Brinkley, FDR and the Creation of the U.N. 6
(1997).
5. 65 The Papers of Woodrow Wilson 71 (Link, ed. 1991).

war power. On March 8, 1920, Wilson wrote to Senator Gilbert Monell Hitchcock (D-Nebr.) explaining why there was no need for the congressional stipulations dealing with Article 10 of the Covenant, under which the League of Nations could take military action. Whatever obligations the U.S. government undertook "would of course have to be fulfilled by its usual and established constitutional methods of action," and there "can be no objection to explaining again what our constitutional method is and that our Congress alone can declare war or determine the causes or occasions for war, and that it alone can authorize the use of the armed forces of the United States on land or on the sea." But to accept the Lodge reservation "would certainly be a work of supererogation," by which Wilson indicated it was superfluous and unnecessary.[6] Events would prove him wrong when President Harry Truman and his successors turned to the UN Security Council for "authority" to use military force against other nations.

Wilson's theory of the treaty process was a simple one: the President proposes, the Senate acquiesces. There was no room in his philosophy of government for independent Senate thinking or the offering of legislative amendments and reservations. His attitude toward the Senate and presidential power had been revealed crisply in two of his books. *Congressional Government* (1885) advocated unilateral presidential negotiation with complete exclusion of the Senate. These executive initiatives would supposedly get the country "into such scrapes, so pledged in the view of the world to certain courses of action, that the Senate hesitates to bring about the appearance of dishonor which would follow its refusal to ratify the rash promises or to support the indiscreet threats of the Department of State."[7] *Constitutional Government in the United States* (1908) reiterated the same line of argument:

> One of the greatest of the President's powers I have not yet spoken of at all: his control, which is very absolute, of the foreign relations of the nation. The initiative in foreign affairs, which the President possesses without any restriction whatever, is virtually the power to control them absolutely. The President cannot conclude a treaty with a foreign power without the consent of the Senate, but he may guide every step of diplomacy, and to guide diplomacy is to determine what treaties must be made, if the faith and prestige of the government are to be maintained. He need disclose no step of nego-

6. Id. at 68.
7. Woodrow Wilson, Congressional Government 233–34 (1885).

tiation until it is complete, and when in any critical matter it is completed the government is virtually committed. Whatever its disincli-
nation, the Senate may feel itself committed also.[8]

This legislative strategy, fully articulated in Wilson's writings, failed
abysmally with the Treaty of Versailles. After excluding the Senate from the
negotiating sessions, he tried to present Senators with a fait accompli. The
result: a resounding political defeat for Wilson. He had never cultivated
sufficient support among Senators to have his handiwork approved, and
the treaty was rejected in November 1919 and again in March 1920. Wilson
appealed to the public in an exhausting campaign across the country, leading to his physical and emotional collapse. The dismal experience of a
President "going it alone" would remain seared in the nation's memory,
casting a shadow over future efforts to create a United Nations.

Creating the UN Charter

America's entry into a world organization was revived in 1943 through a
series of methodical steps: the Ball Resolution, the Connally and Fulbright
Resolutions, and the Moscow Declaration. Those actions were followed by
meetings at Dumbarton Oaks in 1944 and in San Francisco in 1945. The
issue of which branch takes the nation to war—Congress or the President—was ignored at some of the meetings and addressed at others. The
predominant view required prior authorization by Congress (both Houses)
of any commitment of U.S. forces to the United Nations.

On March 16, 1943, Senator Joseph Hurst Ball (R-Minn.) introduced a
resolution calling for the formation of the United Nations. Joined by
Senators Lister Hill (D-Ala.), Harold Burton (R-Ohio), and Carl Hatch (D-
N.Mex.), the bipartisan nature of the resolution commanded respectful
attention. Senator Ball said that the "whole world, and our allies, know
today that it is the United States Senate which will finally decide what will
be the foreign policy of our country when the war ends." He noted that
the Senate's constitutional power in the past had been used "negatively,"
reminding listeners of the rejection of the Treaty of Versailles. Senator Ball
hoped that the decision on the United Nations would not become
embroiled in partisan politics.[9] Senate debate on the Ball Resolution said
nothing about which branch of government would commit U.S. troops.

8. Woodrow Wilson, Constitutional Government in the United States 77–78 (1908).
9. 89 Cong. Rec. 2031 (1943).

On the day that Ball introduced his resolution, Walter Lippmann wrote an article on the Senate's role in giving advice and consent to treaties. Lippmann had long been identified as a defender of foreign policy formulated by elites and executive officials. In an article published in the *Washington Post*, he now urged that President Wilson's mistake with the Treaty of Versailles not be repeated. Ways and means had to be found of "enabling the Senate to participate in the negotiations."[10]

On September 20, the House debated a resolution introduced by J. William Fulbright (D-Ark.) to support the concept of a United Nations. The language was exceedingly brief: "*Resolved by the House of Representatives (the Senate concurring)*, That the Congress hereby expresses itself as favoring the creation of appropriate international machinery with power adequate to establish and to maintain a just and lasting peace, among the nations of the world, and as favoring participation by the United States therein."[11] Rep. Hamilton Fish Jr. (R-N.Y.) proposed that Fulbright's resolution end with the language "favoring participation by the United States therein *through its constitutional processes*."[12] Fish explained that the additional language meant that any commitment to join the United Nations, made either by agreement or by treaty, "must go through in a constitutional way, either by a two-thirds vote of the Senate or by the approval of the entire Congress."[13] He warned that a number of members of Congress were prepared to oppose the Fulbright Resolution because they "are afraid that some secret commitments will be entered into and that the Congress will be by-passed, and that the Constitution will be ignored.[14]

The House passed the Fulbright Resolution, as introduced, 252 to 23.[15] The following day it voted again, after adding the language "through its constitutional processes," and this time the margin was 360 to 29.[16] The House action sharply challenged the Senate's presumed monopoly to define foreign policy for the legislative branch. The debate pointed out that both Houses had acted on the declaration of war for World War II, voted funds to sustain it, and conscripted American soldiers to fight the battles.[17] Recalling the Senate's role in rejecting the Treaty of Versailles, Rep. Mike

10. Id. at 2032 ("Advice and Consent of the Senate," Washington Post, March 16, 1943, at 26).
11. Id. at 7623.
12. Id. at 7646–47 (emphasis added).
13. Id. at 7647.
14. Id.
15. Id. at 7655.
16. Id. at 7728–29.
17. Id. at 7705 (Representative Richards).

Monroney (D-Okla.) said he was "unwilling to surrender to 33 Members of the Senate, one-third of that body, the life or death veto over the security of future generations of Americans."[18]

The Senate ignored the Fulbright Resolution, which had been introduced as a concurrent resolution (H. Con. Res. 25) and therefore needed agreement by the Senate. Instead, the Senate considered a resolution (S. Res. 192) that required only its own action. Debate on this resolution, the Connally Resolution, stretched from October 25 through November 5. Similar to the House resolution, it included the phrase "through its constitutional processes" to prevent the President from joining the United Nations without explicit congressional support.[19] Congressional processes meant the "powers of Congress"—*both* Houses, not just the Senate.[20] A few Senators thought of congressional action solely through the treaty process, excluding the House,[21] but the majority recognized that international commitments (in this case joining the United Nations) could be made either by treaty or by a majority of each House voting on a bill or joint resolution.[22]

The final version of the Connally Resolution, approved 85 to 5, provides that the United States, "acting through its constitutional processes," joins in the establishment of an international authority with power to prevent aggression. The final paragraph states that any treaty made to effect the purposes of the resolution shall be made only with the concurrence of two-thirds of the Senate.[23] Senator Robert Taft (R-Ohio) said that the requirement for Senate action was added because of the fear that the President "has shown some indications of a desire to do by executive agreement things which certainly in my opinion ought to be the subject of a treaty."[24]

Little was said during this lengthy Senate debate about congressional controls over the use of American troops in a UN action. Senator Claude Pepper (D-Fla.) opposed any delegation of Congress's war-declaring power to an international body but believed that it would be permissible for American troops to be used, without prior congressional approval, as a "police force" to combat aggression in small wars.[25] The loose notion of

18. Id. at 7706.
19. Id. at 9187 (Senator Willis, first column).
20. Id. at 8662 (reading by the legislative clerk).
21. Id. at 9187 (Senator Willis, first column); id. at 9189 (Senator Brooks); id. at 9205 (Senator Wherry).
22. Id. at 9207 (Senator Hayden).
23. Id. at 9222.
24. Id. at 9101.
25. Id. at 8742–43.

a "police action" would be later used by President Truman as a legal pretext for going to war in Korea without congressional approval. Truman was a member of the Senate at the time Pepper made that remark.

Senate action on the Connally Resolution occurred during a four-nation conference that endorsed an international peacekeeping organization. On October 30, 1943, the United States, the United Kingdom, the Soviet Union, and China issued the Moscow Declaration, which set forth a number of guiding principles. The declaration recognized "the necessity of establishing at the earliest practicable date a general international organization . . . for the maintenance of international peace and security."

Those same nations met a year later at Dumbarton Oaks, in Washington, D.C., to give further definition to the international organization. Legal specialists who monitored these meetings speculated on the procedures for going to war. Edwin Borchard later surmised: "Constitutionally, the plan seems to assume that the President, or his delegate, without consulting Congress, the war-making and declaring authority, can vote for the use of the American quota of armed forces, if that can be limited when the 'aggressor' resists."[26] Two weeks after the end of the conference at Dumbarton Oaks, President Roosevelt delivered an address in which he indicated the need for advance congressional approval:

> The Council of the United Nations must have the power to act quickly and decisively to keep the peace by force, if necessary. A policeman would not be a very effective policeman if, when he saw a felon break into a house, he had to go to the town hall and call a town meeting to issue a warrant before the felon could be arrested.
>
> It is clear that, if the world organization is to have any reality at all, our representatives must be endowed in advance by the people themselves, by constitutional means through their representatives in the Congress, with authority to act.[27]

But Borchard learned that after Roosevelt's death, President Truman sent a cable from Potsdam stating that all agreements involving U.S. troop commitments to the United Nations would first have to be approved by both Houses of Congress.[28] Borchard, too, believed that the Constitution required

26. Edwin Borchard, "The Dumbarton Oaks Conference," 39 Am. J. Int'l. L. 97, 101 (1945).

27. 11 Dep't of State Bull. 447, 448 (1945).

28. Edwin Borchard, "The Charter and the Constitution," 39 Am. J. Int'l L. 767–68 (1945).

approval by both Houses, not merely the Senate,[29] but another perspective appeared in a letter to the *New York Times*. Six specialists of international law analyzed the President's authority to contribute troops to the United Nations. They recognized the risks for congressional prerogatives: "It is doubtless true that Congress will feel a certain hesitancy in permitting the President, acting through the Security Council, to engage even a small policing force in international action because it will fear that this might commit the United States to further military action and thus might impair the discretion of Congress in respect to engagement in 'war.'" Yet they suggested that Presidents in the past had had broad discretion in the use of military force and had frequently acted without explicit congressional authority. The American constitutional system, they said, relied heavily on good-faith actions and sensitive political judgment by the President: "Congress has always been dependent upon the good faith of the President in calling upon it when the situation was so serious that a large-scale use of force may be necessary."[30]

The meetings at Dumbarton Oaks were followed by a conference in San Francisco in 1945, attended by 50 nations and lasting nine weeks. Unlike Wilson's futile strategy for the Versailles Treaty, half of the eight members of the U.S. delegation came from Congress: Senators Tom Connally (D-Tex.) and Arthur H. Vandenberg (R-Mich.) and Representatives Sol Bloom (D-N.Y.) and Charles A. Eaton (R-N.J.).[31] John Foster Dulles, later to be Secretary of State under President Eisenhower, told the Senate Foreign Relations Committee in 1945 that in the past he had had "some doubts as to the wisdom of Senators participating in the negotiation of treaties." After his experience at the San Francisco conference, he said, those doubts "were dispelled."[32]

Out of the San Francisco conference came the United Nations Charter, submitted to the Senate for approval. The United Nations consisted of a General Assembly representing all member states, an eleven-member Security Council (including China, France, the Soviet Union, the United Kingdom, and the United States as permanent members), a Secretariat, an International Court of Justice, and specialized councils. Chapter VII of the Charter dealt with UN responses to threats to peace, breaches of the peace, and

29. Id. at 770–71.

30. New York Times, November 5, 1944, at 8E. Signers of the letter: John W. Davis, W. W. Grant, Philip C. Jessup, George Rublee, James T. Shotwell, and Quincy Wright.

31. "The Charter of the United Nations," hearings before the Senate Committee on Foreign Relations, 79th Cong., 1st Sess. 197 (1945).

32. Id. at 644.

acts of aggression. Procedures were established to permit the United Nations to employ military force to deal with such threats. All UN members would make available to the Security Council, "on its call and in accordance with a special agreement or agreements," armed forces and other assistance for the purpose of maintaining international peace and security. The agreements were to be concluded between the Security Council and member states and "shall be subject to ratification by the signatory states in accordance with their respective constitutional processes." Thus, the decision of who would grant that approval in the United States— Congress, the President, or the two branches acting jointly—was deliberately deferred. Each nation needed to determine its own "constitutional processes."

From July 9 to July 13, 1945, the Senate Foreign Relations Committee held hearings on the Charter. Leo Pasvolsky, a special assistant to the Secretary of State, was asked whether Congress would have ultimate control over the special agreements to use armed force. Pasvolsky replied: "That is a domestic question which I am afraid I cannot answer."[33] Senator Vandenberg volunteered that, in his opinion, the President would not need "the consent of Congress to every use of our armed forces."[34]

John Foster Dulles, an adviser to the U.S. delegation at San Francisco, testified that the procedure for special agreements would need the approval of the Senate and could not be done unilaterally by the President.[35] Dulles elaborated: "It is clearly my view, and it was the view of the entire United States delegation, that the agreement which will provide for the United States military contingent will have to be negotiated and then submitted to the Senate for ratification in the same way as a treaty." Senator Connally agreed with that interpretation.[36] When Senator Walter F. George (D-Ga.) suggested that congressional approval could be by statute, involving both Houses, Dulles disagreed: "The procedure will be by treaty—agreements submitted to the Senate for ratification."[37] Senator Eugene Millikin (R-Colo.) tried to distinguish between "policing powers" (to be exercised exclusively by the President) and "real war problems" (reserved for congressional action).[38] Dulles replied sympathetically: "If we are talking about a little bit

---

33. "The Charter of the United Nations," hearings before the Senate Committee on Foreign Relations, 79th Cong., 1st Sess. 298 (1945).
34. Id. at 299.
35. Id. at 645–46.
36. Id. at 646.
37. Id. at 652.
38. Id. at 654.

of force necessary to be used as a police demonstration, that is the sort of thing that the President of the United States has done without concurrence by Congress since this Nation was founded."[39]

During floor debate, Senator Scott Lucas (D-Ill.) took sharp exception to Dulles's contention that special agreements would come back to Congress as treaties to be disposed of solely by the Senate. Such agreements, Lucas said, required action by both Houses, and he cited constitutional passages giving to the entire Congress powers to raise and support armies and to make rules for the government and regulation of the land and naval forces.[40] Action by both Houses is required to declare war and to appropriate funds for the military. A number of Senators agreed with Lucas in rejecting the proposition advanced by Dulles.[41]

As the debate continued Senator Vandenberg reached Dulles by phone to clarify his position. Dulles explained that when the issue came up in the hearings, he thought the question was between unilateral action by the President (through executive agreements) or retaining congressional control (which Dulles took to mean action on treaties). The central point he wanted to make, Dulles said, was that "the use of force cannot be made by exclusive Presidential authority through an executive agreement." He was positive about that. On the other issue—whether Congress should act by treaty or by joint resolution—he was less certain.[42]

At other points during the debate Senator Harlan Bushfield (R-S.Dak.) said he had objected, "and I still object, to a delegation of power to one man or to the Security Council, composed of 10 foreigners and 1 American, to declare war and to take American boys into war." Such a proposal "is in direct violation of the Constitution." Congress did not have the power, Bushfield said, "to make such a delegation even if we desired to do so."[43] Senator Burton Wheeler (D-Mont.) was also emphatic on that point: "If it is to be contended that if we enter into this treaty we take the power away from the Congress, and the President can send troops all over the world to fight battles anywhere, if it is to be said that that is to be the policy of this country, I say that the American people will never support any Senator or any Representative who advocates such a policy; and make no mistake about it."[44]

39. Id. at 655.
40. 91 Cong. Rec. 8021 (1945).
41. Id. at 8021–24 (Senators McClellan, Hatch, Fulbright, Maybank, Overton, Hill, Ellender, and George).
42. Id. at 8027–28.
43. Id. at 7156.
44. Id. at 7988.

President Truman, aware of the Senate debate on which branch controlled the sending of armed forces to the United Nations, wired a note from Potsdam to Senator Kenneth McKellar (D-Tenn.) on July 27, 1945, in which he pledged: "When any such agreement or agreements are negotiated it will be my purpose to ask the Congress for appropriate legislation to approve them."[45] In asking "Congress" for legislation, Senators understood that Congress "consists not alone of the Senate but of the two Houses."[46] With that understanding, the Senate approved the UN Charter by a vote of 89 to 2.[47]

Congress now had to pass additional legislation to implement the Charter and determine the precise mechanisms for the use of force. The specific procedures, brought into conformity with "constitutional processes," are included in the UN Participation Act of 1945.

The UN Participation Act

Nothing in the passage of the Fulbright and Connally Resolutions or the history of the UN Charter supports the notion that Congress, by endorsing the structure of the United Nations as an international peacekeeping body, altered the Constitution by reading itself out of the war-making power. Congress did not—it could not—do that, a conclusion driven home sharply by the legislative history of the UN Participation Act.

Under the provisions of the UN charter, in the event of any threat to the peace, breach of the peace, or act of aggression, the UN Security Council may decide under Article 41 of the UN Charter to recommend "measures not involving the use of armed force." If those measures prove inadequate, Article 43 provides that all UN members shall make available to the Security Council—in accordance with "special agreements"—armed forces and other assistance. The agreements would spell out the numbers and types of forces, their degree of readiness and general location, and the nature of the facilities and assistance to be provided. It was anticipated that each nation would ratify these agreements "in accordance with their respective constitutional processes."

The meaning of U.S. constitutional processes is defined by Section 6 of the UN Participation Act of 1945. Without the slightest ambiguity, this

45. Id. at 8185.
46. Id. (Senator Donnell).
47. Id. at 8190.

statute requires that the agreements "shall be subject to the approval of the Congress by appropriate Act or joint resolution." Statutory language could not be more clear. The President must seek congressional approval in advance. Two qualifications are included in Section 6:

> The President shall not be deemed to require the authorization of the Congress to make available to the Security Council on its call in order to take action under Article 42 of said Charter and pursuant to such special agreement or agreements the armed forces, facilities, or assistance provided therein: *Provided,* That nothing herein contained shall be construed as an authorization to the President by the Congress to make available to the Security Council for such purpose armed forces, facilities, or assistance in addition to the forces, facilities, and assistance provided for in such special agreements or agreements.[48]

The first qualification states that once the President receives the approval of Congress for a special agreement, he does not need subsequent approval from Congress to provide military assistance under Article 42 (under which the Security Council determines that peaceful means are inadequate and military action is necessary). Congressional approval is needed for the special agreement, not subsequent implementations of the agreement. The second qualification clarifies that nothing in the UN Participation Act is to be construed as congressional approval of other agreements attempted by the President.

Thus, the qualifications do not eliminate or weaken the need for congressional approval. Presidents could commit armed forces to the United Nations only after Congress gave its explicit consent. That point is crucial. The League of Nations Covenant foundered precisely on the issue of needing congressional approval before using armed force. The framers of the UN Charter recalled that history and very consciously included protections for congressional prerogatives.[49]

The legislative history of the UN Participation Act reinforces the need for advance congressional approval. In his appearance before the House Committee on Foreign Affairs, Under Secretary of State Dean Acheson explained that only after the President receives the approval of Congress is he "bound to furnish that contingent of troops to the Security Council;

48. 59 Stat. 621, sec. 6 (1945).
49. Michael J. Glennon, "The Constitution and Chapter VII of the United States Charter," 85 Am. J. Int'l L. 74, 75–77 (1991).

and the President is not authorized to furnish any more than you have approved of in that agreement."[50] When Edith Rogers (R-Mass.) remarked that Congress "can easily control the [Security] Council," Acheson agreed unequivocally: "It is entirely within the wisdom of Congress to approve or disapprove whatever special agreement the President negotiates."[51] John Kee (D-W.Va.) wondered whether the qualifications in Section 6 of the UN Participation Act permitted the President to provide military assistance to the Security Council without consulting or submitting the matter to Congress. Acheson firmy rejected that possibility. No special agreement, Acheson said, could have any "force or effect" until Congress approved it:

> This is an important question of Judge Kee, and may I state his question and my answer so that it will be quite clear here: The judge asks whether the language beginning on line 19 of page 5, which says the President shall not be deemed to require the authorization of Congress to make available to the Security Council on its call in order to take action under article 42 of the Charter, means that the President may provide these forces prior to the time when any special agreement has been approved by Congress.
>
> The answer to that question is "No," that the President may not do that, that such special agreements refer to the special agreement which shall be subject to the approval of the Congress, so that until the special agreement has been negotiated and approved by the Congress, it has no force and effect.[52]

Other parts of the legislative history support that understanding. In reporting the UN Participation Act, the Senate Foreign Relations Committee anticipated a shared, coequal relationship between the President and Congress:

> Although the ratification of the Charter resulted in the vesting in the executive branch of the power and obligation to fulfill the commitments assumed by the United States thereunder, the Congress must be taken into close partnership and must be fully advised of all phases of our participation in this enterprise. The Congress will be asked annually to appropriate funds to support the United Nations

50. "Participation by the United States in the United Nations Organization," hearings before the House Committee on Foreign Affairs, 79th Cong., 1st Sess. 23 (1945).
51. Id.
52. Id. at 25–26.

budget and for the expenses of our representation. It will be called upon to approve arrangements for the supply of armed forces to the Security Council and thereafter to make appropriations for the maintenance of such forces.[53]

The Senate Foreign Relations Committee further noted that "all were agreed on the basic proposition that the military agreements could not be entered into solely by executive action."[54] Nevertheless, during floor debate, Senators Connally and Taft agreed that in "certain emergencies" the President and the Security Council might be able to act without first obtaining authority from Congress.[55] These comments are interesting, but they do not change the statutory requirement that special agreements be approved in advance by "appropriate Act or joint resolution." Moreover, Connally and Taft seemed to be laboring under concepts left over from the San Francisco conference and the Senate debate over the UN Charter. They were endorsing the President's ability to become engaged in "police actions" without any congressional involvement.

Connally's confusion is evident a few pages later where he agrees with Senator Kenneth Wherry (R-Nebr.) that special agreements could be made by treaty.[56] That misinterpretation, originally pushed by John Foster Dulles and others, was explicitly corrected by the language in Section 6 of the UN Participation Act. Later, an amendment was offered in the Senate to authorize the President to negotiate a special agreement with the Security Council solely with the support of two-thirds of the Senate.[57] Senator Vandenberg opposed the amendment on these grounds:

> If we go to war, a majority of the House and Senate puts us into war. . . . The House has equal responsibility with the Senate in respect of raising armies and supporting and sustaining them. The House has primary jurisdiction over the taxation necessities involved in supporting and sustaining armies and navies, and in maintaining national defense.
>
> . . . [The Senate Foreign Relations Committee] chose to place the ratification of that contract in the hands of both Houses of Congress,

---

53. S. Rept. No. 717, 79th Cong., 1st Sess. 5 (1945).
54. Id. at 8.
55. 91 Cong. Rec. 10965–66 (1945).
56. Id. at 10974.
57. Id. at 11296.

inasmuch as the total Congress of the United States must deal with
all the consequences which are involved either if we have a war or
if we succeeded in preventing one.[58]

Vandenberg's reasoning prevailed. The great majority of Senators, recognizing that the decision to go to war must be made by both Houses of
Congress, defeated the amendment decisively, 57 to 14.[59]

The House of Representatives also designed the UN Participation Act to
protect congressional prerogatives over war and peace. In reporting the
bill, the House Foreign Affairs Committee drew attention to the vote in the
Senate rejecting the idea that special agreements could be handled solely
by the Senate through the treaty process. The committee "believes that it
is eminently appropriate that the Congress as a whole pass upon these
agreements under the constitutional powers of the Congress."[60] During
floor debate, Rep. Sol Bloom (D-N.Y.), one of the delegates at the San
Francisco conference, underscored that point: "The position of the Congress is fully protected by the requirement that the military agreement to
preserve the peace must be passed upon by Congress before it becomes
effective. Also, the obligation of the United States to make forces available
to the Security Council does not become effective until the special agreement has been passed upon by Congress."[61]

The restrictions on the President's power under Section 6 to use armed
force were clarified by amendments adopted in 1949, allowing the
President on his own initiative to provide military forces to the United
Nations for "cooperative action." However, presidential discretion to deploy
these forces is subject to stringent conditions: they can serve only as
observers and guards, can perform only in a noncombatant capacity, and
cannot exceed 1,000 in number.[62] Moreover, in providing these troops to
the United Nations the President shall assure that the troops not involve
"the employment of armed forces contemplated by chapter VII of the
United Nations Charter."[63] Clearly, there is no opportunity in the UN
Participation Act or its amendments for unilateral military commitments by
the President.

58. Id. at 11301.
59. Id. at 11303.
60. H. Rept. No. 1383, 79th Cong., 1st Sess. 7 (1945).
61. 91 Cong. Rec. 12267 (1945).
62. 63 Stat. 735–36, sec. 5 (1949).
63. Id.

Vandenberg Resolution

The capacity of the United Nations to establish a military force, dependent on contributions from each nation, ran into immediate problems when the permanent members of the Security Council exercised their veto power. By 1948, the Senate Foreign Relations Committee reported a resolution in response to "the excessive use of the veto and failure to reach agreement upon the provision of armed forces for the Security Council."[64] The resolution, known as the Vandenberg Resolution, reflected the decision of the Soviet Union to invoke the veto 23 times, eleven of the vetoes related to the admission of new members. "Most of the others related to the pacific settlement of international disputes."[65]

Vandenberg's resolution proposed a voluntary agreement to remove the veto from all questions involving pacific settlements of international disputes. At the same time, and in recognition of problems within the Security Council, the resolution looked to the "progressive development of regional and other collective arrangements for individual and collective self-defense in accordance with the purposes, principles, and provisions of the Charter."[66] The Rio Treaty was already in place; other mutual security treaties, such as NATO, were to come. The committee insisted that "any commitments made pursuant to the resolution must be clearly defined and would require appropriate congressional approval. Thus, if any programs of material assistance are formulated, they will require legislative authorization and appropriations. If any treaty commitments are involved, they will require ratification with the advice and consent of the Senate."[67]

On that point the committee was "unequivocally in agreement."[68] As to the procedure for entering into agreements to provide the United Nations with armed forces, the committee said "it has long been clear" that such agreements "would require congressional approval."[69] The committee reported the Vandenberg Resolution by a vote of 13 to 0.[70] After extensive debate, the Senate passed the resolution 64 to 4.[71]

64. S. Rept. No. 1361, 80th Cong., 2d Sess. 2 (1948).
65. Id. at 4.
66. Id. at 1.
67. Id. at 6.
68. Id. at 8.
69. Id.
70. Id. at 9.
71. 94 Cong. Rec. 6053–54, 7681, 7791–7846 (1948).

The Korean War

With these safeguards supposedly in place to protect congressional pre-rogatives, on June 26, 1950, President Truman announced to the American public that he had conferred with the Secretaries of State and Defense, their senior advisers, and the Joint Chiefs of Staff "about the situation in the Far East created by unprovoked aggression against the Republic of Korea."[72] He said that the UN Security Council had acted to order a withdrawal of the invading forces to positions north of the 38th parallel and that "in accordance with the resolution of the Security Council, the United States will vigorously support the effort of the Council to terminate this serious breach of the peace."[73] At that point, he made no commitment of U.S. military forces.

On the following day, however, President Truman announced that North Korea had failed to cease hostilities and to withdraw to the 38th parallel. He summarized the UN action in this manner: "The Security Council called upon all members of the United Nations to render every assistance to the United Nations in the execution of this resolution. In these circumstances I have ordered United States air and sea forces to give the [South] Korean Government troops cover and support."[74]

In addition, Truman said that "the occupation of Formosa by Communist forces would be a direct threat to the security of the Pacific area and to United States forces performing their lawful and necessary functions in that area."[75] Finally, he advised that all members of the United Nations "will consider carefully" the consequences of Korea's aggression "in defiance of the Charter of the United Nations" and that a "return to the rule of force in international affairs" would have far-reaching effects. The United States, he said, "will continue to uphold the rule of law."[76]

In fact, Truman violated the unambiguous statutory language and legislative history of the UN Participation Act. How could he pretend to act militarily in Korea under the UN umbrella without any congressional approval? The short answer is that he ignored the procedure for special agreements that was the vehicle for assuring congressional control. With the Soviet Union absent, the Security Council voted 9 to 0 to call upon

72. Public Papers of the Presidents, 1950, at 491.
73. Id.
74. Id. at 492.
75. Id.
76. Id.

North Korea to cease hostilities and to withdraw their forces. Two days later the Council requested military assistance from UN members to repel the attack, but by that time Truman had already ordered U.S. air and sea forces to assist South Korea.

Truman's legal authority was nonexistent for two reasons. First, it cannot be argued that the President's constitutional powers vary with the presence or absence of Soviet delegates at the Security Council. As Robert Bork noted in 1971, "the approval of the United Nations was obtained only because the Soviet Union happened to be boycotting the Security Council at the time, and the President's Constitutional powers can hardly be said to ebb and flow with the veto of the Soviet Union in the Security Council."[77]

Second, the Truman administration did not act pursuant to UN authority, even though it strained to make that case. On June 29, 1950, Secretary of State Acheson claimed that all U.S. actions taken in Korea "have been under the aegis of the United Nations."[78] Aegis is a fudge word, meaning shield or protection. Acheson was using the word to suggest that the United States was acting under the legal banner of the United Nations, which was not the case.

Acheson falsely claimed that Truman had done his "utmost to uphold the sanctity of the Charter of the United Nations and the rule of law" and that the administration was in "conformity with the resolutions of the Security Council of June 25 and 27, giving air and sea support to the troops of the Korean government."[79] Truman committed U.S. forces before the Council called for military action. General Douglas MacArthur was immediately authorized to send supplies of ammunitions to the South Korean defenders. On June 26, Truman ordered U.S. air and sea forces to give South Koreans cover and support.[80] After Acheson had summarized the military situation for some members of Congress at noon on June 27, President Truman exclaimed: "But Dean, you didn't even mention the U.N.!"[81] Later that evening the Security Council passed the second resolution. In his memoirs, Acheson admitted that "some American action, said to be in support of the resolution of June 27, was in fact ordered, and pos-

77. Robert H. Bork, "Comments on the Articles of the Legality of the United States Action in Cambodia," 65 Am. J. Int'l L. 79, 81 (1971).
78. 23 Dep't of State Bull. 43 (1950).
79. Id. at 46.
80. Public Papers of the Presidents, 1950, at 529.
81. Glenn D. Paige, The Korean Decision 188 (1968).

sibly taken, prior to the resolution."[82] After he left the presidency, Truman was asked whether he had been prepared to use military force in Korea without UN backing. He replied with customary bluntness: "No question about it."[83]

President Truman did not seek the approval of members of Congress for his military actions in Korea. As Acheson suggested, Truman might only wish to "tell them what had been decided."[84] Truman met with congressional leaders at 11:30 A.M. on June 27, after the administration's policy had been established and implementing orders issued.[85] He later met with congressional leaders to give them briefings on developments in Korea, but never asked for authority.[86] Some consideration was given to presenting a joint resolution to Congress to permit legislators to voice their approval, but the draft resolution never left the administration.[87]

On June 29, at a news conference, Truman was asked whether the country was at war. His response: "We are not at war."[88] Asked whether it would be more correct to call the conflict "a police action under the United Nations," he agreed: "That is exactly what it amounts to."[89] The United Nations exercised no real authority over the conduct of the war. Other than token support from a few nations, it was an American war. The Security Council requested that the United States designate the commander of the forces and authorized the "unified command at its discretion to use the United Nations flag."[90] Truman designated General MacArthur to serve as commander of this so-called unified command.[91] Measured by troops, money, casualties, and deaths, it remained an American war.

Federal and state courts had no difficulty in defining the hostilities in Korea as war. A federal district court noted in 1953: "We doubt very much if there is any question in the minds of the majority of the people of this

82. Dean Acheson, Present at the Creation 408 (1969). See also Edwin C. Hoyt, "The United States Reaction to the Korean Attack: A Study of the Principles of the United Nations Charter as a Factor in American Policy-Making," 55 Am. J. Int'l I. 45, 53 (1961).

83. Merle Miller, Plain Speaking: An Oral Biography of Harry S. Truman 276n (1973).

84 FRUS, 1950. vol. 7, 182 (1976).

85. Id., 200–202.

86. Id., 257.

87. Id., 282–83, nn. 1 and 2; 287–91.

88. Public Papers of the Presidents, 1950, at 504.

89. Id. On July 13, at a news conference, he again called the Korean War a "police action." Id. at 522.

90. Id. at 520.

91. Id.

country that the conflict now raging in Korea can be anything but war."[92] During Senate hearings in June 1951, Secretary of State Acheson conceded the obvious by admitting "in the usual sense of the word there is a war."[93]

Truman's violation of constitutional and statutory requirements may have resulted from a mistaken reading of history. In deciding whether North Korean aggression could go unanswered, he looked, in his own lifetime, to Japan's invasion of Manchuria and Germany's reoccupation of the Rhineland. He did not consider other historical parallels where force had been used, such as the American Civil War or nineteenth-century efforts in Germany for unification. Apparently it did not occur to him that the situation in Korea resembled a civil war more than it did the aggression in Manchuria and the Rhineland.[94]

Even if a case could be made that the emergency facing Truman in June 1950 required him to act promptly without first seeking and obtaining legislative authority, nothing prevented him from returning to Congress and asking for a supporting statute for retroactive authority. John Norton Moore has made this point: "As to the suddenness of Korea, and conflicts like Korea, I would argue that the President should have the authority to meet the attack as necessary but should immediately seek congressional authorization."[95] I would put it a little differently: In a genuine emergency, a President may act without congressional authority (and without express legal or constitutional authority), trusting that the circumstances are so urgent and compelling that Congress will endorse his actions and confer a legitimacy that only Congress, as the people's representatives, can provide. If the President exercises poor judgment and usurps power, he can be impeached.

Political Repercussions

Congress's reaction to Truman's usurpation of the war power was largely passive. Some members offered the weak justification that "history will

92. Weissman v. Metropolitan Life Ins. Co., 112 F.Supp. 420, 425 (S.D. Cal. 1953). See also Gagliomella v. Metropolitan Life Ins. Co., 122 F.Supp. 246 (D. Mass. 1954); Carius v. New York Life Insurance Co., 124 F.Supp. 388 (D. Ill. 1954); Western Reserve Life Ins. Co. v. Meadows, 261 S.W.2d 554 (Tex. 1953); and A. Kenneth Pye, "The Legal Status of the Korean Hostilities," 45 Geo. L. J. 45 (1956).

93. "Military Situation in the Far East" (part 3), hearings before the Senate Committees on Armed Services and Foreign Relations, 82d Cong., 1st Sess. 2014 (1951).

94. Richard S. Kirkendall, Harry S Truman and the Imperial Presidency 11, 16 (1975).

95. John N. Moore, "The National Executive and the Use of the Armed Forces Abroad," 21 Naval War College Rev. 28, 32 (1969).

show that on more than 100 occasions in the life of this Republic the President as Commander in Chief has ordered the fleet or the troops to do certain things which involved the risk of war" without seeking congressional consent."[96] This list of alleged precedents for unilateral presidential action contains not a single military adventure that comes even close to the magnitude of the Korean War. As Edward S. Corwin noted, the list consists largely of "fights with pirates, landings of small naval contingents on barbarous or semi-barbarous coasts, the dispatch of small bodies of troops to chase bandits or cattle rustlers across the Mexican border, and the like."[97]

A few legislators insisted that Truman should have gone to Congress for authority first.[98] Rep. Vito Marcantonio (ALP-N.Y.) delivered this indictment: "When we agreed to the United Nations Charter we never agreed to supplant our Constitution with the United Nations Charter. The power to declare and make war is vested in the representatives of the people, in the Congress of the United States."[99] Senator Taft warned that if the President could intervene in Korea "without congressional approval, he can go to war in Malaya or Indonesia or Iran or South America." Taft conceded that U.S. entry into the United Nations created a new framework, "but I do not think it justifies the President's present action without approval by Congress." Taft referred to Section 6 of the UN Participation Act, noting that no special agreement had ever been negotiated by the Truman administration and submitted to Congress for its approval.[100]

Almost a year after the war began, a number of Senators participated in a lengthy debate that thoroughly shredded the administration's legal pretenses. Truman's commitment of troops to Korea violated the UN Charter, the UN Participation Act, and repeated assurances given to Congress by Acheson and other executive officials. Truman used military force before the second Security Council resolution. It was a war, not a police action, and it was an American, not a UN, operation. On all those points the record is abundantly clear.[101]

Just as the Vietnam War spelled defeat for the Democrats in 1968, so did the Korean War help put an end to 20 years of Democratic control of the

96. 96 Cong. Rec. 9229 (1950); statement of Senator Scott Lucas (D-Ill.).

97. Edward S. Corwin, "The President's Power," New Republic, January 29, 1951, at 16.

98. 96 Cong. Rec. 9233 (1950); statement of Senator Arthur V. Watkins (R-Utah). See also Arthur V. Watkins, "War by Executive Order," 4 West. Pol. Q. 539 (1951).

99. 96 Cong. Rec. 9268 (1951). Marcantonio was a member of the American Labor Party.

100. Id. at 9323.

101. 97 Cong. Rec. 5078–5103 (1951). See Louis Fisher, "The Korean War: On What Legal Basis Did Truman Act?" 89 Am. J. Int'l L. 21 (1995).

White House. "Korea, not crooks or Communists, was the major concern of the voters," wrote Stephen Ambrose.[102] The high point of the 1952 campaign came on October 24, less than two weeks before the election, when Dwight D. Eisenhower announced that he would "go to Korea" to end the war.[103] Two authors of a study on Eisenhower described the crucial influence of the Korean War: "Dissatisfaction with the war destroyed Truman's popularity and had much to do with Eisenhower's emphatic victory in the election of 1952."[104]

Some leading academics rushed to Truman's support but failed to give proper attention to constitutional principles. Henry Steele Commager, a prominent historian, was one. Writing for the *New York Times* on January 14, 1951, Commager remarked that the objections to Truman's unilateral actions "have no support in law or in history."[105] His own research into law and history, on this point, was superficial and misinformed. Consider this reasoning by Commager:

> . . . it is an elementary fact that must never be lost sight of that treaties are laws and carry with them the same obligation as laws. When the Congress passed the United Nations Participation Act it made the obligations of the Charter of the United Nations law, binding on the President. When the Senate ratified the North Atlantic Treaty it made the obligations of that treaty law, binding on the President.
>
> Both of these famous documents require action by the United States which must, in the nature of the case, be left to a large extent to the discretion of the Executive.[106]

Commager not only overstated the President's power under mutual defense treaties but ignored the statutory text and legislative history of the UN Participation Act.

Arthur S. Schlesinger Jr. was also an early defender of Truman's action in Korea. In a letter to the *New York Times* on January 9, 1951, he disputed the statement by Senator Robert Taft that President Truman "had no

---

102. 1 Stephen E. Ambrose, Eisenhower: Soldier, General of the Army, President-Elect 569 (1983).

103. Id.

104. Chester J. Pach Jr. and Elmo Richardson, The Presidency of Dwight D. Eisenhower 46 (1991).

105. Henry Steele Commager, ""Presidential Power: The Issue Analyzed," New York Times, January 14, 1951, at 11.

106. Id. at 24.

authority whatever to commit American troops to Korea without consulting Congress and without Congressional approval" and that by sending troops to Korea he "simply usurped authority, in violation of the laws and the Constitution." Schlesinger said that Taft's statements "are demonstrably irresponsible." Harking back to Jefferson's use of ships to repel the Barbary pirates, Schlesinger claimed that American Presidents "have repeatedly committed American armed forces abroad without prior Congressional consultation or approval."[107]

Schlesinger neglected to point out that Jefferson told Congress he was "unauthorized by the Constitution, without the sanction of Congress, to go beyond the line of defense." It was the prerogative of Congress to authorize "measures of offense also."[108] Congress enacted ten statutes authorizing action by Presidents Jefferson and Madison in the Barbary wars. Schlesinger did not cite, not could he, a similar presidential initiative of the magnitude of the Korean War. Years later he expressed regret that in calling Taft's statement "demonstrably irresponsible," he had responded with "a flourish of historical documentation and, alas, hyperbole."[109]

Edward S. Corwin took Commager and Schlesinger to task by labeling them the "high-flying prerogative men."[110] However, Corwin himself had been careless in earlier publications in describing the scope of presidential war power. Writing in 1949, he said that the original grant of authority to the President to "repel sudden attacks" had developed into an "undefined power—almost unchallenged from the first and occasionally sanctified judicially—to employ without Congressional authorization the armed forces in the protection of American rights and interests abroad whenever necessary.[111] He did note the significance of the UN Participation Act, which he said was based on the theory that American participation in the United Nations "is a matter for Congressional collaboration."[112]

In the late 1960s, with the nation mired in a bitter war in Vietnam, Commager and Schlesinger both publicly apologized for their earlier unreserved endorsements of presidential war power. By 1966 Schlesinger was counseling that "something must be done to assure the Congress a more

---

107. Arthur Schlesinger Jr., "Presidential Powers: Taft Statement on Troops Opposed, Actions of Past Presidents Cited," New York Times, January 9, 1951, at 28.

108. 1 Richardson 315.

109. Arthur M. Schlesinger Jr., The Imperial Presidency 139 (1973).

110. Edward S. Corwin, "The President's Power," New Republic, January 29, 1951, at 15.

111. Edward S. Corwin, "Who Has the Power to Make War?" New York Times Magazine, July 31, 1949, at 14.

112. Id.

authoritative and continuing voice in fundamental decisions in foreign policy."[113] In 1973 he stated that the "idea of prerogative was *not* part of presidential powers as defined by the Constitution," although it "remained in the back of [the framers'] mind[s]."[114] Commager told the Senate in 1967 that there should be a reconsideration of executive-legislative relations in the conduct of foreign relations,[115] and while testifying in 1971 he appealed for stronger legislative checks on presidential war powers.[116]

113. Arthur M. Schlesinger Jr. and Alfred de Grazia, Congress and the Presidency 27–28 (1967).

114. Schlesinger, The Imperial Presidency, at 9 (emphasis in original).

115. "Changing American Attitudes towards Foreign Policy," hearings before the Senate Committee on Foreign Relations, 90th Cong., 1st Sess. 21 (1967).

116. "War Powers Legislation," hearings before the Senate Committee on Foreign Relations, 92d Cong., 1st Sess. 7–74 (1971).

5

TAKING STOCK: 1951–1964

President Truman's commitment of U.S. troops to Korea in 1950 produced an initial jolt to executive-legislative relations. An aftershock hit a year later when he announced the dispatch of U.S. forces to Europe without seeking congressional approval. Led by Senator Taft, the Senate spent three months in a "Great Debate" that focused on the role of Congress in curbing presidential war power. Part of the Senate's concern dealt with inflated executive interpretations of the President's power to send troops abroad pursuant to the North Atlantic Treaty (NATO) and other mutual security treaties.

In 1952, in the Steel Seizure Case, the Supreme Court held that Truman had acted without constitutional or statutory authority when he seized the nation's steel mills, which he had justified under his commander-in-chief powers to prosecute the war in Korea. The protracted war, with no end in sight, cost the Democrats the White House. After Eisenhower's election, he promoted cooperation between the two branches in decisions involving the use of American troops overseas. His policy, implemented through "area resolutions," came to a halt eight years later with the election of John F. Kennedy, who believed he could invoke military force without seeking congressional authority.

Mutual Security Treaties

In addition to invoking authority under the UN Charter, Presidents cite mutual security treaties as an additional source of authority for sending U.S. troops abroad. The problem of defining "constitutional processes" under Article 43 of the UN Charter arises also with language in mutual defense treaties. For example, the NATO treaty was signed in 1949 by the United States, Canada, and ten European countries. Article 5 provides that "an armed attack against one or more of them in Europe or North America shall be considered an attack against them all."[1] It further states that, in the

---

1. 63 Stat. 2244 (1949).

event of an attack, NATO countries may exercise the right of individual or collective self-defense recognized by Article 51 of the UN Charter and assist the country or countries attacked by taking "such action as it deems necessary, including the use of armed force." Article 11 of the North Atlantic Treaty provides that it shall be ratified "and its provisions carried out by the Parties in accordance with their respective constitutional processes."[2]

Similar procedures appear in the Rio Treaty, signed in 1947 by the United States and 18 countries in Central America, South America, and the Caribbean. Nicaragua joined the pact a year later. These nations agreed to assist one another in the event of an attack, with an armed attack against one state considered "as an attack against all the American states."[3]

The principle of an attack on one nation constituting an attack on all nations was rejected in the mutual defense treaty signed between the United States and the Republic of Korea in 1953. The treaty declares the "common determination" of both countries to "defend themselves against external armed attack."[4] Each party recognizes that "an armed attack in the Pacific area on either of the Parties in territories now under their respective administrative control . . . would be dangerous to its own peace and safety and declares that it would act to meet the common danger in accordance with its constitutional processes."[5]

The Southeast Asia treaty was signed in 1954 by a regional alliance called the Southeast Asia Treaty Organization (SEATO), consisting of the United States, Australia, France, New Zealand, Pakistan, the Philippines, Thailand, and the United Kingdom. Each party recognized that armed aggression against one of the parties "would endanger its own peace and safety, and agreed that it will in that event act to meet the common danger in accordance with its constitutional processes."[6] This language was deliberately chosen to avoid the constitutional controversy provoked by the North Atlantic Treaty that "an attack upon one is an attack upon all."[7] As with NATO, the SEATO treaty "shall be ratified and its provisions carried out by the Parties in accordance with their respective constitutional processes."[8] Clearly, these defense treaties require definition and understanding of "constitutional processes."

Mutual defense treaties do not empower the President to use armed

2. Id. at 2246.
3. 62 Stat. 1700 (1947) (Art. 3).
4. 5 UST 2371.
5. Id. at 2372–73.
6. 6 UST 83 (1954) (Art. IV).
7. 101 Cong. Rec. 1051 (1951) (statement by Senator George).
8. 6 UST 84 (Art. IX.2).

force abroad without congressional consent. Treating an attack on one nation as an attack on all does not require an immediate response from any nation. As noted in the Rio Treaty, "no State shall be required to use armed force without its consent."[9] During debate on this treaty, Senator Connally, chairman of the Foreign Relations Committee, noted: "It is left to the discretion and wish of each of the nations to adopt such measures as it may approve in carrying out the obligation to assist the victim of the attack."[10]

NATO's Legislative History

The understanding that mutual security treaties do not require an automatic commitment of war appears in the legislative history. Secretary of State Dean Acheson explained to the Senate Foreign Relations Committee the basic premise in Article V of the NATO treaty that "an armed attack upon any party would so threaten the national security of the other parties as to be in effect an armed attack upon all." He said that the language "does not mean that the United States would automatically be at war if one of the other signatory nations were the victim of an armed attack. Under our Constitution, the Congress alone has the power to declare war."[11] He and Chairman Connally engaged in this exchange:

> THE CHAIRMAN. It is up to each country to determine for itself, is it not, what action it deems necessary to restore the security of the Atlantic Pact area?
>
> SECRETARY ACHESON. There is no question about that, Senator. That is true.[12]

Acheson later entered into the same understanding with Senator Vandenberg, who asked whether there was anything in the treaty "which will lead automatically to the declaration of war on our part." Acheson replied: "No, sir." Vandenberg pressed the issue: "The answer, of course, is unequivocally 'No.'" Acheson shot back: "Unequivocally 'No.'"[13] When Acheson tes-

9. 62 Stat. 1703 (Art. 20).

10. 93 Cong. Rec. 11124 (1947).

11. "North Atlantic Treaty" (part 1), hearings before the Senate Committee on Foreign Relations, 81st Cong., 1st Sess. 11 (1949).

12. Id. at 21.

13. Id. at 25.

tified in 1951 before two Senate committees, he acknowledged that the NATO treaty does not compel any nation "to take steps contrary to its convictions, and none is obligated to ignore its national interests."[14]

In the 1949 hearings, Acheson engaged in some flim-flam about which branch takes the country to war. Senator Forrest C. Donnell (R-Mo.) referred to language in the NATO treaty that it shall be ratified "and its provisions carried out by the Parties in accordance with their respective constitutional processes." Acheson responded: "The words which you just read, so far as the declaration of war is concerned, obviously mean that Congress is the body in charge of that constitutional procedure." Donnell pursued the point: "Obviously, of course, we would agree, would we not, Mr. Secretary, that Congress is the only body that can declare war? That is correct, is it not?" Acheson had no trouble with the answer: "That is correct."[15]

Acheson gave away nothing but the obvious. The express language of the Constitution says that Congress shall declare war. What Acheson did, through omission, was to leave the door open for the President to use military force under NATO *without* a declaration of war. Acheson told Donnell: "Article 5, Senator, does not enlarge, nor does it decrease, nor does it change in any way, the relative constitutional position of the President and the Congress."[16] That was clearly misleading. President Clinton would later use NATO for military action in Bosnia and Yugoslavia, without coming to Congress for authority.

Finally, Donnell asked Acheson: "In other words, the President would have the entire right to send troops to safeguard this country against an attack on New York without any action by Congress; that is correct, is it not?" Acheson: "He would have whatever right the Constitution gives him."[17] Yes, the President has whatever right the Constitution gives him, but the framers intended the President to use military force unilaterally only for defensive operations. There was nothing in Bosnia or Yugoslavia that could be considered defensive. In the Korean War, Acheson would show his true colors on what he thought about congressional authority.

When military force is used pursuant to a mutual defense treaty, it should be unleashed only after following constitutional processes, and that

14. "Assignment of Ground Forces of the United States to Duty in the European Area," hearings before the Senate Committee on Foreign Relations and Armed Services, 82d Cong., 1st Sess. 85 (1951).

15. "North Atlantic Treaty" (part 1), hearings before the Senate Committee on Foreign Relations, 81st Cong., 1st Sess. 80 (1949).

16. Id.

17. Id.

includes Congress (both Houses). The NATO treaty did not give the President any power beyond that provided in the UN Charter. In reporting the North Atlantic Treaty, the Senate Foreign Relations Committee was careful to point out that the provisions of the defense pact "are expressly subordinated to the purposes, principles, and provisions of the United Nations Charter."[18]

By providing that the NATO treaty be carried out according to constitutional processes, the Senate Foreign Relations Committee "intended to ensure that the Executive Branch of the Government should come back to the Congress when decisions were required in which the Congress has a constitutional responsibility."[19] As noted in one study of the NATO treaty, it "does not transfer to the President the Congressional power to make war."[20]

Mutual security treaties do not—they cannot—alter the constitutional allocation of the war power. It would be impermissible for the Senate and the President to use the treaty process to deny the House of Representatives its Article I powers in determining whether the nation should commit itself to war.[21] Senator Walter George said this about SEATO: "The treaty does not call for automatic action; it calls for consultation. If any course of action shall be agreed upon or decided upon, then that course of action must have the approval of Congress, because the constitutional process is provided for."[22]

Congress clarified that point when it enacted the War Powers Resolution of 1973. Section 8(a) provides that authority to introduce U.S. forces into hostilities shall not be inferred "from any treaty heretofore or hereafter ratified unless such treaty is implemented by legislation specifically authorizing" the introduction of American troops.[23] As noted by the Senate Foreign Relations Committee, the purpose of this language is to "ensure that both Houses of Congress must be affirmatively involved in any decision of the United States to engage in hostilities pursuant to a treaty."[24]

In considering the North Atlantic Treaty, the Senate rejected an amendment that would have required explicit, advance congressional approval

18. S. Exec. Rept. No. 8, 81st Cong., 1st Sess. 8 (1949).

19. Richard H. Heindel et al., "The North Atlantic Treaty in the United States Senate," 43 Am. J. Int'l L. 633, 649 (1949).

20. Id. at 650.

21. Michael J. Glennon, "United States Mutual Security Treaties: The Commitment Myth," 24 Colum. J. Transnat'l L. 509 (1986).

22. 101 Cong. Rec. 1051 (1955).

23. 87 Stat. 558 (1973).

24. S. Rept. No. 220, 93d Cong., 1st Sess. 26 (1973).

before the President could use armed force. Senator Arthur Watkins (R-Utah) offered this reservation to the treaty:

> The United States understands and construes article V of the treaty as follows:
> That the United States assumes no obligation to restore and maintain the security of the North Atlantic area or to assist any other party or parties in said area, by armed force, or to employ the military, air, or naval forces of the United States under article V of any article of the treaty, for any purpose, unless in any particular case the Congress, which under the Constitution, has the sole power to declare war or authorize the employment of the military, air, or naval forces of the United States, shall by act or joint resolution so provide.[25]

Watkins's reservation was rejected, 84 Senators voting against and only eleven Senators in favor.[26] However, rejection of the Watkins reservation does not imply that the President has unilateral authority to use armed force without congressional approval. Senate votes do not change the meaning of the Constitution and nullify the prerogatives of the House of Representatives. In legislative history, a negative does not produce a positive. For example, Watkins also offered this reservation, which gained only eight votes with 87 Senators opposed:

> The United States further understands and construes article 5 to the effect that in any particular case or event of armed attack on any other party or parties to the treaty, the Congress of the United States is not expressly, impliedly, or morally obligated or committed to declare war or authorize the employment of the military, air, or naval forces of the United States against the nation or nations making said attack, or to assist with the armed forces the nation or nations attacked, but shall have complete freedom in considering the circumstances of each case to act or refuse to act as the Congress in its discretion shall determine.[27]

Defeat of this second reservation does not imply that the United States has an express or moral obligation to use military force in the event of an

---

25. 95 Cong. Rec. 9806, 9898 (1949).
26. Id. at 9916.
27. Id. at 9901; Senate vote at 9916.

attack on a member of NATO. The legislative history is entirely to the contrary. Despite the rejection of Watkins's second reservation, each nation decides for itself whether to intervene militarily.

The "Great Debate" in 1951

In 1951, President Truman announced that he would send ground forces to Europe. Asked at a press conference on January 4 whether he believed that he needed congressional approval before sending troops abroad, he replied: "No, I do not."[28] A week later, at another news conference, he was asked to respond to the comment by Senator Connally that the executive branch, in the future, would consult with Congress on troop commitments to Europe. Truman read from a prepared statement:

> Under the President's constitutional powers as Commander in Chief of the Armed Forces he has the authority to send troops anywhere in the world. That power has been recognized repeatedly by the Congress and the courts.
>
> This Government will continue to live up to its obligations under the United Nations, and its other treaty obligations, and we will continue to send troops wherever it is necessary to uphold these obligations.[29]

Truman said that Acheson had made it "perfectly plain" to the Senate Foreign Relations Committee that the North Atlantic Treaty did not require that troops be sent, and that each country itself would make up its own mind as to what action to take.[30] He omitted Acheson's reassurance that troop commitments would be made consistent with constitutional processes and that only Congress could declare war. To the extent that Truman would consult with Congress on troop commitments abroad, he identified only the Senate Committees on Foreign Relations and Armed Services, apparently taking the view that these troop commitments would be pursuant to treaty obligations and therefore would exclude the House.[31] He was very explicit on the limited role of these committees: "I don't ask their

28. Public Papers of the Presidents, 1951, at 4 (question 18).
29. Id. at 19.
30. Id.
31. Id. at 20.

permission, I just consult them."[32] Although he excluded the House from these deliberations, he later conceded that "it is necessary for the Congress to appropriate the money for the Government to be carried on."[33]

When Acheson appeared before the Senate Committee on Foreign Relations and Armed Services on February 16, he found the topic of congressional versus executive power plainly annoying. Having assured Congress on numerous occasions that its constitutional prerogatives would be respected, he would now assert, on an impatient if not petulant note:

> It seems to me that perhaps a little more is involved here, and that we are in a position in the world today where the argument as to who has the power to do this, that, or the other thing, is not exactly what is called for from America in this very critical hour, and if we could all agree on the fact that something should be done, we will perform a much greater role in the world, than by quarreling about who ought to do it.[34]

These haughty lectures from the Truman administration helped precipitate a major confrontation with Congress. In an extremely powerful floor statement, Senator Taft delivered a 10,000-word speech urging legislators to defend their prerogatives and arguing that constructive criticism from Congress on foreign policy is essential to the safety of the nation. His speech repudiated the idea that criticism of the administration's foreign policy "is an attack on the unity of the Nation, that it gives aid and comfort to the enemy, and that it sabotages any idea of a bipartisan foreign policy for the national benefit."[35] That mind-set, he said, rested on a dangerous fallacy that threatened the existence of the nation. Members of Congress, and particularly Senators, had "a constitutional obligation to reexamine constantly and discuss the foreign policy of the United States." The trend toward secrecy on the part of recent administrations, combined with the failure of Presidents to consult Congress and seek its advice, deprived members of Congress "of the substance of the powers conferred on them by the Constitution."[36] Taft feared that Truman, having embarked

---

32. Id.

33. Id. at 21.

34. "Assignment of Ground Forces of the United States to Duty in the European Area," hearings before the Senate Committees on Foreign Relations and Armed Services, 82d Cong., 1st Sess. 93 (1951).

35. 97 Cong. Rec. 55 (1951).

36. Id.

on a war in Korea without congressional authority, was about to do the same in Europe.[37] "Mr. Republican," the leading conservative of his time, concluded with these remarks: "And finally the policy we adopt must be approved by Congress and the people after full and free discussion. The commitment of a land army to Europe is a program never approved by Congress, into which we should not drift. The policy of secret executive agreements has brought us to danger and disaster. It threatens the liberties of our people."[38]

For three months in 1951 the Senate debated the scope and limits of presidential power. The principal resolution, S. Res. 99, supported the sending of additional divisions to Europe only on the condition that future commitments would be approved by Congress. As a Senate resolution, the measure was not legally binding, but it gave Senators an opportunity to debate in substantial detail the boundaries of congressional and presidential powers.

Taft believed that Congress had the power to prevent the President from sending troops anywhere in the world if doing so might involve the nation in war. He felt it was "incumbent upon the Congress to assert clearly its own constitutional powers unless it desires to lose them." In what could be read as a precursor to the War Powers Resolution of 1973, Taft urged Congress to assert its powers in the form of a joint resolution (requiring action by both Houses and submission to the President for his signature to veto).[39] Senator Wherry took Taft at his word and offered an amendment to replace the pending Senate resolution with a joint resolution to make it legally binding. Wherry's amendment was ruled out of order.[40] Senator John Bricker (R-Ohio) attempted to recommit the Senate resolution and have it reported back as a joint resolution, but that tactic failed, 31 to 56.[41]

Senators wanted to express their sentiments in a resolution without having to worry about obtaining the concurrence of the House and the President. As a nonbinding resolution, the step was more modest than public opinion, as polls showed that Americans preferred stronger legislative measures. A Gallup poll revealed that the public, by a margin of 64 percent to 28 percent, believed that Presidents should not be allowed to send U.S. troops overseas unless Congress first granted its approval.[42]

37. Id. at 59.
38. Id. at 61.
39. Id. at 2987.
40. Id. at 3065.
41. Id. at 3199.
42. Id. at 3015.

S. Res. 99 served many purposes. To Senator Edward Thye (R-Minn.), it highlighted the need to have "a closer relationship between the executive and legislative branches of our Government with reference to such questions as the assignment of troops abroad. Congress is close to the people and has a definite responsibility."[43] Senator John McClellan (D-Ark.) offered an amendment requiring congressional approval of future plans to send troops abroad. Although the amendment was initially rejected 44 to 45, it was later accepted,[44] 49 to 44. A weak amendment by Senator Herbert Lehman (D-N.Y.) merely calling for the "fullest collaboration" between Congress and the President on future troop actions, was decisively beaten, 35 to 55.[45]

The Senate passed the resolution by a vote of 69 to 21. It approved Truman's sending of four divisions to Europe but stated that "in the interests of sound constitutional processes, and of national unity and understanding, congressional approval should be obtained of any policy requiring the assignment of American troops abroad when such assignment is in implementation of article 3 of the North Atlantic Treaty." No ground troops in addition to the four divisions should be sent "without further congressional approval."[46]

Earlier in the session, Rep. Frederick Coudert (R-N.Y.) introduced legislation to require the authorization of Congress before military forces could be sent abroad.[47] After the Senate had completed action on its resolution, Coudert proposed that no part of the appropriations in the defense appropriations bill could be used for the cost of sending or maintaining additional ground troops in Europe. His amendment failed, 84 to 131.[48]

The 1951 debate provoked both Houses of Congress to rethink the congressional role in foreign affairs and the war power. A report for the House Foreign Affairs Committee in 1951 correctly spotlighted the significance of the Korean War: "The action of the United States in Korea is in one sense unprecedented. For the first time the United States has committed large military forces in a foreign country in response to the action of an international organization. United States forces were committed in Korea by Presidential action."[49]

43. Id. at 3041.
44. Id. at 3082–83, 3095–96.
45. Id. at 3104.
46. Id. at 3283 (para. 6).
47. Id. at 34 (H.J. Res. 9).
48. Id. at 9746.
49. "Background Information on the Use of United States Armed Forces in Foreign Countries," printed for the use of the House Committee on Foreign Affairs, 82d Cong., 1st Sess. 1 (Committee Print 1951).

A House study in 1956 on the President's powers as Commander in Chief drew attention to the fact that the period since the 1930s signaled something fundamentally new and troubling in executive-legislative relations. The study concluded that "in no other period of 20 years of American history have so many different Presidents been called on to exercise this constitutional power [of Commander in Chief] in so many different kinds of situations, each one of major importance."[50]

The Steel Seizure Case

After two years of a costly and apparently unwinnable war, public opposition steadily drained support from the administration, and in the midst of these difficulties Truman faced a nationwide strike of steelworkers. He reacted in 1952 by issuing Executive Order 10340, directing the Secretary of Commerce to take possession of and operate the plants and facilities of 87 major steel companies. As justification for averting a work stoppage, the order referred to Truman's proclamation of December 16, 1950, declaring the existence of a nationwide emergency and the dispatch of American soldiers to Korea. The order called steel "indispensable" for producing weapons and war materials.[51]

Although Truman based the order on authority under "the Constitution and laws of the United States, and as President of the United States and Commander-in-Chief of the armed forces of the United States," the Justice Department later argued in court that Truman had acted solely on inherent executive power without any statutory support. Assistant Attorney General Homer Baldridge told David A. Pine, a federal district judge, that courts were powerless to control the exercise of presidential power when directed toward emergency conditions.[52] At a news conference on April 17, Truman was asked if he could seize the steel mills under his inherent powers, could he "also seize the newspapers and/or radio stations?" Truman answered: "Under similar circumstances the President of the United States has to act for whatever is for the best of the country."[53]

A few days later, recognizing that this theory of virtually limitless presidential power was offensive to the country, Truman wrote a letter to the Senate stating that Congress could, "if it wishes, reject the course of action

50. H. Doc. No. 443, 84th Cong., 2d Sess. viii (1956).
51. 17 Fed. Reg. 3139 (1952).
52. "U.S. Argues President Is Above Courts," New York Times, April 25, 1952, at 1.
53. Public Papers of the Presidents, 1952, at 273.

I have followed in this matter."⁵⁴ At a news conference on April 24, he said that there had been "a lot of hooey" about presidential power to seize the press and the radio.⁵⁵ In a further gesture to defuse the controversy, Truman wrote a letter to a private citizen on April 27, stating that presidential powers are derived from the Constitution and are limited by provisions in the Constitution, "particularly those that protect the rights of individuals."⁵⁶

Those gestures were not enough to undo the damage done in district court. On April 29, Judge Pine wrote a blistering opinion rejecting the Justice Department's analysis of inherent presidential power. In holding Truman's seizure of the steel mills to be unconstitutional, he acknowledged that a nationwide strike could do extensive damage to the country but believed that a strike "would be less injurious to the public than the injury which would flow from a timorous judicial recognition that there is some basis for this claim to unlimited and unrestrained Executive power, which would be implicit in a failure to grant the injunction."⁵⁷

On June 2 the Supreme Court, split 6 to 3, sustained Judge Pine's decision. Each of the five concurring Justices wrote separate opinions, advancing different views of the President's emergency power. Only Justices Hugo Black and William Douglas insisted on specific constitutional or statutory authority to support presidential seizure of private property. The other four concurring Justices (Felix Frankfurter, Robert Jackson, Harold Burton, and Tom Clark) did not try to delimit the President's authority to act in future emergencies.

Jackson's concurrence is the most interesting. He identified three categories of presidential power ranging from actions based on express or implied congressional authorization (putting executive authority at its maximum) to executive measures that were incompatible with congressional policy (reducing presidential power to its lowest ebb). In between lay a "zone of twilight" in which the President and Congress shared authority. Jackson said that congressional inertia, indifference, or quiescence might enable, if not invite, independent presidential action.⁵⁸ Jackson concluded by saying that he had no illusion that any decision by a court "can keep power in the hands of Congress if it is not wise and timely in meeting its problems." Although the power to legislate for emergencies belongs in the hands of Congress, "only Congress itself can prevent power from slipping

54. Id. at 284.
55. Id. at 290.
56. Id. at 301.
57. Youngstown Sheet & Tube Co. v. Sawyer, 103 F.Supp. 569, 577 (D.D.C. 1952).
58. Youngstown Co. v. Sawyer, 343 U.S. 579, 637 (1952).

through its fingers."[59] His concurring opinion remains the most perceptive advice to Congress: the political dynamics of presidential power are such that Congress must invoke the institutional tools at its command rather than expect assistance from the federal judiciary. (The deficiencies of Jackson's opinion are explored more closely in Chapter 11.)

Eisenhower's Philosophy

After these sharp collisions between President Truman and Congress, the Eisenhower administration avoided unilateral moves in dispatching troops abroad. Although Eisenhower initially believed that Truman's decision to intervene in Korea was "wise and necessary,"[60] he came to realize that it was a serious mistake, politically and constitutionally, to commit the nation to war in Korea without congressional approval. Eisenhower thought that national commitments would be stronger if entered into jointly by both branches and therefore asked Congress for specific authority to deal with national security crises. He stressed the importance of *collective* action by Congress and the President: "I deem it necessary to seek the cooperation of the Congress. Only with that cooperation can we give the reassurance needed to deter aggression."[61]

Herbert Brownell, who served as Eisenhower's Attorney General and confidante, described Eisenhower's sensitivity to separation of powers:

[His] view of the president's place within a constitutional system of government allowed him to understand the rightful roles that the various institutions and political actors occupy in our political system so that he did not overextend the scope of presidential interest across the whole gamut of governmental activities. Moreover, it fostered an understanding of the need to establish a sense of comity with those individuals in the other branches with whom a president must necessarily deal. This is an aspect of presidential leadership quite different from the imperial presidency some of his successors would come to embrace.[62]

59. Id. at 654.
60. Dwight D. Eisenhower, Mandate for Change 82 (1963).
61. Public Papers of the Presidents, 1957, at 11.
62. Herbert Brownell with John P. Burke, Advising Ike: The Memoirs of Attorney General Herbert Brownell 289 (1993).

When international emergencies arose, Eisenhower sought the backing of Congress. He did not want to "expose himself to the kind of criticism that Taft and other Republicans had leveled against Truman for entering the Korean War without consulting Congress."[63] In 1954, when Eisenhower was under pressure to intervene in Indochina to save beleaguered French troops, he refused to act unilaterally. He told reporters in a news conference: "There is going to be no involvement of America in war unless it is a result of the constitutional process that is placed upon Congress to declare it. Now, let us have that clear; and that is the answer."[64] Eisenhower told Secretary of State John Foster Dulles that in "the absence of some kind of arrangement getting support of Congress," it "would be completely unconstitutional & indefensible" to give any assistance to the French.[65] Eisenhower's attitude about covert operations was different (see Chapter 10 for his authorization of such actions in Iran, Guatemala, and Cuba without seeking congressional support or authority).

Area Resolutions

Eisenhower's theory of government and international relations invited congressional enactment of area resolutions that authorized presidential action. He believed that the Korean War resulted in part from the Communists' belief that "under no circumstances would the United States move to the assistance of the Korean Republic."[66] To forestall such misconceptions in his administration, he wanted other nations to know that Congress and the President were united in their foreign policy.

Conditions in the Formosa Straits threatened to deteriorate into a military confrontation between the United States and China. In a memorandum in 1954, Secretary of State Dulles noted that "it is doubtful that the issue can be exploited without Congressional approval."[67] One issue was whether President Eisenhower could order an attack on airfields in China. He said that "to do that you would have to get Congressional authorization, since it would be war. If Congressional authorization were not obtained there would be logical grounds for impeachment. Whatever we do must be in a

---

63. 2 Stephen E. Ambrose, Eisenhower the President 232 (1984).
64. Public Papers of the Presidents, 1954, at 306.
65. FRUS, 1952–1954, vol. 13, part 1, 1242.
66. Eisenhower, Mandate for Change, at 467.
67. FRUS, 1952–1954, vol. 14, part 1, 611.

Constitutional manner."[68] Dulles remarked that "if we act without Congress now we will not have anyone in the United States with us."[69]

In 1955, in response to a dangerous turn of events in the Formosa Straits, Eisenhower appealed to Congress for joint action. Communist China had begun shelling the island of Quemoy. It also mounted air attacks against other islands north of Formosa and seized the island of Ichiang. Eisenhower believed that the situation was one "for appropriate action of the United Nations," but unlike Truman he did not go to the United Nations and exclude Congress. Quite the opposite. Instead of waiting for the United Nations to act, he urged Congress "to participate now, by specific resolution, in measures designed to improve the prospects for peace." The resolution would contemplate the use of U.S. armed forces "if necessary to assure the security of Formosa and the Pescadores."[70] While identifying his prerogatives as Commander in Chief, Eisenhower preferred to act jointly with Congress:

> Authority for some of the actions which might be required would be inherent in the authority of the Commander-in-Chief. Until Congress can act I would not hesitate, so far as my Constitutional powers extend, to take whatever emergency action might be forced upon us in order to protect the rights and security of the United States.
>
> However, a suitable Congressional resolution would clearly and publicly establish the authority of the President as Commander-in-Chief to employ the armed forces of this nation promptly and effectively for the purposes indicated if in his judgment it became necessary. It would make clear the unified and serious intentions of our Government, our Congress, and our people.[71]

Eisenhower noted that he did not expect the United States to enlarge "its defensive obligations" beyond Formosa and the Pescadores.[72] How the world of presidential war power had changed since the framers: U.S. *defensive* obligations in the offshore islands of China! But it was settled wisdom in the Eisenhower administration that the western barrier to Communist aggression, consisting of Japan, Formosa, and the Philippines, had to be maintained.

68. Id. at 618.
69. Id. at 620.
70. Public Papers of the Presidents, 1955, at 209.
71. Id. at 209–10.
72. Id. at 209.

During joint hearings before the Senate Committees on Foreign Relations and Armed Services, Secretary of State John Foster Dulles presented the administration's case. He was reminded of Eisenhower's remark that he would not hesitate to act under his own constitutional powers if necessary while awaiting congressional action. Dulles told the committees: "There is at least doubt as to whether or not the President could, without congressional authorization, take the kind of action which I am talking about."[73] Sherman Adams, Eisenhower's chief of staff, later recalled that Eisenhower was determined "not to resort to any kind of military action without the approval of Congress."[74]

Congress responded quickly to Eisenhower's request. On the same day that he addressed Congress, the House Foreign Affairs Committee held a hearing in executive session and reported the resolution unanimously without amendment. With regard to constitutional issues, the committee offered this assessment: "Its conclusion was that the resolution in this form, while making it clear that the people of the United States stand behind the President, does not enter the field of controversy as to the respective limitations of power in the executive and the legislative branches. Acting together, there can be no doubt that all the constitutional powers necessary to meet the situation are present."[75] This position recalls Justice Jackson's concurrence in *Youngstown Co.* v. *Sawyer* (1952), stating that presidential power is "at its maximum" when the President acts on the basis of his constitutional power plus those that Congress delegates to him.[76] The Formosa Resolution passed the House a day later, 410 to 3.[77]

The Senate Foreign Relations Committee also held hearings in executive session and reported the resolution without amendment. The committee vote was 27 to 2 with one Senator absent.[78] After rejecting several floor amendments, the Senate passed the resolution by a margin of 85 to 3, and the resolution become law a day later.[79]

Officials in the Eisenhower administration considered using nuclear weapons against China in the dispute over Formosa. Secretary Dulles sug-

---

73. "Senate Joint Resolution 28—The Formosa Resolution," joint hearings before the Senate Committees on Foreign Relations and Armed Services, 84th Cong., 1st Sess. 87 (1955). Executive sessions of the Senate Foreign Relations Committee (historical series), made public April 1978.
74. Sherman Adams, First-Hand Report 109 (1962).
75. H. Rept. No. 4, 84th Cong., 1st Sess. 4 (1955).
76. 343 U.S. at 635–36.
77. 101 Cong. Rec. 680–81 (1955).
78. S. Rept. No. 13, 84th Cong., 1st Sess. 7 (1955).
79. 101 Cong. Rec. 994–95 (1955); 69 Stat. 7 (1955).

gested that small nuclear weapons could be directed against military targets rather than larger bombs against cities.[80] Smaller nuclear weapons, he said, could be utilized with precision without radioactive fallout problems.[81] At a news conference, President Eisenhower agreed that tactical, small atomic weapons could be used: "Now in any combat where these things can be used on strictly military targets and for strictly military purposes, I see no reason why they shouldn't be used just exactly as you would use a bullet or anything else."[82] The idea of unleashing tactical atomic weapons "sent a shudder through almost every Ambassador" in Washington, D.C. The "overwhelming reaction from press and pulpit was loudly opposed to intervention."[83] The Formosa crisis eventually passed without warfare between the United States and China.

Eisenhower asked for another area resolution in 1957. In an address delivered in person before a joint session, he asked Congress to pass a joint resolution authorizing him to employ armed forces in the Middle East. After alerting Congress to Soviet ambitions in the Middle East, he said that thoughts "naturally turn to the United Nations as a protector of small nations."[84] But he reminded the legislators that Russia had recently used its veto in the Security Council to block UN actions concerning Russia's intervention in Hungary, implying that Russia would also veto any constructive UN response to the situation in the Middle East.

Under these conditions, Eisenhower emphasized the importance of executive-legislative coordination: "I deem it necessary to seek the cooperation of the Congress. Only with that cooperation can we give the reassurance needed to deter aggression."[85] Effective action meant that "basic United States policy should now find expression in joint action by the Congress and the Executive."[86] If military action became necessary he promised "hour-by-hour" contact with Congress if it were in session. If recessed or adjourned, "and if the situation had grave implications," he would "of course, at once" call Congress into special session.[87]

In his memoirs, Eisenhower explained the choice between invoking executive prerogatives or seeking congressional support. On New Year's Day in 1957, he met with Secretary of State Dulles and congressional lead-

---

80. New York Times, March 16, 1955, at 1.
81. Id. at 2.
82. Public Papers of the Presidents, 1955, at 332.
83. James Reston, "Quemoy-Matsu Trend," New York Times, April 7, 1955, at 13.
84. Public Papers of the Presidents, 1957, at 10.
85. Id. at 11.
86. Id. at 12.
87. Id. at 15.

ers of both parties. House Majority Leader John McCormack (D-Mass.) asked Eisenhower whether he, as Commander in Chief, already possessed authority to carry out actions in the Middle East without congressional action. Eisenhower replied that

> greater effect could be had from a consensus of Executive and Legislative opinion, and I spoke earnestly of the desire of the Middle East countries to have reassurance now that the United States would stand ready to help. . . . Near the end of this meeting I reminded the legislators that the Constitution assumes that our two branches of government should get along together.[88]

Congress was not as compliant as it had been in 1955 with the Formosa Resolution. This time legislators objected to giving Eisenhower a blank check. Congressional debate consumed several months and resulted in several restrictions on the delegated authority. For example, the authority in the Formosa Resolution expired whenever the President determined "that the peace and security of the area is reasonably assured by international conditions created by actions of the United Nations or otherwise, and shall so report to the Congress."[89] The 1957 statute kept this provision but also permitted Congress to terminate the authority by passing a concurrent resolution, which requires action by both Houses but is not presented to the President for his signature or veto.[90] As the House Foreign Affairs Committee explained, a concurrent resolution permitted Congress to terminate the President's authority by a simple majority vote of each House, instead of acting by a bill or joint resolution subject to a presidential veto.[91]

Even with that change the Middle East Resolution encountered major congressional opposition. The House Foreign Affairs Committee held hearings morning and afternoon over a period of two weeks and held four executive sessions.[92] After two full days of debate the House passed the resolution by a vote of 355 to 61.[93] Two Senate committees, Foreign Relations and Armed Services, met jointly for almost a month, holding public hearings and meeting in executive session.[94]

88. Dwight D. Eisenhower, Waging Peace 179 (1965).
89. 69 Stat. 7 (1955).
90. 71 Stat. 6, sec. 6 (1957).
91. H. Rept. No. 2, 85th Cong., 1st Sess. 13 (1957).
92. Id. at 2.
93. 103 Cong. Rec. 1323–24 (1957).
94. S. Rept. No. 70, 85th Cong., 1st Sess. 2–3 (1957) (report of the Senate Committees on Foreign Relations and Armed Services).

Several amendments were adopted on the Senate floor while others were rejected. Senator Wayne Morse (D-Oreg.) offered an amendment that built on Eisenhower's promise to meet "hour-by-hour" with Congress and call it in special session if adjourned: "Prior to the employment of armed forces the President shall give notice to Congress. If, in the judgment of the President, an emergency arises in which such notice to Congress is not possible, he shall, upon the employment of armed forces, forthwith inform Congress and submit his action for its approval or disapproval."[95]

The administration opposed the amendment, stating that "it would appear to raise serious question as to the President's power to use the Armed Forces under the resolution, and would impair the effectiveness of the resolution."[96] The Morse amendment failed on a vote of 28 to 64.[97] Senator Carl Curtis (R-Nebr.) proposed a third way to terminate the President's authority under the resolution, letting it expire on a fixed date—February 1, 1961—unless terminated earlier by the President or by Congress. The administration considered the amendment "highly undesirable" because a fixed date would imply that U.S. interests in the region would end on that date and therefore encourage potential aggressors to take advantage of the expiration.[98] The Curtis amendment was rejected 30 to 58.[99] The entire resolution then passed on a vote of 72 to 19,[100] and the House agreed to the Senate amendments, 350 to 60.[101]

On the day that the two Houses finally agreed to the resolution, Eisenhower was asked at a press conference whether he, as Commander in Chief, could send troops wherever he wanted without seeking the approval of Congress. Instead of stressing his independent and inherent powers he pointed to the practical importance of interbranch collaboration.

> Q. . . . Mr. President, in the resolution as passed by the Senate, apparently to be approved today by the House, the original concept suggested in your version of authorizing you to use the Armed Forces was stricken out, and we understand you have approved the substitute voted by the Senate.
>
> Does this mean, sir, that you accept the constitutional interpretation that you have always had, as Commander-in-Chief, the right to

95. 103 Cong. Rec. 3120 (1957).
96. Id. at 3121.
97. Id.
98. Id. at 3123.
99. Id. at 3126.
100. Id. at 3129.
101. Id. at 3265–66.

send the Armed Forces into action in such a situation in the national interest without that specific authorization?

THE PRESIDENT. Well, I don't think . . . that I have to go into the constitutional argument again. I would point out that I haven't spent my life in the study of constitutional law.

I do think the legislative history of this resolution shows that the Senate approves—the Congress approves of what we are trying to do in the area, and that is the important thing.[102]

Upon signing the legislation, Eisenhower followed through on his commitment to interbranch cooperation. He selected James P. Richards, former chairman of the House Foreign Affairs Committee, to head a special mission to the Middle East countries to explain the purpose of the resolution and report back to Eisenhower on the most effective ways of carrying out the purposes of the legislation.[103]

However, when Eisenhower actually sent troops to Lebanon in 1958, he referred only indirectly to the Middle East Resolution by telling Congress that U.S. forces were being deployed "to assist the Government of Lebanon in the preservation of Lebanon's territorial integrity and independence, which have been deemed vital to United States national interests and world peace."[104] (The Middle East Resolution recognized that the United States "regards as vital to the national interest and world peace the preservation of the independence and integrity of the nations of the Middle East."[105]) Eisenhower referred to two other factors: the responsibility to protect and safeguard about 2,500 American citizens in Lebanon and the right of all nations (under the UN Charter) to "work together and to seek help when necessary to preserve their independence" through collective self-defense.[106] He said that he had taken advice from leaders of Congress[107] and that the sending of U.S. forces to Lebanon was not an "act of war."[108]

Eisenhower's general position on the war power was extremely perceptive. He knew that lawyers and policy advisers in the executive branch could always cite a multitude of precedents to justify unilateral presidential action. It was his seasoned judgment, however, that a commitment by

---

102. Public Papers of the Presidents, 1957, at 177–78.
103. Id. at 187.
104. Public Papers of the Presidents, 1958, at 550–51, 556.
105. 71 Stat. 5, sec. 2 (1957).
106. Public Papers of the Presidents, 1958, at 552.
107. Id. at 553.
108. Id. at 549.

the United States would have much greater impact on allies and enemies alike because it would represent the collective judgment of the President and Congress. Single-handed actions taken by a President, without the support of Congress and the people, can threaten national prestige and undermine the presidency. Eisenhower's position was sound then. It is sound now.

Kennedy Reasserts Executive Power

Eisenhower's experiment with interbranch cooperation was short-lived. Unlike Eisenhower, President John F. Kennedy was prepared to act during the Cuban missile crisis solely on his own constitutional authority. At a news conference on September 13, 1962, he warned of a Communist buildup (with Soviet assistance) in Cuba. A series of "offensive missile sites," he said, were in preparation, the purpose of which "can be none other than to provide a nuclear strike capability against the Western Hemisphere."[109] However, he did not request a joint resolution. Under his power as Commander in Chief he said: "I have full authority now to take such action" militarily against Cuba.[110] During the news conference he gave this revealing response:

> Q. Mr. President, you said in your opening statement that you now had full authority to act in the Cuban affair. In view of this, do you think there's any virtue in the Senate or the Congress passing the resolution saying you have that authority?
>
> THE PRESIDENT. No. I think the Members of Congress would, speaking as they do with a particular responsibility—I think it would be useful, if they desired to do so, for them to express their view. And as I've seen the resolutions which have been discussed—a resolution which I think Senator [Mike] Mansfield [D-Mont.] introduced and which Chairman [Carl] Vinson [D-Ga.] introduced in the House—and I would think that—I'd be very glad to have those resolutions passed if that should be the desire of the Congress.[111]

Kennedy imposed a quarantine on all offensive military equipment being shipped to Cuba. Any ship containing cargoes of offensive weapons

109. Public Papers of the Presidents, 1962, at 806.
110. Id. at 674.
111. Id. at 679.

would be turned back. He announced that it would be his policy to regard any nuclear missile launched from Cuba against any nation in the Western Hemisphere "as an attack by the Soviet Union on the United States, requiring a full retaliatory response upon the Soviet Union."[112]

On October 3, Congress passed the Cuba Resolution, stating that the United States is "determined to prevent by whatever means may be necessary, including the use of arms, the Marxist-Leninist regime in Cuba from extending, by force or the threat of force, its aggressive or subversive activities to any part of this hemisphere."[113] The resolution also stated the determination of the United States to prevent in Cuba "the creation or use of an externally supported military capability endangering the security of the United States." The resolution did not, however, authorize presidential action. It merely expressed the sentiments of Congress. Since no authority was delegated, there was no provision for termination by concurrent resolution.

The Senate passed the resolution 86 to 1.[114] Senators deferred broadly to the President's supposed authority in foreign affairs and the war power. Senator George Smathers (D-Fla.) remarked: "We all recognize that the final decision is left to the President of the United States by the Constitution."[115] Precisely when and how the Constitution had been amended he neglected to say. Senator Bourke Hickenlooper (R-Iowa) offered another sweeping assertion: "Basically the Executive has the responsibility for and is in charge of foreign policy operations."[116] He explained that the joint resolution sidestepped any effort to deal with the constitutional issue. The resolution "eliminated the question of whether or not the President or Congress shall declare war."[117] That point, one would think, had been settled in 1788 with ratification of the Constitution.

The two committee reports, by the Senate Committee on Foreign Relations and the House Committee on Foreign Affairs, were brief and perfunctory.[118] House floor debate was similarly sluggish in defending congressional prerogatives. The resolution passed the House with only token opposition, 384 to 7.[119]

112. Id. at 808.
113. 76 Stat. 697 (1962).
114. 108 Cong. Rec. 20058 (1962).
115. Id. at 20026.
116. Id. at 20029.
117. Id. at 20030.
118. S. Rept. No. 2111, 87th Cong., 2d Sess. (1962); H. Rept. No. 2441, 87th Cong., 2d Sess. (1962).
119. 108 Cong. Rec. 20910–11 (1962).

Kennedy acted on October 23 to interdict offensive weapons being delivered to Cuba, basing his action on "the authority entrusted to me by the Constitution as endorsed by the resolution of the Congress."[120] The Organ of Consultation of the American Republics met on that same day to recommend that member states take all measures, individually and collectively, including the use of armed force, to prevent Cuba from receiving threatening weapons from China and Russia. The language in Kennedy's proclamation read: "NOW, THEREFORE, I, JOHN F. KENNEDY, President of the United States of America, acting under and by virtue of the authority conferred upon me by the Constitution and statutes of the United States, in accordance with the aforementioned resolutions of the United States Congress and of the Organ of Consultation of the American Republics."[121]

Little thought was given to the prerogatives of Congress. A proposal to call Congress back to Washington and ask for a declaration of war was quickly discarded. Dean Acheson, part of the administration's team that explored various options, was true to form. This was no time, he counseled, to worry about legal formalities.[122] The Soviet Union removed the missiles, but the prospect of nuclear war led one analyst to estimate that never before "had there been such a high probability that so many lives would end suddenly," risking the deaths of 100 million Americans, more than 100 million Russians, and millions of Europeans.[123]

Next came the fateful Southeast Asia Resolution of 1964, better known as the Tonkin Gulf Resolution. Enacted in the middle of a presidential election year, this massive grant of authority to President Lyndon B. Johnson marked a key step in the escalation of the Vietnam War, a conflict that eventually drove Johnson from office and prepared the way for the War Powers Resolution of 1973.

120. Public Papers of the Presidents, 1962, at 807.

121. Id. at 810.

122. Elie Abel, The Missiles of October: The Story of the Cuban Missile Crisis 84 (1969).

123. Graham T. Allison, Essence of Decision: Explaining the Cuban Missile Crisis 1 (1971).

6

VIETNAM AND THE WAR POWERS RESOLUTION

By the time Lyndon Johnson entered the White House, three American Presidents had taken decisive steps to involve the nation in Vietnam. Truman and Eisenhower provided substantial economic and military assistance to aid the French in Indochina. Under Truman, the United States paid for between one-third and one-half the cost,[1] and American aid climbed to about 75 percent during the Eisenhower years. President Eisenhower made the first commitment of soldiers, sending 200 military personnel to assist the French.[2]

In 1954 Eisenhower told his Secretary of State, John Foster Dulles, to ask Congress to pass a resolution giving the President authority to use American air and sea power in Southeast Asia. Members of Congress balked at the thought of another Korea and insisted that any involvement by the United States would have to include the support of the British and other allies. Faced with those requirements, Dulles decided against submitting the resolution to Congress.[3] The French wanted the United States to intervene with bombing missions, including two or three atomic bombs, but Eisenhower ruled out the use of atomic weapons. He also said that any air strike, without congressional support, would be "completely unconstitutional and indefensible."[4] Eisenhower continued to insist that if the United States ever intervened it would have to be in the company of allies, including Great Britain.

After the French surrendered at Dienbienphu in 1954, Vietnam was divided between the northern part, including Hanoi, and the southern part. President Kennedy continued sending American advisers and providing U.S. weapons to South Vietnam. The number of American military advisers rose from 700 to 16,000. Kennedy initiated the Strategic Hamlet Program in an unsuccessful attempt to build support among the peasants, involved military advisers in combat roles, and supported South Vietnam

---

1. 2 Memoirs by Harry S. Truman, Years of Trial and Hope 337, 339, 519 (1956).
2. 2 Stephen Ambrose, Eisenhower: The President 175–76 (1984).
3. Id. at 178.
4. Id. at 179. See also Chalmers M. Roberts, "The Day We Didn't Go to War," The Reporter, September 14, 1954, at 31–35.

raids against North Vietnam.[5] Armed helicopters, piloted by Americans, were used against the North Vietnamese.[6]

In August 1964, after President Johnson reported attacks against U.S. vessels in the Gulf of Tonkin, Congress hurriedly passed legislation to authorize the use of armed force. Several years later, with U.S. soldiers mired in a land war in Southeast Asia and confronting huge casualties, Congress began the slow process of reevaluating its role in twentieth-century wars. Even for conflicts on the vast scale of Korea and Vietnam, a declaration of war now seemed inappropriate. Without the check, how could Congress limit the President's ability to plunge the nation into war? Out of a long national debate emerged the War Powers Resolution of 1973.

Gulf of Tonkin Resolution

On August 3, 1964, President Lyndon B. Johnson ordered the Navy to take retaliatory actions against the North Vietnamese for their attacks in the Gulf of Tonkin.[7] He acted following an attack on the U.S. destroyer *Maddox* by Communist PT boats. His August 4 radio and television report to the American public provided further details on the incident and described a second attack, this one against two American destroyers. There were no U.S. losses at sea, and American strikes sunk at least two North Vietnamese boats. Air attacks were carried out against gunboats and supporting facilities in North Vietnam, with two U.S. aircraft lost in those missions.

Calling the North Vietnamese attacks an "outrage," Johnson said that the U.S. response would be "limited and fitting."[8] At joint hearings conducted by the Senate Committee on Armed Services and Foreign Relations, Secretary of Defense Robert McNamara testified that the U.S. objective was "to move our forces as rapidly out of Vietnam as that Government can maintain its independence and as rapidly as the North Vietnamese stop their attempts to subvert it."[9]

Johnson met with the leaders of both parties in Congress and asked for a resolution making clear "[our] determination to take all necessary mea-

5. Gary R. Hess, "Commitment in the Age of Counterinsurgency: Kennedy's Vietnam Options and Decisions, 1961–1963," in David L. Anderson, ed., Shadow on the White House: Presidents and the Vietnam War, 1945–1975, at 67–68 (1993).

6. Stanley Karnow, Vietnam: A History 275 (1991).

7. Public Papers of the Presidents, 1963–64, II, at 926.

8. Id. at 927.

9. "Southeast Asia Resolution," joint hearings before the Senate Committees on Foreign Relations and Armed Services, 88th Cong., 2d Sess. 25 (1964).

sures in support of freedom and in defense of peace in southeast Asia."[10] Johnson noted that his opponent for the presidency in 1964, Senator Barry Goldwater (R-Ariz.), was "glad to say that he has expressed his support of the statement that I am making to you tonight."[11] A special message to Congress on August 5 formalized Johnson's request for the joint resolution. In asking Congress to join in affirming the national determination that all attacks by North Vietnam will be met, Johnson said that the United States "intends no rashness, and seeks no wider war."[12] He referred, as models, to previous area resolutions for Formosa, the Middle East, and Cuba.

Although it appeared that the resolution was submitted in response to the incidents in the Tonkin Gulf, it had been conceived as early as February and put in draft form by late May.[13] A draft dated May 25, 1964, included language for dollar limits ("The President is hereby authorized to use for assistance under this joint resolution not to exceed $_____"),[14] but the Tonkin Gulf Resolution submitted to Congress was a blank check.

Congress spent little time debating the resolution. Senate debate started on August 6 and concluded the next day, with an endorsement of the resolution by a vote of 88 to 2. During Senate debate, Gaylord Nelson (D-Wis.) reviewed the statements of his colleagues and discovered that "there is no agreement in the Senate on what the joint resolution means."[15] Some members thought that by acting jointly with President Johnson and by announcing broad, bipartisan support, war with North Vietnam could be avoided. Others saw the need for a vigorous military response to eliminate aggression.

To clarify the resolution, Nelson offered an amendment to state that President Johnson would seek "no extension of the present military conflict" and that "we should continue to attempt to avoid a direct military involvement in the southeast Asian conflict." Senator J. William Fulbright (D-Ark.), acting as floor manager of the resolution, refused to accept the amendment because it would delay enactment. But he remarked that it stated "fairly accurately what the President has said would be our policy, and what I stated my understanding was as to our policy."[16] Fulbright

10. Public Papers of the Presidents, 1963–64, II, at 927.
11. Id. at 928.
12. Id. at 931.
13. Karnow, Vietnam, at 373, 376.
14. The Pentagon Papers, as published by the New York Times 287 (1971 paper ed.).
15. 110 Cong. Rec. 18458 (1964).
16. Id. at 18459.

believed that the resolution "is calculated to prevent the spread of war, rather than to spread it."[17]

The House passed the measure on August 7 without a single dissenting vote, 416 to 0. The Tonkin Gulf Resolution approved and supported the determination of the President, as Commander in Chief, to take "all necessary measures to repel any armed attack against the forces of the United States and to prevent further aggression." The statute further declared that the United States was prepared, "as the President determines, to take all necessary steps, including the use of armed force," to assist any member or protocol state (South Vietnam, Cambodia, and Laos) of SEATO requesting assistance in defense of its freedom. The resolution could expire by two methods: presidential determination or when terminated earlier by concurrent resolution of Congress.[18]

During House debate, no one opposed the legislation or Johnson's initiatives. Rep. Carl Albert (D-Okla.), the House Majority Leader, emphasized the need to set aside party differences and unite behind the President. The House Minority Leader, Charles Halleck (R-Ind.), took the same position. Edwin Adair, Republican from Indiana, responded to the concern that passage of the Tonkin Gulf Resolution would signal that legislators are "abdicating our congressional rights and our congressional responsibilities with respect to the declaration of war and with respect to foreign affairs generally." He said that issue had been raised in committee, "and we were given assurance that it was the attitude of the Executive that such was not the case, that we are not impairing our congressional prerogatives."[19]

Quite an extraordinary statement! Legislators ask executive officials if there has been abdication of congressional duties and are assured that no problem exists. Legislators accepted the word and analysis of executive officials about the protection of congressional prerogatives.

Neither House bothered to conduct independent investigations to verify Johnson's account. Senator Mansfield believed that Johnson had acted "in the hope of restraining the dogs of war."[20] Senator Fulbright, in words he would later regret, said that the facts of the Tonkin Gulf incident "are clear."[21] One of the two opponents in the Senate, Wayne Morse, displayed an uncanny gift for prophecy: "Unpopular as it is, I am perfectly willing to make the statement for history that if we follow a course of action that

17. Id. at 18462.
18. 78 Stat. 384 (1964).
19. 110 Cong. Rec. 18543 (1964).
20. Id. at 18399.
21. Id.

bogs down thousands of American boys in Asia, the administration responsible for it will be rejected and repudiated by the American people. It
should be."[22]

In signing the Tonkin Gulf Resolution, Johnson explained that the military response to North Vietnam "was mine—and mine alone" as Commander in Chief. But as President he said there remained another responsibility: "the responsibility of submitting our course to the representatives
of the people, for them to verity it or veto it."[23]

Subsequent investigations of the Tonkin Gulf incidents cast a heavy
shadow over the account presented by President Johnson and administration officials. Secretary McNamara testified on August 6, 1964, that the
Maddox was engaged in a "routine patrol in International waters."[24] In fact,
those patrols had helped provide support for South Vietnamese attacks on
North Vietnam. In February 1964, Johnson had accelerated attacks on North
Vietnam by using South Vietnamese commandos backed by U.S. warships.[25]

The first attack, on August 2, was too minor to justify asking Congress
for a resolution authorizing military action. The second alleged attack, on
August 4, probably never happened. Conflicting accounts have been given.
The ship's radar showed blips that might have indicated gunfire from North
Vietnamese boats, but the evidence is inconclusive. The commander of the
Maddox sent this cable on August 4: "Review of action makes many record-
ed contacts and torpedoes fired appear doubtful. Freak weather effects and
over-eager sonarman may have accounted for many reports. No actual
visual sightings by *Maddox*. Suggest complete evaluation before any further action."[26] Most, if not all, of the sonar reports identifying torpedoes
were probably reflections from the *Maddox* as it made its evasive weaving
turns.[27]

In a study published in 1996, Edwin E. Moïse concludes on the basis of
documents and interviews that the second attack never took place, but he

22. Id. at 18427.
23. Public Papers of the Presidents, 1963–64, II, at 946.
24. "Southeast Asia Resolution," joint hearing before the Senate Committees on
Foreign Affairs and Armed Services, 88th Cong., 2d Sess. 7 (1964).
25. William Conrad Gibbons, The U.S. Government and the Vietnam War: Executive
and Legislative Roles and Relationships, Part II: 1961–1964, at 228–35 (1986).
26. "The Gulf of Tonkin, The 1964 Incidents," hearing before the Senate Foreign
Relations Committee, 90th Cong., 2d Sess. 54 (1968).
27. Joseph C. Goulden, Truth Is the First Casualty: The Gulf of Tonkin Affairs—
Illusion and Reality (1969); Gibbons, The U.S. Government and the Vietnam War, at
291–92.

attributes the mistaken report to error rather than to an intentional lie by the administration.[28] In 1964, Secretary McNamara was convinced that the second attack occurred. After a trip to Vietnam in 1995, he announced that "I am absolutely positive" the second attack never took place and was prepared to say, "without a doubt, there was no second attack."[29]

Escalation of the War

President Johnson, aware of the hazards of getting involved in Vietnam, worried that the Republicans would exploit any sign of weakness (being "soft on communism") on his part and jeopardize his reelection in 1964. That concern surfaced during House debate on August 7, when Rep. Dante Fascell (D-Fla.) spoke about "our confidence in President Johnson's leadership in time of grave crisis." Johnson's prompt military response, he said, "should put to rest any erroneous idea that the Communists or others may have that the United States has a 'no win policy'; or that the United States is a 'paper tiger.' President Johnson's action also corrects any Communist idea that this administration or this country 'is soft on communism.'"[30]

Johnson shared his misgivings about Vietnam with John S. Knight, chairman of the board of the *Miami Herald,* in a phone call on February 3, 1964. Knight told Johnson that he "never thought we belonged there," and Johnson replied that he had opposed intervention in 1954 and agreed that the odds were against U.S. success: "Anytime you got that many people against you that far from your home base, it's bad."[31]

The instincts of Fulbright also opposed any commitment of U.S. troops to Vietnam. In a conversation with Johnson on December 2, 1963, Fulbright made it plain that a military victory was out of the question: "I just think [Vietnam] is a *hell* of a situation. It involves a lot more talk, but I'll be goddamned if I don't think it is hopeless. . . . I think the whole general situation is against us, as far as a real victory goes. . . . you don't want to send a whole lot more men in there, I don't think."[32] Despite their foreboding and reservations, both Johnson and Fulbright would take steps toward a major commitment in Vietnam.

28. Edwin E. Moïse, Tonkin Gulf and the Escalation of the Vietnam War (1996).
29. Keith B. Richburg, "Mission to Hanoi," Washington Post, November 11, 1995, at A21, A25.
30. 110 Cong. Rec. 18549 (1964).
31. Michael R. Beschloss, ed., Taking Charge: The Johnson White House Tapes, 1963–1964, at 213–14 (1998 ed.).
32. Id. at 88 (emphasis in original).

On May 27, 1964, in a conversation with foreign policy adviser McGeorge Bundy, Johnson confided that "it looks to me like we're getting into another Korea. It just worries the hell out of me. . . . I don't think it's worth fighting for and I don't think we can get out. It's just the biggest damned mess that I ever saw."[33] On June 2, Johnson told Robert Anderson, former Secretary of the Treasury in the Eisenhower administration, "I don't want to get tied down in an Asiatic war."[34]

President Johnson used the incidents in the Tonkin Gulf and the authority derived from the Tonkin Gulf Resolution to widen the war. A few weeks before the election, however, he told an audience in Ohio that "we are not about to send American boys 9 or 10,000 miles away from home to do what Asian boys ought to be doing for themselves."[35] In that speech he estimated that there were about 18,000 American soldiers in Vietnam.

Once elected, he prepared the groundwork for massive intervention. Large bombing runs began in February 1965. By May the troop strength had grown to 42,000, and on July 28 he increased U.S. combat forces from 75,000 to 125,000, promising additional forces if needed.[36] U.S. involvement continued to deepen, eventually putting 500,000 American troops in Vietnam. Officials in the Johnson administration believed that increased application of military power would lead to North Vietnam's breaking point, but appalling casualties on both sides produced a bloody stalemate, spawned a powerful antiwar movement at home, and led to Johnson's announcement in 1968 that he would not run for reelection.

The Vietnam commitment continued to expand because many lawmakers who strongly opposed military intervention refused to say anything in public. The prime example is Senator Richard Russell (D-Ga.), powerful chairman of the Senate Armed Services Committee and an influential adviser to President Johnson. Russell had warned about American involvement in Vietnam from Eisenhower through Johnson but rarely expressed his misgivings. He advised Johnson on December 7, 1963, that, regarding Vietnam, "We should get out, but I don't know any way to get out. I tried my best to keep them from going into Laos and Vietnam."[37]

Overt opposition from Russell would have been pivotal in limiting America's commitment to Southeast Asia, yet he remained silent in public. One scholar suggested two reasons: "First, he had a misguided sense of

---

33. Id. at 370.
34. Id. at 380.
35. Public Papers of the Presidents, 1963–64, II, at 1391.
36. Public Papers of the Presidents, 1965, II, at 795.
37. Beschloss, Taking Charge, at 95.

what was respect for the president, and of the need to support the flag once committed. More important was his total lack of understanding of congressional responsibility in exercising power over the executive under Article 1, § 8, of the Constitution."[38]

Richard Nixon, elected in 1968 to end the war in Vietnam, actually widened it to include Cambodia and Laos. His "incursion" into Cambodia in 1970 triggered nationwide protests and provoked Congress to enact restrictive amendments in 1971 to forbid the introduction of U.S. ground combat troops or advisers into Cambodia.[39] Congress repealed the Tonkin Gulf Resolution in 1971.[40] By denying funds for all combat activities in Southeast Asia in 1973, Congress finally brought the war to an end.

Free World Forces

At the beginning of the Vietnam War, President Johnson made it easy for members of Congress to register their support or opposition. Instead of funding the war through an omnibus defense appropriations bill, which might have been difficult for legislators to vote against, he requested appropriations in a supplemental bill crafted exclusively for Southeast Asia. His message to Congress was clear: "For each Member of Congress who supports this request is voting to continue our effort to try to halt communist aggression."[41] Congress supported this supplemental bill by votes of 408 to 7 in the House and 88 to 3 in the Senate.[42]

Later, in an effort to build support for the war, Johnson resorted to deception and stealth. For example, in September 1966 he expressed his "deep admiration as well as that of the American people for the action recently taken by the Philippines to send a civic action group of 2,000 men to assist the Vietnamese in resisting aggression and rebuilding their country."[43] Other announcements from the White House created the false impression that not only the Philippines but also Thailand, South Korea, and other members of what the administration called the "Free World Forces" had shown a willingness to sacrifice blood and resources in the stand against communism.

38. Ezra Y. Siff, Why the Senate Slept: The Gulf of Tonkin Resolution and the Beginning of America's Vietnam War 56 (1999).

39. 84 Stat. 1943, sec. 7(a) (1971).

40. 84 Stat. 2055, sec. 12 (1971).

41. Public Papers of the Presidents, 1965, I, at 484.

42. 111 Cong. Rec. 9540–41, 9772 (1965); 74 Stat. 109 (1965).

43. Public Papers of the Presidents, 1966, II, at 1029.

Hearings by Senator Stuart Symington (D-Mo.) in 1969 and 1970 discovered a number of secret agreements between the Johnson administration and the Free World Forces. The hearings revealed that the United States had offered sizable subsidies to those countries. For their modest assistance the Philippines received from the United States river patrol craft, engineering equipment, a special overseas allowance for their soldiers sent to Vietnam, and additional equipment to strengthen Philippine forces at home. It cost the United States $38.8 million to send one Filipino construction battalion to Vietnam.[44] Senator Fulbright remarked that it was his own feeling that "all we did was go over and hire their soldiers in order to support our then administration's view that so many people were in sympathy with our war in Vietnam."[45] Although the Philippine government denied that U.S. contributions represented a subsidy or a fee in return for sending the construction battalion, an investigation by the General Accounting Office (GAO) confirmed that quid pro quo assistance had indeed been given to the Philippines.[46]

The Symington subcommittee uncovered an agreement that the Johnson administration had made with the Royal Thai government in 1967 to cover any costs associated with the sending of Thai soldiers to Vietnam. An interim GAO report estimated that the U.S. government had invested "possibly more than $260 million in equipment, allowances, subsistence, construction, military sales concessions, and other support to the Thais for their contribution under the Free World Military Assistance program to Vietnam."[47] Other estimates put the total cost closer to $1 billion to obtain the deployment of a Thai division to fight in South Vietnam.[48] The Foreign Ministry of Thailand denied what evidence amply proved: the United States had offered payments to induce Thailand to send armed forces to Vietnam.[49]

U.S. subsidies were also used to support the sending of South Korean forces to Vietnam. American largesse included equipment to modernize Korean forces at home, equipment and additional costs to cover the deployment of Korean forces in Vietnam (including the payment of overseas

44. "United States Security Agreements and Commitments Abroad: The Republic of the Philippines" (part 1), hearings before the Senate Foreign Relations Committee, 91st Cong., 1st Sess. 255, 358 (1969).

45. Id. at 261.

46. New York Times, November 20, 1969, at 13; 116 Cong. Rec. 9259–60 (1970).

47. 116 Cong. Rec. 40521 (1970); "United States Security Agreements and Commitments Abroad: Kingdom of Thailand" (part 3), hearing before the Senate Foreign Relations Committee, 91st Cong., 1st Sess. 624–25, 657 (1969).

48. New York Times, December 1, 1969, at 1.

49. New York Times, December 16, 1969, at 10.

allowances), loans from the Agency of International Development, and increased ammunition and communications facilities in Korea. For the period from fiscal 1965 to fiscal 1970, Korea's presence in Vietnam cost the United States an estimated $927.5 million.[50]

The legal basis for assistance to Free World Forces in Vietnam derived from legislation passed in 1966. Funds were made available to support Vietnamese "and other free world forces in Vietnam, and related costs . . . on such terms and conditions as the Secretary of Defense may determine."[51] Assistance was broadened in 1967 to include local forces in Laos and Thailand.[52] Reports on such expenditures were submitted only to the Armed Services and Appropriations Committees of both Houses. The general language of the statutes did not reveal the types of financial arrangements the administration might enter into or with what country. Staff members who had access to the reports told me that they did not know the nature and dimension of financing the Free World Forces until hearings were held by the Symington subcommittee.

National Commitments Resolution of 1969

Unilateral executive commitments, both financial and military, caused Senator Fulbright to reverse his position on presidential war power. In 1961 he had written that "for the existing requirements of American foreign policy we have hobbled the President by too niggardly a grant of power."[53] Although it might be "distasteful and dangerous to vest the executive with powers unchecked and unbalanced," he questioned whether "we have any choice but to do so."[54] Having served as the point man in the Senate for the Tonkin Gulf Resolution, Fulbright was stunned in 1965 when President Johnson intervened in the Dominican Republic. In a lengthy speech, Fulbright dissected and repudiated the intervention, accusing the Johnson administration of relying on an exaggerated fear of communism.[55] That speech put an end to the Johnson-Fulbright alliance and freed Fulbright to

50. "United States Security Agreements and Commitments Abroad: Republic of Korea" (part 6), hearings before the Senate Foreign Relations Committee, 91st Cong., 2d Sess. 1529–45 (1970).

51. 80 Stat. 37, sec. 401 (1966); 80 Stat. 82, sec. 102 (1966).

52. 81 Stat. 53, sec. 301 (1967); 81 Stat. 248, sec. 639 (1967).

53. J. William Fulbright, "American Foreign Policy in the 20th Century under an 18th-Century Constitution," 47 Corn. L. Q. 1, 2 (1961).

54. Id. at 7.

55. 111 Cong. Rec. 23858–59 (1965).

challenge the policy in Vietnam.[56] By 1967 Fulbright could see "great merit in the checks and balances of our 18th century Constitution."[57]

The Senate passed a resolution in 1969 challenging the right of the President to commit the nation without congressional action. In an important sense, the resolution marked a return to Eisenhower's philosophy of interbranch cooperation and a recognition that Congress had been derelict in defending its constitutional powers. In reporting the resolution, the Senate Foreign Relations Committee noted the expansion of presidential power and said that if blame is to be apportioned "a fair share belongs to the Congress" because of its acquiescence and passivity.[58] This acquiescence by Congress "is probably the most important single fact accounting for the speed and virtual completeness of the transfer" of the war power from the legislative branch to the President.[59]

The committee report offered an interesting analysis to explain this acquiescence. Partly it was the unfamiliarity of the United States with its new role as a world power after 1900. Legislative decisions were made in an atmosphere of urgency, both real and contrived, and members of Congress might have been "overawed by the cult of executive expertise." Moreover, the Senate's rejection of the Covenant of the League of Nations might have created in Congress "a kind of penance for its prewar isolationism, and that penance has sometimes taken the form of overly hasty acquiescence in proposals for the acceptance of one form or another of international responsibility."[60]

Turning to the Tonkin Gulf Resolution, the report claimed that a discrepancy existed between the language of the resolution and what Congress intended. Although the statutory language appears to endorse a full-scale war in Southeast Asia, should the President determine that was necessary, few members of Congress expected a war of that magnitude. Many thought they were helping to prevent a large-scale conflict by taking a firm stand against aggression. Whatever the motivation, the delegation of such authority to the President was careless and irresponsible:

> In adopting a resolution with such sweeping language, however, Congress committed the error of making a *personal* judgment as to

56. Rowland Evans and Robert Novak, Lyndon B. Johnson: The Exercise of Power 529 (1966).

57. "U.S. Commitments to Foreign Powers," hearings before the Senate Foreign Relations Committee, 90th Cong., 1st Sess. 3 (1967).

58. S. Rept. No. 129, 91st Cong., 1st Sess. 8 (1969).

59. Id. at 15.

60. Id. at 16.

how President Johnson would implement the resolution when it had a responsibility to make an *institutional* judgment, first, as to what *any* President would do with so great an acknowledgment of power, and, second, as to whether, under the Constitution, Congress had a right to grant or concede the authority in question.[61]

The National Commitments Resolution, passed by a vote of 70 to 16, defined a national commitment as the use of U.S. armed forces on foreign territory or a promise to assist a foreign country by using U.S. armed forces or financial resources "either immediately or upon the happening of certain events." The resolution provides that "it is the sense of the Senate that a national commitment by the United States results only from affirmative action taken by the executive and legislative branches of the United States government by means of a treaty, statute, or concurrent resolution of both Houses of Congress specifically providing for such commitment."[62] Passed in the form of a Senate resolution, it had no legal effect. However, it signaled an important expression of constitutional principles by a bipartisan Senate. The Democrats supported it 43 to 3; the Republicans voted in favor 17 to 13.

This new attitude was revealed in 1970, following President Nixon's intervention in Cambodia. Secretary of State William Rogers explained to the Senate Foreign Relations Committee: "I think it is true that when we ask for military assistance and economic assistance for Cambodia we do certainly take on some obligation for some continuity."[63] Congress enacted language to limit that commitment: "Military and economic assistance provided by the United States to Cambodia and authorized or appropriated pursuant to this or any other Act shall not be construed as a commitment by the United States to Cambodia for its defense."[64]

Disputes in the Courts

After intervening in Cambodia in 1970, President Nixon told the nation that the "only remaining American activity in Cambodia after July 1 [1970] will be air missions to interdict the movement of enemy troops and material

61. Id. at 23 (emphasis in original).
62. 115 Cong. Rec. 17245 (1969).
63. "Supplemental Foreign Assistance Authorization, 1970," hearings before the Senate Committee on Foreign Relations, 91st Cong., 2d Sess. 27 (1970).
64. 84 Stat. 1943, sec. 7(b) (1971).

where I find that is necessary to protect the lives and security of our men in South Vietnam."[65] Congress responded with other statutory restrictions. Section 601 of the military authorization bill in 1971 declared it the policy of the United States to terminate "at the earliest practicable date" all military operations in Southeast Asia and to provide for the "prompt and orderly withdrawal of all United States military forces at a date certain," subject to the release of all American prisoners of war. The statutory language placed upon the President the responsibility for establishing a final date for the withdrawal of all U.S. military forces.[66]

In signing the bill, Nixon said that Section 601 "does not represent the policies of this Administration" and was "without binding force or effect."[67] A federal district judge chided Nixon for his language, noting that when the bill embodying Section 601 was signed by the President "it established 'the policy of the United States' to the exclusion of any different executive or administration policy, and had binding force and effect on every officer of the Government. No executive statement denying efficacy to the legislation could have either validity or effect." The judge regarded Nixon's statement as "very unfortunate."[68]

Disagreement continued on the issue of whether appropriation bills are instruments for setting congressional policy. Officials in the Johnson administration argued that Congress had authorized the Vietnam War by appropriating funds for that purpose. Initially, federal judges accepted appropriations statutes as sufficient authority and rejected any claim to the contrary. Said one judge: "That some members of Congress talked like doves before voting with the hawks is an inadequate basis for a charge that the President was violating the Constitution in doing what Congress by its words had told him he might do."[69]

Experts from the academic community challenged that reasoning, advising the judiciary that appropriations bills do not encompass major declarations of policy. They cited House and Senate rules that are designed to prevent substantive legislation from being included in appropriations bills.[70] However, other court decisions endorsed the theory that Congress could

65. Public Papers of the Presidents, 1970, at 478.
66. 85 Stat. 430, sec. 601 (1971).
67. Public Papers of the Presidents, 1971, at 1114.
68. DaCosta v. Nixon, 55 F.R.D. 145, 146 (E.D. N.Y. 1972).
69. Berk v. Laird, 317 F.Supp. 715, 724 (E.D. N.Y. 1970), aff'd sub nom. Orlando v. Laird, 443 F.2d 1039 (2d Cir. 1971), cert. denied, 404 U.S. 869 (1971).
70. Id. at 718, 721 (testimony of Professors Richard F. Fenno Jr. and Don Wallace Jr.).

indirectly assent to war by appropriating the necessary funds.[71] Some of those judges later found this theory unpersuasive. Federal appellate Judge Charles E. Wyzanski commented in a 1973 decision:

> This court cannot be unmindful of what every schoolboy knows: that in voting to appropriate money or to draft men a Congressman is not necessarily approving of the continuation of a war no matter how specifically the appropriation or draft act refers to that war. A Congrssman wholly opposed to the war's commencement and continuation might vote for the military appropriations and for the draft measures because he was unwilling to abandon without support men already fighting. An honorable, decent, compassionate act of aiding those already in peril is no proof of consent to the actions that placed and continued them in that dangerous posture. We should not construe votes cast in pity and piety as though they were votes freely given to express conscnt.[72]

Similarly, federal appellate Judge Arlan Adams argued that it would be impossible to decide whether Congress, through its appropriations, meant to authorize the military activities in Vietnam: "To explore these issues would require the interrogation of members of Congress regarding what they intended by their votes, and then synthesization of the various answers. To do otherwise would call for a gross speculation in a delicate matter pertaining to foreign relations."[73]

The basis for continued U.S. military action seemed to have disappeared with the signing of a cease-fire agreement in Paris on January 27, 1973, and the withdrawal of all American troops from Vietnam by March 28, 1973. Nevertheless, the Nixon administration ordered a massive bombing operation in Cambodia. The State Department submitted an analysis of the President's authority to continue U.S. air combat operations in Cambodia. Part of the justification rested on the "cooperation" of Congress in bringing about the cease-fire agreement: "This cooperation has been shown through

71. Orlando v. Laird, 317 F.Supp. 1013, 1018–19 (E.D. N.Y. 1970); Orlando v. Laird, 443 F.2d 1039, 1042 (2d Cir. 1971); Berk v. Laird, 429 F.2d 302, 305 (2d Cir. 1970); and DaCosta v. Laird, 448 F.2d 1368, 1369 (2d Cir. 1971).

72. Mitchell v. Laird, 476 F.2d 533, 538 (D.C. Cir. 1973). This decision was later withdrawn by court order.

73. Atlee v. Laird, 347 F.Supp. 689, 706 (E.D. Pa. 1972) (three-judge court), aff'd, Atlee v. Richardson, 411 U.S. 911 (1973).

consultations and through the authorization and appropriations process."
The statement noted that Congress had rejected proposals by some members to cut off appropriations for necessary military expenditures and foreign assistance.[74]

On March 21, 1973, President Nixon asked Congress to increase from $750 million to $1.25 billion the Pentagon's authority to transfer funds from one appropriation account to another. John McClellan (D-Ark.), chairman of the Senate Appropriations Committee, asked whether it was correct to say that even if Congress denied the requested additional amount of $500 million in transfer authority, "the Cambodian proceedings and operations will go on anyway, that the administration feels it has the authority to continue these operations and incur the cost involved irrespective of whether the Congress grants this transfer authority." Defense Secretary Elliot Richardson answered: "Yes, that is correct."[75]

The House Appropriations Committee reduced the transfer authority to $430 million. Eight Democratic members of the committee joined in a separate statement expressing strong opposition to the committee's position. They felt it amounted to a "Congressional blank check approving combat activities of the Defense Department which have already taken place and giving Congressional approval to any future combat activities which may be deemed necessary to preserve our flexibility." The grant of transfer authority reminded them of the Gulf of Tonkin Resolution and the erosion of congressional influence in decisions affecting Southeast Asia. To approve the transfer request would start the "entire sordid chain of events in motion once again."[76]

The appropriations bill reached the House floor on May 10. An amendment by Joseph Addabbo (D-N.Y.) to delete the additional transfer authority carried 219 to 188, thus overturning the recommendations of the House Appropriations Committee. In addition, the House adopted an amendment of Clarence Long (D-Md.) to prohibit the use of any funds in the supplemental bill to support directly or indirectly U.S. combat activities in, over, or from off the shores of Cambodia. That amendment passed 224 to 172.[77]

The Senate Appropriations Committee voted to recommend only $170 million in increased transfer authority, prohibiting any transfers for the pur-

74. 68 Dep't of State Bull. 655 (1973).
75. "Second Supplemental Appropriations for Fiscal Year 1973" (part 2), hearings before the Senate Committee on Appropriations, 93d Cong., 1st Sess. 1987 (1973).
76. H. Rept. No. 164, 93d Cong., 1st Sess. 22–23, 122 (1973).
77. 119 Cong. Rec. 15317, 15323 (1973).

pose of supporting combat activities in Cambodia and Laos.[78] Stronger measures would be needed, however. Even if denied transfer authority or access to funds in the supplemental appropriations bill, executive officials could finance the bombing with funds that had been appropriated in prior years. To close that door, the Senate Appropriations Committee adopted a more comprehensive amendment (the Eagleton amendment) to forbid the use of *any* funds to support U.S. combat activities in Cambodia or Laos— a restriction that covered funds contained in the supplemental bill as well as all funds made available by previous appropriations.

The two Houses reached a compromise on the amount of additional transfer authority: $75 million, provided that none of the funds could be used to support U.S. combat activities in Cambodia or Laos. The House also accepted the stronger Eagleton amendment. Nixon vetoed the bill on June 27, claiming that the Cambodia rider would "cripple or destroy the chances for an effective negotiated settlement in Cambodia and the withdrawal of all North Vietnamese troops." He also warned that the bill contained a number of appropriations that were essential for the continuation of governmental operations. Within a day, he said, nine agencies would exhaust their authority to pay the salaries and expenses of their employees.[79]

A stalemate loomed as the dispute moved to its climax. An attempt to override the veto in the House of Representatives failed by a vote of 241 to 173, short of the necessary two-thirds.[80] A revised supplemental bill was drafted to delay the effect of the Eagleton amendment until August 15, allowing the President to bomb Cambodia for another 45 days. Nixon signed that bill, which retained the substance of the Long amendment by prohibiting the use of any funds in the bill for combat activities in Southeast Asia. The additional $75 million in transfer authority was stricken from the bill.[81]

The August 15 compromise affected litigation that had been progressing in the federal courts. Rep. Robert Drinan (D-Mass.) and three other members of the House asked that the 1973 bombing of Cambodia be declared a violation of domestic and international law. Judge Joseph Tauro, a federal judge in Massachusetts, ruled that only in situations when a conflict between the executive and legislative branches appeared to be incapable of resolution should the courts intervene. Adoption of the August 15 compromise, he said, "demonstrates clearly and objectively that the branches

78. S. Rept. No. 160, 93d Cong., 1st Sess. 21 (1973).
79. Public Papers of the Presidents, 1973, at 621–22.
80. 119 Cong. Rec. 21778 (1973).
81. 87 Stat. 129, sec. 307 (1973).

were not in resolute conflict." Had Congress indicated an unwillingness to compromise, "we would have a clear issue of conflict before us that would have required judicial determination."[82]

Rep. Elizabeth Holtzman (D-N.Y.) filed a separate suit to have the courts determine that the President could not engage in combat operations in Cambodia and elsewhere in Southeast Asia in the absence of congressional authorization. Judge Orrin Judd, a federal judge in New York, held that Congress had not authorized the bombing of Cambodia. Its inability to override the veto and its subsequent adoption of the August 15 deadline could not be taken as an affirmative grant of authority: "It cannot be the rule that the President needs a vote of only one-third plus one of either House in order to conduct a war, but this would be the consequence of holding that Congress must override a Presidential veto in order to terminate hostilities which it has not authorized."[83] Judd enjoined President Nixon from engaging in combat operations in Cambodia but postponed the injunction for 48 hours to permit the administration to apply for a stay.

When the Second Circuit ordered a stay of the injunction until August 13, Holtzman appealed to the Supreme Court. Justice Marshall, assigned to oversee the proceedings of the Second Circuit, denied the Holtzman motion to vacate the stay. Marshall noted that once the August 15 date was reached, "the contours of this dispute will then be irrevocably altered. Hence, it is difficult to justify a stay for the purpose of preserving the status quo, since no action by this Court can freeze the issues in their present form."[84]

The Judd order was reversed on August 8 by the Second Circuit, which treated the dispute as basically a political question to be resolved by the executive and legislative branches. However, the Second Circuit did note that the August 15 date constituted congressional approval of the bombing in Cambodia.[85]

The War Powers Resolution

After decades of intense debate, Congress passed legislation in 1973 in an effort to limit presidential war power. The statute calls for "collective judg-

---

82. Drinan v. Nixon, 364 F.Supp. 854, 860, 861 (D. Mass. 1973).

83. Holtzman v. Schlesinger, 361 F.Supp. 553, 565 (E.D. N.Y. 1973).

84. Holtzman v. Schlesinger, 414 U.S. 1304, 1310 (1973). On August 4, Justice Douglas vacated the stay, 414 U.S. 1316, but later that same day Justice Marshall reinstated the stay and announced that other members of the Court were unanimous in overruling the Douglas order, 414 U.S. 1321.

85. Holtzman v. Schlesinger, 484 F.2d 1307, 1313–14 (2d Cir. 1973).

ment" by Congress and the President before U.S. troops are sent into combat, especially for long-term military engagements. The War Powers Resolution has had the effect of allowing the President to make war unilaterally for up to 90 days. Congressional approval was supposedly required after that period, but that part of the resolution has not worked out as planned. The statute also requires the President to report to Congress and encourages the President to consult with legislators before taking action.

The War Powers Resolution is usually described as a concerted effort to "reassert" congressional prerogatives. In fact, by recognizing that the President may use armed force for up to 90 days without seeking or obtaining legislative authority, the resolution legalizes a scope for independent presidential power that would have astonished the framers. According to Section 2(a) of the resolution, the measure is intended "to fulfill the intent of the framers" and to "insure that the collective judgment of both the Congress and the President" will apply to the introduction of U.S. forces to foreign hostilities. The statute has had no such effect. Instead, it violates the intent of the framers and does not in any sense ensure collective judgment. Presidents from Ronald Reagan to Bill Clinton made repeated use of military force without either seeking or obtaining authority from Congress.

Given the institutionally humiliating lesson of the Tonkin Gulf Resolution and the thoughtful deliberations that led to the National Commitments Resolution, how could Congress pass such a misguided measure as the War Powers Resolution? In part, it represented an effort to blend House and Senate versions that were incompatible in constitutional principle. As Senator Thomas F. Eagleton (D-Mo.) remarked, the two chambers "marched down separate and distinct roads, almost irreconcilable roads."[86]

Action by the House of Representatives in 1970 on the War Powers Resolution conceded a measure of war power to the President. Passed by a vote of 289 to 39, the resolution recognized that the President "in certain extraordinary and emergency circumstances has the authority to defend the United States and its citizens without specific prior authorization by the Congress." Instead of trying to define the precise conditions under which Presidents may act, the House opted for procedural safeguards. The President would be required, "whenever feasible," to consult with Congress before sending American forces into armed conflict. He was also to report the circumstances necessitating the action; the constitutional, legislative, and treaty provisions authorizing the action, together with his reasons for not seeking specific prior congressional authorization; and the estimated

86. 119 Cong. Rec. 33555 (1973).

scope of activities.[87] The House passed the same resolution a year later,[88] but the Senate did not act on either measure.

Both Houses later passed the War Powers Resolution that went beyond mere reporting requirements. The House of Representatives, adhering to its earlier practices, did not try to define or codify presidential war powers. It directed the President "in every possible instance" to consult with Congress before sending forces into hostilities or situations in which hostilities might be imminent. If unable to do so, he was to report to Congress within 72 hours, setting forth the circumstances and details of his action. Unless Congress declared war within 120 days or specifically authorized the use of force, the President had to terminate the commitment and remove the troops. Congress could also direct disengagement at any time during the 120-day period by passing a concurrent resolution.[89]

The Senate thought it could identify the precise conditions under which Presidents could act unilaterally. Armed force could be used in three situations: (1) to repel an armed attack upon the United States and its territories and possessions, retaliate in the event of such an attack, and forestall the direct and imminent threat of such an attack; (2) to repel an armed attack against U.S. armed forces located outside the United States and its territories and possessions, and forestall the direct and imminent threat of such an attack; and (3) to rescue endangered American citizens and nationals in foreign countries or at sea. The first situation (except for the final clause) agrees with the understanding reached at the Philadelphia convention. The other situations reflect the changes in presidential power that developed later, including the broad concept of defensive war and actions taken to protect American lives and property.

The Senate bill required the President to cease military action unless Congress, within 30 days, specifically authorized him to continue. A separate provision allowed the President to sustain military operations beyond the 30-day period if he determined that "unavoidable military necessity respecting the safety" of the armed forces required their continued use for purposes of "bringing about a prompt disengagement."[90] This attempt to codify presidential war powers carried a number of risks. Because of ambiguities in the language, legislation might broaden presidential power instead of restricting it. Executive officials could give broad interpretations of such

87. 116 Cong. Rec. 37398–408 (1970).
88. 117 Cong. Rec. 28870–78 (1971).
89. 119 Cong. Rec. 24653–708 (1973).
90. Id. at 25051–120.

terms as "necessary and appropriate retaliatory actions," "imminent threat," and "endangered citizens."

After meeting in conference the two Houses developed a bill that included a mix of House and Senate provisions. President Nixon vetoed that bill because he believed it encroached upon the President's constitutional responsibilities as Commander in Chief. He also thought it was impractical and dangerous to try to fix in a statute the procedures by which the President and Congress would share the war power. He told Congress that the "only way in which the constitutional powers of a branch of the Government can be altered is by amending the Constitution—and any attempt to make such alterations by legislation alone is clearly without force."[91]

Both Houses overrode the veto, the House narrowly (284 to 135), the Senate by a more comfortable margin (75 to 18). Some of the congressional support for the War Powers Resolution was based more on partisan motivations than on constitutional analysis. Fifteen members of the House voted against the House bill and the conference version, arguing that it gave the President too much power. They should have sustained the veto to prevent the bill from becoming law, yet they voted to override.[92] In part they may have feared that a vote to sustain might have indirectly endorsed the views advanced by Nixon in his veto message. A failure to enact the bill could have been interpreted as support for the constitutional claims of Johnson and Nixon.

Other legislators used the override vote as part of the effort to impeach Nixon. One of those who voted against the House resolution and conference version, yet switched to override the veto, was Rep. Bella Abzug (D-N.Y.). She predicted that the override "could be a turning point in the struggle to control an administration that has run amuck. It could accelerate the demand for the impeachment of the President."[93] Another factor unrelated to the substance of the War Powers Resolution was the desire of Democrats to override Nixon, who had vetoed bills successfully eight straight times during the 93d Congress, with the two Houses unable to override. These legislators saw the War Powers Resolution as a way to test congressional power.[94]

Some Democrats in the House recognized that the conference report tilt-

91. Public Papers of the Presidents, 1973, at 893.

92. Representatives Abzug, Drinan, Duncan, Flynt, Harsha, Hechler, Holtzman, Hungate, Landrum, Lott, Maraziti, Milford, Natcher, Stubblefield, and Whitten.

93. 119 Cong. Rec. 36221 (1973).

94. Thomas F. Eagleton, War and Presidential Power 213–20 (1974).

ed power dangerously toward the President.[95] Senator Eagleton, a principal sponsor of the resolution, denounced the bill that emerged from conference as a "total, complete distortion of the war powers concept."[96] Instead of the three exceptions specified in the Senate bill, the conference version gave the President "carte blanche" authority to use military force for up to 90 days. To Eagleton, the bill was a sellout, a surrender. He confessed to being "dumbfounded." With memories so fresh about presidential expansion of the war in Southeast Asia, he asked "how can we give unbridled, unlimited total authority to the President to commit us to war?" Eagleton charged that the bill, after being nobly conceived, "has been horribly bastardized to the point of being a menace."[97]

The vote on the War Powers Resolution was clouded by the Watergate scandal. The "Saturday Night Massacre," which sent Special Prosecutor Archibald Cox, Attorney General Elliot Richardson, and Deputy Attorney General William Ruckelshaus out of the government, occurred just four days before Nixon's veto of the War Powers Resolution. Ten days before the Saturday Night Massacre, Spiro Agnew had resigned as Vice President in the face of criminal charges.

Strengths and Weaknesses

Section 2(a) states that the purpose of the resolution is "to insure the collective judgment" of both branches when U.S. forces are introduced into hostilities. Surely that principle fits foursquare with the text of the Constitution and the intent of the framers. Two other sections—on consultation and reporting—are consistent with constitutional principles. The President is to consult with Congress "in every possible instance," leaving considerable discretion to the President but placing the emphasis on interbranch collaboration. The legislative history makes it clear that consultation goes beyond simply being informed that the President has made a decision. Consultation means that "a decision is pending on a problem and that Members of Congress are being asked by the President for their advice and opinions and, in appropriate circumstances, their approval of action contemplated."[98] After introducing forces into hostilities, the President is required to report to Congress within 48 hours.

95. Louis Fisher and David Gray Adler, "The War Powers Resolution: Time to Say Goodbye," 113 Pol. Sci. Q. 1, 5 (1998).
96. 119 Cong. Rec. 36177 (1973).
97. Id. at 36178.
98. H. Rept. No. 287, 93d Cong., 1st Sess. 6–7 (1973).

The War Powers Resolution contemplated two means of legislative control: a supposed deadline of 60 to 90 days on presidential initiatives to use force and the use of a concurrent resolution to require him to remove troops engaged in hostilities. Neither control has been effective. The effort to combine elements of House and Senate bills resulted in a statute that is internally inconsistent.

For example, Section 2(c) attempts to define the President's constitutional powers as Commander in Chief to introduce U.S. forces into hostilities "or into situations where imminent involvement in hostilities is clearly indicated by the circumstances." The President may introduce troops *only* pursuant to (1) a declaration of war, (2) specific statutory authorization, or (3) "a national emergency created by attack upon the United States, its territories, or its armed forces."[99] Those three conditions are fairly much in accord with the Constitution and the framers' intent.

However, Section 4, governing reports to Congress, is not consistent with Section 2(c). Presidents may report under a broad range of circumstances unrelated to attacks on the United States, its territories, or its armed forces. Presidents may report when U.S. troops are introduced

(1) into hostilities or into situations where imminent involvement in hostilities is clearly indicated by the circumstances;

(2) into the territory, airspace or waters of a foreign nation, while equipped for combat, except for deployments which relate solely to supply, replacement, repair, or training of such forces; or

(3) in numbers which substantially enlarge United States Armed Forces equipped for combat already located in a foreign nation.[100]

This language appears to sanction presidential use of military force in situations wholly unrelated to attacks against U.S. territory and troops. Under this broader reading, the President may dispatch troops to intervene in Grenada, invade Panama or Haiti, or assist in Somalia and Bosnia.

Congressional control is further weakened by awkward language that fails to start the 60-to-90-day clock. According to the War Powers Resolution, if the President introduces troops into hostilities he is to remove them unless Congress approves within 60 days. The President may extend the deadline by an additional 30 days if he determines that an extension is necessary to protect and remove the troops. The problem with this procedure

99. 87 Stat. 555, sec. 2(c) (1973).
100. Id. at 555–56.

is that the clock does not start ticking for the 60-to-90-day limit unless the President reports under a very specific section: Section 4(a)(1). For fairly obvious reasons, Presidents do not submit reports under that section. Instead, they report more generally. For example, when President Reagan reported to Congress on his air strikes against Libya in 1986, he reported "consistent with the War Powers Resolution."[101] The clock never started.

Only twice has Section 4(a)(1) been used. President Ford reported under Section 4(a)(1) to describe the capture of the U.S. merchant ship *Mayaguez* by Cambodian forces. However, by the time his report reached Congress, the military operation was already over. Reporting under Section 4(a)(1) did not restrict his actions. The second time Section 4(a)(1) was used was in 1983 when Congress passed the Lebanon Resolution. Enacted on October 12, 1983, the statute declared that Section 4(a)(1) had been activated on August 29, 1983. There were two weaknesses with this approach. It took a statute to start the clock rather than a presidential report. Moreover, Congress authorized President Reagan to keep troops in Lebanon not for three months but for up to *eighteen* months.[102] He removed most of the U.S. Marines in February 1984.

The second form of congressional control—passage of a concurrent resolution—has been challenged on constitutional grounds. The legal adviser to the State Department told a House committee in 1975 that if the President has the power to put U.S. troops into combat, "that power could not be taken away by concurrent resolution because the power is constitutional in nature."[103] That position appeared to be strengthened by the Supreme Court in *INS* v. *Chadha* (1983), which held that Congress can control executive actions only by presenting a bill or joint resolution to the President for signature or veto.[104] Concurrent resolutions pass the House and Senate but are not submitted to the President.

Even if the clock does not tick on the 60-to-90-day deadline, executive officials sometimes *behave* as though it does. Military operations in Grenada and Panama were conducted as though the 60-day limit was enforceable— if not legally, then politically. A former high-ranking member of the Joint Chiefs of Staff during the Reagan years revealed that as the 60-day deadline drew near, administrative officials believed "it would not be political-

101. Public Papers of the Presidents, 1986, I, at 478.

102. 97 Stat. 805 (1983).

103. "War Powers: A Test of Compliance," hearings before the House Committee on International Relations, 94th Cong., 1st Sess. 91 (1975).

104. 462 U.S. 919 (1983).

ly wise" to challenge Congress on this particular issue.[105] For longer and more dangerous operations, such as in the Middle East in 1983, Iraq in 1991, Afghanistan in 2001, and Iraq in 2003, Presidents have come to Congress to seek authorization.

Efforts to Amend the WPR

The War Powers Resolution has remained unchanged since 1973, despite efforts in 1983 and 1995 to amend it. The first amendment would have removed the procedure that permits Congress to disapprove military commitments by concurrent resolution. The second would have repealed all of the War Powers Resolution except for the consultation and reporting provisions.

Objections had long been leveled against the concurrent resolution, which must be adopted by a majority of each House but is not submitted to the President for his signature or veto. The case against this type of "legislative veto" was measurably strengthened in 1983 when the Supreme Court struck down the legislative veto as unconstitutional.[106] The Court ruled that whenever Congress wants to alter the legal rights, duties, or relations outside the legislative branch, it must act by both Houses in a bill or joint resolution that is presented to the President for his signature or veto.

In response to the Court's decision, an amendment was offered to the WPR to require Congress to act not by concurrent resolution but by joint resolution. As enacted, however, this amendment did not alter the WPR. Instead, it became a freestanding procedure available to Congress to act by joint resolution to require the President to withdraw troops.[107] The concurrent resolution remains in the War Powers Resolution.

In 1995, House Republicans proposed an amendment that would have repealed all of the WPR except for the sections on consultation and reporting. Opposition to the WPR came from both flanks: those who said it usurps presidential power and those who believed it abdicates congressional prerogatives. As written, the amendment left the impression

105. Christopher B. Howard, "The Role of the House Armed Services and Foreign Affairs Committees in Force Employment Policymaking: 97th–100th Congresses" (Master's thesis, Oxford University, 1993), chap. 3, 55.

106. INS v. Chadha, 462 U.S. 919 (1983).

107. 97 Stat. 1062–63, sec. 1013 (1983); 50 U.S.C. 1546a (2000). See 129 Cong. Rec. 28406–8, 28673–74, 28683–84, 28686–89, 33385, 33395–96 (1983).

that Presidents could do pretty much as they pleased in initiating military operations so long as they consulted a few people in Congress and submitted regular reports. Rep. David Skaggs (D-Colo.) expressed concern that the amendment carried "an unfortunate implication" that presidential authority in war "is restrained only by a consultative and reporting requirement."[108]

Toward the end of the debate, it appeared that a significant motivation behind partial repeal was an effort to augment presidential power. Speaker Newt Gingrich appealed to the House "to, at least on paper, increase the power of President Clinton." He said he wanted to "strengthen the current Democratic President because he is the President of the United States. And the President of the United States on a bipartisan basis deserves to be strengthened in foreign affairs and strengthened in national security."[109] Forty-four Republicans, repelled by that objective, abandoned Gingrich. With their exodus the amendment fell short of votes, 201 to 217.

One proposal, never put to vote, would replace the WPR with a Use of Force Act, which would delegate to the President a number of authorities, including the right to "protect and extricate citizens and nationals of the United States located abroad in situations involving a direct and imminent threat to their lives, provided they are being evacuated as rapidly as possible."[110] Such language could have been used to justify U.S. invasions of the Dominican Republic in 1965, Grenada in 1983, Panama in 1989, and Haiti in 1994. Americans abroad are abused and threatened every year.

The Use of Force Act would also authorize the President to use force abroad "to participate in multilateral actions undertaken under urgent circumstances and pursuant to the approval of the United Nations Security Council." Language of that nature would have sanctioned Truman's use of military force against North Korea in 1950, Bush's military operations against Iraq in 1990–1991, and Clinton's invasion of Haiti in 1994. In each of those situations the administration was able to get resolutions adopted by the UN Security Council authorizing the use of military force. Rather than forcing the President to seek authority from Congress, the Use of Force Act accepts a UN resolution as a perfectly acceptable substitute.

The Use of Force Act would permit the President to use force abroad "to participate in multilateral actions undertaken in cooperation with dem-

108. 141 Cong. Rec. 15203 (1995).
109. Id. at 15209.
110. Joseph R. Biden Jr. and John B. Ritch III, "The War Power at a Constitutional Impasse: A 'Joint Decision' Solution," 77 Geo. L. J. 367, 398 (1988).

ocratic allies under urgent circumstances wherein the use of force could have decisive effect in protecting existing democratic institutions in a particular nation against a severe and immediate threat." That language would have given legal cover to President Clinton's use of military force in Bosnia and Yugoslavia once he secured the approval of NATO countries. All of those provisions read Congress (and its constituents) out of the picture.

7

MILITARY INITIATIVES FROM FORD TO BUSH I

From Gerald Ford through George H. W. Bush, Presidents used military force on numerous occasions by citing their power as Commander in Chief. Although they challenged the constitutionality of the War Powers Resolution, the record since 1973 was fairly uniform. Presidents acted unilaterally when using force for short-term operations in areas of the world that are relatively isolated, with little chance of the conflict spreading. For military operations in regions that pose extreme danger of involving other nations, such as in the Middle East, they sought congressional approval in advance (without fully admitting that they needed it).

The pattern of reports under the War Powers Resolution indicates an increased reliance on U.S. military forces. Presidents Ford and Carter reported only five uses of armed forces, and three of the occasions under Ford involved military efforts to evacuate American citizens and foreign nationals from Southeast Asia. Ignoring those operations, in the six and a half years of Ford's and Carter's terms of office there were only two presidential initiatives to use armed forces: Ford's effort to rescue the *Mayaguez* crew in 1975 and Carter's attempt to rescue American hostages in Iran in 1980.

Military activity accelerated during the Reagan and Bush I administrations. President Reagan submitted 14 reports under the War Powers Resolution and President Bush six. Several reports covered major military operations: the dispatch of U.S. Marines to Lebanon in 1982, the invasion of Grenada in 1983, air strikes against Libya in 1986, military actions in the Persian Gulf in 1987 and 1988, the invasion of Panama in 1989, and the war against Iraq in 1991.

Evacuations from Southeast Asia

Early drafts of the War Powers Resolution discussed the President's responsibility to protect the lives and property of Americans. A bill introduced by Senator Jacob Javits (R-N.Y.) in 1971 would have permitted the President to use armed force "to protect the lives and property, as may be required, of United States nationals abroad." Javits later deleted the words "and

154

property" for fear that they might be interpreted in nineteenth-century fashion to protect American businesses in other countries.[1] The rest of his language disappeared in the House-Senate negotiations leading to final passage of the War Powers Resolution.

This lack of explicit statutory authority, combined with other statutory restrictions on the use of force in Southeast Asia, produced a difficult decision for President Ford in 1975. He asked Congress to clarify the statutory restrictions to permit him to evacuate American citizens and foreign nationals from South Vietnam and Cambodia. Congress was given nine days to produce the desired legislation.[2] Instead of trying to act while a presidential timer ticked away, party leaders in Congress could have issued a statement saying that the President had sufficient authority for the evacuations provided he used a minimum of force and did not spread the conflict. Ford had already announced that the War Powers Resolution, as he interpreted it, gave the President "certain limited authority to protect American lives. And to that extent, I will use that law."[3] Why then ask Congress for clarifying authority with such a short deadline? The legal issue was complicated by the need to rescue foreign nationals as well, but it was politically unreasonable and unrealistic to expect Congress to complete legislation on such an explosive issue in nine days.

Members agonized for weeks, searching for language that would give Ford the authority he needed for the evacuations without possibly inviting military reinvolvement in Southeast Asia. Given the limitations of language and the history of bad-faith relations between the branches, it was unlikely that the legislative process would be successful. Legislators were whipsawed by conflicting emotions. On the one hand they wanted to relate all military operations to the procedures established in the War Powers Resolution; on the other, they were apprehensive that any legislation, no matter how meticulously drawn, would become anachronous and ambiguous because of the rapidly changing conditions in Southeast Asia.

While Congress anguished over the wording of the legislation, Ford went ahead with the evacuations from Cambodia and South Vietnam. In each case he based his action on the President's "executive power" under the Constitution and his authority as Commander in Chief.[4] He took action before Congress could deliver the "clarifying authority," but even after the

1. "War Powers Resolution," hearings before the Senate Committee on Foreign Relations, 92d Cong., 1st Sess. 35–36, 95–96, 128 (1971).
2. Public Papers of the Presidents, 1975, I, at 464.
3. Id. at 414–15.
4. H. Doc. Nos. 105 and 124, 94th Cong., 1st Sess. (1975).

evacuations were over some members of Congress insisted that the legislation should still be passed. They reasoned that the President had conducted the evacuations within the limitations of the legislation under consideration (although Ford cited only constitutional sources in his reports) and therefore Congress should enact the legislation and legalize the President's action. Other legislators believed that the bill was moot because the evacuations were over. Passage of the legislation, they feared, would merely lift the restrictions that barred any reintroduction of troops into Southeast Asia. The House, capping three weeks of legislative frenzy, voted down the conference report—an ignominious finale to an ill-conceived legislative exercise.[5]

Following the evacuations from Southeast Asia, Senator Thomas F. Eagleton introduced legislation explicitly recognizing the President's right to protect American lives (but not property) and stipulating various conditions to limit this presidential power. The citizens to be rescued would have to be involuntarily held with the express or tacit consent of the foreign government; there would have to be a direct and imminent threat to their lives; the foreign government either could not or would not protect the individuals; and the evacuations would have to take place as expeditiously as possible and with a minimum of force.[6] Congress took no action on this legislation.

The *Mayaguez* Capture

In May 1975, the U.S. merchant ship *Mayaguez,* traveling from Hong Kong to Sattahip, Thailand, was seized by Cambodians. Two days later the United States recovered the vessel and its crew after President Ford ordered air strikes against Cambodia and introduced U.S. Marine ground forces. Ford reported to Congress in accordance with Section 4(a)(1) of the War Powers Resolution, thereby triggering the 60-day clock, but only after the operation was over. Thus, invoking 4(a)(1) had no practical effect. He said that the operation was ordered and conducted "pursuant to the President's constitutional Executive power and his authority as Commander-in-Chief of the United States Armed Forces."[7] Ford acted in light of North Korea's capture

---

5. 121 Cong. Rec. 12752–64 (1975). For a GAO decision holding that the evacuation of Vietnamese nationals was necessarily incident to the rescue of Americans, see 55 Comp. Gen. 1081 (1976).

6. 121 Cong. Rec. 15579–82 (1975).

7. Public Papers of the Presidents, 1975, I, at 670.

of the USS *Pueblo* in 1968, when the American crew was held captive for more than a year.

Although months would pass by before members of Congress had an adequate picture of what had taken place, on the very day of the recovery they rushed forward with glowing words of praise. With a spirit of jingoism filling the air, the episode became a "proud new chapter in our history." Legislators expressed pride in their country and in their President, exclaiming with youthful enthusiasm that it was "great to be an American."[8]

A few members reserved judgment, which was sensible, because no one knew exactly what had happened or why. A legislator could have announced: "I am happy that the crew is back. Unfortunately, many lives were lost in the rescue effort. It is still too early, and the facts too incomplete, for us to make a judgment." Most members, however, felt compelled to outdo each other with words of commendation and jubilation.

As details of the incident trickled in, Ford's action looked less and less appealing. Approximately 41 Americans had lost their lives trying to rescue 39 crewmen. The administration spent little effort probing diplomatic avenues before resorting to force, and the quality of military intelligence was not reassuring. U.S. Marines suffered heavy casualties during the assault on Koh Tang Island under the erroneous impression that the crewmen were detained there. As noted in one study, "18 of the 41 Marines who died . . . were killed raiding the wrong place."[9] A punitive spirit seemed to infuse the operations. The United States bombed the Cambodian mainland *after* the crew had been released. A 15,000-pound bomb—the largest conventional bomb in America's arsenal—was dropped on a Cambodian island that measured just a few square miles.[10]

Administration officials insisted that this use of force contained valuable lessons regarding America's determination to meet its international commitments.[11] How that solitary event could help guide future emergencies is difficult to envision. Anthony Lewis of the *New York Times* said that for "all the bluster and righteous talk of principle, it is impossible to imagine

8. See especially the Congressional Record of May 15, 1975.

9. Charles F. Bennett, "The Mayaguez Re-examined: Misperception in an Information Shortage," 1 Fletcher Forum 15, 16 (1976).

10. "Seizure of the Mayaguez" (parts I and II), hearings before the House Committee on International Relations, 94th Cong., 1st Sess. (1975); 121 Cong. Rec. 18312–13 (1975) (statement by Senator Javits); Jordan J. Paust, "The Seizure and Recovery of the Mayaguez," 85 Yale L. J. 774 (1976).

11. "Seizure of the Mayaguez" (part 1), hearings before the House Committee on International Relations, 94th Cong., 1st Sess. 61–130 (1975).

the United States behaving that way toward anyone other than a weak, ruined country of little yellow people who have frustrated us."[12] An editorial in the *Washington Post* noted with alarm that the use of force by the greatest power in the world against a small country could serve as such a tonic in the nation's capital: "That anyone could find the Mayaguez affair a valid or meaningful guide to the requirements of post-Vietnam foreign policy at other times and places defies common sense."[13]

It is remarkable that one month after the costly disengagement from Southeast Asia, after the United States had finally broken free from a lengthy and violent war that had racked the country, there could be such a celebration of force. What happened to the "deliberative process" of Congress? The vaunted independent legislative capability? The promise of closer scrutiny of executive actions? Unless members take the time personally to analyze a President's decision, Congress cannot expect a coequal status or a share in "collective judgment." Instead, legislators will become prematurely associated with a war policy they may later find unworthy of support.[14]

A federal district judge received a case in which former crewmen of the *Mayaguez* brought an action seeking damages for personal injuries suffered during the rescue effort. They claimed that U.S. agencies had knowledge of previous hostile acts by Cambodia and failed to give proper warning to the *Mayaguez*. They also argued that the military operation was executed in a negligent fashion. After stating that the "responsibility for the use of military forces is clearly committed to the President by the Constitution" and citing *Durand* v. *Hollins* (1860) as good law on the President's authority to implement military decisions without having to undergo judicial scrutiny, the judge held that Ford's action was immune from judicial review under the political question doctrine.[15]

Desert One Rescue Effort

In November 1979, Iranian militants seized the U.S. embassy in Tehran and took more than 50 American citizens as hostage. They were held captive for the next 444 days, throughout the remainder of the Carter administra-

12. New York Times, May 19, 1975, at 29.
13. Washington Post, May 16, 1975, at A26.
14. Robert Zutz, "The Recapture of the S.S. Mayaguez: Failure of the Consultation Clause of the War Powers Resolution," 8 N.Y.U. J. Int'l L. & Pol. 457 (1976).
15. Rappenecker v. United States, 509 F.Supp. 1024, 1029, 1030 (N.D. Cal. 1980).

tion. Unable to obtain the release of the hostages by diplomatic efforts, Carter ordered a military raid that involved sending eight American helicopters to Iran to a remote staging area called Desert One. The helicopters were supposed to join up with six C-130 cargo planes carrying 90 commandos, leading to a military raid into Tehran. However, two of the helicopters malfunctioned and never reached Desert One. When a third developed a serious hydraulic problem, Carter canceled the operation. In leaving the site, a helicopter and a cargo plane collided, killing eight Americans and injuring several others. The surviving personnel were placed aboard the remaining cargo planes, leaving the abandoned helicopters at the staging site.

When President Carter reported to Congress on the use of military force in this rescue attempt, he reported "consistent" with the War Powers Resolution and relied on the President's authority as Chief Executive and Commander in Chief.[16] Secretary of State Cyrus Vance, who believed that several remaining political and diplomatic options should be considered before resorting to military force, was angry that the administration had decided on the rescue mission while he was out of town for a weekend.[17] He resigned in protest.

Vance believed that Carter should have notified the Democratic and Republican leaders in Congress about the planned raid, but Carter decided to consult with legislators only after the rescue operation had reached the point of no return.[18] On the evening prior to the operation, Carter met with Senate Majority Leader Robert C. Byrd (D-W.Va.) to discuss possible military action in Iran and told Byrd that before he took any of the military actions mentioned in the press (mining, blockade, and so forth) he would consult first with Congress. Carter said that Byrd made a "sharp distinction" between consulting with Congress on military plans and informing Congress "at the last minute" about covert operations. Carter had planned to let Byrd know about the impending rescue attempt at the end of the conversation but chose to delay that briefing until the following evening after the U.S. team was actually in place and ready to enter Tehran. After Byrd left the White House, Carter wondered if it would have been better to confide in him: "His advice would have been valuable to me then—and also twenty-four hours later."[19]

16. Public Papers of the Presidents, 1980–81, I, at 779.
17. Cyrus Vance, Hard Choices 409 (1983).
18. Jimmy Carter, Keeping Faith 511 (1982).
19. Id. at 514.

Lebanon

Military initiatives by President Reagan in 1982 revealed severe weaknesses in the War Powers Resolution. Initially, Reagan intervened in Lebanon
as part of a three-nation peacekeeping force (including France and Italy).
The announced goal was to assure the withdrawal of the Palestine Liberation Organization (PLO) and to restore the sovereignty of the Lebanese government. He explained on August 20 that U.S. troops would play a "carefully limited, noncombatant role," remaining in Lebanon for no longer than
30 days.[20] He ordered the deployment solely under what he called his
"constitutional authority with respect to the conduct of foreign relations
and as Commander in Chief."[21]

The noncombatant, peacekeeping mission turned violent. A terrorist
bomb on April 18, 1983, killed 16 Americans at the U.S. embassy in Beirut,
and other fatalities of U.S. Marines occurred on August 29 and September
6. Although hostilities were not merely "imminent" in Lebanon but had
actually broken out, Reagan sent in troops without reporting under Section
4(a)(1) of the War Powers Resolution. Consistent with Ford and Carter, he
deployed troops pursuant to his "constitutional authority."[22] Because
Reagan refused to trigger the clock under the War Powers Resolution, Congress passed legislation on October 12, 1983, providing that the requirements of Section 4(a)(1) became operative on August 29, 1983.[23] However,
instead of confining Reagan to 60 or 90 days, Congress authorized military
action for 18 months.[24]

Members supported this massive delegation partly on the assumption
that Reagan, by signing the bill, would concede the legitimacy of the procedures established by the War Powers Resolution. Several of his public
statements indicated the need and desirability of joint executive-legislative
action. Writing to Congress on September 27, 1983, before enactment of
the resolution triggering Section 4(a)(1), Reagan said it was his intention to
"seek Congressional authorization" if it became necessary to substantially
expand the number or role of U.S. armed forces in Lebanon.[25] After House
action on the resolution, he announced that a "spirit of cooperation
between members of the two parties, and between the executive and the

20. Public Papers of the Presidents, 1982, II, at 1063.
21. Id. at 1079.
22. Public Papers of the Presidents, 1982, II, at 1238.
23. 97 Stat. 805, sec. 2(b) (1983).
24. Id. at 807, sec. 6.
25. Public Papers of the Presidents, 1983, II, at 1368.

legislative branches of our Government, has been the traditional hallmark of a successful foreign policy."[26] A day later he praised the Senate for passing the resolution, observing that the votes by the two Houses send a signal that "we speak with one voice."[27]

However, in signing the resolution he took exception to many of its provisions. With regard to the clock beginning on August 29, 1983, he noted that "the initiation of isolated or infrequent acts of violence against the United States Armed Forces does not necessarily constitute actual or imminent involvement in hostilities, even if casualties to those forces result."[28] As to the 18-month deadline, he thought it unwise and unconstitutional for Congress to establish precise periods for presidential use of force. He made it clear that he felt no constitutional obligation to seek congressional authorization after the expiration of the 18-month period if, in his view, further use of military action was necessary.[29]

A few weeks after enactment of the bill authorizing military force for 18 months, a suicide truck carrying explosives broke through barriers surrounding U.S. military headquarters in Beirut and killed 241 marines. A separate suicide mission killed more than 50 French soldiers. As hostilities continued to mount, Reagan ordered military strikes against Druze, Shiite, and Syrian positions. The posture of neutrality had now disappeared. On March 30, 1984, long before the 18-month period had expired, Reagan terminated U.S. participation in the multinational force. What began as a humanitarian, peacekeeping, noncombatant mission, to last 30 days, deteriorated into a war of almost two years.[30]

Invasion of Grenada

On October 25, 1983, President Reagan announced that he had ordered U.S. troops to Grenada as part of a multilateral effort. A coup on October 12 led to the murder of Prime Minister Maurice Bishop, three cabinet members, two labor leaders, and other citizens. Bishop's murder on October 19 raised questions about the safety of American medical students present on the island. Participating in this invasion were contingents from

26. Id. at 1384.
27. Id. at 1389.
28. Id. at 1444.
29. Id. at 1444–45.
30. For U.S. military miscalculations in Lebanon, see Peter Huchthausen, America's Splendid Little Wars 45–63 (2003).

Antigua, Barbados, Dominica, Jamaica, St. Lucia, and St. Vincent. These countries, with the exception of Barbados and Jamaica, were members of the Organization of Eastern Caribbean States (OECS), which voted unanimously for the military intervention. Reagan gave three justifications for the invasion: (1) the protection of lives, including up to 1,000 Americans, (2) forestalling "further chaos," and (3) assisting in the restoration of "conditions of law and order and of governmental institutions" to the island of Grenada.[31]

The UN Security Council drafted a resolution "deeply deploring" the invasion of Grenada, eleven members voting in favor and the United States exercising its veto. Britain, Togo, and Zaire abstained on the vote. A number of U.S. allies, including France, the Netherlands, and Pakistan, voted for the resolution. On the key language of legality, the Security Council "DEEPLY DEPLORES the armed intervention in Grenada, which constitutes a flagrant violation of international law and of the independence, sovereignty and territorial integrity of that state."[32]

President Reagan reported to Congress, "consistent with the War Powers Resolution," on the deployment of U.S. forces to Grenada. A total of 1,900 U.S. Army and Marine Corps personnel landed in Grenada, supported by elements of the U.S. Navy and Air Force. Member states of the OECS provided approximately 300 personnel. Reagan stated that he deployed U.S. forces pursuant to his constitutional authority "with respect to the conduct of foreign relations and as Commander-in-Chief of the United States Armed Forces."[33] In a later address he said that Grenada "was a Soviet-Cuban colony, being readied as a major military bastion to export terror and undermine democracy."[34] Intervention in Grenada permitted Reagan to shift attention away from mounting problems in Lebanon. On October 23, two days before his action in Grenada, a terrorist attack in Beirut resulted in the death of 241 American soldiers.[35]

Although Presidents regularly object to the constitutionality of the War Powers Resolution, the Reagan administration seemed to accept the 60-day limit. The House of Representatives passed legislation stating that the requirements of Section 4(a)(1) of the War Powers Resolution became

31. Public Papers of the Presidents, 1983, II, at 1505–6.
32. "U.S. Vetoes U.N. Resolution, 'Deploring' Grenada Invasion," New York Times, October 29, 1983, at A1.
33. Public Papers of the Presidents, 1983, II, at 1513.
34. Id. at 1521.
35. Denise M. Bostdorff, "The Presidency and Promoted Crisis: Reagan, Grenada, and Issue Management," 21 Pres. Stud. Q. 737 (1991).

operative on October 25, 1983. This legislation, passed by a vote of 403 to 23, required the Reagan administration to conclude military operations within 60 days, with an additional 30 days for removal of troops if needed.[36] The Senate was about to pass the same type of legislation.[37]

With this legislative activity under way, the administration announced that it planned to withdraw all combat troops from Grenada by December 23. Because of this timetable, the administration said there was no need for Congress to complete action on the bill triggering Section 4(a)(1). Larry Speakes, White House press secretary, announced that the administration did not anticipate "any additional hostilities, and combat troops will be out, as Department of Defense said, before the 60-day period expires."[38]

Eleven members of Congress went to court, claiming that President Reagan violated the Constitution. A district judge held that it would be unwise for courts to intrude into this dispute until Congress, as an entire body, had used all of the institutional remedies available to it. Suits by individual legislators, representing a fraction of the institution, would not be favored.[39] Upon appeal, it was held that the issue was moot because the invasion had been terminated.[40]

Air Strikes against Libya

On March 24, 1986, the Reagan administration announced that U.S. naval aircraft and ships in the Gulf of Sidra had been the subject of attack by six surface-to-air missiles launched by Libyan forces. U.S. forces fired back, sinking three Libyan patrol boats and damaging another. There were no American casualties or loss of aircraft or ships.[41] President Reagan reported to Congress that he had taken the actions pursuant to his authority as Commander in Chief.[42] He defended the air strikes as an act of "self-defense" and a preemptive strike designed to "deter acts of terrorism by Libya."[43]

On April 14, Reagan ordered a series of air strikes against targets in Libya: command and control systems, intelligence, communications, logis-

36. 129 Cong. Rec. 29994–99, 30285 (1983).
37. Id. at 30600.
38. New York Times, November 17, 1983, at 3.
39. Conyers v. Reagan, 578 F.Supp. 323 (D.D.C. 1984).
40. Conyers v. Reagan, 765 F.2d 1124 (D.C. Cir. 1985).
41. Public Papers of the Presidents, 1986, at 394, 395.
42. Id. at 407.
43. Id. at 478.

tics, and training facilities. Air strikes were also directed against targets that jeopardized U.S. forces engaged in this mission. A White House announcement explained that the strikes were in retaliation for the bombing of the LaBelle, a West Berlin disco, that resulted in the death of a U.S. soldier and injury to about 50 American servicemen. The administration attributed the bombing to Libyan terrorists.[44] In an address to the nation, President Reagan stated that whenever U.S. citizens are "abused or attacked anywhere in the world on the direct orders of a hostile regime, we will respond so long as I'm in the Oval Office. Self-defense is not only our right, it is our duty. It is the purpose behind the mission undertaken tonight, a mission fully consistent with Article 51 of the United Nations Charter."[45]

In his report to Congress on the air strikes, President Reagan gave a brief description of the raids and repeated the claim that the action was taken as self-defense under Article 51 of the UN Charter. He also said that the strikes were designed to deter acts of terrorism by Libya. The measures were undertaken "pursuant to my authority under the Constitution, including my authority as Commander in Chief of United States Armed Forces."[46]

Reagan received the approval of Prime Minister Margaret Thatcher, who permitted American planes to take off from British soil to make the attack.[47] However, he did not consult with Congress or seek the permission of any of its members. Congressional leaders were called to the White House only as U.S. bombers were approaching Libya.[48] Dante B. Fascell (D-Fla.), chairman of the House Committee on Foreign Affairs, objected to this circumvention of the War Powers Resolution. Given the relations between the United States and Libya, the presence of American warships in the Gulf of Sidra involved imminent hostilities and should have produced a Section 4(a)(1) report from President Reagan.[49]

Escort Operations in the Persian Gulf

On May 17, 1987, the USS *Stark* was hit by an Iraqi missile in the Persian Gulf, killing 37 American sailors. In response, the Reagan administration

44. Id. at 468.
45. Id. at 469.
46. Id. at 478.
47. CQ Weekly Rept., April 19, 1986, at 882.
48. Id. at 1023.
49. "War Powers, Libya, and State-Sponsored Terrorism," hearings before the House Committee on Foreign Affairs, 99th Cong., 2d Sess. 2 (1986).

adopted the policy of "reflagging" Kuwaiti oil tankers (registering them under the U.S. flag) to provide safe naval escort in the Gulf. The U.S. fleet gradually increased to include warships, minesweepers, and small patrol boats. Despite the presence of hostilities in the Gulf and the potential for further military conflicts, President Reagan did not report to Congress. The USS *Bridgeton* was seriously damaged by a mine on July 24 and the U.S.-chartered *Texaco-Caribbean* hit a mine on August 10. Still Reagan did not report.

Not until U.S. naval forces on September 21 fired at an Iranian Navy ship that was laying mines did Reagan begin reporting to Congress under the War Powers Resolution. He justified the military actions as an exercise of the right of self-defense under Article 51 of the UN Charter, citing his "constitutional authority with respect to the conduct of foreign affairs and as Commander-in-Chief."[50] Congress considered passing an authorizing resolution, as it had for Lebanon in 1983, but no final action was taken.

Rep. Mike Lowry (D-Wash.) and 112 other members of Congress filed suit in federal court asking the court to declare that a presidential report under Section 4(a)(1) was required as a result of the U.S. escort operations beginning on July 22 and the September 21 attack on the Iranian ship. The court dismissed the suit as nonjusticiable. Prudential considerations and the political question doctrine convinced the court that the issue had to be returned to the elected branches. The determination of what constitutes "hostilities" was a question for the executive and legislative branches, not for the courts. Only in the event of a "true confrontation" between the branches marked by the passage of legislation to enforce the War Powers Resolution would the courts have jurisdiction to hear and decide such a case.[51]

Panama

In December 1989, with Congress out of session, President Bush ordered 11,000 troops into Panama to join up with 13,000 American troops already in the Canal Zone. Bush cited a number of reasons for intervening with Operation Just Cause. He said that General Manuel Noriega's threats and

---

50. Public Papers of the Presidents, 1987, II, at 1074.
51. Lowry v. Reagan, 676 F.Supp. 333 (D.D.C. 1987); on appeal, the D.C. Circuit dismissed the case on grounds that it was moot and presented a nonjusticiable political question.

attacks upon Americans in Panama created "an imminent danger" to the 35,000 American citizens there and that, as President, he had "no higher obligation than to safeguard the lives of American citizens." He also felt an obligation "to bring General Noriega to justice in the United States." Other justifications cited by Bush included defending democracy in Panama, combating drug trafficking, and protecting the integrity of the Panama Canal treaty.[52]

Through this military intervention the United States was able to restore to office President Guillermo Endara and Vice Presidents Ricardo Arias Calderon and Guillermo Ford, who had been elected in May 1989 but removed from power by Noriega. In his report to Congress, Bush cited the right of self-defense under Article 51 of the UN Charter (protecting American lives), fulfilling U.S. responsibilities under the Panama Canal treaties, and his authority with respect to foreign relations and as Commander in Chief.[53]

Noriega, who surrendered on January 3, 1990, was taken to the United States to be tried on various criminal charges. Beginning on that date, U.S. combat troops started leaving Panama.[54] In an address to a joint session of Congress on January 31, Bush announced that the American troops sent to Panama would be out by the end of February.[55] Whether consciously or not, the administration appeared to be restricting itself to the 60-to-90 day clock of the War Powers Resolution.

On February 7, the House of Representatives passed a resolution stating that Bush had acted "decisively and appropriately in ordering United States forces to intervene in Panama after making substantial efforts to resolve the crisis in Panama by political, economic, and diplomatic means in order to avoid resorting to military action." While praising Bush with this language, the House also sought to prevent the Panama invasion from becoming a precedent for U.S. intervention elsewhere, especially in regions that had been subject to such interventions in the past (Central America, Mexico, and the Caribbean). The resolution cautioned: "Whereas the United States' action in Panama was a response to a unique set of circumstances, and does not undermine the commitment of the government of the United States to the principle of non-intervention in the internal affairs of other countries."[56]

---

52. Public Papers of the Presidents, 1989, II, at 1722–23.
53. Id. at 1734.
54. Public Papers of the Presidents, 1990, I, at 8.
55. Id. at 130.
56. 136 Cong. Rec. 1507 (1990).

The resolution passed the House 389 to 26 but was not acted upon by the Senate. During House debate, Robert Kastenmeier (D-Wis.) took "great exception to that provision of the resolution which gratuitously commends President Bush for ordering the invasion of Panama, an independent and sovereign nation, an action which, in my view, does violate international law and which has been condemned by 20 or 21 Latin American countries."[57]

Those observations by Kastenmeier anticipated some of the legal criticisms that later appeared in professional journals. The isolated incidents in Panama involving American citizens did not justify the use of military force for "self-defense." The 13,000 American troops already stationed in the Canal Zone were a sufficient force to protect U.S. citizens. If the United States has the right to invade whenever American citizens are threatened or mistreated in another country, it would have cause for intervening in dozens of other sovereign countries.[58] But such actions are prohibited by the Organization of American States (OAS) Charter, which the United States and Panama signed. Article 20 provides that the territory of a nation is inviolable and it "may not be the object, even temporarily, of military occupation or of other measures of force taken by another State, directly or indirectly, on any grounds whatsoever." The OAS condemned the invasion of Panama by a vote of 20 to 1.

With regard to the claim that U.S. action was necessary to protect the Panama Canal, the operation of the canal was not jeopardized until U.S. troops intervened. Panama "had not breached its duty to permit the free transit of ships through the Canal; and even if it had, the Canal treaties do not give the United States a right to intervene militarily against Panama."[59]

Another justification offered by President Bush—intervening in Panama to protect democracy—has rather obvious problems. The United States would not accept that rationale if Nazi Germany or the Soviet Union used it to invade nearby countries under the pretext of protecting democracy. The UN Charter does not sanction invading another country to safeguard its political processes. If such a premise were adopted, the United States would be busy intervening in other countries to bring their governments up to what it considered to be minimum democratic standards. Louis Henkin remarked: "There are many illegitimate, undemocratically elected and undemocratically maintained governments . . . whose territories the

---

57. Id. at 1511.
58. John Quigley, "The Legality of the United States Invasion of Panama," 15 Yale J. Int'l L. 276, 281–97 (1990).
59. Id. at 299.

United States has not invaded and which the U.S. government indeed has continued to treat as friends."[60]

Abraham D. Sofaer, who served as legal adviser to the State Department during the time of the Panama invasion, acknowledged that the United States "does not accept the notion that a state is entitled to use force to overthrow the dictator of another state."[61] However, he made the case for "humanitarian intervention," especially when the population of the invaded country "broadly approved of the action."[62] Ambassador Luigi R. Einaudi, in his address to the OAS on December 22, 1989, made a similar distinction: "I am not here this morning to claim a right on behalf of the United States to enforce the will of history by intervening in favor of democracy where we are not welcomed."[63] This is tenuous ground. As Henkin noted, the fact that the Panamanian people might have "welcomed" the American invasion is legally irrelevant. In 1938, citizens of Austria supposedly gave Hitler's troops a "tumultuous welcome."[64]

The final justification cited by Bush—intervening to combat drug trafficking—collapses with the merest scrutiny. In his appearance before the UN Security Council on December 20, 1989, Ambassador Thomas R. Pickering tried to analogize drug operations in Panama with military attacks on the United States:

> Countries that provide safe haven and support for the international drug trafficking cartels menace the peace and security just as surely as if they were using their own conventional military forces to attack our societies. The truth is, and every one of us knows it, General Noriega turned Panama into a haven for drug traffickers and a center for money laundering and transshipment of cocaine. General Noriega could not be permitted falsely to wrap himself in the flag of Panamanian sovereignty while the drug cartels with which he is allied intervene throughout this hemisphere. That is aggression. It is aggression against us all, and now it is being brought to an end.[65]

60. Louis Henkin, "The Invasion of Panama under International Law: A Gross Violation," 29 Colum. J. Transnat'l L. 293, 298 (1991).

61. Abraham D. Sofaer, "The Legality of the United States Action in Panama," 29 Colum. J. Transnat'l L. 281, 288 (1991).

62. Id.

63. U.S. Department of State, Bureau of Public Affairs, "Panama: A Just Cause," Current Policy No. 1240, at 3.

64. Henkin, "The Invasion of Panama under International Law," at 300 n. 30.

65. U.S. Department of State, Bureau of Public Affairs, "Panama: A Just Cause," Current Policy No. 1240, at 2.

Acceptance of that argument would provide a green light for American military intervention in Mexico, Colombia, Turkey, and other nations that contribute to the flow of drugs to the United States. Obviously that is not U.S. policy. Simply to pursue the logic is to reject it.

The Gulf War

After Saddam Hussein invaded Kuwait on August 2, 1990, President Bush sent several hundred thousand troops to Saudi Arabia and the Middle East. At that point the operation was purely defensive (to deter further Iraqi aggression), but Bush's decision in November to double the size of U.S. forces gave him the capacity to wage offensive war. The constitutional issue was clear-cut: May the President take the nation from a defensive posture to an offensive operation without congressional authority?

The Bush administration made no effort to seek authority from Congress. Instead, it created a multinational alliance and encouraged the Security Council to "authorize" the use of military force. The strategic calculations were later explained by James A. Baker, III, who served as Secretary of State in the Bush administration. Baker realized that military initiatives by Reagan in Grenada and Bush in Panama had reinforced the impression in the international community that American foreign policy seemed animated by a "cowboy mentality." In response to those concerns, Baker helped Bush assemble a broad coalition. Baker notes: "From the very beginning, the President recognized the importance of having the express approval of the international community if at all possible."[66]

This coalition was willing to cover most of the costs of military action. Saudi Arabia, Kuwait, the United Arab Emirates, Japan, Germany, France, Great Britain, and other nations agreed to shoulder the financial burden. The administration wanted those financial contributions to go directly to the Defense Department as "gifts" to be later allocated as the administration determined.[67] Such a system would bypass the appropriations power of Congress. Senator Robert C. Byrd (D-W.Va.) intervened to scotch that idea. Contributions from foreign governments would go first to the Treasury, subject to appropriation by Congress.[68]

The next step was to secure the support of the United Nations. On

---

66. James A. Baker III, The Politics of Diplomacy 304 (1995).
67. H. Doc. No. 101–237, 101st Cong., 2d Sess. (1990).
68. 136 Cong. Rec. 25067–68 (1990).

November 29, 1990, under the urging of the Bush administration, the Security Council passed Resolution 678, authorizing member states to use "all necessary means" to force Iraqi troops out of Kuwait. The phrase "all necessary means" is diplomatic talk for military force. What role would Congress have?

After the Security Council vote on November 29, Professor Thomas M. Franck of the New York University Law School wrote an article for the *New York Times* in which he argued that a congressional declaration of war "is inapplicable to U.N. police actions."[69] Franck claimed that the UN Charter "does not leave room for each state, once the Council has acted, to defer compliance until it has authority from its own legislature," but the legislative histories of the UN Charter and the UN Participation Act do not support Franck's position. Although a declaration of war by Congress is not required for UN actions, clearly Congress was expected to approve the use of military commitments to the United Nations. It did not surrender its constitutional power. Franck is further in error by suggesting that the contemplated action against Iraq was a "U.N. police action." It was, instead, a military action dominated by the United States with the financial assistance of a number of allies.[70]

Franck's willingness to remove Congress from the decision to go to war is remarkable. In an article published in 1991, he conceded that the purpose of the war-declaring clause "was to ensure that this fateful decision did not rest with a single person." Does that mean that Congress therefore has a role? Not to Franck. "The new system vests that responsibility in the Security Council, a body where the most divergent interests and perspectives of humanity are represented and where five of fifteen members have a veto power. This Council is far less likely to be stampeded by combat fever than is Congress."[71] In short, although the framers expected Congress to share the war power with the President, contemporary conditions permit that power to be shared between the Security Council and the President. Contemporary convenience does not exclude Congress from its constitutional responsibility.

69. Thomas M. Franck, "Declare War? Congress Can't," New York Times, December 11, 1990, at A27.

70. See the letter to New York Times, December 29, 1990, at 22, by John M. Hillebrecht, and also Michael J. Glennon, "The Constitution and Chapter VII of the United Nations Charter," 85 Am. J. Int'l L. 74 (1991).

71. Thomas M. Franck and Faiza Patel, "UN Police Action in Lieu of War: 'The Old Order Changeth,'" 85 Am. J. Int'l L. 74 (1991).

Secretary of Defense Dick Cheney testified before the Senate Armed Services Committee on December 3, 1990, that President Bush did not require "any additional authorization from Congress" before attacking Iraq.[72] The phrase "additional authorization" implied that Security Council approval was sufficient. Reacting to Cheney's claim, the House Democratic Caucus on the following day adopted a resolution stating that the President must first seek authorization from Congress unless American lives were in danger. The resolution passed 177 to 37.[73]

The Justice Department argued in court that President Bush could order offensive actions in Iraq without seeking advance authority from Congress. The case was brought by 54 members of Congress, who challenged the constitutional authority of the President to initiate war in the Persian Gulf. Although the court held that the case was not ripe for judicial determination, it rejected many of the sweeping interpretations advanced by the administration for independent presidential war powers. The Justice Department maintained that definitions of the war power were left to the elected branches, not the judiciary. Courts were excluded from such judgments, according to the Justice Department. Judge Harold H. Greene rejected that argument, noting that if the President

> had the sole power to determine that any particular offensive military operation, no matter how vast, does not constitute war-making but only an offensive military attack, the congressional power to declare war will be at the mercy of a semantic decision by the Executive. Such an "interpretation" would evade the plain language of the Constitution, and it cannot stand.[74]

Judge Greene disagreed with other propositions advanced by the administration. The Justice Department insisted that the judiciary had no place in deciding such questions because it would have to "inject itself into foreign affairs, a subject which the Constitution commits to the political branches."[75] That argument, Greene said, "must fail."[76] Other passages in his opinion repudiated the administration's position on the war power.

72. "Crisis in the Persian Gulf Region: U.S. Policy Options and Implications," hearings before the Senate Committee on Armed Services, 101st Cong., 2d Sess. 701 (1990).
73. 1990 CQ Almanac 742.
74. Dellums v. Bush, 752 F.Supp. 1141, 1145 (D.D.C. 1990).
75. Id. at 1146.
76. Id.

Either because of the court's decision or other factors, on January 8, 1991, President Bush asked Congress to pass legislation supporting his policy in the Persian Gulf. He was asked by reporters the next day whether he needed a resolution from Congress. He replied: "I don't think I need it. . . . I feel that I have the authority to fully implement the United Nations resolutions."[77] The legal crisis was avoided on January 12 when Congress authorized President Bush to take offensive actions against Iraq. In signing the legislation two days later,[78] he indicated that he could have acted without congressional authority:

> As I made clear to congressional leaders at the outset, my request for congressional support did not, and my signing this resolution does not, constitute any change in the long-standing positions of the executive branch on either the President's constitutional authority to use the Armed Forces to defend vital U.S. interests or the constitutionality of the War Powers Resolution.[79]

After the war was over, Bush offered his views on presidential power in a speech given at Princeton University. Of his power to take the country to war without congressional authority he said: "Though I felt after studying the question that I had the inherent power to commit our forces to battle after the U.N. resolution, I solicited congressional support before committing our forces in the Gulf War."[80] His attitude toward Congress is reflected in a more mean-spirited way in a speech given in Texas during the 1992 campaign. Bush said that some people asked why he couldn't bring the same kind of purpose and success to domestic policy as he did to the war in Iraq. His answer: "I didn't have to get permission from some old goat in the United States Congress to kick Saddam Hussein out of Kuwait. That's the reason."[81]

Bush's signing statement and his speeches at Princeton and in Texas do not alter the fact that the resolution passed by Congress specifically authorized him to act. In a war of the magnitude contemplated in the Persian Gulf, President Bush needed *authority* (not merely "support") from Congress. The resolutions adopted by the Security Council were insufficient legal sanction. The UN Charter does not take from Congress the constitu-

---

77. Public Papers of the Presidents, 1991, I, at 20.
78. 105 Stat. 3 (1991).
79. Public Papers of the Presidents, 1991, I, at 40.
80. Id. at 497.
81. Public Papers of the Presidents, 1992–93, I, at 995.

tional responsibilities and duties vested in the representative branch. Under no interpretation could the Charter do that. As the people's branch, Congress must debate and authorize all major military, political, and financial commitments, including the decision to go to war. Those determinations may not be left to judgments reached merely between the Security Council and the President.

Bush's decision to pull out of Iraq after the military victory, rather than continue on to Baghdad, was later criticized for allowing Saddam Hussein to regroup and remain in power. However, Bush knew that the UN Security Council resolutions and the congressional statute supported military action only to remove Iraqi troops from Kuwait. The statute authorized the President to use U.S. armed forces pursuant to Security Council resolution 678 in order to achieve implementation of resolutions 660–62, 664–67, 669–70, 674, and 677, all of which were directed to oust Iraqi troops from Kuwait. The broad coalition he assembled for military action would have fractured had Bush gone beyond the Security Council mandate.

In a book he later wrote with Brent Scowcroft, Bush states plainly why he ceased military operations after ejecting Iraqi troops from Kuwait. His position is of special interest when compared to the more ambitious plans of his son, who chose in 2003 to occupy Iraq after losing support from many nations, including France, Germany, and Russia. Here are Bush's calculations, published in 1998:

> I firmly believed that we should not march into Baghdad. Our stated mission, as codified in UN resolutions, was a simple one—end the aggression, knock Iraq's forces out of Kuwait, and restore Kuwait's leaders. To occupy Iraq would instantly shatter our coalition, turning the whole Arab world against us, and make a broken tyrant into a latter-day Arab hero. It would have taken us way beyond the imprimatur of international law bestowed by the resolutions of the Security Council, assigning young soldiers to a fruitless hunt for a securely entrenched dictator and condemning them to fight in what would be an unwinnable urban guerrilla war. It could only plunge that part of the world into even greater instability and destroy the credibility we were working so hard to reestablish.[82]

After the military victory against Iraq by President George W. Bush in 2003, many of those issues would reappear: the difficulty of finding Saddam Hussein, the outbreak of guerrilla war, and the loss of U.S. credibility.

82. George Bush and Brent Scowcroft, A World Transformed 464 (1998).

Early in 1999, while driving home from work, I turned on the radio and happened to catch George H. W. Bush giving a talk to the Senate. He discussed the different opinions as to who has the power to declare war. Different opinions? The Constitution expressly vests that power in Congress. I wondered if he had departed from the text of his speech and was offering some ad-lib remarks. The next day, I read his speech and was startled to see these words: "There was a fundamental difference of opinion between the Senate and the White House over the Senate's role in declaring war—one that dated back to the War Powers Act."[83] Of course, the issue dates back quite a bit earlier (to the Constitution), and it is not the Senate's role but the Congress's role "to declare war."

83. 145 Cong. Rec. S959 (daily ed., January 23, 1999).

8

MILITARY ACTIONS BY CLINTON

Throughout Bill Clinton's 1992 presidential campaign, he spoke out force-fully on behalf of an activist, interventionist foreign policy. Repeatedly he expressed a willingness to use military force. His image as a credible Com-mander in Chief had been damaged by conflicting stories about his draft record during the Vietnam War. Various accounts surfaced on his efforts to avoid military service. Yet in an interview in June 1992, he insisted that he could be trusted to be Commander in Chief, serving notice of his willing-ness to use military force in Bosnia.[1]

Clinton's capacity to serve credibly as Commander in Chief came to a head shortly after he took office and proposed that gays be allowed to serve in the military. Objections to that policy came from the Joint Chiefs of Staff and from prominent Senators. At a news conference on March 23, 1993, Clinton was asked: "Mr. President, you seem to be having some dif-ficulty with the Pentagon. When you went to the U.S.S. *Theodore Roosevelt,* the sailors there were mocking you before your arrival, even though you are Commander in Chief. The services have been undercutting your pro-posal for permitting gays to be in the military. . . . Do you have a problem, perhaps because of your lack of military service or perhaps because of issues such as gays in the military, in being effective in your role as Commander in Chief, and what do you propose to do about it?"[2] Clinton denied that he had a problem being Commander in Chief. Within a few months, he would have what White House officials considered an oppor-tunity to demonstrate his military "toughness."

Launching Missiles against Baghdad

On June 26, 1993, President Clinton ordered air strikes against Iraq. In an address to the nation, he reviewed the attempted assassination of former

---

1. Louis Fisher, "President Clinton as Commander in Chief," in Rivals for Power, ed. James A. Thurber 215 (1996).
2. Public Papers of the Presidents, 1993, I, at 337.

President Bush during a visit to Kuwait. Sixteen suspects, including two Iraqi nationals, had been arrested. Although the trial of those suspects was still under way in Kuwait, the CIA concluded that there was "compelling evidence that there was, in fact, a plot to assassinate former President Bush and that this plot, which included the use of a powerful bomb made in Iraq, was directed and pursued by the Iraqi intelligence service." Clinton called the attempted assassination of Bush "an attack against our country and against all Americans."[3] In a message to Congress, he said that the attack was ordered "in the exercise of our inherent right of self-defense as recognized in Article 51 of the UN Charter and pursuant to my constitutional authority with respect to the conduct of foreign relations and as Commander in Chief."[4]

Clinton did not consult with members of Congress before ordering the launching of 23 Tomahawk cruise missiles against the Iraqi intelligence service's principal command-and-control facility in Baghdad. The facility was badly damaged, but three of the missiles destroyed homes in the surrounding neighborhood, killing eight people and wounding at least 12 others. News analyses suggested that the White House appreciated that the use of force would help rebuild Clinton's image into that of a strong and decisive leader. After Clinton's ragged start as President, members of Congress and the public had questioned his ability to lead the nation. A White House aide noted that the cruise missile attack would "serve notice to one and all that Americans are prepared first of all to exercise leadership and to remain engaged and to act with military force as appropriate." A senior administration official remarked: "We were showing that Bill Clinton can take the challenge." Aides disclosed to the press that Clinton, shortly after making an address from the Oval Office on the bombing, returned to the White House residence to watch a movie with his wife and slept "a solid eight hours."[5] The word was out: Clinton could make the tough military calls and not look back.

President Clinton said that the attack on Baghdad "was essential to protect our sovereignty, to send a message to those who engage in state-sponsored terrorism, to deter further violence against our people, and to affirm the expectation of civilized behavior among nations." He further noted that there should be no mistake about the message being sent to Iraq and other

3. Public Papers of the Presidents, 1993, I, at 938.
4. Id. at 940.
5. Ruth Marcus and Daniel Williams, "Show of Strength Offers Benefits for Clinton," Washington Post, June 28, 1993, at A1.

nations: "We will combat terrorism. We will deter aggression. We will protect our people."[6] That argument is not credible. As two attorneys of constitutional law noted, "calling the U.S. bombing of Iraq an act of self-defense for an assassination plot that had been averted two months previously is quite a stretch."[7] If the United States had evidence of terrorist activity by Syria, it would not have launched cruise missiles against intelligence facilities in Damascus. Other responses, less confrontational, would have been used. Iraq was attacked because—like Cambodia, Grenada, and Libya—it fell into the category of a weak and isolated nation that could be punished militarily with little fear of retaliation.

Combat Operations in Somalia

Civil war and famine in Somalia reached the point in 1992 that the United Nations and the Bush administration were under pressure to avert a humanitarian disaster. A quarter of a million people had died in the famine, and another million or more were at risk of starving to death. On December 3, 1992, the UN Security Council adopted Resolution 794 to authorize the use of peacekeeping troops to address the deteriorating crisis.

On the following day, President Bush agreed to dispatch U.S. troops to Somalia as part of a multinational relief effort. He explained to the nation that the mission had a limited objective: "To open the supply routes, to get the food moving, and to prepare the way for a U.N. peacekeeping force to keep it moving. This operation is not open-ended. We will not stay one day longer than is absolutely necessary."[8] There were no plans "to dictate political outcomes."[9] In a letter to congressional leaders he said that there was no intention for U.S. armed forces in Somalia to become "involved in hostilities."[10]

Also on December 4, the Justice Department advised President Bush that he possessed constitutional authority to commit U.S. troops to Somalia. Citing an earlier opinion by Attorney General Robert Jackson, the department concluded that Bush had authority "to commit troops overseas without specific prior Congressional approval 'on missions of good will or res-

6. Public Papers of the Presidents, 1993, I, at 938–39.
7. Michael Ratner and Jules Lobel, "Bombing Baghdad: Illegal Reprisal or Self-Defense?" Legal Times, July 5, 1993, at 24.
8. Public Papers of the Presidents, 1992–93, II, at 2175.
9. Id. at 2176.
10. Id. at 2180.

cue, or for the purpose of protecting American lives or property or American interests.'"[11] Apart from constitutional authority, the department told Bush that he had "ample statutory authority" for the mission and that the deployment of U.S. forces would help implement Security Council Resolution 794.

Early the following year, with Bill Clinton now President, Congress debated the need for authorizing legislation. On February 4, 1993, Senate Majority Leader George Mitchell (D-Maine) spoke in favor of a Senate joint resolution to authorize the deployment of American troops to Somalia, pointing out that "U.N. Security Council resolutions are no substitute for congressional authorization."[12] The joint resolution passed on voice vote.[13] With some amendments, the Senate resolution passed the House on May 25.[14] However, the two Houses could not agree on compromise language.

The humanitarian effort turned bloody in June 1993 when 23 Pakistani peacekeepers were killed. After UN military officials blamed their deaths on a Somali political figure, Mohamed Farah Aideed, U.S. warplanes launched a retaliatory attack, hitting a radio station and four weapons-storage sites. What began as a nonpolitical effort to help starving Somalis now turned into a personal operation against Aideed. President Clinton explained that armed force was needed

> to undermine the capacity of Aideed to wreak military havoc in Mogadishu. He murdered 23 U.N. peacekeepers. And I would remind you that before the United States and the United Nations showed up, he was responsible for the deaths of countless Somalis from starvation, from disease, and from killing.
>
> The military back of Aideed has been broken. A warrant has been issued for his arrest.[15]

In August 1993, four U.S. soldiers were killed when a land mine blasted apart their Humvee vehicle in Mogadishu. The killings were again attributed to Aideed, who remained at large. Earlier conflicts had killed four other American soldiers. Because of the transformed nature of the effort

---

11. 16 Op. O.L.C. 6 (1992), citing 40 Op. Att'y Gen. 58, 62 (1941).

12. 139 Cong. Rec. 2272 (1993).

13. Id. at 2275.

14. Id. at 11017–38. For House and Senate action on this legislation, see Ryan C. Hendrickson, The Clinton Wars: The Constitution, Congress, and War Powers 21–31 (2002).

15. Public Papers of the Presidents, 1993, I, at 870.

in Somalia, the Pentagon began awarding American soldiers "hostile fire pay" for service in Somalia and authorized U.S. Army troops to wear a combat patch on their uniforms. Moreover, officials in the Clinton administration began to talk of "nation building": rebuilding political structures in Somalia to form a stable order.

By September 1993, members of Congress were drafting legislation that would require Clinton to remove American troops within a fixed period of time unless Congress enacted legislation authorizing that they remain. Rep. Lee Hamilton (D-Ind.), chairman of the House Foreign Affairs Committee, objected to the new mission of U.S. troops in Somalia: "I do not believe that the United States should be engaged in nation building in Somalia. That is the task of the United Nations."[16] Rep. Ron Dellums (D-Calif.) added: "Who gave us the right—as peacekeepers—to determine which political figure or faction deserves to emerge victorious in Somalia?"[17] On October 3, about a week after this debate, 18 Army soldiers were killed. Aideed's forces captured an American pilot and displayed him, battered and dazed, to TV cameras. An angry mob dragged the body of a dead U.S. soldier through the streets of Mogadishu.

Under pressure from Congress, Clinton announced on October 7 that all American troops would be out of Somalia no later than March 31, 1994, except for a few hundred support personnel in noncombat roles.[18] He repeated the March 31 pledge a week later in a message to Congress, at which time he said the U.S. military mission "is not now, nor was it ever one of 'nation building.'"[19]

President Clinton and Congress forged a compromise arrangement. The defense appropriations bill provided that no funds for the operations of U.S. armed forces in Somalia could be used for expenses after March 31, 1994, although that date could be extended "if so requested by the President and authorized by the Congress." The legislation further provided that funds could be used after the March 31 date to protect American diplomatic facilities and American citizens. Moreover, to assure that American forces would not be under UN control, the measure provided that U.S. combat forces in Somalia "shall be under the command and control of United States commanders under the ultimate direction of the President of the United States."[20]

16. 139 Cong. Rec. 22748 (1993).
17. Id. at 22754.
18. Public Papers of the Presidents, 1993, II, at 1705.
19. Id. at 1740.
20. 107 Stat. 1475–77, sec. 8151 (1993).

Troops to Haiti

Jean-Bertrand Aristide, the first democratically elected president of Haiti, was ousted on September 30, 1991, in a military coup. On June 16, 1993, the UN Security Council adopted an oil, arms, and financial embargo against Haiti in an effort to force the military regime to step down. On July 3, at Governors Island in New York, the coup's leader, Lt. Gen. Raoul Cedras, signed an agreement promising Aristide's return by October 30.

To encourage this peaceful transition, the Security Council passed Resolution 867 on September 23, allowing for up to 567 UN police monitors and a military construction unit of approximately 700, including 60 military trainers, to enter Haiti. On October 12, President Clinton sent about 600 U.S. soldiers to Haiti to assist in restoring the deposed government of President Aristide. The troops were largely military engineers, sent to work on roads, bridges, and water supplies, but the operation was part of a UN-brokered agreement to force Haiti's military rulers to resign by October 15. When the ships arrived, a group of armed civilians prevented the troops from landing. On October 15, President Clinton implied that he might have to use military force against Haiti, ticking off the telltale signs of an impending U.S. intervention: 1,000 American citizens lived in Haiti, Americans helped to operate the embassy, and the United States had "an interest in promoting democracy in this hemisphere."[21]

To enforce economic sanctions imposed by the UN Security Council, Clinton ordered six destroyers to patrol the waters off Haiti and reported this fact to Congress under the War Powers Resolution. He also ordered an infantry company to be on standby at the Guantanamo Naval Base in Cuba. Madeleine K. Albright, U.S. Ambassador to the United Nations, said that the administration had "not ruled out" a unilateral use of force in Haiti. Lieutenant General Cedras, the Haitian Army commander, made clear that there was "no threat against any American on Haitian soil."[22] Congress debated placing a limit on Clinton's power to send troops to Haiti unless specifically authorized by statute, but in the end settled for nonbinding language making it the "sense of Congress" that funds appropriated should not be expended for U.S. military operations in Haiti unless authorized in advance by Congress. There were two exceptions for advance authorization: when necessary to protect or evacuate U.S. citizens from a situation of "imminent danger" and when "vital to the national security interests of

21. Public Papers of the Presidents, 1993, II, at 1755.
22. Washington Post, October 18, 1993, at A16.

the United States" and there "is not sufficient time" to seek and receive congressional authorization.[23]

In May 1994, Clinton said that with regard to Haiti "we cannot afford to discount the prospect of a military option."[24] In expressing a desire to work peacefully with nations in the Caribbean and Latin America, he announced that the United States "never will interfere in the affairs of another country to try to seek to thwart the popular will there. This is a different case."[25] Later that month, the House of Representatives debated several amendments designed to limit Clinton's military options in Haiti. The amendment that passed, 223 to 201, declared it to be the sense of Congress "that the United States should not undertake any military action directed against the mainland of Haiti unless the President first certifies to Congress that clear and present danger to citizens of the United States or United States interests requires such action."[26] Even that amendment, weak as it is, was voted down two weeks later on a separate vote.[27]

Congress continued to express uncertainty about its authority to constrain Clinton. On June 29, 1994, the Senate rejected an amendment stating that funds could not be used for any U.S. military operations in Haiti unless authorized in advance by Congress. However, that limitation would not apply if the President reported to Congress that deployment of armed forces in Haiti "is justified by United States national security interests."[28] What appears to be a prohibition on the use of funds could be lifted simply by a presidential statement that U.S. force is necessary for national security interests. In effect, the amendment contemplated delegating legislative prerogatives and duties to the President. That procedure was later adopted by the Senate, on a vote of 93 to 4, after making the amendment a nonbinding "sense of Congress."[29]

By late July, there were strong rumors that the UN Security Council was about to pass a resolution authorizing an invasion of Haiti. Dante Caputo, the UN's special envoy to Haiti, wrote a "confidential" memo to UN Secretary General Boutros Boutros-Ghali describing political calculations within the Clinton White House. This memo, placed in the *Congressional Record,* states that Clinton's advisers believed that an invasion of Haiti would be

23. 107 Stat. 1474, sec. 8147 (1993).
24. Public Papers of the Presidents, 1994, I, at 823.
25. Id.
26. 140 Cong. Rec. 11632–33 (1994).
27. Id. at 12420–21.
28. Id. at 15016.
29. Id. at 15047, 15052.

"politically desirable" because it would highlight for the American public "the President's decision making capability and the firmness of leadership in international political matters."[30]

On July 31, the UN Security Council adopted a resolution "inviting" all states, particularly those in the region of Haiti, to use "all necessary means" to remove the military leadership on that island. On this occasion the Senate spoke promptly and with a clear voice, passing a "sense of the Senate" amendment that the Security Council resolution "does not constitute authorization for the deployment of United States Armed Forces in Haiti under the Constitution of the United States or pursuant to the War Powers Resolution (Public Law 93-148)." This amendment passed by a vote of 100 to 0.[31] At a news conference on August 3, President Clinton once again denied that he needed authority from Congress to invade Haiti: "Like my predecessors of both parties, I have not agreed that I was constitutionally mandated" to obtain the support of Congress.[32]

In a nationwide televised address on September 15, President Clinton told the American public that he was prepared to use military force to invade Haiti, referring to the UN resolution of July 31 and his willingness to lead a multinational force "to carry out the will of the United Nations."[33] An invasion became unnecessary when former President Jimmy Carter negotiated an agreement in which the military leaders in Haiti agreed to step down to permit the return of Aristide. U.S. troops were sent in to occupy Haiti and provide stability. It was also reported that President Clinton had signed a secret contingency plan that authorized the CIA to engage in political activities for the purpose of countering the opponents of Aristide.[34]

House and Senate debates were strongly critical of Clinton's insistence that he could act militarily against Haiti without legislative authority. Both Houses passed legislation stating that "the President should have sought and welcomed Congressional approval before deploying United States Forces to Haiti."[35] Even legislators who voted against this legislation agreed that Clinton should have gotten approval from Congress.[36]

30. Id. at 18451.
31. Id. at 19306–24.
32. Public Papers of the Presidents, 1994, II, at 1419.
33. Id. at 1559.
34. New York Times, September 28, 1994, A8.
35. 140 Cong. Rec. 28239 (1994), passing S. J. Res. 229; id. at 28565–78, passing H. J. Res. 416. A day later the House, by voice vote, agreed to S. J. Res. 229; 140 Cong. Rec. 29223–24 (1994).
36. For example, of the eight Senators who voted against S. J. Res. 229, at least four agreed that Clinton should have first obtained approval from Congress: Baucus (140

Air Strikes in Bosnia

In addition to using military force against Iraq and Somalia and considering an invasion of Haiti, President Clinton periodically threatened to order air strikes in Bosnia. Age-old rivalries between Serbs, Croats, and Muslims precipitated a huge number of deaths from fighting and famine in former Yugoslavia. In concert with the United Nations and NATO, the United States participated in humanitarian airlifts into Sarajevo and helped enforce a "no-fly zone" (a ban on unauthorized flights over Bosnia-Herzegovina). The U.S. forces initially assigned included 13 F-15 and 12 F-18A fighter aircraft, equipped for combat and ready to fire in self-defense. Clinton reported to Congress on these flights.[37]

In other statements, Clinton sketched out some general policies: the United States would act not alone but only as part of a multilateral force; he would not consider the introduction of American ground forces; and the United States would not become involved as a partisan for one side.[38] Although in these statements Clinton indicated that he would consult closely with Congress and seek its "support," he did not state that prior authorization from Congress would be required before ordering air strikes. He did say, at one point, that for air strikes "Congress would have to agree."[39] Later he stated that he would "welcome and encourage congressional authorization of any military involvement in Bosnia."[40]

Congress considered various restrictions on military initiatives by Clinton in Bosnia. One amendment, never enacted, sought to prevent the deployment of additional U.S. forces to Bosnia and Herzegovina unless Congress gave advance approval.[41] In response to pending amendments to restrict presidential actions in Bosnia and Haiti, Clinton objected that they would infringe on his constitutional authority to make foreign policy and deploy troops. He promised to "strenuously oppose such attempts to encroach on the President's foreign policy powers."[42] When asked whether he would veto legislation requiring him to obtain congressional consent before using troops in Haiti and Bosnia, he replied:

Cong. Rec. 28236–37), Bradley (id. at 28233), Byrd (id. at 28212–16), and Feingold (id. at 28205–6, 28208). For further details on Clinton's policy in Haiti, see Hendrickson, The Clinton Wars, at 43–67.

37. Public Papers of the Presidents, 1993, I, at 429–30.
38. Id. at 484, 486, 487, 429–93, 631–32, 984–85.
39. Id. at 1455.
40. Id. at 1781.
41. 139 Cong. Rec. 22304–5 (1993).
42. Public Papers of the Presidents, 1993, II, at 1764.

All I can tell you is that I think I have a big responsibility to try to appropriately consult with Members of Congress in both parties—whenever we are in the process of making a decision which might lead to the use of force. I believe that. But I think that, clearly, the Constitution leaves the President, for good and sufficient reasons, the ultimate decisionmaking authority. . . .

The President should be very circumspect and very careful in committing the welfare and the lives of even our All-Volunteer Army. We need to have a clear American interest there, and there needs to be clearly-defined conditions of involvement, and the burden is on the President to provide those. But still the President must make the ultimate decision, and I think it's a mistake to cut those decisions off in advance.[43]

In a message to Congress a day later, Clinton expressed his "grave concern" about a number of amendments designed to restrict the use of American troops in Haiti, Bosnia, and UN peacekeeping operations. He was "fundamentally opposed" to amendments that "improperly limit my ability to perform my constitutional duties as Commander-in-Chief, which may well have unconstitutional provisions." Adversaries and allies, he said, must know with certainty that the United States can respond decisively "to protect the lives of Americans and to address crises that challenge American interests." Amendments regarding "command and control" of U.S. forces "would insert Congress into the detailed execution of military contingency planning in an unprecedented manner."[44] Clinton's objections were misplaced. Congress has full constitutional authority to place limits on the deployment of American soldiers even when such restrictions affect "command and control." Such statutory restrictions are not unprecedented. Indeed, they are consistent with constitutional principles.

After substantial debate on various amendments, Congress and the administration compromised on sense-of-Congress (nonbinding) observations about the placement of U.S. troops under foreign commanders and conditions for such engagements.[45] Congress also stated its sense that funds appropriated for defense should not be available for deploying U.S. forces to participate in the implementation of a peace settlement in Bosnia-Herzegovina "unless previously authorized by Congress."[46]

43. Id. at 1768.
44. Id. at 1770.
45. 107 Stat. 1478–80, sec. 9001 (1993). See also 107 Stat. 1839–40, sec. 1511 (1993).
46. 107 Stat. 1474, sec. 8146 (1993).

In 1994, Clinton continued to threaten air strikes to bomb Serbian militias in Bosnia. Such actions would be taken in response to UN Security Council resolutions, operating through NATO's military command. As Clinton explained: "The authority under which air strikes can proceed, NATO acting out of area pursuant to U.N. authority, requires the common agreement of our NATO allies."[47] In other words, Clinton would have to obtain approval from England, Italy, and other NATO allies, but not from Congress.

In late February, U.S. jets shot down four Serbian bombers over Bosnia. Clinton reported to Congress: "U.S. Armed Forces participate in these operations pursuant to my constitutional authority to conduct U.S. foreign relations and as Commander in Chief."[48] This was the first time in the history of NATO that its forces had been engaged in combat. In April 1994, U.S. planes bombed Bosnian Serb forces involved in laying a siege around the Muslim-held city of Gorazde. UN officials requested the air strikes ostensibly to protect twelve international peacekeepers deployed in the city.[49] In August 1994, U.S. jets again hit Serbian positions.[50]

Using military force under NATO auspices raises the perennial issue of the meaning of "constitutional processes." To claim that the President, acting in concert with NATO allies, has the power to order military strikes without advance congressional authority would mean that the President and the Senate, through the treaty process, can obliterate the constitutional power of the House of Representatives to decide whether to take the nation to war. That position, no matter how asserted, is untenable.

NATO conducted limited air strikes during the first half of 1995. When Bosnian Serb forces overran the UN-designated "safe area" of Sbrebrenica, NATO carried out the war's biggest air raid at the end of August, 1995.[51] On September 1, Clinton explained to congressional leaders the procedures for ordering air strikes on Bosnia. The UN and NATO participated in the decision; Congress did not. The North Atlantic Council (NAC) "approved" a number of measures and "agreed" that any direct attacks against remaining safe areas would justify air operations as determined "by the common judgment of NATO and U.N. military commanders."[52] The "common judg-

47. Public Papers of the Presidents, 1994, I, at 186.
48. Id. at 355.
49. "U.S. Jets Strike Serb Forces Near Bosnian Town," Washington Post, April 11, 1994, at A1; "U.S. Planes Blast Serb Forces Again," Washington Post, April 12, 1994, at A1.
50. "U.S. Jets Hit Serbs after Raid on Arms," Washington Post, August 6, 1994, at A1.
51. Rick Atkinson and John Pomfret, "NATO Bombs Serbs in War's Biggest Air Raid," Washington Post, August 30, 1995, at A1.
52. Public Papers of the Presidents, 1995, II, at 1280.

ment" had nothing to do with Congress. On September 12, Clinton stated that he regarded the bombing attacks as "authorized by the United Nations."[53]

Ground Troops to Bosnia

As the next escalation of U.S. military power, Clinton decided in 1995 to introduce ground forces to Bosnia. The initial number of American soldiers was put at 25,000. On September 29, the Senate debated ways of limiting the deployment, but once again chose legally nonbinding language. It would be the "sense of the Senate" that no funds should be used to deploy combat-equipped U.S. forces for any ground operations in Bosnia and Herzegovina unless "Congress approves in advance the deployment of such forces." Exceptions were allowed to permit the President to deploy U.S. ground forces if needed to evacuate U.S. peacekeeping forces from a "situation of imminent danger, to undertake emergency air rescue operations, or to provide for the airborne delivery of humanitarian supplies."[54]

Debate on this amendment illustrates how much legislators deferred to the President on troop deployment. The author of the amendment, Senator Judd Gregg (R-N.H.), argued that "it is appropriate that we as a Congress act to either approve that action or disapprove that action." He suggested this allocation of constitutional power: "Clearly, the power to undertake actions which put American soldiers' lives in harm's way lies primarily and first with the President, but obviously we as a Congress also play a major role, not only on the appropriating side but, more importantly, on the side of being concerned for our soldiers, many of whom will obviously be our constituents."[55] Gregg felt "strongly that prior to the President taking this action, he should come to the Congress and ask for our approval."

However, nothing in his amendment required congressional approval. Senator Sam Nunn (D-Ga.) supported the amendment only because it lacked legal effect: "If it did tie the President's hands at this critical juncture while the peace negotiations are underway, I would oppose it and vote against it."[56] Senator John Kerry (D-Mass.) agreed that if the amendment's language had been legally binding, many Senators would have opposed it.[57] Senator Paul Simon (D-Ill.) opposed the amendment even

---

53. Id. at 1353.
54. 141 Cong. Rec. 27050 (1995).
55. Id.
56. Id.
57. Id. at 27052.

though it was a "sense of the Senate," explaining that foreign policy cannot be effective "if Congress micromanages it." Senator Bill Cohen (R-Maine) disputed that point, noting that Clinton was about to deploy 25,000 troops "to one of the most hostile regions in the world" and "without having any sort of defined plan presented to us."[58] The Senate agreed to the Gregg amendment, 94 to 2.[59]

Clinton continued to claim broad powers over troop deployment. At a news conference on October 19, a reporter asked: "Would you go ahead, then, and send the troops, even if Congress does not approve?" His response: "I am not going to lay down any of my constitutional prerogatives here today. I have said before and I will say again, I would welcome and I hope I get an expression of congressional support. I think it's important for the United States to be united in doing this. . . . I believe, in the end, the Congress will support this operation."[60]

That support would never come, although both the House and the Senate took many votes on the President's authority to commit ground troops to Bosnia. On October 30, by a vote of 315 to 103, the House passed a nonbinding resolution stating that U.S. troops should not be deployed without congressional approval.[61] Ninety-three Democrats—nearly half of those in the House—joined 222 Republicans to support the resolution. Although House Minority Leader Dick Gephardt (D-Mo.) voted against the resolution, he said that "none of us wants to see American troops in Bosnia without the prior approval of this body."[62] He supported the second part of the resolution requiring congressional authorization, but not the first part that dealt with negotiations over a peace agreement. He thought that part of the resolution was too disruptive of ongoing negotiations. Other Democrats, like Lee Hamilton and James Moran, voted against the resolution while agreeing that Congress needed to approve the sending of U.S. troops to Bosnia.[63]

The House majority of 315 to 103 slipped considerably on November 17, when the House voted on legislation that would have legal effect. The bill prohibited the use of funds to deploy U.S. ground troops in Bosnia unless Congress specifically appropriated money for that purpose. The

58. Id.
59. Id. at 27057.
60. Public Papers of the Presidents, 1995, II, at 1630.
61. 141 Cong. Rec. 30738–50, 30763 (1995).
62. Id. at 30743.
63. Id. at 30745, 30748–49.

margin was now 243 to 171.[64] Instead of the 93 Democrats who supported the measure on October 30, only 28 Democrats backed a legally binding requirement.

Hamilton's position expressed in the past—that the President needed
prior authorization from Congress for military deployments—had changed.
He now opposed the bill on the ground that it "ties the hands of the
President. It tells the commander in chief that he cannot deploy troops to
Bosnia, period. When you are the commander in chief, you have the
power to deploy troops. That is fundamental, and this bill takes away that
power."[65] Yet it is also fundamental that Congress has the power of the
purse and can use it to deny funds for military deployments. Moreover, the
bill did not say that Clinton could not "deploy troops to Bosnia, period."
He could deploy them, but only after Congress had appropriated funds
specifically for that purpose. As Benjamin Gilman (R-N.Y.), chairman of the
House Committee on International Relations, noted: "This resolution does
not rule out the deployment of United States forces to Bosnia, but it does
make certain that the President come to the Congress first."[66]

Some Democrats who had voted for the October 30 measure now withdrew their support from the November 17 version because it was legally
binding. John Spratt of South Carolina remarked: "We have to and can send
the President strong signals, as we did when we passed McHale-Buyer,
315-to-103. But this bill is more than a warning signal; it flat-out prohibits
the President from sending any U.S. ground troops to Bosnia as part of any
peacekeeping operation unless funds are specifically appropriated."[67] As a
lawmaking body, it was entirely appropriate for Congress to send the clear-
est possible signal—no deployment without funds first—and to make it
legally binding.

Twelve Republicans voted against the November 17 alternative. James
B. Longley Jr. (R-Maine) said he was "not a supporter of putting American
troops on the ground in Bosnia. I think it would be a terrible mistake."
Nevertheless, he deferred to Clinton: "I have to respect the authority of the
Commander in Chief to conduct foreign policy. . . . I think there is no
greater threat to American lives than a Congress that attempts to micro-
mangage foreign policy. I have told the President that I would respect his
authority as Commander in Chief."[68]

64. Id. at 33845.
65. Id. at 33820.
66. Id. at 33825–26.
67. Id. at 33827.
68. Id. at 33835.

Respect for the President is important, but far more important is respect for the Constitution and checks and balances. Members of Congress have not merely a right but a duty to reach independent judgments on war-making and to place legal limits on presidential power. If a lawmaker opposes sending American troops abroad and regards it as a "terrible mistake," the way to avert the mistake is by enacting binding statutory constraints. Sending 20,000 ground troops to Bosnia was never an issue of "micromanagement," nor do congressional limits on troop deployments threaten American lives. Instead, those lives are threatened when a President places them in harm's way.

Clinton expressed interest in obtaining legislative support but never legislative authority. In a letter to Senator Robert C. Byrd (D-W.Va.) on October 19, Clinton invited "an expression of support by Congress."[69] He told reporters on October 31 that if a peace agreement were reached it would request "an expression of support" in Congress for committing U.S. troops to a NATO implementation force.[70] In a letter to Speaker Newt Gingrich on November 13, Clinton continued to avoid any suggestion that he needed authorization from Congress before sending U.S. ground forces to Bosnia.[71]

Addressing the nation on November 27, Clinton justified the deployment as a way of stopping "the killing of innocent civilians, especially children, and at the same time, to bring stability to Central Europe, a region of the world that is vital to our national interests. It is the right thing to do."[72] That language parallels Clinton's justification for invading Haiti: It was the right thing, even if not the legal thing or constitutional thing. On December 6, having approved the NATO operation plan for sending ground troops to Bosnia, he said he would be requesting "an expression of support from the Congress."[73] The support never came.

The congressional response depended greatly on what Bob Dole, the Senate Majority Leader, would do. On November 27, he made it clear that legislative prerogatives were subordinate to presidential interests. It was Dole's view that Clinton had "the authority and the power under the Constitution to do what he feels should be done regardless of what Congress does."[74] Dole told CBS News: "No doubt about it, whether Congress agrees

69. Id. at 28718.
70. Public Papers of the Presidents, 1995, II, at 1702.
71. 141 Cong. Rec. 33823–25 (1995).
72. Public Papers of the Presidents, 1995, II, at 1784.
73. Id. at 1857.
74. 141 Cong. Rec. 34504 (1995).

or not, troops will go to Bosnia."[75] That is a remarkable statement for a legislative leader. No matter "what Congress does"—even in passing language to deny funds without express legislative approval—the President may do whatever "he feels." Under this political system and distribution of power, Congress does not exist as an independent branch. It is not remotely coequal. The checks and balances essential to constitutional government disappear.

Dole spoke as the Republican front-runner for President in 1996. Instead of demonstrating leadership and protecting institutional and constitutional interests, he looked to the President and to polls. He said: "We need to find some way to be able to support the President and I think we need to wait and see what the American reaction is."[76] Other Republican candidates were similarly guarded. Steve Forbes opposed the deployment but said that Clinton had the authority to send troops to Bosnia, and, if that happened, "We have to support the troops while they're there." The issue was never supporting the troops, but whether they should be sent. Another Republican contender for President, Lamar Alexander, said this about Clinton: "I intend to continue to listen to him and do my best to support him, but I believe he's wrong." Why support a President you think is wrong? Pat Buchanan was the only Republican candidate to say flatly that Clinton lacked constitutional authority to send troops to Bosnia without approval from Congress.[77]

On December 13 and 14, the Senate considered several measures regarding the commitment of U.S. troops to Bosnia. One approach was a nonbinding resolution with two parts: expressing congressional opposition to sending the troops, while also "strongly" supporting the troops.[78] The resolution fell, 47 to 52. The Senate also rejected a House bill prohibiting the use of defense funds for the deployment of ground troops to Bosnia unless the funds were specifically appropriated by law. That bill failed, 22 to 77.[79] The Senate then passed, 69 to 30, a multipart bill providing support for American troops but expressing "reservations" about sending them to Bosnia.[80] This compromise bill was incoherent. If the Senate had reser-

75. Ann Devroy and Helen Dewar, "U.S. Troops Vital to Bosnia Peace Plan, Clinton Says," Washington Post, November 28, 1995, at A1.

76. Dan Balz, "As Dole Equivocates on Troop Deployment, Most GOP Rivals Oppose Plan," Washington Post, November 28, 1995, at A9.

77. Id.

78. 141 Cong. Rec. 36921 (1995).

79. Id. at 36824.

80. Id. at 36908.

vations about sending troops to Bosnia and wanted to support the troops, the logical policy would have been to prohibit deployment.

Senator Dole explained some of the purposes of the bill that passed. One was to shift responsibility from Congress to the President. Dole said that Clinton "made this decision and he takes responsibility. It was his decision to send troops and his decision alone."[81] Translation: If anything went wrong it would be Clinton's fault, not Congress's. Second, the Senate was expressing doubts about the merits of sending troops to Bosnia. As Dole put it: "This resolution does not endorse the President's decision. It does not endorse the agreement reached in Dayton."[82] Dole elaborated: "We can posture and complain about the President's decision. I do not like it. He knows I do not like it. I told him I do not like it."[83] Essentially, the bill was a way for Senators to oppose Clinton's policy but praise the soldiers who would carry it out. It made no sense.

On the same day as these Senate votes, the House acted on a series of measures related to Bosnia. By 210 to 218, the House failed to pass a bill prohibiting funds from being used to deploy troops to Bosnia. It next voted 287 to 141 to pass a nonbinding House resolution regarding enforcement of the peace agreement. The resolution expressed "serious concerns and opposition to the President's policy" but declared that the House was confident that U.S. troops "will perform their responsibilities with professional excellence, dedicated patriotism, and exemplary courage." Like the Senate, the House wanted to have it both ways. Another House resolution, "unequivocally" supporting American troops but omitting direct criticism of Clinton's policy, lost 190 to 237.[84]

In the end, Clinton was able to deploy 20,000 American ground troops to Bosnia without first seeking or obtaining authority from Congress. On December 21, 1995, he said he expected that the military mission to Bosnia "can be accomplished in about a year."[85] No one following the issue could have believed that. A year later, on December 17, 1996, Clinton extended the troop deployment for "another 18 months."[86] The 18-month extension came and went, with the Clinton administration no longer attempting to set an endpoint to the commitment in Bosnia. On March 3, 1998, Clinton told Congress that he did not propose "a fixed end-date" for U.S. troops in

81. Id. at 36905.
82. Id.
83. Id. at 36906.
84. Id. at 36384–85.
85. Public Papers of the Presidents, 1995, II, at 1917.
86. Public Papers of the Presidents, 1996, II, at 2221.

Bosnia.[87] Efforts by Congress to force withdrawal of troops by a date certain or to require authorization for continued deployment failed.[88] By the fall of 2003, U.S. troops were still in Bosnia.

If it was the right thing to intervene militarily in Bosnia, it was wrong for Clinton to act unilaterally. Multibillion-dollar commitments should not be entered into simply because a President says it is "the "right thing" and is determined to proceed with or without Congress. That is a superficial foundation for national policy, domestic or foreign. Far more important than doing the right thing is doing things the right way: following constitutional procedures, developing a national consensus and public support, and working with the legislative branch instead of circumventing it.[89]

Continued Strikes against Iraq

Clinton's launching of missiles against Baghdad in June 1993 marked the beginning of successive military operations against Iraq. In September 1996, he ordered the launching of more cruise missiles against Iraq in response to an attack by Iraqi forces against the Kurdish-controlled city of Irbil in northern Iraq. Cruise missiles also hit air defense systems in southern Iraq. Clinton explained that the missiles "sent the following message to Saddam Hussein: When you abuse your own people or threaten your neighbors, you must pay a price."[90]

That justification for military action bore no relationship to arguments offered by previous Presidents, such as self-defense or the need to protect the lives of Americans. Clinton's justification was both novel and startling: Whenever foreign leaders abuse their people and threaten their neighbors, an American President can unleash military attacks to punish them. Adopting that standard, how many nations could a President attack? Start with Russia and China and then turn to smaller but still substantial countries in Asia, Africa, and other continents. Clinton's argument here was even less credible than his cruise missile attack against Baghdad. His decision to launch cruise missiles in 1996 coincided with his reelection race and preparations to deliver an acceptance speech at the Democratic convention.

87. Public Papers of the Presidents, 1998, I, at 325.
88. 144 Cong. Rec. S2506–32 (daily ed., March 25, 1998); 144 Cong. Rec. S3810–17, S3840, S3843 (daily ed., April 30, 1998).
89. Louis Fisher, "The Bosnia Commitment: Binding the United States by Unilateral Executive Action," Legal Times, March 11, 1996, at 22–23.
90. Public Papers of the Presidents, 1996, II, at 1469.

Toward the end of January 1998, Clinton threatened once again to bomb Iraq, this time because Saddam Hussein had refused to give UN inspectors full access to examine Iraqi sites for possible nuclear, chemical, and biological weapons. He delayed the bombing after UN Secretary General Kofi Annan visited Baghdad in February to negotiate a settlement with Iraq. The Clinton administration accepted the settlement, with reservations, but made clear that military force remained an option if Iraq failed to comply with the new agreement.

In January 1998, congressional leaders drafted a resolution (S. Con. Res. 71) that condemned Iraq and urged Clinton to take "all necessary and appropriate actions to respond." The language held an eerie resemblance to the sweeping transfer of legislative power in the Tonkin Gulf Resolution. Senator Max Cleland (D-Ga.) led a handful of Democrats in opposing the resolution. It was never adopted.[91]

The closest anyone ever came to a legal justification for the bombing relied on two sources: the January 1991 statute that authorized war against Iraq and a succession of resolutions passed by the UN Security Council. Those arguments were presented by the Clinton administration in 1998 and again by the Bush administration in 2002. In both cases, executive officials insisted that when Congress passed the 1991 statute, it gave advance blessing to whatever the Security Council might do in the future when issuing resolutions on Iraq. Yet Congress had no right to delegate war in perpetuity, nor could it surrender to an international organization its prerogatives over war and foreign policy.

Here are the specifics. On January 15, 1991, Congress enacted P.L. 102-1 to authorize military action against Iraq. The President could use military force pursuant to UN Security Council Resolution 678 "in order to achieve implementation of Security Council Resolutions 660, 661, 662, 664, 665, 666, 667, 669, 670, 674, and 677."[92] The 1991 statute therefore authorized military force to drive Iraq out of Kuwait, which was the purpose of Resolution 678, adopted on November 29, 1990. All of the earlier resolutions, from 660 to 677, prepared the way for 678. Resolution 660, passed on August 2, 1990, condemned Iraq's invasion of Kuwait and demanded immediate withdrawal. Resolution 661 imposed economic sanctions. Resolutions 662 to 677 reinforced the earlier resolutions and added other restrictions.

How can it be argued that Congress, on January 14, 1991, transferred its

91. Donna Cassata, "Cleland Warns against Repeating Tonkin Gulf Mistake," CQ Weekly Report, January 31, 1998, at 247; Helen Dewar, "Iraq Resolution Sends Chills through Some in Congress," Washington Post, February 3, 1998, at A13.

92. 105 Stat. 3, sec. 2(a) (1991).

constitutional power to the Security Council? Here is the reasoning of some executive officials. Resolution 678 authorized member states to use all necessary means "to uphold and implement 660 (1990) and all subsequent relevant resolutions and to restore international peace and security in the area."[93] Supporters of presidential power concluded that the phrase "all subsequent relevant resolutions" meant that whatever the Security Council promulgated after January 14, 1991, would be automatically sanctioned by P.L. 102-1. By such reasoning, U.S. lawmakers authorized the Security Council to define the future scope of military operations against Iraq without further participation by Congress. That is unsupportable, practically and constitutionally.

As to the language of the Security Council resolution, how should one interpret the word "subsequent"? Does it refer to any resolution issued after 678, or only to the resolutions issued after 660 but before 678? The natural reading is the latter one, because the objective was to oust Iraq from Kuwait, not to sanction ongoing military operations in the future. In 1991, President Bush lacked authority (either from Congress or the Security Council) to send ground troops north to Baghdad. He understood that in 1991 and later, when he wrote *A World Transformed* (1998) with Brent Scowcroft. Such initiatives would have exceeded his statutory authority and violated the understanding of other nations that had joined the multinational alliance.

The most unnatural reading would be to conclude that Congress, in passing P.L. 102-1, had placed its constitutional authority with the Security Council, and that the future magnitude of U.S. military actions in Iraq would be decided by UN resolutions, not congressional statutes. Under this strained legal theory, whatever the Security Council decided would compel Congress to vote the necessary appropriations. Congressional debate on P.L. 102-1 provides no support for that analysis.

On February 19, 1998, during a visit to Tennessee State University, Secretary of State Albright was asked how Clinton could order military action against Iraq after opposing American policy in Vietnam. Her response: "We are talking about using military force, but we are not talking about a war. That is an important distinction."[94] Through her argument, the framers' effort to keep the war power with Congress and its elected representatives could be nullified simply by describing presidential action as military force rather than war. The Constitution would be suspended by mere semantics.

93. CQ Weekly Report, December 1, 1990, at 4007.
94. Barton Gellman, "Students Receive Albright Politely," Washington Post, February 20, 1998, at A19.

In December 1998, Clinton ordered four days of bombing in Iraq. He justified the military action as an effort to attack Iraq's nuclear, chemical, and biological weapons programs and because Iraq has failed to cooperate fully with UN weapons inspectors.[95] He also explained that U.S. credibility would suffer if it did not fulfill its earlier threat to use military action if Iraq interfered with UN inspectors: "if Saddam can cripple the weapons inspection system and get away with it, he would conclude that the international community, led by the United States, has simply lost its will. . . . If we turn our backs on his defiance, the credibility of U.S. power as a check against Saddam will be destroyed."[96]

As a result of the December bombing, there were now no UN inspectors to monitor chemical, biological, and nuclear capability in Iraq. In place of an imperfect inspection system was no system at all. The purpose of the bombing (removing weapons of mass destruction) was also in question. The Pentagon disclosed that American and British forces were "taking care to avoid hitting Iraqi factories suspected of producing chemical and biological weapons" for fear of unleashing plumes of poisons on civilians.[97]

In a letter to Congress, Clinton argued that the military operation in Iraq was "consistent with and has been taken in support of numerous U.N. Security Council resolutions, including Resolutions 678 and 687." In this same message, he claimed that he acted under "the Authorization for Use of Military Force Against Iraq Resolution (Public Law 102-1) enacted in January 1991."[98] That argument, for reasons given above, lacks legal merit. Moreover, the Clinton administration apparently jettisoned its legal reliance on UN Security Council resolutions. Secretary of State Albright and Secretary of Defense William S. Cohen warned that the United States and Britain would continue to act militarily against Iraq with or without the approval of other allies or the UN Security Council.[99]

In the midst of the four-day bombing in December, the House passed a nonbinding resolution supporting the armed forces and reaffirming the policy of removing Saddam Hussein. Rep. David Skaggs (D-Colo.) faulted both Clinton and Congress for violating the war power provisions of the Constitution:

95. Public Papers of the Presidents, 1998, II, at 2182.
96. Id. at 2183.
97. Steven Lee Myers, "Jets Said to Avoid Poison Gas Sites," New York Times, December 18, 1998, at A1.
98. Public Papers of the Presidents, 1998, II, at 2195–96.
99. Thomas W. Lippman, "U.S. Warns Iraq of More Raids," Washington Post, December 21, 1998, at A1.

Mr. Speaker, of course we want to support American troops as they carry out this dangerous and important mission. But let us not lose sight of the sad fact that President Clinton has acted in violation of the Constitution in ordering these attacks without authority of Congress. And let us not forget as well that the decision to go to war is vested in Congress and not in the Commander in Chief and that we too share blame for this violation of the Constitution because we have time and time again defaulted in our responsibility and obligation to insist on our proper constitutional role.[100]

For the remainder of the Clinton administration, the United States and Britain conducted repeated air strikes against Iraq, firing more missiles and hitting more targets than during the four-day operation in December 1998.[101]

Afghanistan and Sudan

President Clinton took other military actions in 1998, again without congressional authorization. In August, he ordered cruise missiles into Afghanistan to attack paramilitary camps and into Sudan to destroy a pharmaceutical factory. He justified this use of military force as a retaliation for bombings earlier in the month against U.S. embassies in Africa. The administration claimed that Osama bin Laden was behind the embassy attacks, that he used the training complex in Afghanistan, and that he was somehow related to the pharmaceutical plant. The last assertion was the most suspect.

Clinton said he selected the two targets because "of the imminent threat they presented to our national security."[102] It was never clear why the pharmaceutical plant represented a threat. Although Clinton claimed it produced "materials for chemical weapons,"[103] the chemical in question (Empta) was a precursor capable of making either a nerve gas or an agricultural insecticide.[104] Evidence supported the latter. The Pentagon later conceded that it was unaware that the plant produced "a large share of the medicine

100. 144 Cong. Rec. H11727 (daily ed., December 17, 1998).

101. E.g., Steven Lee Myers, "In Intense but Little-Noticed Fight, Allies Have Bombed Iraq All Year," New York Times, August 13, 1999, at A1.

102. Public Papers of the Presidents, 1998, II, at 1460.

103. Id. at 1461.

104. Steven Lee Myers and Tim Weiner, "Possible Benign Use Is Seen for Chemical at Factory in Sudan," New York Times, August 27, 1998, at A1.

used in the Sudan."[105] Why did the U.S. government not know that? The plant was not restricted. Anyone in Khartoum could have entered the plant and learned that it was producing pharmaceuticals.

In February 1999, a Saudi businessman who owned the plant went to court to demand that the Clinton administration compensate him for the facility and release millions of dollars of assets frozen by U.S. officials on the ground that he was linked to bin Laden. He denied that he had any such relationship and also denied that the plant produced chemicals for a nerve gas.[106] In May, the administration agreed to release $24 million of his assets but refused to clear his name. Instead, a senior White House official said that the administration continued to have "concerns" about him, but that the concerns were based on sensitive intelligence sources and methods that the administration did not want to disclose in court. His attorney responded: "We deal in a world of facts and evidence; the government appears to be hiding behind suggestion and innuendo."[107] Long after the missile attack on Sudan, news reports continued to question the legitimacy of bombing the plant.[108]

The owner pressed his case for compensation, seeking $50 million for the destruction of the plant. In 2003, the U.S. Court of Federal Claims decided that his company had standing to bring a case. The issue was whether there had been an unconstitutional "taking" of property in violation of the Fifth Amendment, which allows for "just compensation" when private property is taken for public use. The court also ruled that the takings clause extends to disputes about property located outside the United States and owned by noncitizens.

However, the claims court ruled that the takings clause does not cover claims arising when an alleged enemy war-making property is destroyed by American military action.[109] The court explained that the "legitimacy or

105. Tim Weiner and Steven Lee Myers, "Flaws in U.S. Account Raise Questions on Strike in Sudan," New York Times, August 29, 1998, at A1, A4; Tim Weiner and Steven Lee Myers, "U.S. Notes Gaps in Data about Drug Plant," New York Times, September 3, 1998, at A6.

106. Vernon Loeb, "Saudi Demands Compensation for Destroyed Plant," Washington Post, February 4, 1999, at A9.

107. Vernon Loeb, "U.S. Unfreezes $24 Million in Assets of Saudi Who Owned El Shifa Plant," Washington Post, May 4, 1999, at A11.

108. Vernon Loeb, "U.S. Wasn't Sure Plant Had Nerve Gas Role," Washington Post, August 21, 1999, at A1; James Risen, "To Bomb Sudan Plant, or Not: A Year Later, Debates Rankle," New York Times, October 27, 1999, at A12.

109. El-Shifa Pharmaceutical Industries Co. v. United States, 55 Fed.Cl. 751 (Fed. Claims 2003).

authority of the Government's action must be conceded in takings proceedings before this Court," and that the exercise of military power "falls outside the Fifth Amendment and beyond this Court's jurisdiction."[110] The place to challenge the destruction of the plant "is elsewhere, presumably the District Court in ordinary cases."[111] Thus, even if Clinton's national security advisers relied on faulty intelligence about the plant, the court refused to second-guess Clinton's decision that the plant represented an enemy war-making property.[112] The court "may not look behind the President's discharge of his Constitutional duties as Commander in Chief, including his declaration of what constitutes an enemy target and his determination to use military force to destroy that target."[113]

War against Yugoslavia

Presidents have undertaken a number of military actions without seeking authority from Congress. For the most part, they involved short-term actions modest in scope. As to major U.S. wars, all except two have been either declared or authorized by Congress. The two clearly unconstitutional wars are the Korean War, initiated by President Truman, and the war against Yugoslavia in 1999, ordered by President Clinton.

By October 1998, the Clinton administration was once again threatening the Serbs with air strikes, this time because of Serb attacks on the ethnic Albanian majority in Kosovo. At a news conference on October 8, Clinton stated: "Yesterday I decided that the United States would vote to give NATO the authority to carry out military strikes against Serbia if President Milosevic continues to defy the international community."[114] Note the language: "*I* decided that the United States. . . ." Clinton alone would decide America's policy. The decision to go to war against another country rested in the hands of one person, exactly what the framers thought they had avoided. Moreover, Clinton would be giving *NATO* authority, instead of Congress giving the *President* authority.

Clinton's foreign policy advisers went to Capitol Hill to consult with lawmakers but not to obtain their approval.[115] Although Congress was to be

110. Id. at 766, 767.
111. Id. at 766.
112. Id. at 771.
113. Id. at 774.
114. Public Papers of the Presidents, 1998, II, at 1765.
115. Helen Dewar and John M. Goshko, "Hill Signals Support for Airstrikes," Washington Post, October 2, 1998, at A35.

given no formal role in the use of force against the Serbs, legislatures in other NATO countries took votes to authorize military action in Yugoslavia. The Italian Parliament had to vote approval for the NATO strikes.[116] The German Supreme Court ruled that the Bundestag, which had been dissolved with the election that ousted Chancellor Helmut Kohl, would have to be brought back into session to approve deployment of German aircraft and troops to Kosovo.[117] The U.S. Congress, supposedly the strongest legislature in the world, watched from the sidelines.

On March 11, 1999, with Clinton close to unleashing air strikes against Serbia, the House voted on a resolution to support U.S. armed forces as part of a NATO *peacekeeping* operation. The resolution, designed to authorize U.S. forces to implement a peace agreement, passed 219 to 191.[118] However, the legislative measure was a concurrent resolution (H. Con. Res. 42). Congress cannot authorize anything in a concurrent resolution, which passes each House but is not presented to the President to become a public law. To be legally binding, the measure would have to be a bill or joint resolution, both of which are presented to the President for his signature or veto. Lawmakers actually voted on something that originated as a joint resolution but changed at some point to become a concurrent resolution without anyone changing the word "authorize" to something more appropriate, like "support."

Members of the House clearly anticipated a peace agreement between the Serbs and the Kosovars. The House vote did not register any support for military action. The Kosovars eventually accepted the plan, but the Serbs did not. Nothing in the House action implied support for the bombing operation that would begin within two weeks.

By the time the Senate voted on March 23, negotiations had collapsed and air strikes were imminent. The Senate voted 58 to 41 to support military air operations and missile strikes against the Federal Republic of Yugoslavia (Serbia and Montenegro).[119] As with the House, the Senate used the word "authorize" in a concurrent resolution (S. Con. Res. 21). A congressional staffer involved with the legislation told me why the mistake occurred: "stupidity." The war against Yugoslavia began on March 24, without any statutory or constitutional support.

116. Alessandra Stanley, "Italy's Center-Left Government Is Toppled by One Vote," New York Times, October 10, 1998, at A3.

117. William Drozdiak, "Allies Grim, Milosevic Defiant amid Kosovo Uncertainty," Washington Post, October 8, 1998, at A32.

118. 145 Cong. Rec. H1249–50 (daily ed., March 11, 1999).

119. Id. at S3118 (daily ed., March 23, 1999).

On April 28, the House took several votes on the war in Yugoslavia. It voted 249 to 180 to prohibit the use of appropriated funds for the deployment of U.S. ground forces unless first authorized by Congress. A motion to direct the removal of U.S. armed forces from Yugoslavia failed, 139 to 290. A resolution to declare a state of war between the United States and Yugoslavia was rejected, 2 to 427. A fourth vote, to authorize the air operations and missile strikes, lost on a tie vote, 213 to 213.

Some newspaper editorials and commentators derided the House for what they considered an incoherent voting pattern, but the House announced two clear positions: insisting that Congress authorize the introduction of ground troops and refusing to authorize the air strikes. Lawmakers noted the irony of President Clinton seeking the approval of 18 NATO nations but not the approval of Congress. Rep. Ernest Istook (R-Okla.) remarked, "President Clinton asked many nations to agree to attack Yugoslavia, but he failed to get permission from one crucial country, America."[120]

After the House votes, Clinton explained his policy on the introduction of ground troops: "I can assure you that I would fully consult with the Congress. Indeed, without regard to our differing constitutional views on the use of force, I would ask for Congressional support before introducing U.S. ground forces into Kosovo into a non-permissive environment."[121] Some interpreted this statement as a commitment to seek congressional authority, but Clinton never went beyond a promise to "consult" and to request legislative "support." Had Congress withheld its support, nothing in Clinton's statement or other remarks would have stopped him from acting unilaterally.

In contrast to the specific votes taken by the House, the Senate decided to duck the issue once hostilities were under way. Senator John McCain (R-Ariz.) offered a joint resolution to authorize Clinton to use "all necessary force and other means, in concert with United States allies, to accomplish United States and North Atlantic Treaty Organization objectives in the Federal Republic of Yugoslavia (Serbia and Montenegro)." Rather than debate the substance of this amendment, the Senate chose to fall back on procedure and simply tabled it, 78 to 22.[122] The Senate tabled another amendment, this one by Senator Arlen Specter (R-Pa.) to direct the President to seek approval from Congress before introducing ground troops

---

120. Id. at H2419 (daily ed., April 28, 1999).
121. Id. at S4531 (daily ed., May 3, 1999). Letter of April 28, 1999.
122. Id. at S4616 (daily ed., May 4, 1999). Most of the debate on the McCain resolution occurred on May 3 (S4510–70).

into Yugoslavia. Failure to obtain approval would have denied the President funds to conduct the operation.[123] The amendment was tabled, 52 to 48. Yet another amendment from Senator Bob Smith (R-N.H.) would have prohibited funding for military operations in Yugoslavia unless Congress enacted specific authorization. A tabling motion prevailed, 77 to 21.[124]

During the bombing of Serbia and Kosovo, Rep. Tom Campbell (R-Calif.) went to court with 25 other colleagues to seek a declaration that President Clinton had violated the Constitution and the War Powers Resolution by conducting the air offensive without congressional authorization. A district judge held that Campbell lacked standing to raise his claims. Although each House had taken a number of votes—sometimes supporting Clinton, sometimes not—Congress had never acted as an entire institution to order the President to cease military operations. For that reason, there was no "constitutional impasse" or "actual confrontation" for the court to resolve. Instead, the court was faced with a typical congressional lawsuit where a small group of lawmakers objected to presidential conduct. As the court noted: "If Congress had directed the President to remove forces from their positions and he had refused to do so or if Congress had refused to appropriate or authorize the use of funds for the air strikes in Yugoslavia and the President had decided to spend that money (or money earmarked for other purposes) anyway, that likely would have constituted an actual confrontation sufficient to confer standing on legislative plaintiffs."[125] That decision was affirmed by the D.C. Circuit.[126]

Clinton's military initiatives were remarkable both for their frequency and the absence of any institutional checks, either legislative or judicial.

123. Id. at S5809 (daily ed., May 24, 1999).
124. Id. at S6034–40 (daily ed., May 26, 1999).
125. Campbell v. Clinton, 52 F.Supp.2d 34, 43 (D.D.C. 1999).
126. Campbell v. Clinton, 203 F.3d 19 (D.C. Cir. 2000). See Louis Fisher, "Litigating the War Power with *Campbell* v. *Clinton*," 30 Pres. Stud. Q. 564 (2000).

9

GEORGE W. BUSH

During the 2000 presidential campaign, George W. Bush spoke cautiously about using military force abroad and engaging in nation-building. He recognized the threat of terrorism and weapons of mass destruction, but his program for national security centered on deployment of a missile defense system. That model of government changed radically on September 11, 2001, when terrorists from the Middle East hijacked four U.S. commercial airliners, flying two of them into the World Trade Center. The south and north towers collapsed, with the loss of almost 3,000 people. Another plane crashed into the Pentagon. The fourth plane, apparently destined for Washington, D.C., was forced down by passengers in rural Pennsylvania, killing all onboard. In a proclamation on September 13, President Bush referred to the terrorist attacks as "acts of war."[1]

After 9/11, President Bush moved quickly to obtain legislative authorization for military action against Afghanistan and later against Iraq, requiring in each instance the rebuilding of civil and economic structures in those countries. Bush articulated much more ambitiously than Presidents before him the concept of "preemptive action." At times he acted unilaterally, such as authorizing the creation of military tribunals to try those responsible for 9/11. Congress and the courts provided few legislative and judicial checks to his military initiatives.

The Preemption Doctrine

The potential sweep of presidential war power is reflected in a document called "National Security Strategy," released by the Bush administration in September 2002. It articulates the doctrine of preemption and perhaps an even broader concept: preventive war. President Bush warned against enemies seeking weapons of mass destruction, pledging to "act against such

---

1. 37 Weekly Compilation of Presidential Documents 1308.

emerging threats before they are fully formed."[2] History, he said, "will judge harshly those who saw this coming danger but failed to act. In the new world we have entered, the only path to peace and security is the path of action."[3]

The tone of the document, which championed "a single sustainable model for national success: freedom, democracy and free enterprise," seemed to some as giving the United States "a nearly messianic role in making the world 'not just safer but better.'"[4] One editorial thought the new doctrine "sounds more like a pronouncement that the Roman Empire or Napoleon might have produced."[5] European nations were concerned that the new doctrine favored unilateral U.S. military action at the cost of multilateral institutions and broad-based alliances.[6]

The concept of preemptive war is not new. The right of a state to use military force for self-defense has always included the use of force in anticipation of an attack, such as troops massing on one's border or an armada gathering off the coast. Secretary of State Daniel Webster identified the basic principles of international law after the British, in 1837, sank an American ship, the *Caroline,* in U.S. waters because it was being used to supply insurrectionists against British rule in Canada. Webster acknowledged that a nation could use military force in the territory of another nation, but only in those "cases in which the 'necessity of that self-defense is instant, overwhelming, and leaving no choice of means, and no moment for deliberation.'"[7] International law places other restraints on nations. The use of military force must be proportional to the threat. Article 51 of the UN Charter sanctions military force for self-defense "if an armed attack occurs." Is this limited to self-defense after being attacked, or does it also allow for "anticipatory self-defense"?

However one answers those questions, President Bush proposed a policy that goes well beyond self-defense or preemptive war, where the test

2. The National Security Strategy of the United States of America [hereafter "National Security Strategy"], September 2002, page 2 of introductory statement by President Bush, September 17, 2002.

3. Id.

4. Karen DeYoung and Mike Allen, "Bush Shifts Strategy from Deterrence to Dominance," Washington Post, September 21, 2002, at A1.

5. "The Bush Doctrine," Washington Post, September 22, 2002, at WK 12.

6. Glenn Frankel, "New U.S. Doctrine Worries Europeans," Washington Post, September 30, 2002, at A1.

7. 2 A Digest of International Law 412 (John Bassett Moore, ed. 1906) (letter from Secretary of State Daniel Webster to Lord Ashburton, August 6, 1842).

is a threat that is imminent, direct, and offers no alternative but the use of force. Bush advocated something much more sweeping: the legitimacy of using military force against a nation that could be a threat in the near future. As he stated in "National Security Strategy," the United States "will act against such emerging threats before they are fully formed." That crosses the line from imminent or immediate threats to *emerging* threats and places the United States in a new posture that some call "preventive war." As noted by Miriam Sapiro, the war against Iraq in 2003 was "not designed to pre-empt a specific, imminent threat, but to prevent Saddam Hussein from threatening the United States in the future."[8]

Whether the concept is preemption or preventive war, the world would be at great risk if nations felt free to use military force against emerging threats. In his address at West Point on June 1, 2002, President Bush cautioned that he would "not use force in all cases to preempt emerging threats, nor should nations use preemption as a pretext for aggression." Yet he then acknowledged that in a world where enemies seek destructive technologies, "the United States cannot remain idle while dangers gather."[9]

If America is unwilling to remain idle, what of India, Pakistan, and other countries that might want to use nuclear weapons first? The Bush administration counsels them to rely on diplomacy to defuse military confrontations while at the same time reserving to the United States the moral and legal right to use military force—including nuclear weapons—unilaterally. This policy differs from the preemption doctrine developed in the past, which relied on universal principles that apply to all nations, not just to one.

There have been clear cases of preemptive action in the past, such as Israel's military response in 1967 to Syria, Iraq, Jordan, and Saudi Arabia massing troops on its borders. Examples of preemptive action by the United States are more difficult to find. Frequently cited is the Cuban Missile Crisis of 1962, when President Kennedy ordered a U.S. naval "quarantine" to prevent Cuba from receiving missile shipments from the Soviet Union and other military supplies. However, Kennedy did not use military force in anticipation of an imminent threat. He selected the quarantine as an intermediate strategy to settle the matter diplomatically and peacefully, which is what occurred.

8. Miriam Sapiro, "War to Prevent War," Legal Times, April 7, 2003, at 43 (emphasis in original).
9. National Security Strategy, at 15.

Military Tribunals

Before using military force against Afghanistan and Iraq, President Bush, after gaining statutory support, acted unilaterally on what he considered to be his independent constitutional power to create military tribunals (commissions). On November 13, 2001, he issued a military order to authorize the creation of military tribunals to try any individual "not a United States citizen" (a population of about 18 million inside U.S. borders) who pro vided assistance to the 9/11 attacks. He acted without touching base with anyone on Capitol Hill, including the Judiciary and Armed Services Committees.

The military order closely tracks the model established by President Franklin D. Roosevelt, who appointed a military tribunal in 1942 to try eight German saboteurs. The Bush administration cited with confidence a unanimous ruling by the Supreme Court in *Ex parte Quirin* (1942), which upheld Roosevelt's tribunal. William P. Barr, former Attorney General in the first Bush administration, coauthored an article in which he called the 1942 decision the "most apt precedent" for what the Bush administration wanted to do in 2001.[10]

Military tribunals have been used for centuries to try individuals of offenses when civil courts are either not open or considered not suitable. Tribunals are most justified when civil courts are unavailable or not functioning, and least justified when they are. Careful scrutiny of the 1942 experience rebuts the notion that the Nazi saboteur case is a reliable or attractive precedent for the Bush initiative in 2001. The Roosevelt administration was so torn by its handling of the case that it adopted an entirely different procedure in 1945 to deal with two other German spies.

The Bush administration misapplied the *Ex parte Quirin* precedent when it held U.S. citizens (Yasser Esam Hamdi and Jose Padilla) as "enemy combatants." In 1942, the Supreme Court referred to the eight Germans as "unlawful combatants," a term for those who enter the country in civilian dress to execute an enemy's policy. Any U.S. citizen who associates himself with the military arm of an enemy government and enters the country for the purpose of committing hostile acts is an enemy combatant subject to a military tribunal. There the similarity ends. The eight Germans were charged, assigned defense attorneys, subjected to a trial, and allowed to challenge the tribunal's jurisdiction before the Supreme Court. In contrast,

10. William P. Barr and Andrew G. McBride, "Military Justice for al Qaeda," Washington Post, November 18, 2001, at B7.

the Bush administration after 9/11 designated U.S. citizens as "enemy combatants" but refused to charge them with a crime, allow counsel, or bring the matter to trial. Nothing in *Quirin* justifies holding a U.S. citizen indefinitely without access to counsel or a trial.

In June 1942, eight German saboteurs came to the United States by submarine, intent on using explosives against railroads, factories, bridges, and other strategic targets. One of the Germans, George John Dasch, turned himself in to the Federal Bureau of Investigation and helped the agency round up the others. President Roosevelt issued Proclamation 2561 on July 2, 1942, to create a military tribunal, and on July 2, 1942, he issued a military order appointing the members of the military commission, the prosecutors, and the defense counsel. He appointed seven generals to sit on the commission. After the commission reached a judgment, the matter came back to Roosevelt as the final reviewing authority.

Compare that process with adjudication in a civil court, which involves all three branches. Congress decides what is a crime and what the sentence should be; the executive branch prosecutes the case; and the court functions as an independent agency to decide guilt or innocence. The Roosevelt proclamation and military order packed all three functions in a single branch. Roosevelt appointed the tribunal, selected the judges, prosecutors, and defense counsel, and served as the final reviewing authority. The generals on the tribunal, the colonels serving as defense counsel, and the two prosecutors (Attorney General Francis Biddle and Judge Advocate General Myron C. Cramer) were all subordinate to the President. "Crimes" related to the law of war came not from the legislative branch, enacted by statute, but from executive interpretations of the "law of war."

The unanimous opinion of the Supreme Court is less impressive when one analyzes how the Justices performed their task. A federal district court denied the petition for writ of habeas corpus, brought by the defense counsel of the German saboteurs, at 8:00 PM on July 28. Oral argument began the next day before the Supreme Court at noon, before the appellate court had participated. The briefs from both sides were dated on the first day of oral argument, which lasted nine hours over a two-day period. The Justices had little preparation to hear a matter of military law largely foreign to them.

On the third day, just before the Court was about to issue its decision, the papers came over from the D.C. Circuit. The Court granted cert from the appellate court and released a short per curiam, upholding the jurisdiction of the military tribunal. The per curiam promised a "full opinion" that would set forth the legal reasoning. It took the Court three months to craft a decision that would avoid any concurrences or dissents, even though the Justices were well aware that Roosevelt had violated several Articles of War.[11] In the first week of this drafting process, the tribunal completed its work and found all eight Germans guilty as charged. Six were electrocuted on August 8 and two were given prison terms.

With six dead, the Court's full opinion issued on October 29 could hardly imply that the per curiam rested on shaky legal grounds, or that the administration had not acted with adequate authority. Assembling the Court in the middle of the summer, in emergency session and with briefs hurriedly prepared and read, sent a message of inconsiderateness, not careful judicial deliberation. In 1953, when the Court was considering whether to sit in summer session to hear the espionage case of Ethel and Julius Rosenberg, someone recalled the 1942 case as a possible model. Justice Felix Frankfurter, who sat on the *Quirin* Court, remarked that the experience "was not a happy precedent."[12] Justice William O. Douglas, also a member of the 1942 Court, reached a similar conclusion: "The experience with *Ex parte Quirin* indicated, I think, to all of us that it is extremely undesirable to announce a decision on the merits without an opinion accompanying it. Because once the search for the grounds, the examination of the grounds that had been advanced is made, sometimes those grounds crumble."[13]

In 1944, Nazi Germany sent two more saboteurs to the United States by submarine. Two men reached the coast of Maine on November 29 and made their way to New York City, where they were apprehended by the FBI. Initially, it appeared that the two men would be tried in the same manner as the eight Nazi agents in 1942: by a military tribunal sitting on the fifth floor of the Justice Department in Washington, D.C., with Biddle and Cramer handling the prosecution. However, Secretary of War Henry L. Stimson objected to their service as prosecutors in 1942, and this time forcefully intervened to block their participation. On January 12, 1945, Roosevelt issued a military order to try the two German spies, but he did not name the members of the counsel or the counsel for the prosecution

11. Louis Fisher, Nazi Saboteurs on Trial: A Military Tribunal and American Law 109–17 (2003). See this book for further details on the 1942 trial and its application to the Bush military order.

12. Memorandum Re: Rosenberg v. United States, Nos. 111 and 687, October Term 1952, June 4, 1953; Felix Frankfurter Papers, Harvard Law School, Part I, Reel 70, Library of Congress.

13. Conversation between Justice Douglas and Professor Walter F. Murphy, June 6, 1962; Seeley G. Mudd Manuscript Library, Princeton University.

and defense. Instead, he empowered the commanding generals, under the supervision of the Secretary of War, to appoint the military commission. The trial record went not to Roosevelt, as in 1942, but to the Judge Advocate General's office. The trial took place not in Washington, D.C., but at Governors Island in New York City.[14]

For other reasons, *Quirin* serves as a poor precedent for the Bush military order of 2001. When Roosevelt created military tribunals in 1942 and again in 1945, they applied to the people apprehended, a total of ten. The Bush military order applied to all non–U.S. citizens (a population of about 18 million). Admittedly, the order applies only to those who assisted the 9/11 terrorists, but many non–U.S. citizens make charitable contributions, and the Justice Department may determine after the fact that the charitable organization provided some assistance to terrorist groups. The potential reach of the Bush military order is vastly greater that those issued by Roosevelt.

Military Action in Afghanistan

Unlike President Clinton, President George W. Bush twice came to Congress for statutory action to commit U.S. troops to combat: in Afghanistan in 2001 and in Iraq the following year. Military action against Afghanistan attracted broad support among American citizens and from the international community. The war against Iraq, however, provoked much greater opposition from Congress, the American public, and U.S. allies. The two military operations illustrated that American citizens are willing to use force, and use it unilaterally, when necessary for national security. They were united in supporting action against the terrorist structures in Afghanistan, but more doubtful about Iraq representing an imminent threat and skeptical about the justifications offered by the Bush administration.

After 9/11, the administration submitted a Use of Force Act, authorizing military action against the terrorists. The bill, passing both Houses on September 14, was enacted four days later. It passed the Senate 98 to zero and the House 420 to one. The statute authorizes the President to use "all necessary and appropriate force against those nations, organizations, or persons he determines planned, authorized, committed, or aided" the 9/11 attacks.[15] The White House wanted Congress to authorize the President "to

14. Fisher, Nazi Saboteurs on Trial, at 138–44.
15. 115 Stat. 224 (2001).

deter and pre-empt any future acts of terrorism or aggression against the United States."[16] Congress declined to grant that authority. Instead, the administration language appears in a "whereas clause" at the top of the statute: "the President has authority under the Constitution to take action to deter and prevent acts of international terrorism against the United States." Other than the significant change from "pre-empt" to "prevent," the whereas language appears before the section that authorizes the use of military force.

U.S. intelligence connected 9/11 to al Qaeda, a terrorist organization led by Osama bin Laden with the assistance of the Taliban regime in Afghanistan. Al Qaeda had been linked to earlier terrorist attacks, including the bombing of U.S. embassies in Tanzania and Kenya in 1998, and the attack on the *U.S.S. Cole* in Yemen two years later. The Taliban, a fundamentalist Islamic sect, banned television, popular music, and dancing and required men to leave their beards untrimmed. Taliban rule prohibited women from working outside their home, except in health care, and closed schools to girls. Women had to wear a head-to-toe garment (burqa) in public and could not ride in a vehicle unless accompanied by a male relative.

In a speech to Congress on September 20, 2001, President Bush described al Qaeda's presence in more than 60 countries. Their members were brought to places like Afghanistan for training in the tactics of terror. Bush issued an ultimatum to the Taliban: "Deliver to United States authorities all the leaders of al Qaeda who hide in your land. Release all foreign nationals, including American citizens, you have unjustly imprisoned." He also directed the Taliban to immediately close every training camp in Afghanistan and give U.S. forces access to the camps to assure that they were no longer operating.[17]

After the Taliban rejected those conditions, the stage was set for U.S. military action. At the time of the U.S. intervention, Afghanistan was in the midst of a civil war, with the Northern Alliance (composed primarily of Tajiks and Uzbeks) fighting against the Taliban. To prepare for military operations, Bush sent a team of covert CIA paramilitary officers into Afghanistan, carrying cash to enlist the support of members of the Northern Alliance.[18] The United States also needed forces on the ground to direct air strikes.

On October 7, 2001, President Bush addressed the nation on military action in Afghanistan. The purpose of military action, he said, was "to dis-

16. 147 Cong. Rec. S9950–51 (daily ed., October 1, 2001).
17. 37 Weekly Compilation of Presidential Documents 1348.
18. Bob Woodward, Bush at War 139–54 (2002).

rupt the use of Afghanistan as a terrorist base of operations and to attack the military capability of the Taliban regime."[19] Several allies, including Great Britain, Australia, Canada, Germany, and France, pledged forces. More than 40 countries granted air transit or landing rights. While conducting air strikes, the United States also dropped food, medicine, and supplies to the Afghans.

Two days later, Bush sent a letter to congressional leaders on combat activities in Afghanistan. He said he took the actions "pursuant to my constitutional authority to conduct U.S. foreign relations as Commander in Chief and Chief Executive."[20] For some reason, the legal authority he cited consisted only of what he considered to be constitutional grants while ignoring the authority in P.L. 107-40, the Use of Force Act, which had provided him with specific statutory authority to use military action against those responsible for 9/11. Bush referred to P.L. 107-40, but only for reporting purposes and as a source of "support," not authority:

> I am providing this report as part of my efforts to keep the Congress informed, consistent with the War Powers Resolution and Public Law 107-40. . . . I appreciate the continuing support of Congress, including its enactment of Public Law 107-40, in these actions to protect the security of the United States of America and its citizens, civilian and military, here and abroad.[21]

Northern Alliance forces captured Kabul, the capital of Afghanistan, on November 12, 2001. Other regions of the country gradually fell, leaving small remnants of Taliban and al Qaeda forces operating throughout Afghanistan, particularly in the south and near the border with Pakistan. After the fall of Kabul, delegates of the major Afghan factions met in Bonn, Germany, to sign an agreement for an interim government. Hamid Karzai, a Pashtun from the south, was selected as President. Ambitious plans for the reconstruction of Afghanistan were delayed, in part because of security problems outside Kabul. With the new Afghan government unable to exercise power throughout the country, fundamentalist Islamic leaders in the south began to reassert their control. The pattern in Afghanistan—a quick military victory with little follow-through afterward—would reappear in Iraq.

19. 37 Weekly Compilation of Presidential Documents 1432.
20. Id. at 1447.
21. Id. at 1448.

War against Iraq

After the military victory in Afghanistan, Bush considered military action against Iraq, eventually persuading Congress to pass the Iraq Resolution of October 2002 that granted him authority to use "the Armed Forces of the United States as he determines to be necessary and appropriate in order to (1) defend the national security of the United States against the continuing threat posed by Iraq; and (2) enforce all relevant United Nations Security Council resolutions regarding Iraq." It would be incorrect to say that Congress decided on war. It decided only that President Bush should decide. Military operations, which began on March 19, 2003, were completed within a month.

Following the swift military triumph, teams of experts conducted careful searches to discover the weapons of mass destruction that President Bush offered as the principal justification for war. He claimed that the weapons represented a direct and immediate threat. Months after hostilities had ended, little evidence had been found nor was there much reason to expect anything significant to emerge. Stories began to circulate that perhaps the Bush administration had misled allies, Congress, and the American public.

However, charges of exaggeration and hype had surrounded administration efforts for the past year. Executive officials had been unable to present a persuasive, credible, or consistent case for war. Claims were exploded on a regular basis by the press. In justifying war in that manner, plans for a stable, functioning Iraqi civil society seemed to be an afterthought. Having proved itself skilled in military combat, the Bush administration was unprepared for predictable looting and violence. After the experience in Afghanistan, it should have been obvious that a military victory had to be followed quickly by a secure environment and visible reconstruction efforts. For its part, Congress seemed incapable of analyzing a presidential proposal and protecting its institutional powers. The decision to go to war cast a dark shadow over the health of U.S. political institutions and the celebrated system of democratic debate and checks and balances.

Making the Case for War

When the administration first began talking about war against Iraq, White House spokesman Ari Fleischer cautioned on a number of occasions that President Bush was not rushing into war. Instead, he was described as a deliberate man who moved with great care. On August 21, 2002, President Bush called himself "a patient man. And when I say I'm a patient man, I mean I'm a patient man, and that we will look at all options, and we will consider all technologies available to us and diplomacy and intelligence."[22]

A war plan, the administration emphasized, was not "on the President's desk."[23] At that same press conference on August 21, Bush noted that "there is this kind of intense speculation that seems to be going on, a kind of a—I don't know how you would describe it. It's kind of a churning—." Secretary of Defense Donald Rumsfeld, standing next to him, supplied the missing word: "frenzy." Bush agreed. The country was too preoccupied, he said, with military action against Iraq.

Yet within five days, the administration adopted a frenzied mode. Vice President Dick Cheney delivered a forceful speech that offered a single option: going to war. He warned that Saddam Hussein would "fairly soon" have nuclear weapons, and that it would be useless to seek a Security Council resolution requiring Iraq to submit to weapons inspectors. Hussein's threat, Cheney said, made preemptive attack against Iraq imperative.[24] The press interpreted his speech as "ruling out anything short of an attack."[25] Newspaper editorials concluded that Cheney's speech "left little room for measures short of the destruction of Saddam Hussein's regime through preemptive military action."[26] On September 6, two reporters for the *Washington Post* underscored the abrupt transition: "This week's frenzy of attention to Iraq was entirely generated by a White House whose occupants returned from the August recess anxious and ready to push the debate to a new level."[27] Where were the options being weighed by Bush?

In that first month, the administration had not yet produced a united front. Secretary of State Colin Powell, in a September 1 interview with BBC, recommended that weapons inspectors should return to Iraq as a "first step" in resolving the dispute with Iraq. Ari Fleischer, asked whether Powell's statement signaled a conflict within the administration, told reporters that Cheney and Powell agreed on fundamentals: "that arms inspectors in Iraq

22. 38 Weekly Compilation of Presidential Documents 1393–94.

23. Elizabeth Bumiller, "U.S. Must Act First to Battle Terror, Bush Tells Cadets," New York Times, June 2, 2002, at A1.

24. Elizabeth Bumiller and James Dao, "Cheney Says Peril of a Nuclear Iraq Justifies Attack," New York Times, August 27, 2002, at A1.

25. Dana Milbank, "Cheney Says Iraqi Strike Is Justified," Washington Post, August 27, 2002, at A1.

26. "Mr. Cheney on Iraq" (Editorial), Washington Post, August 27, 2002, at A14.

27. Dan Balz and Dana Milbank, "Iraq Policy Shift Follows Pattern," Washington Post, September 6, 2002, at A19.

are a means to an end, and the end is knowledge that Iraq has lived up to its promises that it made to end the Gulf War, that it has in fact disarmed, that it does not possess weapons of mass destruction."[28] However, the conflict within the administration was evident. Cheney had already announced that Iraq *did* possess weapons of mass destruction.

On September 3, Senate Minority Leader Trent Lott (R-Miss.) acknowledged the disarray within the administration: "I do think that we're going to have to get a more coherent message together."[29] Asked whether he was comfortable with the White House's presentation of the case for war against Iraq, he responded gamely: "I'd like to have a couple more days before I respond to that."[30]

The meaning of "regime change" changed several times. On April 4, 2002, in an interview with a British television network, Bush said: "I made up my mind that Saddam needs to go. . . . The policy of my Government is that he goes. . . . [T]he policy of my Government is that Saddam Hussein not be in power."[31] Clear enough. On August 1, he stated that the "policy of my Government . . . is regime change—for a reason. Saddam Hussein is a man who poisons his own people, who threatens his neighbors, who develops weapons of mass destruction."[32] Without equivocation, Hussein had to go.

A different view of regime change appeared on September 12 when President Bush addressed the United Nations. After cataloguing Saddam Hussein's noncompliance with Security Council resolutions, apparently building a case for regime change and military operations, Bush then laid down five conditions for a peaceful resolution. If Iraq wanted to avoid war, it would have to immediately and unconditionally pledge to remove or destroy all weapons of mass destruction, end all support for terrorism, cease persecution of its civilian population, release or account for all Gulf War personnel, and immediately end all illicit trade outside the oil-for-food program.[33] The underlying message: If Iraq complied with those demands, Saddam Hussein could stay in power. On October 21, after Congress had passed the Iraq Resolution, Bush again said that Hussein could stay. He

28. Dana Milbank, "No Conflict on Iraq Policy, Fleischer Says," Washington Post, September 3, 2002, at A14.

29. Alison Mitchell and David E. Sanger, "Bush to Put Case for Action in Iraq to Key Lawmakers," New York Times, September 4, 2002, at A1.

30. Helen Dewar and Mike Allen, "Senators Wary about Action against Iraq," Washington Post, September 4, 2002, at A16.

31. 38 Weekly Compilation of Presidential Documents 573.

32. Id. at 1295.

33. Id. at 1532.

announced that if Hussein complied with every UN mandate, "that in itself will signal the regime has changed."[34] Saddam Hussein could stay if he changed.

After the September 12 UN speech, offering peace to Iraq if it complied with the five demands, Iraq agreed four days later to unconditional inspections. Given Iraq's record since 1991, there was good cause to be skeptical of its promises. Its sincerity could have been tested by sending inspection teams to learn—on the ground—whether Iraq would give full access to buildings and presidential palaces. Instead, the administration began to make light of inspections. Pentagon spokeswoman Victoria Clarke warned that inspections would be difficult if not impossible to carry out.[35] If so, why did Bush go to the United Nations and place that demand on Iraq and the Security Council?

On September 26, during a campaign speech in Houston, Texas, Bush remarked, "This is a guy that tried to kill my dad at one time."[36] The comment made some wonder whether the impulse for war reflected careful considerations of national security or was, instead, a "family grudge match."[37] The administration offered many reasons for war, often going beyond concerns about weapons of mass destruction. Senator Paul Sarbanes (D-Md.) questioned the claims by Secretary Powell that Iraq, to avoid military action, would have to comply with a number of UN resolutions, including one directed against prohibited trade. Sarbanes asked: "Are we prepared to go to war to make sure they comply with UN resolutions on illicit trade outside the oil for food program? Will we take military action or go to war in order to make them release or account for all Gulf war personnel whose fate is still unknown? Would we do that?"[38] No answer was forthcoming. Senator Richard Lugar (R-Ind.) criticized the undifferentiated laundry list of charges against Saddam Hussein, such as brutality toward his own people. In conversations with top officials of the administration, Lugar was satisfied that they recognized that such conduct could not justify a U.S. war.[39]

34. David E. Sanger, "Bush Declares U.S. Is Using Diplomacy to Disarm Hussein," New York Times, October 22, 2002, at A15.

35. Todd A. Purdum and David Firestone, "Chief U.N. Inspector Backs U.S., Demanding Full Iraq Disclosure," New York Times, October 5, 2002, at A1.

36. 38 Weekly Compilation of Presidential Documents 1633.

37. Mike Allen, "Bush's Words Can Go to the Blunt Edge of Trouble," Washington Post, September 29, 2002, at A22.

38. Todd S. Purdum, "The U.S. Case against Iraq; Counting Up the Reasons," New York Times, October 1, 2002, at A14.

39. David E. Sanger and Carl Hulse, "Bush Appears to Soften Tone on Iraq Action," New York Times, October 2, 2002, at A13.

In public statements, however, the administration did not differentiate between major and minor concerns. Various claims seemed to be on the same level.

Going to war is meant to be a serious enterprise, requiring consistency, clarity, and coherence. In an op-ed piece in the *Washington Post* on October 11, 2002, Michael Kinsley acknowledged that ambiguity can be useful in dealing with other nations. Sending mixed signals can keep an enemy off balance. Yet Kinsley concluded: "The cloud of confusion that surrounds Bush's Iraq policy is not tactical. It's the real thing. And the dissembling is aimed at the American citizenry, not at Saddam Hussein." Kinsley said that arguments that "stumble into each other like drunks are not serious. Washington is abuzz with the 'real reason' this or that subgroup of the administration wants this war."[40]

Enlisting Legislative Support

Initially, the administration announced that President Bush did not need authority from Congress to mount an offensive war against Iraq. The White House Counsel's office offered a broad reading to the President's power as Commander in Chief and argued that the 1991 Iraq Resolution provided continuing military authority to the President, transferring the authority neatly from father to son.[41] As explained in the previous chapter, such arguments would allow Congress to shift, on a permanent basis, its constitutional authority to the Security Council.[42] The framers made the President Commander in Chief, not a monarch.

The White House also claimed that Congress, by passing the Iraq Liberation Act of 1998, had already approved U.S. military action against Iraq for violations of Security Council resolutions.[43] The statute begins by itemizing a number of congressional findings about Iraq: the invasion of Iran and Kuwait, the killing of Kurds, the use of chemical weapons against civilians, and other offenses. It supported, as a legally nonbinding "sense of Congress," efforts to remove Saddam Hussein from power and replace him with a democratic government. The law states that none of its provisions

40. Michael Kinsley, "War for Dummies," Washington Post, October 11, 2002, at A37.
41. Mike Allen and Juliet Eilperin, "Bush Aides Say Iraq War Needs No Hill Vote," Washington Post, August 26, 2002, at A1.
42. See also Louis Fisher, "The Road to Iraq," Legal Times, September 2, 2002, at 34.
43. "Bush Rejects Hill Limits on Resolution Allowing War," Washington Post, October 2, 2002, at A12.

"shall be construed to authorize or otherwise speak to the use of United States Armed Forces (except as provided in section 4(a)(2)) in carrying out this Act."[44] That section authorized up to $97 million in military supplies to Iraqi opposition groups as part of the transition to democracy in Iraq. By its explicit terms, the statute did not authorize war.

For one reason or another, Bush decided in early September 2002 to seek authorization from Congress. On several Sunday talk shows on September 8, administration officials abandoned the unilateralist rhetoric and began building a case for a broad coalition. Cheney, having advocated preemptive strikes against Iraq a few weeks earlier, now embraced an entirely different strategy: "We're working together to build support with the American people, with the Congress, as many have suggested we should. And we're also, as many have suggested we should, going to the United Nations."[45]

Although the administration had debated going to war against Iraq ever since 9/11, Congress was expected to act quickly. According to one newspaper story, White House officials "have said that their patience with Congress would not extend much past the current session." The administration wanted Congress to pass an authorizing resolution before it adjourned for the November elections. There would be little time for independent legislative debate and analysis.

Senator Robert C. Byrd deplored "the war fervor, the drums of war, the bugles of war, the clouds of war—this war hysteria has blown in like a hurricane."[46] What explained the shift from a measured policy in August to an accelerated schedule a month later? White House Chief of Staff Andrew Card gave an interesting reason for waiting until September to advocate military action against Iraq: "From a marketing point of view, you don't introduce new products in August."[47] A careless, flippant remark or an inadvertent disclosure of motivation?

Bush was unable to rely on precedents established by his father. In 1990, after Iraq had invaded Kuwait, the administration did not ask Congress for authority before the November elections. Instead, it first went to the Security Council and requested a resolution to authorize military operations, which passed on November 29. Only in January 1991, after lawmakers returned, did they debate and pass legislation to authorize war

44. 112 Stat. 3181, § 8 (1998).
45. Mike Allen, "War Cabinet Argues for Iraq Attack," Washington Post, September 9, 2002, at A1.
46. 148 Cong. Rec. S8966 (daily ed., September 20, 2002).
47. Dana Milbank, "Democrats Question Iraq Timing," Washington Post, September 16, 2002, at A6.

against Iraq. Senate Majority Leader Tom Daschle (D-S.D.) suggested that Bush would have an easier time getting congressional support if he first gained Security Council approval, but the administration opposed any delays.[48] Congress had to act and act quickly. There was no constitutional requirement for Congress to wait until the Security Council met and voted, but acting in the months before the November elections placed lawmakers in a subordinate position.

Democrats, unable to develop a counterstrategy, appeared to favor a prompt vote on the Iraq Resolution to get that issue "off" the table. It was reported that Senator Daschle hoped to expedite action on the Iraq Resolution "to focus on his party's core message highlighting economic distress before the November midterm elections."[49] Senator John Edwards (D-N.C.) counseled quick action: "In a short period of time, Congress will have dealt with Iraq and we'll be on to other issues."[50]

That approach had multiple drawbacks, both moral and practical. Could Democrats credibly authorize a war merely to draw attention to their domestic agenda? That seems unconscionable. As noted by Senator Mark Dayton (D-Minn.), trying to gain "political advantage in a midterm election is a shameful reason to hurry decisions of this magnitude."[51] Second, voting on the Iraq Resolution could never erase the White House's advantage in controlling the headlines, if not through the Iraq Resolution then through ongoing, cliffhanging negotiations with the UN Security Council. Third, although these Democrats said they wanted to put the issue of war against Iraq behind them, it would always be in front.

Legislative action before the November elections invited partisan exploitation of the war issue. Several Republican nominees in congressional contests made a political weapon out of Iraq, comparing their "strong stand" on Iraq to "weak" positions by Democratic campaigners. Some of the key races in the nation appeared to turn on what candidates were saying about Iraq.[52] Because of the steady focus on the war, Democrats were unable to

48. Bradley Graham, "Cheney, Tenet Brief Leaders of Hill on Iraq," Washington Post, September 6, 2002, at A1.

49. David Firestone, "Liberals Object to Bush Policy on Iraq Attack," New York Times, September 28, 2002, at A1.

50. Dana Milbank, "In President's Speeches, Iraq Dominates, Economy Fades," Washington Post, September 25, 2002, at A6.

51. Mark Drayton, "Go Slow on Iraq," Washington Post, September 28, 2002, at A23.

52. Jim VandeHei, "GOP Nominees Make Iraq a Political Weapon," Washington Post, September 18, 2002, at A1.

redirect the political agenda to corporate crime, the state of the stock market, and the struggling economy.[53]

The partisan flavor intensified when President Bush, in a speech in Trenton, N.J., on September 23, said that the Democratic Senate "is more interested in special interests in Washington and not interested in the security of the American people."[54] That was a stunning charge, invoking national security to brand Democrats as corrupt if not traitorous. Recognizing that it might have stepped over the line, the administration quickly explained that Bush's remark was delivered in the context of the legislative delay on the Department of Homeland Security, but Democrats faulted Bush for using the war as leverage in the House and Senate races.[55]

After the Trenton speech, Democrats could have announced that Bush had so politicized and poisoned the debate on the Iraq Resolution that it could not be considered with the care and seriousness it deserved. Daschle, in particular, could have used his position as Senate Majority Leader to delay a vote until after the elections. Perhaps he lacked the votes in the Senate Democratic Caucus to prevail. If he failed to rally his troops, he would have highlighted his weakness as a leader and advertised the divisions within his own ranks. In the end, however, as evidenced by the vote on the Iraq Resolution, Senate Democrats were divided anyway. Several Senate Democrats criticized Daschle for working too closely with Bush on the Iraq Resolution and getting nothing in return. Bush's comments on September 23, they said, made it look like Daschle was being "played for a fool."[56]

Unsubstantiated Executive Claims

Bush and other top officials invited members of Congress to sessions where they would receive confidential information about the threat from Iraq, but the lawmakers said they heard little that was new. After one of the briefings, Senator Bob Graham (D-Fla.) remarked, "I did not receive any new

53. Dana Milbank, "Democrats Question Iraq Timing," Washington Post, September 16, 2002, at A1.

54. 38 Weekly Compilation of Presidential Documents 1598.

55. Carl Hulse and Todd S. Purdum, "Daschle Defends Democrats' Stand on Security of U.S.," New York Times, September 26, 2002, at A1.

56. Jim VandeHei, "Daschle Angered by Bush Statement," Washington Post, September 26, 2002, at A6.

information."[57] House Minority Whip Nancy Pelosi (D-Calif.), who also served as ranking Democrat on the House Intelligence Committee, announced that she knew of "no information that the threat is so imminent from Iraq" that Congress could not wait until January to vote on an authorizing resolution.[58] None of the charges against Iraq in Bush's address to the UN were new. After a "top secret" briefing by Defense Secretary Rumsfeld in a secure room in the Capitol, Senator John McCain (R-Ariz.) soon rose and walked out, saying "It was a joke."[59]

The administration tried repeatedly to establish a connection between Iraq and al Qaeda, but the reports could never be substantiated. On September 25, Bush claimed that Saddam Hussein and al Qaeda "work in concert."[60] On the following day, he claimed that the Iraqi regime "has longstanding and continuing ties to terrorist organizations, and there are Al Qaida terrorists inside Iraq."[61] Ari Fleischer tried to play down Bush's remark, saying he was talking about what he feared *could* occur.[62] Did the ties and links exist, as Bush claimed, or were they merely future possibilities?

Senator Joseph Biden (D-Del.), after attending a classified briefing that talked about the relationship between Iraq and al Qaeda, said that credible evidence had not been presented.[63] There was possible al Qaeda activity in the northeastern part of Iraq—the community of Ansar al-Islam—but that was Kurdish territory made semiautonomous because of American and British flights over the no-fly zones. Saddam Hussein was not in a position to do anything about Ansar. Besides, members of al Qaeda are present in some 60 countries. Presence alone would not justify military force.

Allies in Europe, active in investigating al Qaeda and radical Islamic cells, could find no evidence of links between Iraq and al Qaeda. Interviews with top investigative magistrates, prosecutors, police, and intelligence officials could uncover no information to support the claims by the

57. Mike Allen and Karen DeYoung, "Bush to Seek Hill Approval on Iraq War," Washington Post, September 5, 2002, at A1.

58. Jim VandeHei and Juliet Eilperin, "Democrats Unconvinced on Iraq War," Washington Post, September 11, 2002, at A1.

59. Jim VandeHei, "Iraq Briefings: Don't Ask, Don't Tell," Washington Post, September 15, 2002, at A4.

60. 38 Weekly Compilation of Presidential Documents 1619.

61. Id. at 1625.

62. Mike Allen, "Bush Asserts That Al Qaeda Has Links to Iraq's Hussein," Washington Post, September 26, 2002, at A29.

63. Karen De Young, "Unwanted Debate on Iraq-Al Qaeda Links Revived," Washington Post, September 27, 2002, at A19.

Bush administration. Investigative officials in Spain, France, and Germany, after dismissing a connection between Iraq and al Qaeda, worried that a war against Iraq would increase the terrorist threat rather than diminish it.[64]

On September 27, Secretary Rumsfeld announced that the administration had "bulletproof" evidence of Iraq's links to al Qaeda. He said that declassified intelligence reports, showing the presence of senior members of al Qaeda in Baghdad in "recent periods," were "factual" and "exactly accurate." It sounded like solid evidence. However, when reporters sought to substantiate his claim, officials offered no details to back up the assertions. Having claimed bulletproof support, Rumsfeld admitted that the information was "not beyond a reasonable doubt." Senator Chuck Hagel (R-Nebr.) cautioned Secretary of State Powell: "To say, 'Yes, I know there is evidence there, but I don't want to tell you any more about it,' that does not encourage any of us. Nor does it give the American public a heck of a lot of faith that, in fact, what anyone is saying is true."[65]

In his speech to the nation on October 7, on the eve of the congressional vote, President Bush said that Iraq "has trained Al Qaida members in bombmaking and poisons and deadly gases."[66] Intelligence officials, however, played down the reliability of those reports.[67] After the vote, the administration promoted a story about Mohamed Atta, the leader of the 9/11 attacks, meeting with an Iraqi intelligence officer in Prague in April 2001. Czech President Vaclav Havel and the Czech intelligence service said that there was no evidence that the meeting ever took place. CIA Director George Tenet told Congress that his agency had no information that could confirm the meeting.[68]

On February 11, 2003, Secretary Powell cited an audiotape believed to be of Osama bin Laden as evidence that he was "in partnership with Iraq."[69] The tape offered no support for that interpretation. It specifically

64. Sebastian Rotella, "Allies Find No Links between Iraq, Al Qaeda," Los Angeles Times, November 4, 2002, at A1.
65. Eric Schmitt, "Rumsfeld Says U.S. Has 'Bulletproof' Evidence of Iraq's Links to Al Qaeda," New York Times, September 28, 2002, at A8.
66. 38 Weekly Compilation of Presidential Documents 1717.
67. Karen De Young, "Bush Cites Urgent Iraqi Threat," Washington Post, October 8, 2002, at A21.
68. James Risen, "Prague Discounts an Iraqi Meeting," New York Times, October 21, 2002, at A1; James Risen, "How Politics and Rivalries Fed Suspicions of a Meeting," New York Times, October 21, 2002, at A9; Peter S. Green, "Havel Denies Telephoning U.S. on Iraq Meeting," New York Times, October 23, 2002, at A11.
69. Dan Eggen and Susan Schmidt, "Bin Laden Calls Iraqis to Arms," Washington Post, February 12, 2003, at A1, A14.

criticized "pagan regimes" and the "apostasy" practiced by socialist governments like Iraq. In a military contest between the United States and Iraq, the tape certainly supported Iraq, but that was not evidence of partnership. Al Qaeda merely detested the United States more than Iraq. In an op-ed article for the *Washington Post* on February 13, Richard Cohen wondered why Powell had to "gild the lily. The case for war is a good one." He reminded Powell that in the war against Vietnam, the U.S. government's exaggerations and decisions eventually "lost the confidence of the people." The Bush administration, Cohen said, had a habit of tickling the facts and expunging caveats, doubts, and conditional clauses from the record.[70] An editorial in the *New York Times* warned that there was "no need for the administration to jeopardize its own credibility with unproved claims about an alliance between Iraq and Al Qaeda."[71] Nevertheless, on May 1, 2003, while standing on the deck of the *Abraham Lincoln* carrier to announce military victory over Iraq, Bush announced: "We've removed an ally of Al Qaida."[72]

The administration released various accounts to demonstrate why Iraq posed an imminent threat. On September 7, 2002, President Bush cited a report by the International Atomic Energy Agency (IAEA) that the Iraqis were "6 months away from developing a weapon. I don't know what more evidence we need."[73] More evidence was needed because the report he referred to did not exist.[74] In his October 7 speech, President Bush claimed that satellite photographs revealed that Sadam Hussein was "rebuilding facilities at sites that have been part of his nuclear program in the past."[75] The administration decided to declassify two before-and-after photos of the Al Furat manufacturing facility.[76] Five busloads of 200 reporters descended on the site and received a 90-minute tour by Iraqi generals. The reporters found few clues to indicate a weapons program.[77]

The visit by reporters was not decisive. They had neither time nor

70. Richard Cohen, "Powellian Propaganda?" Washington Post, February 13, 2003, at A31.
71. "Elusive Qaeda Connections" (Editorial), New York Times, February 14, 2003, at A30.
72. 39 Weekly Compilation of Presidential Documents 517.
73. 38 Weekly Compilation of Presidential Documents 1518.
74. Dana Milbank, "For Bush, Facts Are Malleable," Washington Post, October 22, 2002, at A1, A22.
75. 38 Weekly Compilation of Presidential Documents 1718.
76. "Al Furat Manufacturing Facility, Iraq," Washington Post, October 8, 2002, at A21.
77. John Burns, "Iraq Tour of Suspected Sites Gives Few Clues on Weapons," New York Times, October 13, 2002, at A1.

expertise to explore all the buildings and examine them carefully. But it was equally true that satellite photos could not penetrate buildings and analyze their interiors. Only a ground search by experienced inspectors could do that. When the UN inspection teams reached Iraq in November 2002, they could find no evidence of a nuclear weapons program at Al Furat or anywhere else in Iraq.[78]

The Bush administration claimed that Iraq had bought aluminum tubes and planned to use them to enrich uranium to produce nuclear weapons. Specialists from UN inspection teams concluded that the specifications of the tubes were consistent with tubes used for rockets. The tubes could have been modified to serve as centrifuges for enriching uranium, but the modifications would have had to be substantial. Moreover, there was no evidence that Iraq had purchased materials needed for centrifuges, such as motors, metal caps, and special magnets.[79]

On February 5, 2003, in his statement to the UN Security Council, Secretary Powell laid out his case for going to war against Iraq, citing what he considered to be evidence of weapons of mass destruction. He claimed that Iraq had mobile production facilities "used to make biological agents."[80] In a matter of months, he said, these mobile facilities "can produce a quantity of biological poison equal to the entire amount that Iraq claimed to have produced in the years prior to the Gulf War."[81] After hostilities were over, U.S. forces discovered two mobile labs in Iraq, but it was uncertain what they had been used for.[82] A May 28, 2003, report by the intelligence community, discussed later in this chapter, found nothing definitive.

The British government released a 19-page report entitled "Iraq: Its Infrastructure of Concealment, Deception and Intimidation," posting it on No. 10 Downing Street's Web site. It appeared to be a thorough analysis prepared

78. "Nuclear Inspection Chief Reports Finding No New Weapons," New York Times, January 28, 2003, at A11.

79. Michael R. Gordon, "Agency Challenges Evidence against Iraq Cited by Bush," New York Times, January 10, 2003, at A10; Joby Warrick, "U.S. Claim on Iraqi Nuclear Program Is Called into Question," Washington Post, January 24, 2003, at A1.

80. Michael Dobbs, "Powell Lays Out Case against Iraq," Washington Post, February 6, 2003, at A1, A25.

81. Id. at A25.

82. Walter Pincus and Michael Dobbs, "Suspected Bioweapon Mobile Lab Recovered," Washington Post, May 7, 2003, at A1; "A Suspected Weapons Lab Is Found in Northern Iraq," New York Times, May 10, 2003, at A9; Judith Miller, "Trailer Is a Mobile Lab Capable of Turning Out Bioweapons, a Team Says," New York Times, May 11, 2003, at 11; Judith Miller and William J. Broad, "U.S. Analysts Link Iraq Labs to Germ Arms," New York Times, May 21, 2003, at A1.

by the British intelligence agencies. In fact, the report had its own problems with concealment and deception. In February 2003, the British government admitted that much of the report had been lifted from magazines and academic journals, some of it verbatim. Spelling and punctuation errors in the originals were faithfully reproduced in the government's report. Although the government claimed that the report contained "up-to-date details of Iraq's network of intelligence and security," much of it was based on an article by a postgraduate student who focused on events a dozen years old, in the 1990–1991 period.[83] After initially defending the report, the British government in June 2003 conceded that including the student's article was "regrettable."[84]

In his State of the Union address on January 28, 2003, President Bush said that the British government "has learned that Saddam Hussein recently sought significant quantities of uranium from Africa."[85] The British government relied on evidence that its intelligence agencies thought unreliable. The documents turned out to be a fabrication, containing crude errors that undermined their credibility.[86] A U.S. official admitted: "We fell for it."[87] The point was not an unfortunate mistake but rather the willingness of the administration to go public with information that was tenuous and suspect.

Over the space of several weeks in July 2003, the Bush administration offered conflicting explanations of how the uranium claim was included in the State of the Union address. On July 7, the White House acknowledged that President Bush should not have alleged that Iraq had sought to buy uranium in Africa.[88] The administration then blamed the CIA for the error, prompting CIA Director George Tenet to draft a statement accepting responsibility.[89] Two days later, Defense Secretary Rumsfeld and National Security Adviser Condi Rice weighed in by arguing that Bush's claim in the State of the Union address was "technically correct" because the British govern-

83. Sarah Lyall, "Britain Admits That Much of Its Report on Iraq Came from Magazines," New York Times, February 8, 2003, at A8; Glenn Frankel, "Blair Acknowledges Flaws in Iraq Dossier," Washington Post, February 8, 2003, at A15.

84. Jane Wardell, "Blair Aide Concedes Error on Iraq Dossier," Washington Post, June 26, 2003, at A20.

85. 39 Weekly Compilation of Presidential Documents 115.

86. Joby Warrick, "Some Evidence on Iraq Called Fake," Washington Post, March 8, 2003, at A1.

87. Id. at A18.

88. Walter Pincus, "White House Backs Off Claim on Iraqi Buy," Washington Post, July 8, 2003, at A1.

89. Walter Pincus, "Bush, Rice Blame CIA for Iraq Error," Washington Post, July 12, 2003, at A1.

ment believed it to be true.[90] If technically correct, why the White House apology?

Initially, in June, Rice said that "no one in our circles knew that there were doubts and suspicions this might be a forgery."[91] That position was undermined on July 23 when Stephen Hadley, Rice's deputy in the National Security Council, revealed that the CIA had sent him two memos in October 2002 warning that evidence about Iraqi efforts to obtain uranium in Africa was weak.[92] It was now Hadley's turn to take the blame. At a July 30 news conference, when asked about the erroneous uranium claim in the State of the Union address, President Bush responded: "I take personal responsibility for everything I say."[93] Rice also stated that she felt "personal responsibility."[94] With so many people responsible, no one was.

White House efforts to put the story to bed inevitably backfired. On July 18, 2003, a "senior administration official" held a background briefing on weapons of mass destruction (WMDs) in Iraq. A reporter asked the official why Rice was unaware that the State Department, in a National Intelligence Estimate prepared by intelligence agencies, had expressed concerns about the quality of the intelligence supporting the uranium claim. The official said she "did not read footnotes in a 90-page document."[95] Yet a reporter told the official that the State Department analysis was not buried in a footnote but appeared in "the very first paragraph of the key judgments."[96]

Voting on the Iraq Resolution

In the midst of confusing and contradictory claims about Iraqi WMDs, Congress was under pressure to pass the Iraq Resolution to authorize mil-

---

90. James Risen, "Bush Aides Now Say Claim on Uranium Was Accurate," New York Times, July 14, 2003, at A7.

91. Walter Pincus, "CIA Says It Cabled Key Data to White House," Washington Post, June 13, 2003, at A16.

92. David E. Sanger and Judith Miller, "National Security Aide Says He's to Blame for Speech Error," New York Times, July 23, 2002, at A11; Dana Milbank and Walter Pincus, "Bush Aides Disclose Warnings from CIA," July 23, 2003, at A1.

93. Richard W. Stevenson, "President Denies He Oversold Case for War with Iraq," New York Times, July 31, 2003, at A1.

94. Id. at A11.

95. "Senior Administration Official Holds Background Briefing on Weapons of Mass Destruction in Iraq, as Released by the White House," July 18, 2003, at 10; www.fas.org/irp/news/2003/07/wh071803.html.

96. Id. at 16; see also Dana Milbank and Dana Priest, "Warning in Iraq Report Unread," Washington Post, July 19, 2003, at A1, A13.

itary force. There was little doubt that President Bush would gain approval in the Republican House. The question was whether the vote would divide along party lines. Some of the partisan issue blurred when House Minority Leader Dick Gephardt (D-Mo.) broke ranks with many in his party and announced support for a slightly redrafted resolution. He said: "We had to go through this, putting politics aside, so we have a chance to get a consensus that will lead the country in the right direction."[97]

Of course, politics could not be put aside. Even when leaders of the two parties and the two branches appealed for nonpartisan or bipartisan conduct, their comments were generally viewed as calculated to have some partisan benefit. Gephardt's interest in running for the presidency was well known, as was Daschle's and that of several other members of Congress. Democratic Senators John Edwards and Joseph Lieberman, both interested in a 2004 bid for the presidency, endorsed the Iraq Resolution. Senator John Kerry, about to announce his bid for the presidency, initially expressed doubts about the resolution but later voted for it.[98] One Democratic lawmaker concluded that Gephardt, by supporting Bush, had "inoculated Democrats against the charge that they are antiwar and obstructionist."[99]

Why were Democrats so anxious about being seen as antiwar? There was no evidence that the public, in any broad sense, supported immediate war against Iraq. A *New York Times* poll published on October 7, 2002, indicated that 69 percent of Americans believed that Bush should be paying more attention to the economy. Although support was high for military action (with 67 percent approving U.S. military action against Iraq with the goal of removing Hussein from power), when it was asked, "Should the U.S. take military action against Iraq fairly soon or wait and give the U.N. more time to get weapons inspectors into Iraq?" 63 percent preferred to wait. To the question "Is Congress asking enough questions about President Bush's policy toward Iraq?" only 20 percent said too many, while 51 percent said not enough. Asked whether Bush was more interested in removing Hussein than weapons of mass destruction, 53 percent said Hussein and only 29 said weapons.[100]

97. "For Gephardt, Risks and a Crucial Role," Washington Post, October 3, 2002, at A15.

98. Dan Balz and Jim VandeHei, "Democratic Hopefuls Back Bush on Iraq," Washington Post, September 14, 2002, at A4.

99. David E. Rosenbaum, "United Voice on Iraq Eludes Majority Leader," New York Times, October 4, 2002, at A12.

100. Adam Nagourney and Janet Elder, "Public Says Bush Needs to Pay Heed to Weak Economy," New York Times, October 7, 2002, at A1, A14.

A *Washington Post* story on October 8 described the public's enthusiasm for war against Iraq as "tepid and declining."[101] Americans gave Bush
the benefit of the doubt but were not convinced by his arguments. Because
of those doubts, "support could fade if the conflict in Iraq becomes bloody
and extended."[102] These public attitudes led the *New York Times* to wonder, "Given the cautionary mood of the country, it is puzzling that most
members of Congress seem fearful of challenging the hawkish approach to
Iraq."[103]

The vote on the Iraq Resolution could never be anything other than a
political decision, probably the most important congressional vote of the
year. Inescapably it called for a political judgment. Lawmakers would be
voting on whether to commit as much as $100 billion or $200 billion to a
war stretching over a period of years. Their actions would stabilize or desta-
bilize the Middle East, strengthen or weaken the war against terrorism,
enhance or debase the nation's prestige. Politics would always be present,
as would partisan calculations and strategy.

When the House International Relations Committee reported the resolution, it divided 31 to 11. Democrats on the committee split 10 to 9 in
favoring it. Two Republicans, Jim Leach of Iowa and Ron Paul of Texas,
opposed it. The 47-page committee report consists of only five pages of
text analyzing the resolution.[104] President Bush's speech to the United
Nations occupies another five pages. Twenty-one pages are devoted to an
administration document called "A Decade of Deception and Defiance:
Saddam Hussein's Defiance of the United Nations" (September 12, 2002),
which was prepared as a background paper for Bush's UN speech. Some
of it describes what was supposedly the administration's main concern: the
development of weapons of mass destruction. Other sections focused on
conditions in Iraq that, while deplorable, could hardly justify war: Iraq's
refusal to allow visits by human rights monitors, the expulsion of UN
humanitarian relief workers, violence against women, child labor and forced
labor, the lack of freedom of speech and press, and the refusal to return
to Kuwait state archives and museum pieces.

A key section of the report reads: "The Committee hopes that the use
of military force can be avoided. It believes, however, that providing the

101. Dana Milbank, "With Congress Aboard, Bush Targets a Doubtful Public," Washington Post, October 8, 2002, at A21.
102. Id.
103. "A Nation Wary of War" (Editorial), New York Times, October 8, 2002, at A30.
104. H. Rept. No. 107-721, 107th Cong., 2d Sess. (2002).

President with the authority he needs to use force is the best way to avoid its use. A signal of our Nation's seriousness of purpose and its willingness to use force may yet persuade Iraq to meet its international obligations, and is the best way to persuade members of the Security Council and others in the international community to join us in bringing pressure on Iraq or, if required, in using armed force against it."[105] Thus, the legislation would decide neither for nor against war. That judgment, which the Constitution places in Congress, was left in the hands of the President.

Acting as it did, the House International Relations Committee both authorized military force and hoped it would not be necessary. That kind of calculation recalls the Tonkin Gulf Resolution of 1964. Members of Congress thought that by offering broad, bipartisan support to President Lyndon B. Johnson, war with North Vietnam could be avoided. Like the Iraq Resolution, the legislative vote in 1964 was neither for war nor against it. During Senate debate in 1964, Gaylord Nelson reviewed the statements by his colleagues and noticed that "every Senator who spoke had his own personal interpretation of what the joint resolution means." He found that "there is no agreement in the Senate on what the joint resolution means."[106] To clarify the intent of the resolution, he offered an amendment to state that President Johnson would seek "no extension of the present military conflict" and that "we should continue to attempt to avoid a direct military involvement in the southeast Asian conflict."

Senator J. William Fulbright, floor manager of the resolution, refused to accept the amendment because it would force the two Houses to go to conference to resolve the differences between the versions passed by each chamber. Fulbright didn't want Congress taking another week or so to clarify the resolution. Nevertheless, he felt satisfied that Nelson's amendment expressed "fairly accurately what the President has said would be our policy, and what I stated my understanding was as to our policy." Fulbright believed that the resolution "is calculated to prevent the spread of the war, rather than to spread it."[107] What counts, however, is not what lawmakers say during debate but what the President does with broad statutory authority. The military expansion that began in February 1965 led to the deaths of 58,000 Americans and several million in Southeast Asia.

Congressional debate in 2002 contains some similarities and differences to the Tonkin Gulf Resolution. The House passed the Iraq resolution 296

105. Id. at 4–5.
106. 110 Cong. Rec. 18458 (1964).
107. Id. at 18462.

to 133, compared to the unanimous House vote in 1964. Yet the resolutions are virtually identical in transferring to the President the sole decision to go to war and determine its scope and duration. In each case, lawmakers chose to trust in the President, not in themselves. Instead of acting as the people's representatives and preserving the republican form of government, they gave the President unchecked power.

After the House vote in 2002, Senate Majority Leader Daschle announced his support for the resolution. Although he suggested that Senators might "go back and tie down the language a little bit more if we can," he insisted that "we have got to support this effort. We have got to do it in an enthusiastic and bipartisan way." Placing trust in the President or calling for bipartisanship are not substitutes for independently analyzing the need for military force against another country. Senator Kerry, who had earlier raised substantive arguments against going to war against Iraq, now accepted presidential superiority over Congress: "We are affirming a president's right and responsibility to keep the American people safe, and the president must take that grant of responsibility seriously."[108]

With that interpretation of the Constitution, Congress had little role other than to offer words of encouragement and support to a President who already seemed to possess all the constitutional authority he needed to act single-handedly. Far from being a coequal branch, Congress was distinctly junior varsity. It no longer functioned as an authorizing body. Its task was simply to endorse what the President had already decided.

A similar position appears in Daschle's statement that "it is important for America to speak with one voice at this critical moment."[109] Comparable statements were made by Senators in 1964 when they endorsed the Tonkin Gulf Resolution. Legislators should not consider agreement with the President more important than conscientious and individual allegiance to their constitutional duties. The framers counted on collective judgment, the deliberative process, and checks and balances. All of that is lost when lawmakers decide to join with the President and subordinate their positions to his. A member of Congress takes an oath to support and defend the Constitution, not the President. The experience with the Tonkin Gulf Resolution demonstrated that unity and lockstep decision making do not assure wise policy.

108. Helen Dewar and Juliet Eilperin, "Iraq Resolution Passes Test, Gains Support," Washington Post, October 10, 2002, at A16.
109. Jim VandeHei and Juliet Eilperin, "House Passes Iraq War Resolution," Washington Post, October 11, 2002, at A6.

This issue played out in other contexts. During debate on the Department of Homeland Security, Senator Daschle said he intended "to give the President the benefit of the doubt." His Democratic colleague, Robert Byrd, took sharp exception: "I will not give the benefit of the doubt to the President. I will give the benefit of the doubt to the Constitution."[110] Byrd watched the congressional debate drift from an initial willingness of lawmakers to analyze issues and weigh the merits to wholesale legislative abdication to the President. To Byrd, the fundamental question of why the United States should go to war was replaced by "the mechanics of how best to wordsmith the president's use-of-force resolution in order to give him virtually unchecked authority to commit the nation's military to an unprovoked attack on a sovereign nation." Having followed the arguments presented by Bush and after questioning the top executive branch officials responsible for crafting the resolution, Byrd did not find the threat from Iraq "so great that we must be stampeded to provide such authority to this president just weeks before an election."[111]

Republican Senators Lugar, Hagel, and Specter, after raising serious questions about the Iraq Resolution, decided by October 7 to support it.[112] On October 10, the Senate voted 77 to 23 for the resolution. The only Republican voting against the resolution was Lincoln Chafee of Rhode Island. An Independent, James Jeffords of Vermont, also voted No.

In signing the resolution, President Bush said that "Congress has now authorized the use of force."[113] In a separate statement, he referred to the "resolution of support" and said that the signing of the resolution did not "constitute any change in the long-standing positions of the executive branch on either the President's constitutional authority to use force to deter, prevent, or respond to aggression or other threats to U.S. interests or on the constitutionality of the War Powers Resolution."[114] In March 2003, when he ordered troops into combat, he would cite as authority not the resolution but what he considered to be his independent constitutional powers.

Six members of Congress, along with soldiers and parents, filed a lawsuit to challenge Bush's legal authority to wage war under the Iraq Resolu-

---

110. 148 Cong. Rec. S9187, S9188 (daily ed., September 25, 2002).

111. Robert C. Byrd, "Congress Must Resist the Rush to War," New York Times, October 10, 2002, at A35.

112. Helen Dewar, "Armey, Lugar Reverse Stand on Resolution," Washington Post, October 8, 2002, at A21.

113. 38 Weekly Compilation of Presidential Documents 1777.

114. Id. at 1779.

tion. A district court in Massachusetts held that the dispute involved political questions beyond the authority of the judiciary to resolve: "Absent a clear abdication of this constitutional responsibility by the political branches, the judiciary has no role to play."[115] Only if the political branches were "clearly and resolutely in opposition as to the military policy to be followed by the United States" would the issue pose a question that could be resolved by the courts.[116] Whatever the ambiguity of the Iraq Resolution, "it is clear that Congress has not acted to bind the President with respect to possible military activity in Iraq."[117]

When this decision was appealed, the lawsuit had the support of twelve members of Congress. The First Circuit affirmed the district court ruling, but not on the political question doctrine, which it found "famously murky."[118] Instead, it based its analysis on ripeness: "Diplomatic negotiations, in particular, fluctuate daily. The President has emphasized repeatedly that hostilities still may be averted if Iraq takes certain actions."[119] Although the First Circuit agreed that the "amalgam of powers" involved in war envisage "the joint participation" of Congress and the President in determining "the scale and duration of hostilities,"[120] it found no evidence of the President acting "without apparent congressional authorization, or against congressional opposition."[121]

After Military Victory

On March 19, 2003, President Bush notified the nation on the deployment of combat forces to Iraq.[122] Two days later, he reported to Congress on the commencement of military operations. He based his action on the President's powers under the Constitution, not on statutory authority conferred by Congress. He made reference to the two Iraq Resolutions of 1991 and 2002: "I now inform you that pursuant to my authority as Commander in Chief and consistent with the Authorization for Use of Military Force Against Iraq Resolution (Public Law 102-1) and the Authorization for Use

115. Doe v. Bush, 240 F.Supp.2d 95, 96 (D. Mass. 2002).
116. Id.
117. Id.
118. Doe v. Bush, 323 F.3d 133, 140 (1st Cir. 2003).
119. Id. at 139.
120. Id. at 142 (quoting Massachusetts v. Laird, 451 F.2d 26, 31–32 [1st Cir. 1971]).
121. Id. at 143.
122. 39 Weekly Compilation of Presidential Documents 342.

of Military Force Against Iraq Resolution of 2002 (Public Law 107-243), I directed U.S. Armed Forces, operating with other coalition forces, to commence combat operations on March 19, 2003, against Iraq."[123]

The United States triumphed militarily over Iraq in less than a month, but with severe costs to constitutional government in the United States and reconstruction efforts in Iraq. The euphoria and celebrations in the United States were not unexpected. No one doubted that U.S. forces would prevail over an Iraqi military that lacked an air force and had few ground troops willing to fight. Understandably, great pride was placed in the American men and women who put their lives at stake in Iraq and accomplished their military mission. But the issue was never whether the United States would win the war. It was whether war was necessary, and what would happen in Iraq and the region after military operations had ceased.

Congress failed to discharge its constitutional duties when it passed the Iraq Resolution. Instead of making a decision about whether to go to war and spend billions for a multiyear commitment, it transferred those legislative judgments to the President. Legislators washed their hands of the key decisions to go to war and for how long. Congress should not have voted on the resolution before the election, which colored the votes and the political calculations. Voting under that pressure benefited the President.

It would have been better for Congress as an institution, and for the country as a whole, to first wait for President Bush to request the Security Council to authorize inspections in Iraq. Depending on what the Security Council did or did not do, and on what Iraq agreed or did not agree to do, Congress could then have debated whether to authorize war. Having learned what the Security Council and Iraq actually did rather than speculate on what they might do, Congress would have been in the position to make an informed choice. Instead, it voted under partisan pressures, with inadequate information, and thereby abdicated its constitutional duties to the President. Congress suffered a loss, as did popular control and the democratic process. Congress should not allow any President to dictate the timing of a vote on war.

In the end, Congress had two models to choose from. It could have acted after the election as it did in 1990–1991. Or it could have acted in the middle of an election as in 1964. The first maintained the integrity of the legislative institution by minimizing partisan tactics and scheduling legislative debate after the Security Council voted. The second placed Con-

123. Id. at 348.

gress in a position of voting hurriedly without the information it needed and with the information it did receive (the two "attacks" in Tonkin Gulf) of dubious quality. In 2002, Congress picked the Tonkin Gulf model. There may be times when Congress might have to authorize war in the middle of an election. The year 2002 was not one.

Rather than proceed with deliberation and care, the two branches rushed to war on a claim of imminent threat that lacked credibility. The Bush administration never made a convincing case why the delay of a few months would injure or jeopardize national security. By acting hastily and without just cause, the administration did damage to what President Bush highlighted in his September 12, 2002, address: the relevance of the United Nations. Unwilling to wait an extra month or two to allow UN inspectors to continue their work, the Bush administration missed an opportunity to attract the support of other nations. In place of a multinational effort to remove Saddam Hussein and rebuild Iraq, the United States found itself almost solely responsible for an occupation that has uncertain goals, heavy financial costs, and an open-ended duration.

Doctoring Intelligence Reports

The failure to find weapons of mass destruction in Iraq raised the question whether the Bush administration misread or misrepresented intelligence reports to exaggerate the nature of the Iraqi threat. That charge assumes that reports prepared by the intelligence agencies are professionally crafted when presented to administration officials and that distortions begin at that point. Yet the reports might already be manipulated.

Consider the CIA report of October 2002, "Iraq's Weapons of Mass Destruction Programs." It was released at a critical time when Congress was considering whether to authorize military operations. On October 2, President Bush announced a bipartisan agreement on a joint resolution to authorize armed force against Iraq. He stated that Iraq "has stockpiled biological and chemical weapons."[124] In his address to the nation on October 7, from Cincinnati, he said that Iraq "possesses and produces chemical and biological weapons."[125]

Those remarks reflected an analysis prepared by the Central Intelligence Agency. The unclassified version, available on the CIA's web site

---

124. 38 Weekly Compilation of Presidential Documents 1670.
125. Id. at 1716.

(www.cia.gov), states unequivocally: "Baghdad has chemical and biological weapons." The impact of any report depends on its opening line, since readers are apt to skim the rest. Yet the detailed analytical section that follows contradicts the flat assertion, providing statements that are much more cautious and qualified:

- "Iraq has the ability to produce chemical warfare (CW) agents within its chemical industry."
- "Iraq probably has concealed precursors, production equipment, documentation, and other items necessary for continuing its CW effort."
- "Baghdad continues to rebuild and expand dual-use infrastructure that it could divert quickly to CW production."
- "Iraq has the capability to convert quickly legitimate vaccine and biopesticide plants to biological warfare (BW) production and already may have done so."

None of the statements in the analytical section support the striking claim in the first paragraph of the CIA report and in Bush's statements to the nation. The same gap between the front material and the internal analysis appears in a May 28, 2003, publication on mobile labs, jointly authored by the CIA and the Defense Intelligence Agency (DIA). Entitled "Iraqi Mobile Biological Warfare Agent Production Plans," it can also be found on CIA's Web site.

The first sentence is eye-catching: "Coalition forces have uncovered the strongest evidence to date that Iraq was hiding a biological warfare program." The analysis within the report does not support such a dramatic claim. The report notes instead that one of the mobile labs was "equipped to produce BW agent." Was it equipped for that purpose and no other? Elsewhere the report acknowledges that a mobile lab "could be used to support BW or legitimate research." Use of "equipped" provided no evidence of WMDs. The report refers to other findings, but in guarded terms.

The CIA/DIA report concedes that some of the features of the labs "are consistent with both bioproduction [of BW agents] and hydrogen production" for artillery weather balloons. Clearly, much more analysis is necessary. What was evident in these declassified CIA reports is that intelligence analysts prepare a report, complete with caveats and qualifications, and someone comes along and puts a screamer up front. Was the classified report more professional and nuanced? When it was decided to put an unclassified version on the Web site, did someone think it important—with public consumption in mind—to rewrite the lead?

On June 18, 2003, Deputy Defense Secretary Paul Wolfowitz appeared before the House Armed Services Committee, where Rep. Gene Taylor (D-Miss.) asked whether the intelligence about the threat from Iraq's weapons was wrong. Taylor said he voted for the Iraq Resolution because of the administration's warning that Iraq had weapons of mass destruction. He now told Wolfowitz: "A person is only as good as his word. This nation is only as good as its word. And if that's the reason why we did it—and I voted for it—then we need some clarification here." Wolfowitz replied: "If there's a problem with intelligence . . . it doesn't mean that anybody misled anybody. It means that intelligence is an art and not a science."[126] In July, Wolfowitz talked about the "nature of terrorism intelligence as intrinsically murky."[127]

That modest tone was absent during the debate on the Iraq resolution. The administration treated intelligence as a science that yields certitude, not doubt. There was no admission of murkiness. The position was not merely that Iraq had WMDs in the past. It had them now. On March 6, 2003, shortly before going to war, President Bush said that Iraq "has weapons of mass destruction."[128] On March 15 he said that Saddam Hussein "possesses the weapons of mass destruction."[129] Bush, Cheney, Rumsfeld, and other top administration officials spoke with great conviction and certainty that Iraq currently had WMD capability, particularly chemical and biological weapons. According to their analysis, the threat was imminent, not in the future.

Democracy depends on laws but much more on trust. Constitutions and statutes are necessarily general in scope, placing a premium on judgment and discretion. Without confidence in what public officials say and do, laws are easily twisted to satisfy private ends. Leaders who claim to act in the national interest may, instead, pursue personal or partisan agendas. The opportunity for harm is especially great in the field of national security. Approximately $40 billion in secret funds are spent by the U.S. intelligence community whose mission is to supply reliable analysis for policymakers, both executive and legislative, including whatever caveats and qualifications are appropriate. When those reports are doctored, either before they leave the agency or afterward, government is likely to blunder.

126. Walter Pincus and Dana Priest, "Lawmakers Begin Iraq Intelligence Hearings," Washington Post, June 19, 2003, at A16.
127. Walter Pincus, "Wolfowitz: Iraq Key to War on Terrorism," Washington Post, July 28, 2003, at A12.
128. 39 Weekly Compilation of Presidential Documents 299.
129. Id. at 330.

In an age of terrorism, especially after 9/11, the public needs full trust in the integrity of its elected leaders and in the intelligence agencies that guide crucial decisions. For all the sophistication of the U.S. political and economic system, if trust is absent so is popular control. The United States cannot install democracy abroad if it lacks it at home.

U.S. political institutions failed in their constitutional duties when they authorized war against Iraq. The Bush administration never presented sufficient and credible information to justify statutory action in October 2002 and military operations in March 2003. Statements by executive officials were regularly punctured by press disclosures. The call to war demands a careful marshaling of evidence to build public confidence. The record of the Bush administration on war-making created distrust of the spoken word and the declassified document. For its part, Congress failed to insist on reliable arguments and evidence before passing the Iraq Resolution. There was no need for Congress to act when it did. Instead of passing legislation to authorize war, members of Congress agreed to compromise language that left the decisive judgment with the President. Placing the power to initiate war in the hands of one person was precisely what the framers hoped to avoid when they drafted the Constitution.

10

COVERT OPERATIONS

From modest beginnings, covert activities of the federal government proliferated after World War II. At first an exception to the rule, they became more frequent and disturbing, more aggressive abroad and intrusive at home. Minor incidents of spying over the first three-quarters of American history were later eclipsed by attempted assassinations of foreign leaders and interventions (political and military) into the internal affairs of other countries. Tactics included sabotage, propaganda, support for opposition groups, destruction of economic facilities, mining of harbors, and conducting guerrilla operations. Private citizens, American and foreign, were recruited for these operations. After World War II, Congress authorized secret funding for the intelligence agencies, making it easier to conceal abuses.

Congressional oversight of covert operations, largely desultory in earlier years, gradually led in the 1970s to the creation of separate intelligence committees in the House and the Senate and the enactment of specific restrictions and procedures. The purpose: to make the President personally accountable for covert actions (previous Presidents hid behind the doctrine of "plausible deniability") and to provide for regular reporting to Congress. Legislative control remains inadequate and episodic, as witnessed by the Iran-Contra debacle during the Reagan years.

Seeds of Secrecy

Two constitutional provisions open the door to some covert activity. One is the authority to grant letters of marque and reprisal, permitting the use of private individuals to commit military action against foreign governments. This constitutional power to substitute private parties for regular military forces was lodged solely in Congress, but in later years the executive branch turned to private citizens to conduct secret and "paramilitary" operations. The other constitutional provision giving some support to covert actions is the statement and account clause, which requires Congress to make a regular accounting of public funds to the people "from time to time." Those four words invite an element of secret funding. Neither provision led to much covert activity throughout most of American history. The problems are recent, dating from World War II.

Article I grants Congress the power to "grant Letters of Marque and Reprisal." At a time when the United States lacked a standing army and a strong navy, Congress could authorize these letters to permit private individuals and privately owned warships to make war against other nations. This power is given expressly to Congress, not to the President. As Jefferson noted in 1793, if reprisal is invoked "Congress must be called on to take it; the right of reprisal being expressly lodged with them by the constitution, & not with the executive."[1] In the Quasi-War with France in 1798, Congress authorized the President to grant to the owners of private armed ships special commissions, giving them "the same license and authority for the subduing, seizing and capturing [of] any armed French vessel."[2] In the wars against Tripoli and the Barbary pirates, Congress frequently authorized the President to grant commissions to the owners of private armed vessels.[3]

Congress jealously guarded this power. An amendment in 1802 to empower the President to grant letters of marque and reprisal was rejected.[4] In 1834, President Andrew Jackson asked Congress to delegate to him authority to issue letters of marque and reprisal for the purpose of redressing a debt owed by France to the United States. The repeated failure of France to appropriate funds to discharge the debt convinced Jackson that the United States should invoke a remedy sanctioned by the laws of nations:

It is a well-settled principle of the international code that where one nation owes another a liquidated debt which it refuses or neglects to pay the aggrieved party may seize on the property belonging to the other, its citizens or subjects, sufficient to pay the debt without giving just cause of war.

. . . I recommend that a law be passed authorizing reprisals upon French property in case provisions shall not be made for the payment of the debt at the approaching session of the French Chambers. Such a measure ought not to be considered by France as a menace.[5]

The Senate Foreign Relations Committee concluded that Congress could not, and should not, delegate such power to any President. Although reprisals

1. 6 The Writings of Thomas Jefferson 259 (Paul Leicester Ford, ed. 1892–1899).
2. 1 Stat. 579, sec. 2 (1798).
3. 2 Stat. 130, sec. 3 (1802); 3 Stat. 230, sec. 3 (1815).
4. Annals of Cong., 7th Cong., 1st Sess. 431 (1802).
5. 3 Richardson 1325.

"do not of themselves produce a state of public war . . . they are not unfrequently the immediate precursor of it." The committee believed that U.S. reprisals would provoke retaliation by France, plunging both nations into war. It noted that the authority to issue letters of marque and reprisal is associated in the same clause that grants Congress the power to declare war. Since that authority was specifically delegated to Congress, the legislative branch "ought to retain to itself the right of judging of the expediency of granting them, under all the circumstances existing at the time when they are proposed to be actually issued."[6]

A second source of covert authority lies in the statement and account clause. In the interest of financial accountability, the Constitution requires that a regular statement and account of the receipts and expenditures of all public money shall be published "from time to time." Open budgeting permits accountability to citizens in a democratic society. But what is meant by the phrase "from time to time?" Does that allow for some secrecy?

Toward the end of the Philadelphia convention, George Mason proposed that "an Account of the public expenditures should be annually published."[7] Gouverneur Morris and Rufus King objected that publication would be "impossible in many cases" and that periodic statements might be so general that they "would afford no satisfactory information."[8] James Madison proposed to strike "annually" and insert "from time to time." He thought this change would "enjoin the duty of frequent publications and leave enough to the discretion of the Legislature."[9] James Wilson, supporting Madison, remarked that many operations of finance "cannot be properly published at certain times."[10] The delegates unanimously adopted Madison's phrase "from time to time."

During the Virginia ratifying convention in 1788, George Mason objected that the phrase "from time to time" was too loose an expression, noting that one justification for this language was that "there might be some matters which require secrecy."[11] Although he conceded that secrecy was necessary sometimes for matters relative to military operations and foreign negotiations, he did not "conceive that the receipts and expenditures of the public money ought ever to be concealed." The people "had a right to know the expenditures of their money." Accounting from time to time "might

---

6. S. Rept. No. 40, 23d Cong., 2d Sess. 21–22 (1835).
7. 2 Farrand 618.
8. Id.
9. Id. at 618–19.
10. Id.
11. 3 Elliott 459.

afford opportunities of misapplying the public money, and sheltering those who did it." These comments suggest that Mason merely supported some delay in publishing sensitive material, not suppressing it entirely.

Madison also seemed to endorse full disclosure. By giving Congress the opportunity to publish from time to time, "they would be more full and satisfactory to the public, and would be sufficiently frequent."[12] Publication of governmental expenditures was essential for popular control. As Robert Livingston told his colleagues at the New York ratifying convention, the statement and account clause operated as a check against political corruption: "Congress are to publish, from time to time, an account of their receipts and expenditures. These may be compared together; and if the former, year after year, exceed the latter, the corruption may be detected, and the people may use the constitutional mode of redress."[13]

James McHenry, a member of the constitutional convention, advised the Maryland House of Delegates that "the People who give their Money ought to know in what manner it is expended."[14] Notwithstanding this history and intent, covert spending in 2003 for the Central Intelligence Agency and other elements of the intelligence community runs in the neighborhood of $40 billion a year.

Early Departures from Openness

Confidential spending began with a single statutory precedent in 1790, providing the President with a $40,000 account "for the support of such persons as he shall commission to serve the United States in foreign parts."[15] The President could account for such expenditures "as in his judgment may be made public, and also for the amount of such expenditures as he may think it advisable not to specify." Congress granted the President this discretion to avoid publicizing different salaries for foreign ministers and thereby make "invidious distinctions between foreign nations."[16] The statute was extended in 1793, allowing the President to use certificates instead of vouchers.[17] With certificates, Presidents simply state that funds have been spent appropriately; documents or vouchers are not required.

12. Id. at 460.
13. 2 Elliot 345.
14. 3 Farrand 150.
15. 1 Stat. 128–29 (1790).
16. 1 Annals of Cong. 1089 (1790) (statement of Representative Scott).
17. 1 Stat. 300 (1793).

Confidential funding provoked only three controversies in the nineteenth century. The first case of secret funding involved President Madison. Concerned that certain territory south of Georgia might pass from Spain to another foreign power, he asked Congress for authority to take temporary possession. Voting in secret session in 1811, Congress provided $100,000 for that purpose. The public did not know of this action until 1818, when Congress published the secret statute.[18]

The second controversy arose in 1846, when the House of Representatives asked President Polk to furnish an account of all payments made on presidential certificates for the contingent expenses of foreign intercourse from March 4, 1841, to May 8, 1843. Polk refused to release the information on the ground that Congress had given the President statutory authority to decide whether such expenditures should be made public.[19]

The last dispute in the nineteenth century, arising after the Civil War, involved the use of confidential funds by President Lincoln. The heirs of a spy who had served under Lincoln during the Civil War tried to recover compensation. The Supreme Court decided that Lincoln, as Commander in Chief, could properly employ secret agents to cross Confederate lines and obtain reconnaissance information. The Court, holding that the contract between Lincoln and the spy had to remain forever confidential, denied the claim for compensation.[20]

By the end of the nineteenth century, Congress had authorized and funded only one confidential account. Congress established three other confidential funds in the early decades of the twentieth century: a $25,000 travel fund for the President in 1906, $50,000 for the Secretary of the Navy in 1916 to obtain information from abroad, and $20,000 for the Federal Bureau of Investigation "to meet unforeseen emergencies."[21] In this lengthy period—from 1789 to 1935—Congress deviated from the statement and account clause only four times and for relatively small amounts.

World War II triggered a sharp rise in confidential spending, decreasing the visibility and accountability of the federal budget. The President and other cabinet officials were given broad discretion in spending emergency and confidential funds.[22] The Roosevelt administration hid money in appropriations accounts during World War II to fund the Manhattan Proj-

18. 3 Stat. 471–72 (1818). See David Hunter Miller, Secret Statutes of the United States (1918).
19. 5 Richardson 2283.
20. Totten v. United States, 92 U.S. 105 (1875).
21. 34 Stat. 454 (1906); 39 Stat. 557 (1916); 49 Stat. 78 (1935).
22. 55 Stat. 682, 818 (1941); 56 Stat. 611, 704, 995–96 (1942).

ect, which developed and produced the atomic bomb. Only a handful of legislators knew of the more than $2 billion spent on this project.[23]

Over the next few decades, Congress created confidential funds for a number of agencies and appropriations accounts: the Atomic Energy Commission, defense operation and maintenance, defense contingencies, the Attorney General, the Drug Enforcement Administration, the Food and Drug Administration, the U.S. Coast Guard, the Bureau of Customs, the U.S. Secret Service, the Immigration and Naturalization Service, the District of Columbia, and several accounts for the White House.[24] The dollar figures for these accounts were modest. The major portion of secret funding involved the various agencies that make up the intelligence community.

The Intelligence Community

During World War II, the Office of Strategic Services (OSS) engaged not only in intelligence gathering but also in covert actions involving sabotage, assassination, and commando operations. Unlike contemporary practices for the intelligence community, the OSS appropriation was published in federal statutes.[25] The National Security Act of 1947 established the Central Intelligence Agency (CIA) to give advice on intelligence activities related to national security and to perform "such other functions and duties related to intelligence affecting the national security as the National Security Council may from time to time direct."[26]

The general phrase "other functions and duties" would be used later as legal authority for covert operations. A report to the National Security Council in 1948, "taking cognizance of the vicious covert activities of the USSR," stated that the overt foreign activities of the U.S. government "must be supplemented by covert operations." That responsibility was placed in the CIA under a new Office of Special Projects. Covert operations were supposed to be planned and conducted "in a manner consistent with US foreign and military policies." The report defined covert operations to mean activities conducted or sponsored by the U.S. government in such a way that its responsibility "is not evident to unauthorized persons and that

23. Louis Fisher, "Confidential Spending and Governmental Accountability," 47 G. W. L. Rev. 347, 361–62 (1979).
24. Id. at 362–82.
25. 57 Stat. 526–27 (1943); 58 Stat. 534–35 (1944); 59 Stat. 483 (1945).
26. 61 Stat. 498, sec. 102(d)(5) (1947).

if uncovered the US Government can plausibly disclaim any responsibility for them."[27] Other reports over the next few years amplified this policy.[28]

Statutory support for secret funding awaited the Central Intelligence Act of 1949, which contained extraordinary authority over the transfer and application of funds. Sums made available to the CIA "may be expended without regard to the provisions of law and regulations relating to the expenditure of Government funds." For objects of a confidential nature, expenditures can be accounted for solely on the certificate of the CIA Director, with each certificate deemed a sufficient voucher for the amount spent.[29] In addition, rather than appropriating funds directly to the CIA, Congress authorized the agency to transfer to and receive from other government agencies "such sums as may be approved" by the Bureau of the Budget (later the Office of Management and Budget [OMB]) for the performance of any functions or activities authorized by the National Security Act of 1947. Other agencies were authorized to transfer to or receive from the CIA such sums "without regard to any provisions of law limiting or prohibiting transfers between appropriations."[30]

Funds for the "intelligence community" (Central Intelligence Agency, National Security Agency, Defense Intelligence Agency, National Reconnaissance Office, and other agencies) are initially concealed in several appropriations bills, the main one being defense. Appropriations accounts must be artificially inflated to hide the amounts destined for the intelligence community. After enactment of these bills, the OMB transfers the appropriate amounts to the intelligence agencies.

Current criticism of the CIA results from its evolution from an intelligence-gathering agency, confined to foreign activities, to that of a participant/catalyst in military and political operations that often affect domestic affairs. Harry Howe Ransom, a leading scholar on the subject, concluded that nothing in the public record or in public archives (for example, the Truman Library) "suggests that Congress ever intended to create or knew that it was creating an agency for para-military operations and a wide range of foreign political interventions."[31] Certainly the use of an intelligence agency for domestic operations was never anticipated, but OSS prece-

27. A Report to the National Security Council by Executive Secretary on Office of Special Projects, NSC 10/1, June 15, 1948, secs. 1, 3a, 3e(1), 5.
28. NSC 10/2, June 18, 1948; NSC 5412/1, March 12, 1955.
29. 63 Stat. 213, sec. 10 (1949).
30. 63 Stat. 211, sec. 6 (1949); 50 U.S.C. 403 (2000).
31. Harry Howe Ransom, "Secret Intelligence Agencies and Congress," Society, March/April 1975, at 34.

dents and the early documents creating the CIA looked to an intelligence agency capable of conducting subversive operations abroad.

Beginning in the late 1940s, some of the power to use private individuals for war-making purposes shifted from legislative to executive control, and the CIA used paramilitary troops against foreign governments on numerous occasions. In 1953, the CIA was instrumental in undermining the Mossadegh regime in Iran and returning the Shah to his throne. In such countries as Guatemala, Cuba, and Nicaragua, the Agency hired mercenaries and directed them to carry out U.S. foreign policy. In Guatemala the CIA helped oust the Arbenz government in 1954 and orchestrated the ill-conceived Bay of Pigs invasion in Cuba in 1961.

Although President Eisenhower sought congressional support in advance of possible military action in Formosa and the Middle East, relying on area resolutions for executive-legislative cooperation, he readily sanctioned covert operations in Iran and Guatemala without seeking legislative authority. Planning for the Bay of Pigs invasion was initiated by his administration. CIA activities in the 1950s reflected the attitudes of the Doolittle Committee, a special study group created by Eisenhower in 1954 to examine covert operations by the CIA. Its report cited the need for a gloves-off policy:

> Another important requirement is an aggressive covert psychological, political and paramilitary organization more effective, more unique and, if necessary, more ruthless than that employed by the enemy. No one should be permitted to stand in the way of the prompt, efficient and secure accomplishment of this mission.
>
> . . . It is now clear that we are facing an implacable enemy whose avowed objective is world domination by whatever means and at whatever cost. There are no rules in such a game. Hitherto acceptable norms of human conduct do not apply. If the United States is to survive, long-standing American concepts of "fair play" must be reconsidered.[32]

In the early 1970s, the CIA spent millions trying to discredit Salvador Allende, the Marxist-socialist leader in Chile, and from 1963 to 1973, the Agency supported the Meo hill tribes of North Laos in a war against the Communist Pathet Lao. The CIA also sponsored guerrilla wars in the Ukraine,

---

32. Special Study Group on Covert Activities of the Central Intelligence Agency, September 30, 1954, at 6–7 (declassified in part in 1976).

Poland, Albania, Hungary, Indonesia, China, Oman, Malaysia, Iraq, the Dominican Republic, Venezuela, North Korea, Bolivia, Thailand, Haiti, Greece, Turkey, Vietnam, Afghanistan, and Angola.[33]

The CIA has been involved in a number of plots to assassinate foreign leaders: Fidel Castro in Cuba, Patrice Lumumba in the Congo (now Zaire), Rafael Trujillo in the Dominican Republic, Ngo Dinh Diem in South Vietnam, and General Rene Schneider of Chile. The efforts against Castro failed, a rival Congolese faction murdered Lumumba before CIA operatives could carry out their plan, and the other murders were accomplished without full Agency control.[34] The Church Committee, established by the Senate to investigate abuses by intelligence agencies, recommended in 1975 that Congress enact legislation "making it a Federal crime to commit or attempt an assassination, or to conspire to do so."[35]

In 1976, President Ford issued Executive Order 11905 on "United States Foreign Intelligence Activities." One of the sections prohibited assassinations: "No employee of the United States Government shall engage in, or conspire to engage in, political assassination."[36] President Carter continued that ban in 1978 with Executive Order 12036,[37] as did President Reagan in 1981 with Executive Order 12333.[38] Nonetheless, in 1984 Congress learned of a CIA-approved manual that advocated that government officials in Nicaragua be "neutralized." As translated by the Congressional Research Service, the manual read:

> It is possible to neutralize carefully selected and planned targets, such as court judges . . . police and state security officials, CDA (Sandinista Defense Committee) chief, etc. For psychological purposes, it is necessary to take extreme precautions and it is absolutely necessary to gather together the population affected, so that they will be present, take part in the act, and formulate accusations against the oppressor.[39]

---

33. Loch J. Johnson, America's Secret Power: The CIA in a Democratic Society 26 (1989); Jules Lobel, "Covert War and Congressional Authority: Hidden War and Forgotten Power," 134 U. Pa. L. Rev. 1035, 1056, 1076 n. 178 (1986).

34. Johnson, America's Secret Power 27–28; John Ranelagh, The Agency: The Rise and Decline of the CIA 336–45 (1987); "Alleged Assassination Plots Involving Foreign Leaders," S. Rept. No. 465, 94th Cong., 1st Sess. 4–5 (1975).

35. S. Rept. No. 465, 94th Cong., 1st Sess. 281 (1975).

36. 41 Fed. Reg. 7733 (1976).

37. 43 Fed. Reg. 3687 (Sec. 2.305) (1978).

38. 46 Fed. Reg. 59952 (Sec. 2.11) (1981).

39. 1984 CQ Almanac 91.

The word "neutralize," especially in the context used, appeared to mean assassination. More charitable interpretations were offered, such as advocating "restraint" on certain officials. The CIA sanctioned six employees for their role in producing the manual.[40]

Even with assassinations supposedly prohibited by executive order, military operations can "indirectly" kill the leader of a foreign country. In the air raids on Libya in 1986, the headquarters of Muammar el-Qaddafi was damaged in the attack, but administration officials denied that the intent was to kill the Libyan leader.[41] There have been reports that the Bush administration in 1990–1991 gave some consideration to a plan to kill Saddam Hussein during his travels between Baghdad and Kuwait City,[42] and the Clinton administration's plan to "capture" Mohamed Farah Aideed in Somalia came very close to killing him.[43] During the war against Iraq in 2003, several U.S. strikes destroyed buildings that the administration thought sheltered Saddam Hussein.

Statutory Controls on the CIA

The War Powers Resolution of 1973 placed restrictions only on the President's power to dispatch *armed service personnel* into hostilities. Not covered are activities by civilian combatants and "paramilitary operations." The resolution does cover, however, instances in which military personnel are temporarily detailed to the CIA, but it does not cover the CIA's use of civilian or ex-military personnel.[44]

Senator Thomas Eagleton proposed that covert operations be explicitly covered by the War Powers Resolution. He had in mind the CIA advisers who organized indigenous Laotian forces to engage in hostilities to carry out the policy objectives established by the executive branch of the U.S. government.[45] Another example was the covert military operation, under the code name Operation Plan 34A, initiated by President Johnson in

40. Id.

41. Pat Towell, "After Raid on Libya, New Questions on Hill," CQ Weekly Report, April 19, 1986, at 838.

42. "The Plan to Kill Saddam Hussein," Newsweek, January 10, 1994, at 31.

43. Patrick J. Sloyan, "How the Warload Outwitted Clinton's Spooks," Washington Post, April 3, 1994, at C3.

44. 4A Op.O.L.C. 197 (1983).

45. 119 Cong. Rec. 25079 (1973).

February 1964 to provoke the enemy and justify the bombing of North Vietnam.[46] Eagleton's amendment was defeated, 34 to 53.[47]

In 1974, Congress attempted to monitor covert operations by requiring timely reporting by the President. As a general limitation on intelligence activities, the Hughes-Ryan Amendment of 1974 provided that no funds appropriated may be expended by or on behalf of the CIA for operations in foreign countries, other than activities intended solely for obtaining necessary intelligence, "unless and until the President finds that each operation is important to the national security of the United States and reports, in a timely fashion, a description and scope of such operations" to the appropriate committees of Congress, including the Senate Committee on Foreign Relations and the House Committee on Foreign Affairs. The Armed Services and the Appropriations Committee also received the reports. This procedure would not apply during military operations initiated by the United States under a declaration of war approved by the Congress "or an exercise of powers by the President under the War Powers Resolution."[48]

The Hughes-Ryan Amendment responded to reports about the CIA's involvement in the overthrow of the Allende regime in Chile in 1973. The amendment had several purposes. One was to provide some assurance that designated congressional committees would be notified of covert activities. However, the opportunity for executive evasion was evident in the vague language requiring that the President report to Congress "in a timely fashion." The second purpose was to require that the President be personally responsible for approving these operations. Instead of a system of "plausible denial," permitting the President to feign ignorance of actions taken by the executive branch, the Hughes-Ryan Amendment required the President to "find" that these operations were important to U.S. national security. Findings had to be signed by the President.

In 1975, Congress enacted legislation to prohibit a CIA operation in Angola. The Angolan civil war involved a Cuban- and Soviet-supported faction fighting against an opposition force assisted by the CIA. The Agency spent an estimated $32 million for arms and equipment, communications gear, political action support, and other items.[49] Toward the end of 1975, Senator John Tunney offered an amendment to strike $33 million

46. Id. at 25080.
47. Id. at 25092. Senator Eagleton reintroduced his amendment two years later; 121 Cong. Rec. 40884 (1975).
48. 88 Stat. 1804, sec. 32 (1974); H. Rept. No. 1471, 93d Cong., 2d Sess. 43–44 (1974).
49. Stephen R. Weissman, "CIA Covert Action in Zaire and Angola: Patterns and Consequences," 94 Pol. Sci. Q. 263, 283–84 (1979).

in CIA money hidden in an account in the defense appropriations bill to restrict CIA activities in Angola to intelligence gathering.[50] The reduction was not accepted, but the restriction on CIA actions in Angola became law in early 1976.[51] Having finally extricated the United States from Southeast Asia, Congress was in no mood to approve military involvement in Africa.

The Senate acted partly in response to duplicity within the Ford administration. During hearings held by the Senate Foreign Relations Committee, the CIA deputy director of operations admitted that the agency was sending arms to Angola. Shortly after he left the room, the deputy assistant secretary of state for African affairs testified that arms were not being sent to Angola (the administration's cover story). Confronted with the earlier admission by the CIA, the State Department witness switched his position. The committee then unanimously agreed to terminate U.S. military involvement in Angola.[52]

Also in 1976, Congress enacted what became known as the Clark Amendment (named after Senator Dick Clark) to place further restrictions on CIA activities in Angola. The legislative language provided that no assistance "of any kind may be provided for the purpose, or which would have the effect, of promoting or augmenting, directly or indirectly, the capacity of any nation, group, organization, movement, or individual to conduct military or paramilitary operations in Angola unless and until the Congress expressly authorizes such assistance by law."[53]

The Clark Amendment did not prohibit U.S. intervention in Angola. It merely required that U.S. assistance "be provided openly, through authorizations approved by Congress."[54] If the administration wanted to intervene in Angola it had to come to Congress, present its views, and answer questions. In 1976, Congress also used its power of the purse to deny funds to military activities in Angola: "None of the funds appropriated or made available pursuant to this Act shall be obligated or expended to finance directly or indirectly any type of military assistance to Angola."[55] The Clark Amendment was repealed in 1985.[56]

Following a series of disclosures in the 1970s about CIA violations and abuses, both at home and abroad, Congress created intelligence commit-

50. 121 Cong. Rec. 41141, 42213–19 (1975); 122 Cong. Rec. 1035–57 (1976).
51. 90 Stat. 166 (1976).
52. John Stockwell, In Search of Enemies: A CIA Story 230 (1978).
53. 90 Stat. 757, sec. 404 (1976).
54. S. Rept. No. 97–83, 97th Cong., 1st Sess. 79 (1981).
55. 90 Stat. 776, sec. 109 (1976).
56. 99 Stat. 264, sec. 811 (1985).

tees in each House to review and authorize Agency operations. Congress passed legislation in 1980 to regulate the President's power to engage in covert actions. The Intelligence Oversight Act of 1980 repealed Hughes-Ryan and reduced the number of congressional committees entitled to be notified of covert actions from eight to two.[57] The 1980 statute required the Director of Central Intelligence and the heads of all other agencies or entities of the United States involved in intelligence activities to keep the two intelligence committees "fully and currently informed" of all intelligence activities. If the President determined that it was essential to limit prior notice to meet "extraordinary circumstances affecting vital interests of the United States," he could limit notice to eight members of Congress: the chair and ranking minority members of the intelligence committees, the Speaker and Minority Leader of the House, and the Majority and Minority Leaders of the Senate.[58] This so-called Gang of Eight was never notified of the Iran-Contra operations. Under the 1980 statute, if the President did not give notice to Congress, he had to "fully inform" the intelligence committees "in a timely fashion" and explain the failure to provide notice, but President Reagan never notified the intelligence committees of the events, separate or combined, that became known as the Iran-Contra affair. After ten months had elapsed some of the facts spilled out in Lebanese and U.S. newspapers.

Covert Action in the Open

CIA involvement in Angola illustrates how "covert" operations can become the topic of public debate. So prevalent is this pattern that it suggests a basic principle: Covert operations should be conducted with the understanding that they will become public knowledge, probably within a short time. Policymakers need to act in ways that are defensible once the operation comes to light, and covert actions should be consistent with the declared policy of government and with the values of the nation.

A conspicuous example of a covert action that did not withstand public scrutiny is the Bay of Pigs. On April 7, 1961, the *New York Times* ran an article entitled "Anti-Castro Units Trained to Fight at Florida Bases," describing an effort by the Kennedy administration to train 5,000 to 6,000 Cuban exiles at camps located in Florida, Louisiana, and Guatemala to overthrow

---

57. 94 Stat. 1981, sec. 407(a) (1980).
58. Id. at 1981, sec. 407(b).

Premier Fidel Castro. A subhead in the lengthy story, supplying many details of the plan, read: "Invasion Reported Near."[59]

On April 12, President Kennedy was asked whether a decision had been made to invade Cuba. He dissembled: "First, I want to say that there will not be, under any conditions, an intervention in Cuba by the United States Armed Forces. This Government will do everything it possibly can, and I think it can meet its responsibilities, to make sure that there are no Americans involved in any actions inside Cuba."[60] Later in the news conference, when asked whether the U.S. government would "oppose any attempt to mount an offensive against Castro from this country," Kennedy responded: "If your phrase 'to mount an offensive' is as I understand it, I would be opposed to mounting an offensive."[61]

Undisclosed in these remarks, of course, was the administration's ongoing effort to use the CIA to train Cuban exiles, supply them with equipment and arms, and direct the planned invasion. At the news conference, Kennedy publicly tied his hands. Having pledged that the United States would not intervene in Cuba and would not be involved in any actions inside Cuba, he was in no position to provide key air support to the Cuban exiles when they went ashore at the Bay of Pigs. The result was a quick and humiliating defeat.

After the Soviet Union invaded Afghanistan in 1979, the United States gave weapons and support to the Afghan resistance, the Mujahedeen. Special emphasis was placed on building a rebel antiaircraft capability to shoot down Soviet jet fighters and helicopters. The assistance was publicly debated in Congress, year in and year out.[62] Both Houses endorsed U.S. support for the Afghan rebels, even to the point of passing a sense of Congress resolution in 1984.[63] However, political and diplomatic factors prohibited official admission of American involvement. Denying the covert war, no matter how fictional, protected U.S. relations with Pakistan, which served as the conduit for assistance to Afghan rebels. Open acknowledgment would have threatened Pakistan's relationship with its northern neighbor, the Soviet Union.[64]

During the early 1980s, the Reagan administration conducted a suppos-

59. New York Times, April 7, 1961, at 2.
60. Public Papers of the Presidents, 1961, at 256 (question 4).
61. Id. at 264 (question 20).
62. E.g., 130 Cong. Rec. 15526–28 (1984).
63. 130 Cong. Rec. 28983–85 (1984). See also 128 Cong. Rec. 26665–67 (1982).
64. Gregory F. Treverton, Covert Action: The Limits of Intervention in the Postwar World 213 (1987).

edly secret war against the Sandinistas in Nicaragua. Legislation in 1981 and 1982 provided covert assistance to the Contra rebels, but the operation was too large to remain hidden. By December 1982, Rep. Tom Harkin (D-Iowa) was able to introduce legislation to deny funds to the CIA and the Defense Department to furnish any military assistance to groups and individuals in Nicaragua.[65] Harkin could point to a variety of stories in newspapers and national magazines that publicly discussed military activities in Nicaragua.

During debate on the Harkin amendment, Rep. Edward Boland (D-Mass.) disclosed that the House Intelligence Committee had already put restrictive language in the classified annex that accompanies the intelligence authorization bill. The committee decided that no funds authorized by the intelligence bill should be used "to overthrow the Government of Nicaragua or to provoke a military exchange between Nicaragua and Honduras."[66] Congress enacted language prohibiting the CIA or the Defense Department from furnishing military equipment, military training or advice, or other support for military activities "to any group or individual, not part of a country's armed forces, for the purpose of overthrowing the Government of Nicaragua or provoking a military exchange between Nicaragua and Honduras."[67]

The 1982 curb proved ineffective. The insurgents in Nicaragua openly acknowledged their goal of overthrowing the Sandinistas and provoking a military confrontation.[68] In a May 1983 report, the House Intelligence Committee admitted: "This is no longer a covert operation. The public can read or hear about it daily. Anti-Sandinista leaders acknowledge U.S. aid."[69] Congress discovered early in 1984 that the administration, operating through the CIA, had mined the harbors of Nicaragua. Congress responded with this statutory language: "It is the sense of the Congress that no funds heretofore or hereafter appropriated in any Act of Congress shall be obligated or expended for the purpose of planning, directing, executing, or supporting the mining of the ports or territorial waters of Nicaragua."[70]

Later in 1984, Congress enacted the Boland Amendment to delete all funds for the Contras. The language was intended to be all-embracing to prevent any further evasion by executive officials:

65. 128 Cong. Rec. 29457 (1982).
66. Id. at 29466.
67. 96 Stat. 1865, sec. 793 (1982).
68. H. Rept. No. 122 (part 1), 98th Cong., 1st Sess. 11 (1983).
69. Id. at 12.
70. 98 Stat. 1210, sec. 2907 (1984).

During fiscal year 1985, no funds available to the Central Intelligence Agency, the Department of Defense, or any other agency or entity of the United States involved in intelligence activities may be obligated or expended for the purpose or which would have the effect of supporting, directly or indirectly, military or paramilitary operations in Nicaragua by any nation, group, organization, movement, or individual.[71]

Congress devised this tortured language because the Reagan administration had demonstrated a disposition to exploit every possible loophole. It was the intention of Congress to close them all.

Even with this explicit language, some legislators suspected that the Reagan administration might find some indirect way of assisting the Contras. During hearings on March 26, 1985, Senator Christopher Dodd (D-Conn.) said that there "have been a number of rumors or news reports around this town about how the administration might go about its funding of the contras in Nicaragua. There have been suggestions that it would be done through private parties or through funneling funds through friendly third nations, or possibly through a new category of assistance and asking the Congress to fund the program openly."[72]

The administration's spokesman, Ambassador Langhorne A. Motley, assured Senator Dodd that there would be no attempt to circumvent the Boland Amendment by soliciting funds from private parties or from foreign governments. He pledged that the amendment would be complied with fully: "Nobody is trying to play games with you or any other Member of Congress. That resolution stands, and it will continue to stand; and it says no direct or indirect. And that is pretty plain English; it does not have to be written by any bright, young lawyers. And we are going to continue to comply with that."[73]

Motley provided similar statements to the House Committee on Appropriations on April 18, 1985, testifying that the administration would not attempt to solicit funds from outside sources to assist the Contras.[74] When President Reagan signed the continuing resolution that contained the strict

---

71. 98 Stat. 1935, sec. 8066(a) (1984).

72. "Security and Development Assistance," hearings before the Senate Committee on Foreign Relations, 99th Cong., 1st Sess. 908 (1985).

73. Id. at 910. At the time he testified, Ambassador Motley was Assistant Secretary of State for Inter-American Affairs.

74. "Department of Defense Appropriations for 1986" (part 2), hearings before the House Committee on Appropriations, 99th Cong., 1st Sess. 1092 (1985).

language of the Boland Amendment, he did not issue a statement claiming that Congress had overstepped its powers and that the administration would pursue its course in Nicaragua. The Attorney General did not challenge the constitutionality of the Boland Amendment, and the Office of Legal Counsel in the Justice Department did not conclude in any internal memorandum or report that the amendment was invalid or nonbinding.

Nevertheless, at the very moment Motley was testifying before two congressional committees, executive branch officials were actively soliciting funds from private parties and from foreign governments to assist the Contras. Working closely with the White House and the National Security Council, private citizens raised money from private contributors to provide military weapons and supplies to the Contras.[75] This subterfuge eventually degenerated into the Iran-Contra affair.

The Iran-Contra Affair

Illegal assistance to the Contras became linked with another Reagan initiative: supplying arms to Iran. The Reagan administration had issued a number of policy declarations covering the war between Iran and Iraq. Executive officials repeatedly told the American public and allies that all nations should remain neutral in the conflict. Weapons were not supposed to be sent to either country (Operation Staunch). The Reagan administration emphasized that it was firmly opposed to giving any concessions to terrorists, much less providing them arms in exchange for hostages.

In November 1986, the American public received the first details of the Iran-Contra affair from a newspaper in Beirut. The Reagan administration had sold arms to Iran (violating its declared policy) and had sent weapons to the Contras (violating the Boland Amendment). New twists and turns emerged, describing a complex covert operation carried out by a mixture of executive officials and private citizens. Some of the profits from the sale of arms to Iran had been diverted to the Contras. Congressional hearings added insights, as did investigation and prosecution by Independent Counsel Lawrence E. Walsh. The resulting picture cast a permanent shadow over the two terms of Ronald Reagan. Either he knew of the effort and deliberately defied the law and the Constitution, or he was unaware of a high-

---

75. Report of the Congressional Committees Investigating the Iran-Contra Affair, H. Rept. No. 433 and S. Rept. No. 216, 100th Cong., 1st Sess. 85–103 (1987) (hereafter referred to as Iran-Contra Report).

level national security initiative operating within his own office. Neither interpretation adds luster to his public service.

Only one document from the administration asserted that the Boland Amendment permitted some executive officials to assist the Contras. Bretton G. Sciaroni, counsel to the President's Intelligence Oversight Board, issued a memorandum on September 12, 1985, concluding that the National Security Council (NSC) was not covered by the amendment.[76] This memorandum was never made available to Congress or to the public. Its existence was revealed only after the Iran-Contra affair became public in November 1986. According to the legal analysis in the memorandum, John Poindexter, Robert McFarlane, Oliver North, and other members of the NSC staff could do what the intelligence community, the Defense Department, and "any other agency or entity" had been prohibited from doing by the Boland Amendment.

The Sciaroni memo is deficient in several respects. First, under the terms of the Boland Amendment, the NSC is an "entity . . . involved in intelligence activities." The National Security Act provides that there "is established under the National Security Council a Central Intelligence Agency."[77] If a subordinate body (the CIA) is involved in intelligence activities, so is the controlling body (the NSC). Second, the NSC-CIA relationship is elaborated in Executive Order 12333, issued by President Reagan in 1981. The order states that the NSC "shall act as the highest Executive Branch entity that provides review of, guidance for and direction to the conduct of all national foreign intelligence, counterintelligence, and special activities [covert operations], and attendant policies and programs."[78] This provides clear evidence that the NSC is "involved in intelligence activities" within the meaning of the Boland Amendment. Moreover, the Director of Central Intelligence "shall be responsible directly to the President and the NSC,"[79] and the CIA shall "conduct services of common concern for the Intelligence Community as directed by the NSC."[80] The principal responsibility for implementing the order, entitled "United States Intelligence Activities" falls to the NSC.[81] Finally, even if one were to reject this analysis, the plain fact

76. Memorandum from Bretton G. Sciaroni to Robert C. McFarlane, Assistant to the President for National Security Affairs, September 12, 1985, reprinted in "Iran-Contra Investigation," joint hearings by the Iran-Contra Committees, 100th Cong., 1st Sess., vol. 100–5 at 1158 (hereafter referred to as Iran-Contra Hearings).

77. 50 U.S.C. sec. 403(a) (2000).

78. 46 Fed. Reg. 59942 (Sec. 1.2) (1981).

79. Id. at 59943 (Sec. 1.5).

80. Id. at 59946 (Sec. 1.8[f]).

81. Id. at 59952 (Sec. 3.2).

is that the NSC under North and company *was* "involved in intelligence activities."

The idea that North and other members of the NSC could carry out a covert operation to assist the Contras collides with Section 1.8(e) of Executive Order 12333. No agency except the CIA "may conduct any special activity [covert operation] unless the President determines that another agency is more likely to achieve a particular objective." President Reagan never determined that the NSC should conduct a covert action to replace the CIA. Such a determination would have deliberately undermined the Boland Amendment, shifting the operating responsibility from an agency proscribed by law to one that attempts, by stealth and proxy, to achieve an end prohibited by Congress.

The NSC would have a conflict of interest if called upon to present, in objective fashion, national security options to the President while conducting covert operations. It cannot be both analyst and agent. An operational role undermines the NSC's function as a coordinating body and honest broker between the various departments that have responsibility for national security affairs. When Frank Carlucci became National Security Adviser after the Iran-Contra affair became public, he barred the NSC from conducting covert operations.[82] National Security Decision Directive 266, issued by President Reagan on March 31, 1987, stipulated that "the NSC staff itself will not undertake the conduct of covert activities."[83]

The Iran-Contra affair illustrates how the executive branch can usurp the power of Congress by using private parties for military purposes (marque and reprisal). Private citizens involved in the scandal included Carl R. "Spitz" Channell and Richard Miller, who helped raise money for the Contras. They pleaded guilty to tax fraud. Richard V. Secord, a former Air Force officer, pleaded guilty to making false statements to congressional investigators about assistance to the Contras. Thomas G. Clines, a former CIA agent who assisted with arms sales to the Contras, was convicted of tax violations. Another member recruited from the private sector, Albert Hakim, assisted with arm sales to Iran. Hakim pleaded guilty to a misdemeanor charge of helping to supplement Oliver North's government salary by arranging to pay for his home security system.

Major administration figures included North, National Security Adviser Poindexter, and former National Security Adviser McFarlane. McFarlane

82. John Felton, "Tower Panel Lays Out Reagan Policy Failures," CQ Weekly Report, February 28, 1987, at 339, 349.
83. Reprinted in H. Doc. No. 58, 100th Cong., 1st Sess. 3 (1987).

pleaded guilty to four misdemeanor charges of withholding information from Congress. North was convicted of obstructing Congress, unlawfully mutilating government documents, and taking an illegal gratuity. Poindexter was convicted of conspiracy, making false statements to Congress, destroying and removing records, and obstructing Congress. The convictions of North and Poindexter were later overturned by an appellate court, which ruled that new trials would have to demonstrate that evidence against them had not been tainted by the congressional hearings. The difficulty of this hurdle convinced Independent Counsel Walsh not to retry North and Poindexter. Elliott Abrams, former Assistant Secretary of State, pleaded guilty to withholding information from Congress about covert assistance to the Contras. Casper W. Weinberger, former Secretary of Defense, was charged with four counts of false statements and perjury. He was pardoned before trial by President Bush.

The CIA was deeply involved. Before investigators could learn about the full influence of its Director, William Casey, he died of a brain tumor on May 6, 1987. Clair George, CIA deputy director for operations, was convicted of false statements and perjury before Congress. Alan D. Fiers, chief of the Agency's Central American Task Force, pleaded guilty to withholding information from Congress. Duane (Dewey) Clarridge, former chief of the CIA's Latin American Division, was indicted on seven counts of perjury and false statements, but he too was pardoned before trial by President Bush. The pardon also covered George and Fiers. Another CIA employee, Joseph Fernandez, was indicted on four counts of obstruction and making false statements relating to his assistance to the Contras. His case was dropped when Attorney General Dick Thornburgh refused to declassify information needed for the trial.

Precisely what happened in the Iran-Contra affair, and why, may never be determined. Administration officials destroyed documents, declined to tell the truth to investigators, and key trials (like Fernandez's) were aborted by executive branch decisions. When Independent Counsel Walsh brought indictments against former Secretary of Defense Caspar Weinberger, there was an opportunity to learn more about the responsibility of President Reagan and Vice President Bush for the Iran-Contra affair. Weinberger was scheduled to go on trial on January 5, 1993; a likely witness to be called was President Bush. Two weeks before the trial, Bush issued pardons for Weinberger and five other federal officials involved in the Iran-Contra affair. Three had already pleaded guilty (Abrams, Fiers, and McFarlane), and the pardons of Clarridge and George eliminated any chance of discovering the full extent of CIA participation.

Congressional Reforms

Congress enacted legislation in 1991 to reduce the likelihood of future Iran-Contras. A key issue is presidential notification to Congress. The Intelligence Oversight Act of 1980 required Presidents to make a "finding" on the necessity of a covert operation. In the course of the Iran-Contra affair, President Reagan made an "oral" finding on one occasion and at another point issued a finding that tried to retroactively authorize what the CIA had done. At no time did he notify the intelligence committees. The 1991 statute requires that presidential findings must be in writing and cannot have retroactive effect. Moreover, findings may not authorize any action that violates federal law or the Constitution and must identify any third party (foreign nation) that is involved in the covert action.[84]

One of the most disturbing theories to emerge from the Iran-Contra affair was the claim that Presidents, denied funds by Congress, may finance foreign policy goals by using nonappropriated funds obtained from private citizens and foreign governments. In their effort to provide military assistance to the Contras after enactment of the Boland Amendment, officials in the Reagan administration sought funds from private individuals, Saudi Arabia, and other countries. At the congressional hearings, both Poindexter and North defended the constitutionality of these initiatives, claiming that these efforts did not violate the Boland Amendment because that amendment applied only to appropriations.[85]

The Poindexter-North theory raises two issues, one constitutional, the other political. As explained in Chapter 1, the framers took great pains to keep the legislative purse separate from the presidential sword. They did not want a single branch to both make and fund war. Allowing the President to carry out foreign policy with private or foreign contributions would create what the framers feared most: union of purse and sword. If President Reagan had authorized the theory propounded by Poindexter and North, he would have invited, and deserved, impeachment proceedings. He would have failed in his constitutional duty to see that the laws are faithfully executed and would have precipitated a major constitutional crisis by merging purse and sword.

Moreover, soliciting funds from foreign governments to promote U.S. foreign policy opens the door to widespread compromise and corruption. Accepting funds from foreign governments to sustain the Contras created

84. 105 Stat. 441–45 (1991).
85. Iran-Contra Hearings, vol. 100–8, at 158, and vol. 100–7, part II, at 37.

an implicit quid pro quo, requiring the United States to reciprocate by giving donor countries special consideration in such tangible forms as foreign assistance, military assistance, arms sales, and trade concessions.[86] Instead of national policy being articulated by Congress through an open legislative process, it became the net product of secret agreements. Government went underground.

Congress had passed legislation to stop these quid pro quos. The Pell Amendment in 1985 prohibited the use of any U.S. funds to provide "assistance of any kind, either directly or indirectly, to any person or group engaging in an insurgency or other act of rebellion against the Government of Nicaragua." The purpose was to prevent recipients of U.S. funds and materials from giving assistance to the Contras as a condition, or quid pro quo, for obtaining aid.[87] In 1989, President Bush vetoed a bill that contained criminal sanctions to punish quid pro quos.[88] In the same year he vetoed another bill establishing restrictions on quid pro quos, even though this measure omitted criminal sanctions.[89] In each of his veto messages Bush stated that he was "sensitive to the concerns" that prompted Congress to add such language.[90] The principle that Congress advocated merited presidential support. It was a matter of finding the right language.

Bush signed a revised bill aimed at quid pro quos. The new law states that appropriated funds for foreign assistance may not be provided to "any foreign government (including any instrumentality or agency thereof), foreign person, or United States person in exchange for that foreign government or person undertaking any action which is, if carried out by the United States Government, a United States official or employee, expressly prohibited by a provision of United States law."[91] In signing the legislation, Bush agreed that the section prohibited quid pro quo transactions "in which U.S. funds are provided to a foreign nation on the express condition that the foreign nation provide specific assistance to a third country, which assistance U.S. officials are expressly prohibited from providing by U.S. law."[92]

The House and Senate Iran-Contra Committees' joint report, released in November 1987, stresses that Congress as well as the President has impor-

86. Iran-Contra Hearings, vol. 100–2, at 25, 201, 279–80.
87. 99 Stat. 254, sec. 722(d) (1985).
88. Public Papers of the Presidents, 1989, II, at 1567–69.
89. Id. at 1546.
90. Id. at 1546, 1569.
91. 103 Stat. 1251, sec. 582 (1989).
92. Public Papers of the Presidents, 1989, II, at 1573.

tant powers in the areas of foreign policy and national security. Foreign policy cannot be successful in the long run unless it has bipartisan congressional support.[93] The "misrepresentations, half-truths, and concealment" employed by executive officials in the Iran-Contra affair reflected an attitude "based on a view of Congress' role in foreign policy that is without historical or legal foundation."[94]

Another legislative-executive struggle over information in the intelligence community took place in 1998, when Congress wanted to sanction access by the intelligence committees to "whistleblowers" in the intelligence community. Lawmakers understood the importance of receiving information directly from the rank-and-file of agency employees. The Justice Department objected that the bill was unconstitutional because it interfered with the President's control over the dissemination of national security information. Both Houses of Congress rejected the theory that the President exercised exclusive and unreviewable authority over such information. National security, they insisted, was "a shared responsibility, requiring joint efforts and mutual respect by Congress and the President." As a coequal branch of government, Congress "is empowered by the Constitution to serve as a check on the executive branch; in that capacity, it has a 'need to know' of allegations of wrongdoing within the executive branch, including allegations of wrongdoing in the Intelligence Community."[95]

Actions against Terrorism

The CIA was regularly involved in antiterrorism efforts, supporting programs in Iraq, Afghanistan, and the Middle East. One objective was to weaken and overthrow President Saddam Hussein in Iraq. In 1991, President Bush ordered the CIA to encourage the Shiites in the south and the Kurds in the north to rise up against him. Those efforts were crushed by Hussein. Under President Clinton, the CIA engaged in radio propaganda, paramilitary plots, and sabotage, all for the purpose of toppling Hussein. The CIA worked with Iraqi exiles in London and Iraqi military defectors living in Jordan. As with other "covert" activities, these operations were regularly reported in the press.[96]

93. Iran-Contra Report 19, 20.
94. Id. at 387.
95. 112 Stat. 2423, sec. 701(b) (1998). See Thomas Newcomb, "In from the Cold: The Intelligence Community Whistleblower Protection Act," 53 Adm. L. Rev. 1235 (2001).
96. Tim Weiner, "C.I.A. Drafts Covert Plan to Topple Hussein," New York Times, February 26, 1998, at A11.

After the bombing of U.S. embassies in Kenya and Tanzania in 1998, President Clinton authorized the CIA to disrupt and preempt terrorist operations under the direction of Osama bin Laden. In 2001, President Bush reaffirmed the Clinton directive.[97] The CIA was deeply involved in military operations in Afghanistan in 2001. Shortly after 9/11, CIA agents were flown into northeastern Afghanistan to meet with members of the Northern Alliance. They came with communications equipment and $3 million in U.S. bills, ready to be distributed to tribal leaders willing to do battle against the Taliban and al Qaeda forces. The agents later received $10 million in cash to help tribal leaders buy food and weapons. These early efforts helped build a small landing strip and develop a capacity for selecting bombing targets.[98]

The CIA also assisted in the war against Iraq in 2003. At least three months before military operations began in March, the CIA helped forge alliances with Iraqi military leaders and persuade them not to fight. Jordanian intelligence officers worked with American Special Forces and CIA agents, helping them make contact with Iraqi officers. The CIA was assisted by an Iraqi-American businessman, a former Iraqi general, a Shiite Muslim guerrilla leader, and a Sunni Muslim. Iraqi opponents of Saddam Hussein met in Kuwait City in February 2003 to plan operations against Hussein.[99]

Future Presidents may decide to ignore statutory procedures that strengthen the ability of Congress to oversee covert operations. Still, it is important for Congress to express its sense of prerogatives and constitutional duties. Otherwise, executive officials (and courts) are likely to interpret congressional passivity as support for the President's unilateral and independent assertion of power.

The Iran-Contra affair was not an aberration. Given the attitudes within the executive branch, it was a disaster waiting to happen. It progressed because of a series of carefully calculated, conscious choices, all designed to concentrate foreign policymaking within the presidency. Any impediments to that goal—the Constitution, Congress, opposition within the exec-

97. Bob Woodward and Vernon Loeb, "CIA's Covert War on Bin Laden," Washington Post, September 14, 2001, at A1.

98. Bob Woodward, Bush at War 139–55, 184–85, 190–91, 238–39, 249–50, 265–66 (2002).

99. Douglas Jehl with Dexter Filkins, "U.S. Moved to Undermine Iraqi Military before the War," New York Times, August 10, 2003, at 1.

utive branch—were systematically swept aside by the individuals in charge of the operations and those at a higher level who assisted with winks and nods. The lesson from recent decades is that the temptation of executive officials to exceed constitutional limits in covert operations is ever-present, always pushing, and in constant need of checks from other institutions and the public.

11

RESTORING CHECKS AND BALANCES

The drift of the war power from Congress to the President after World War II is unmistakable. The framers' design, deliberately placing in Congress the decision to expend the nation's blood and treasure, has been radically transformed. Presidents now regularly claim that the commander-in-chief clause empowers them to send American troops anywhere in the world, including into hostilities, without first seeking legislative approval. Congress has made repeated efforts since the 1970s to restore legislative prerogatives, with little success. Presidents continue to wield military power single-handedly, agreeing only to consult with legislators and notify them of completed actions. That is not the framers' model.

Many justifications are advanced to defend this fundamental shift in constitutional power. Champions of executive power cite the need for secrecy and prompt action, qualities supposedly associated in some unique fashion with the Executive. The framers knew about dangers and emergencies, and they understood the virtues of speed and secrecy. They lived at risk also but drafted a charter that vested in Congress the crucial responsibility for moving the nation from peace to war. Contemporary justifications for presidential dominance must be examined closely to challenge explanations that initially may have superficial allure.

Contemporary Justifications

It is often argued that presidential power must be defined more broadly today than the model formulated by the framers. They agreed that the President could "repel sudden attacks," but advocates of executive power in recent decades want more elbow room than that. The climate after World War II, they say, is far more dangerous and much more in need of decisive presidential action. Promptness, we are told, is a quality of the Executive, not the Legislature.

It is simplistic to claim that the conditions of the modern world make it necessary to vest in the President the crucial decision to go to war. If the current risk to national security is great, so is the risk of presidential miscalculation and aggrandizement—all the more reason for insisting that military decisions be thoroughly examined and approved by Congress. Contemporary presidential judgments need more, not less, scrutiny.

The framers also lived at a dangerous time, possibly more hazardous than today. After granting the President power to repel sudden attacks, they relied for their safety primarily on Congress. In a succession of statutes, Congress authorized the President to respond to emergencies involving Indians, domestic rebellions, the Barbary conflicts, and other national security issues. Presidents acted on statutory, not inherent, authority. As noted in one study:

> Despite glib assertions of the novelty and gravity of the post-Korean war period, the threats confronting the United States during the first quarter century of government under the Constitution imperiled the very independence and survival of the nation. The United States Government fought wars against France and England, the two greatest powers of that period, to protect its existence, preserve the balance of power, and defend its commerce. Notably, both conflicts, the Franco-American War [the Quasi-War of 1798–1800] and the War of 1812, were authorized by statute.[1]

In the years following World War II, there has been more than enough time to seek authorization in advance from Congress before committing the nation to war. Even if one could argue that President Truman needed to take immediate "police action" to respond to North Korea's provocation, he had time after that to ask Congress to authorize extended hostilities. Presidents find time to seek advice from executive officials, often over a period of months, before acting. They even reach out to inform allies of planned attacks. Few uses of unilateral force by the President can be explained by genuine emergencies. Contrived emergencies, perhaps, but not real ones. In the period since World War II, only *one* situation justified presidential action in the absence of congressional authority: President Ford's evacuation of American and foreign nationals from Vietnam.

Does the specter of nuclear war—unknown to the framers—require concentrating in the President the sole responsibility for launching missiles? That is a beguiling, but misleading, proposition. There is a difference between first use of nuclear weapons (any initiation of war requires prior congres-

---

1. David S. Friedman, "Waging War against Checks and Balances—The Claim of an Unlimited Presidential War Power," 57 St. John's L. Rev. 213, 228 (1983).

sional authority) and retaliatory second strikes (a unilateral presidential power pursuant to the executive duty to repel sudden attacks). Policymakers generally assume that nuclear weapons would be used only after a conventional war escalates, over a period of weeks or months, to a nuclear confrontation. Time is available within the executive branch to debate and decide the use of nuclear weapons, permitting adequate opportunity for a congressional role.[2]

If Presidents decide that an emergency requires action without first obtaining approval from Congress, it is far better for them to use military force on suspect authority and come later to Congress to explain what they did, why they acted, and request Congress to provide retroactive authorization. The burden is wholly on the President to make the case. Congress is the only branch that can confer legitimacy on an emergency measure. That is the procedure Lincoln used in the Civil War. It is the proper model for all Presidents. Congress should not attempt to provide advance authority for every type of emergency action. Having been burned on the Tonkin Gulf Resolution, the Senate Foreign Relations Committee concluded in 1969:

> Finally, should the President find himself confronted with a situation of such complexity and ambiguity as to leave him without guidelines for constitutional action, it would be far better for him to take the action he saw fit without attempting to justify it in advance and leave it to Congress or the courts to evaluate his action in retrospect. A single unconstitutional act, later explained or pronounced unconstitutional, is preferable to an act dressed up in some spurious, precedent-setting claim of legitimacy.[3]

The concept of "defensive war" has expanded in recent decades beyond any definition familiar to the framers. During the nineteenth century, defensive war was confined to protective action along the borders of the United States and ships at sea. Notions of defensive war today are far more ambitious. As a result of World War II, American military bases are now dispersed around the globe. By 1966, the legal adviser to the State Depart-

---

2. Peter Raven-Hansen, ed., First Use of Nuclear Weapons: Under the Constitution, Who Decides? (1987); Allan Ides, "Congressional Authority to Regulate the Use of Nuclear Weapons," 13 Hastings Const. L. Q. 233 (1986); Jeremy J. Stone, "Presidential First Use Is Unlawful," 56 Foreign Policy 94 (1984). See also James M. Lindsay, Congress and Nuclear Weapons (1991).

3. S. Rept. No. 129, 91st Cong., 1st Sess. 32 (1969).

ment, Leonard C. Meeker, could offer this open-ended concept of presidential power:

> In 1787 the world was a far larger place, and the framers probably had in mind attacks upon the United States. In the 20th century, the world has grown much smaller. An attack on a country far from our shores can impinge directly on the nation's security. In the SEATO treaty, for example, it is formally declared that an armed attack against Viet-Nam would endanger the peace and safety of the United States.[4]

That statement distorts the significance of SEATO and other mutual security pacts. Each nation, in accordance with its "constitutional processes," decides for itself the appropriate response. Nothing in those pacts defines constitutional processes to mean whatever the President wants to do. The Senate, in agreeing to those treaties, did not abandon its constitutional responsibilities or attempt to deny to the House of Representatives its constitutional role in authorizing war. A shrinking globe is no reason to shrink congressional power or the Constitution.

Defenders of presidential war power point to more than 200 instances in which Presidents have used military force without authorization from Congress. Those actions were minor adventures done in the name of protecting American lives or property, taken at a time when U.S. intervention in neighboring countries was considered routine and proper. Today, such invasions violate international law and regional treaties. The bombardment of Greytown, Nicaragua, in 1854 is not an acceptable "precedent" for the current use of American military power. Nor should we be comfortable citing America's occupation of Haiti from 1915 to 1934 or the repeated interventions in Nicaragua from 1909 to 1933. It is error to speak nonchalantly about "more that 200 precedents," assuming that such numbers, by themselves, justify unilateral military action by the President. We need to examine the specific instances. Are they attractive precedents for the use of force today? None of the 200 incidents comes close to justifying military actions of the magnitude and risk of Korea in 1950, Panama in 1989, Iraq in 1990, Bosnia and Haiti in 1994, or Yugoslavia in 1999.

As another justification for executive power, Presidents have told the American public that mutual defense treaties (like NATO) and resolutions passed by the UN Security Council provide sufficient legal support for pres-

4. 54 Dep't of State Bull. 474, 484 (1966).

idential military actions. There is no basis for those claims. Treaties entered into by the President and the Senate—whether for NATO or the UN Charter—cannot strip from the House of Representatives its constitutional duties over military commitments.

President Bush invaded Panama because he and his advisers concluded that Panama was too weak and isolated to resist American force. His action parallels President Wilson's invasion of Veracruz in 1914. At that time Felix Frankfurter was a young attorney working in the War Department. Enoch H. Crowder, the Judge Advocate General, asked for his advice after the White House requested a memorandum on whether Wilson's action should be treated as an act of war. Frankfurter recalled this conversation:

> General, I'm going to ask to be excused. I don't have to work on that. I know the answer to that.
> You do?
> Yes, I do.
> What is the answer?
> It would be an act of war against a great nation; it isn't against a small nation.
> I can't give him that.
> I know you can't but that's the answer.[5]

Frankfurter's analysis has a cynical edge, but it captures a recurring flavor of U.S. foreign policy. American troops have been used repeatedly against small nations over incidents that would have been considered too minor to justify the use of force against larger powers. Targets of American military power are typically weak and isolated nations, including Cambodia, Libya, Grenada, Panama, Iraq, Haiti, Yugoslavia, and Afghanistan.

Jackson's Zone of Twilight

In his concurring opinion in the Steel Seizure Case in 1952, Justice Jackson identified three scenarios for presidential power. When the President acts pursuant to an express or implied authorization of Congress, his authority "is at its maximum, for it includes all that he possesses in his own right plus all that Congress can delegate." The President's power is "at its lowest ebb" when he takes measures incompatible with the expressed or

---

5. Felix Frankfurter Reminisces 60 (1960).

implied will of Congress, for then he relies only upon his own constitutional powers minus any constitutional powers possessed by Congress.[6]
Jackson's third scenario, in which Congress neither grants nor denies
power, is of special interest:

> When the President acts in absence of either a congressional grant
> or denial of authority, he can rely upon his own independent pow-
> ers, but there is a zone of twilight in which he and Congress may
> have concurrent authority, or in which its distribution is uncertain.
> Therefore, congressional inertia, indifference or quiescence may some-
> times, at least as a practical matter, enable, if not invite, measures on
> independent presidential responsibility. In this area, any actual test of
> power is likely to depend on the imperatives of events and contem-
> porary imponderables rather than on abstract theories of law.[7]

In this same case, Justice Frankfurter also explored the impact of custom and practice on presidential power. Legislative and executive power
were not defined purely on the basis of textual grants. The behavior of
each branch added meaning to constitutional power:

> Deeply embedded traditional ways of conducting government cannot
> supplant the Constitution or legislation, but they give meaning to the
> words of a text or supply them. It is an inadmissibly narrow concep-
> tion of American constitutional law to confine it to the words of the
> Constitution and to disregard the gloss which life has written upon
> them. In short, a systematic, unbroken, executive practice, long pur-
> sued to the knowledge of the Congress and never before questioned,
> engaged in by Presidents who have also sworn to uphold the Con-
> stitution, making as it were such exercise of power part of the struc-
> ture of our government, may be treated as a gloss on "executive
> Power" vested in the President by § 1 of Art. II.[8]

These observations by Jackson and Frankfurter seem innocent enough:
Custom helps shape the Constitution. However, they also give some encouragement to presidential raids of power, done with the knowledge that the
additional power seized will be successful and permanent unless Congress

6. Youngstown Co. v. Sawyer, 343 U.S. 579, 635–37 (1952).
7. Id. at 637.
8. Id. at 610–11.

effectively defends itself. Jackson and Frankfurter provide an incentive for aggression similar to disputes between nations. When one nation expands its territory by violating surrounding borders, the burden is placed on neighboring countries to resist.

To a certain extent, this dynamic describes the U.S. constitutional system. If one branch encroaches, the branch under attack must respond. It must fight back out of a sense of institutional survival. However, in recognizing these struggles as part of the system of checks and balances, legitimacy should not be conferred on illegitimate actions. Illegal and unconstitutional actions, no matter how often repeated, do not build a lawful foundation. If Presidents withdrew funds from the Treasury without an appropriation from Congress, those actions would have no constitutional legitimacy, regardless of the number of infractions. As Gerhard Casper has remarked: "unconstitutional practices cannot become legitimate by the mere lapse of time."[9] Justice Frankfurter noted: "Illegality cannot attain legitimacy through practice."[10] Presidential acts of war can never be accepted as constitutional or as a legal substitute for congressional approval.

Revisiting War Powers

Critics of the War Powers Resolution argue that it has failed to work as planned and trenches upon the constitutional powers of the President. The core principle of the War Powers Resolution is sound. The decision to commit U.S. troops to hostilities should be a matter for "collective judgment" entered into by both branches. Only after Congress authorizes military action, reaching that decision through parliamentary deliberations, may the President as Commander in Chief order troops into combat. That principle was well-grounded in 1787. It remains so today.

Does the War Powers Resolution trench upon presidential authority? No one has identified a military initiative, desired by the President after 1973, that has been canceled or restricted because of this legislation. Where else did Presidents want to intervene? The historical record is silent. Presidents have generally done what they wanted to do, notwithstanding the War Powers Resolution. Their actions have been hurried in some instances (as

9. Gerhard Casper, "Constitutional Constraints on the Conduct of Foreign and Defense Policy: A Nonjudicial Model," 43 U. Chi. L. Rev. 463, 479 (1976).
10. Inland Waterways Corp. v. Young, 309 U.S. 517, 524 (1940).

in Grenada) and restricted in others (El Salvador).[11] If anything, the resolution recognizes too much latitude for presidential war power. An expansive reading implies that the President may use military force unilaterally for up to 60 days—anywhere, anytime, for any reason. The framers would never have allowed that kind of open-ended discretion.

Congressional (and public) control would be greatly strengthened if tied to the power of the purse. Legislation could prohibit the President from obligating or spending any funds to initiate military action unless Congress passes legislation appropriating funds. Such language would give the President some latitude in responding to an emergency, subject to the condition that Congress must provide funds and authority for military conflicts. The burden would be on the President, as it should be, to seek congressional authority.[12]

In 1998, the House added language to the defense appropriation bill, providing that no funds appropriated in that act "may be used to initiate or conduct offensive military operations" by U.S. forces except in accordance with the war powers clause of the Constitution, "which vests in Congress the power to declare and authorize war."[13] That language was tabled in the other chamber because Senators were scrambling to get out of town for the August recess.[14] If legislators want to reclaim constitutional powers that have drifted to the President and restore Congress as a coequal branch, holding hearings on this amendment and subjecting it to full legislative debate would be a constructive step.

As another option, Congress could pass a concurrent resolution disapproving a presidential war, automatically triggering a point of order against any measure that contains funds to perpetuate the conflict. Operating as an internal mechanism (one part of Congress controlling another part), no constitutional objection can be raised that the concurrent resolution is a "legislative veto" prohibited by *INS* v. *Chadha*.[15] The legislative veto applies

11. Ellen C. Collier, "Statutory Constraints: The War Powers Resolution," in Gary M. Stern and Morton H. Halperin, eds., The Constitution and the Power to Go to War 65–66 (1994).

12. Michael J. Glennon, "Strengthening the War Powers Resolution: The Case for Purse-Strings Restrictions," 60 Minn. L. Rev. 1, 32 (1975); Cyrus R. Vance, "Striking the Balance: Congress and the President under the War Powers Resolution," 133 U. Pa. L. Rev. 79, 93–94 (1984); John Hart Ely, War and Responsibility 121 (1993).

13. 144 Cong. Rec. H5247 (daily ed., June 24, 1998).

14. Id. at S9386–92 (daily ed., July 30, 1998).

15. Louis Fisher, "The Legislative Veto: Invalidated, It Survives," 56 Law and Contemp. Prob. 273, 283–84 (1993).

to congressional efforts to control the executive branch, not its own internal proceedings.

Consultation

Presidents regularly promise to brief members of Congress and consult with them about military commitments. Many legislators seem satisfied by these offers. However, "consultation" does not satisfy the Constitution. Congress is a legislative body and discharges its constitutional duties by passing statutes that authorize and define national policy. Congress exists to legislate and legitimate, not to have Presidents and executive officials simply touch base with it.

There may be some merit in creating a congressional consultative group, consisting of perhaps 18 members: Speaker of the House, House Majority Leader, House Minority Leader, President Pro Tempore of the Senate, Senate Majority Leader, Senate Minority Leader, and the chairman and ranking members of six committees: Senate Foreign Relations, House International Relations, the Senate and House Armed Services Committees and the Senate and House Intelligence Committees.[16] This core group could be expanded, depending on the issue, to include other members of Congress who have special expertise and experience. However, consultation is not a *legal substitute* for full congressional action. Congress cannot delegate to a subunit the constitutional decision to go to war. A House bill providing for a consultative group explains that consultations "shall not be construed as a grant of authority from the Congress to the President to conduct such military action."[17]

A Forbidden Legislative Veto?

Some critics of the War Powers Resolution argue that the concurrent resolution is unconstitutional because it is not submitted to the President. In 1975, the legal adviser to the State Department told a House committee that if the President has the power to put men into combat, "that power could not be taken away by concurrent resolution because the power is consti-

16. Joseph R. Biden Jr. and John B. Ritch III, "The War Power at a Constitutional Impasse: A 'Joint Decision' Solution," 77 Geo. L. J. 367, 402–3 (1988).

17. H.R. 3405, 103d Cong., 1st Sess (October 28, 1993), sec. 2.

tutional in nature."[18] The Justice Department reached the same conclusion in 1980.[19] Those positions appeared to be strengthened in 1983 when the Supreme Court, in *INS* v. *Chadha,* struck down the legislative veto as unconstitutional. The Court held that whenever Congress wants to control the executive branch, it must act by both Houses in a bill or joint resolution that is presented to the President for his signature or veto.[20]

During hearings in 1988, the legal adviser to the State Department testified that the concurrent resolution in the War Powers Resolution was "clearly" unconstitutional and should be repealed.[21] In a committee report in 1987, the Senate Foreign Relations Committee also stated that the concurrent resolution in the War Powers Resolution "has been effectively nullified" by *Chadha.*[22]

Replacing the concurrent resolution in the War Powers Resolution with a joint resolution is both unnecessary and undesirable. As used by the Supreme Court in *Chadha,* the term "legislative veto" should be restricted to the following meaning: a condition placed on delegated authority, such as the one-House legislative veto that accompanied the delegation of reorganization power to the President, or the two-House veto attached to rule-making authority for the Federal Trade Commission. The War Powers Resolution does not delegate legislative authority to the President. No legislative veto exists as a condition on that authority. Section 8(d)(2) expressly states that nothing in the War Powers Resolution "shall be construed as granting any authority to the President with respect to the introduction of United States Armed Forces into hostilities or into situations wherein involvement in hostilities is clearly indicated by the circumstances which authority he would not have had in the absence of this joint resolution."

The constitutional disadvantage of acting by joint resolution is profound. If Congress passed a joint resolution ordering the President to withdraw troops and the President exercised his veto, Congress would need a two-thirds majority in each House to override the veto. In other words, the President could continue to prosecute a war he started even if a majority of each House is opposed. He would simply need one-third plus one in a

18. "War Powers: A Test of Compliance," hearings before the House Committee on International Relations, 94th Cong., 1st Sess. 91 (1975).

19. 4A Op.O.L.C. 185, 197 (1980).

20. 462 U.S. 919 (1983).

21. "The War Power after 200 Years," hearings before the Senate Committee on Foreign Relations, 100th Cong., 2d Sess. 1061 (1988).

22. S. Rept. No. 106, 100th Cong., 1st Sess. 6 (1987).

single House to prevent the override. It does violence to the Constitution to place that burden on Congress.

The issue can be more clearly understood by reviewing the specific situation in 1973 when Congress tried to use its power of the purse to end the war in Vietnam. President Nixon vetoed a bill directing that no appropriated funds could be used to support combat activities in Cambodia or Laos. Congress, unable to override the veto, agreed to give Nixon 45 additional days to bomb Cambodia. Rep. Elizabeth Holtzman (D-N.Y.) filed a suit asking a federal court to determine that the President could not engage in combat operations in Southeast Asia without express authorization from Congress. Judge Orrin G. Judd ruled that Congress had not authorized the bombing in Cambodia and that its inability to override the veto could not be interpreted as an affirmative grant of authority. Said Judd: "It cannot be the rule that the President needs a vote of only one-third plus one of either House in order to conduct a war, but this would be the consequence of holding that Congress must override a Presidential veto in order to terminate hostilities which it has not authorized."[23] His order was stayed and eventually reversed because Congress had entered into the compromise with Nixon.[24]

The concurrent resolution remains a useful and appropriate means for expressing congressional policy. If Congress passed such a resolution, the President might well argue that it was legally null and void because of *Chadha.* How would that fare politically? Would a President keep troops in hostilities after a majority in each House told him to bring the soldiers home? A majority vote should suffice, especially to rein in a war initiated by the President. Congress should not have to regain control by securing a two-thirds majority in both Houses.[25]

Even critics of the War Powers Resolution seem to concede that Congress does not need a two-thirds majority in each House to stop a presidential war. After leaving the White House, Gerald R. Ford said that it was the framers' intention that a President "could not initiate a war without the

23. Holtzman v. Schlesinger, 361 F.Supp. 553, 565 (E.D. N.Y. 1973).

24. Holtzman v. Schlesinger, 414 U.S. 1304, 1316, 1321 (1973); Holtzman v. Schlesinger, 484 F.2d 1307 (2d Cir. 1973), cert. denied, 416 U.S. 936 (1974).

25. For those who support the constitutionality of the concurrent resolution in the War Powers Resolution, see Ely, War and Responsibility, at 119–20; G. Sidney Buchanan, "In Defense of the War Powers Resolution: *Chadha* Does Not Apply," 22 Houston L. Rev. 1155 (1985); Vance, "Striking the Balance: Congress and the President under the War Powers Resolution," at 86–87; and Casper, "Constitutional Constraints on the Conduct of Foreign and Defense Policy: A Nonjudicial Model," at 484–85.

approval of both houses of Congress."[26] If a President needs the support
of both Houses in advance, that means that either House can disapprove
and leave the President with no authority. In essence, the framers anticipated a one-House veto over the war power. Robert F. Turner, another crit-
ic of the War Powers Resolution, concludes that the concurrent resolution
is invalid under *Chadha*.[27] Yet Turner also states that the Constitution, as
intended by the framers, gives Congress a one-House veto over presidential wars. One of the checks "incorporated to protect against executive
abuse [is] the power of either house of Congress to veto a decision to initiate a war."[28] That is the correct principle; the requirement of a two-thirds
majority in each House is constitutionally excessive.

In vetoing the War Powers Resolution, President Nixon objected that the
procedure for a 60–90-day limit meant that Congress did not have to vote.
It could control by inaction: "No overt Congressional action would be
required to cut off these powers—they would disappear automatically
unless the Congress extended them. In effect, the Congress is here attempting to increase its policymaking role through a provision which requires it
to take absolutely no action at all."[29] There is nothing unusual or unconstitutional about Congress controlling the President through inaction. If
Congress doesn't want to vote funds or authority for something the President wants, there is no obligation to act. A failure by the President to persuade Congress that the proposal has merit means that it dies. Congress
need not even report the proposal out of committee. Such are the hazards
of the legislative process—perhaps unfortunate for the President but fully
constitutional.

Compelling Court Action

In recent decades, federal courts have consistently refused to reach the
merits in war power cases. Throughout the Vietnam period such cases
were regarded as political questions to be resolved by the elected branches.[30] Federal judges began to offer other reasons to avoid a decision: the

---

26. Foreword to Robert F. Turner, Repealing the War Powers Resolution: Restoring
the Rule of Law in U.S. Foreign Policy vii (1991).
27. Id. at 116–18.
28. Id. at xiv.
29. Public Papers of the Presidents, 1973, at 894.
30. E.g., Luftig v. McNamara, 373 F.2d 664 (D.C. Cir. 1967); Velvel v. Johnson, 287
F.Supp. 846 (D. Kans. 1968); Berk v. Laird, 317 F.Supp. 715 (E.D. N.Y. 1970); Orlando

issue was moot,[31] it was not ripe,[32] plaintiffs lacked standing,[33] a variety of doctrines on judicial prudence and "equitable discretion,"[34] and a finding of nonjusticiability because judicial resolution would require fact-finding better done by Congress.[35]

Several proposals would try to force a judicial decision. One recommendation would authorize any member of Congress to bring an action in federal court for declaratory judgment and injunctive relief on the grounds that the President had violated statutory policy.[36] In such actions, courts "shall not decline to make a determination on the merits based upon the doctrine of political question, remedial discretion, equitable discretion, or any other finding of nonjusticiability, unless such declination is required by Article III of the Constitution."[37] Another variation of the court-forcing idea would give members of Congress standing to go to court whenever the President fails to start the clock by reporting under Section 4(a)(1). Under this proposal, judges could not invoke standing, political question, ripeness, or any other threshold to avoid deciding the matter.[38]

Federal courts have decided many cases involving foreign affairs and the war power. Depending on the circumstances, they can help clarify constitutional issues and monitor the relationships between Congress and the President. But efforts to *compel* judges to decide cases are unwise and unconstitutional. Most of the thresholds used by courts to avoid a decision (standing, mootness, ripeness, and so forth) are derived from the case-or-controversy test in Article III.[39] Judges alone must decide what is a case or controversy. Congress cannot compel them to decide a case, especially when it is not in their institutional interest to act. For any number of sound reasons (including lack of judicial competence), judges may

v. Laird, 443 F.2d 1039 (2d Cir. 1971); Atlee v. Laird, 347 F.Supp. 689 (E.D. Pa. 1972); Gravel v. Laird, 347 F.Supp. 7 (D.D.C. 1972); DaCosta v. Laird, 471 F.2d 1146 (2d Cir. 1973); and Mitchell v. Laird, 488 F.2d 611 (D.D.C. 1973).

31. Conyers v. Reagan, 765 F.2d 1124 (D.C. Cir. 1985).

32. Dellums v. Bush, 752 F.Supp. 1141, 1149–52 (D.D.C. 1990); Ange v. Bush, 752 F.Supp. 509, 515–17 (D.D.C. 1990).

33. Dornan v. U.S. Secretary of Defense, 851 F.2d 450 (D.C. Cir. 1988)

34. Lowry v. Reagan, 676 F.Supp. 333, 337–39 (D.D.C. 1987); Conyers v. Reagan, 578 F.Supp. 324 (D.D.C. 1984).

35. Crockett v. Reagan, 558 F.Supp. 893, 898 (D.D.C. 1982); Sanchez-Espinoza v. Reagan, 568 F.Supp. 596, 600 (D.D.C. 1983).

36. Biden and Ritch, "The War Power at a Constitutional Impasse: A 'Joint Decision' Solution," at 409.

37. Id. at 410.

38. Ely, War and Responsibility, at 60–63, 125, 135.

39. Louis Fisher, American Constitutional Law 75–114 (2003).

properly conclude that disputes over the war power are best left to the elected branches.

As noted by Harold Koh, statutes cannot require federal judges to "surrender their discretion to dismiss those suits in which concerns about separation of powers proved particularly intense, for example, suits brought by constitutionally inappropriate plantiffs."[40] Even for techniques of judicial abstention that supposedly lack an Article III basis, such as prudential consideration and equitable discretion, a judge's decision not to decide is rooted in an institutional judgment that abstention is necessary for the continued independence and health of the courts.

Furthermore, members of Congress (and the President) should not press for a judicial decision without knowing what it will be, and they cannot know that ahead of time. It is standard courtroom practice for attorneys not to ask a question of a witness unless they know that the answer will assist their case. Federal courts have often expanded, not restricted, presidential power. If courts in a particular case decide that the President acted properly in initiating military action without first seeking congressional authority, the cause of Congress (and the Constitution) would be gravely compromised. Lawmakers would now face not one branch, acting on suspect authority, but two branches agreed on the use of force.

The framers' basic theory, guiding us for two centuries, is that "ambition must be made to counteract ambition."[41] Each branch must protect its own territory. Congress cannot go to the courts, hat in hand, asking judges to do what legislators are fully capable of doing: Check the President. Congress should not entrust to the judiciary the duty of protecting legislative prerogatives. As Justice Jackson said in the Steel Seizure Case, "only Congress itself can prevent power from slipping through its fingers."[42] The problem over the past half century is that Congress has failed to protect its institutional powers.[43]

Statutory Restrictions

Instead of relying on unpredictable court decisions, Congress must learn to invoke the powerful weapons at its command. Through its prerogative to

---

40. Harold Hongju Koh, The National Security Constitution: Sharing Power after the Iran-Contra Affair 223 (1990).

41. James Madison, Federalist no. 51, The Federalist 356 (Benjamin Fletcher Wright, ed. 1961).

42. Youngstown Co. v. Sawyer, 343 U.S. at 654.

43. Louis Fisher, Congressional Abdication on War and Spending (2000).

authorize programs and appropriate funds, it can define and limit presidential power. In domestic as well as in foreign affairs, Congress can withhold all or part of an appropriation and may attach riders to appropriations measures to proscribe certain actions.[44]

Some claim that the power of the purse is ineffective in restraining presidential wars. Senator Jacob Javits (R-N.Y.) said that Congress "can hardly cut off appropriations when 500,000 American troops are fighting for their lives, as in Vietnam."[45] The short answer is that Congress can, and has, used the power of the purse to restrict presidential war power. If members of Congress are worried about American troops fighting for their lives in a futile war, those lives are not protected by voting for continued funding. The proper and responsible action is to terminate appropriations and bring the troops home. Members need to make that case to their constituents. It can be done.

The Supreme Court has held that the President as Commander in Chief "is authorized to direct the movements of the naval and military forces placed by law at his command, and to employ them in the manner he may deem most effectual to harass and conquer and subdue the enemy."[46] The power to move forces "placed *by law*" at his command implies that Congress can, by statute, control the scope of the commander-in-chief powers. Many such restrictions have been enacted. Following are some contemporary examples.

In 1973, Congress used the power of the purse to end the war in Vietnam. Three years later it prohibited the CIA from operating in Angola other than to gather intelligence. Legislation also prohibited the Agency from conducting military or paramilitary operations in Angola and denied any appropriated funds to finance directly or indirectly any type of military assistance to Angola.[47]

In 1984, Congress adopted the Boland Amendment to prohibit assistance of any kind by the Reagan administration to support the Contras in Nicaragua. The all-embracing language read: "During fiscal year 1985, no funds available to the Central Intelligence Agency, the Department of

44. Eli E. Nobelman, "Financial Aspects of Congressional Participation in Foreign Relations," 289 The Annals 145 (1953); Louis Fisher, "How Tightly Can Congress Draw the Purse Strings?" 83 Am. J. Int'l L. 758 (1989).

45. Jacob K. Javits, "The War Powers Resolution and the Constitution: A Special Introduction," in The President's War Powers: From the Federalists to Reagan 3 (Demetrios Caraley, ed. 1984).

46. Fleming v. Page, 50 U.S. (9 How.) 602, 614 (1850).

47. 90 Stat. 166 (1976); 90 Stat. 757, sec. 404 (1976); 90 Stat. 776, sec. 109 (1976).

Defense, or any other agency or entity of the United States involved in intelligence activities may be obligated or expended for the purpose or which would have the effect of supporting, directly or indirectly, military or paramilitary operations in Nicaragua by any nation, group, organization, movement, or individual."[48] No constitutional objection to this provision was ever voiced publicly by President Reagan, the White House, the Justice Department, or any other agency of the executive branch.

Two years later, Congress restricted the President's military role in Central America by stipulating that U.S. personnel "may not provide any training or other service, or otherwise participate directly or indirectly in the provision of any assistance, to the Nicaraguan democratic resistance pursuant to this title within those land areas of Honduras and Costa Rica which are within 20 miles of the border with Nicaragua."[49] The statute defined U.S. personnel to mean "any member of the United States Armed Forces who is on active duty or is performing inactive duty training" and any employee of any department, agency, or other component of the executive branch.[50] The clear purpose was to prevent military activities in Honduras and Costa Rica from spilling over into Nicaragua. The Reagan administration never offered any constitutional objections to this statutory restriction.

Also in 1986, Congress passed this prohibition on placing U.S. personnel in Nicaragua: "No member of the United States Armed Forces or employee of any department, agency, or other component of the United States Government may enter Nicaragua to provide military advice, training, or logistical support to paramilitary groups operating inside that country. Nothing in this title shall be construed as authorizing any member or unit of the Armed Forces of the United States to engage in combat against the government of Nicaragua."[51]

In 1991, when Congress authorized President Bush to use military force against Iraq, the authority was explicitly linked to UN Security Council Resolution 678, which was adopted to expel Iraq from Kuwait.[52] Thus, the legislation did not authorize any wider action, such as using U.S. forces to invade and occupy Iraq. In 1993, Congress established a deadline for troops to leave Somalia. No funds could be used for military action after

48. 98 Stat. 1935, sec. 8066(a) (1984).
49. 100 Stat. 3341-307, sec. 216(a) (1986).
50. Id. at sec. 216(b).
51. 100 Stat. 1783-297, sec. 203(e) (1986).
52. 105 Stat. 3 (1991).

March 31, 1994, unless the President requested an extension from Congress and received legislative authority.[53]

Thinking National Interest

It is in the nature of the White House that Presidents will be surrounded by aides who advocate heavy reliance on executive powers and inherent authority, thus eliminating the need to build congressional support. Watergate and the Iran-Contra affair teach us that executive officials have great capacity for self-inflicted injuries. The loyalty of political appointees to the President gives them little stake in the long-term operations of government. Quick to bridle at the frustrations of orderly, constitutional procedures, executive officials are tempted to circumvent laws with interpretations they regard as clever.

Political appointees are often willing to initiate actions that come at great cost to Congress, the President, and the political system. Eager for results and ignorant of constitutional processes, they seek immediate action regardless of long-term damage. By the time the offense is uncovered they are likely to be back in the private sector. Contemptuous of government, they make government contemptible by their conduct. The task of cleaning up the debris is then left to careerists and professionals in Congress and the executive branch. They have done it before and can do it again, but the political system is inevitably poisoned. Afterward there is less good faith, trust, and confidence between the branches—qualities indispensable in a government of divided powers, general grants of constitutional authority, and broadly drawn statutes that demand sound judgment from administrators.

Power has been shifting from career executives to short-term political appointees. The latter are more loyal to the President than to the federal policies that Congress enacts into law, and they have less of a stake in healthy executive-legislative relations. Political appointees "have enough time to make mistakes, but not enough time to learn from them."[54] Increased numbers of political appointees pose serious risks: a layer of inexperienced

53. 107 Stat. 1476, sec. 8151(b)(2)(B) (1993).

54. James P. Pfiffner, "Political Appointees and Career Executives: The Democracy-Bureaucracy Nexus in the Third Century," 47 Pub. Adm. Rev. 57, 63 (1987). See also Patricia W. Ingraham, "Building Bridges or Burning Them? The President, the Appointees, and the Bureaucracy," 47 Pub. Adm. Rev. 425 (1987).

policymakers subject to frequent turnover, the exclusion of many career professionals from agency deliberations, and greater administrative instability and incompetence. The result is that Congress enacts legislation but has less confidence that laws will be carried out faithfully.

In its report released in 1989, the Volcker Commission studied the relationship between political appointees and career executives and recommended that the number of political appointees be reduced by about one-third.[55] Unfortunately, that proposal was not adopted, and the reforms pushed by the Clinton administration, particularly the National Performance Review (the Gore Report on "reinventing government"), will make the ratio worse. Careerists will be reduced by about 252,000 over five years without any decrease in political appointees. Congress later increased the personnel cut to 272,900.

This climate will invite short-term political appointees to augment presidential war power and ignore congressional controls. Democrats who eagerly supported President Clinton as Commander in Chief, pressing those powers to the limit, should have reviewed earlier experiences with that strategy. President Wilson's entry into World War I cost the Democrats control of Congress in the 1918 elections and the loss of the White House in 1920. Truman's war in Korea resulted in the election of Eisenhower, ending 20 years of Democratic control of the White House. Lyndon Johnson's entanglement in Vietnam set the stage for Richard Nixon's victory in 1968. This is not a winning pattern.

Republicans, especially those with monarchical leanings, should also reflect on the costs to their party when presidential war power is unchecked. Dwight Eisenhower understood the need to share the war power with Congress. He served for two full terms. Under Richard Nixon, exaggerated notions of national security and a refusal to recognize congressional prerogatives led to Watergate and Nixon's resignation. The Iran-Contra fiasco discredited the Reagan administration and the Republicans' traditional claim that they can manage the executive branch. President Reagan said he did not know what was being done within his own National Security Council. Even Bush's "popular" actions in Panama in 1989 and Iraq in 1991 yielded no benefits for his reelection effort in 1992. The military triumphs by President George W. Bush in Afghanistan and Iraq have left in their wake new problems of terrorism and long-term financial burdens for the U.S. taxpayer. Activists in both parties need to rethink the merits of presidential wars.

55. Task Force Reports to the National Commission on the Public Service, Leadership in America: Rebuilding the Public Service 158–90 (1989).

For its part, Congress needs to rediscover its institutional and constitutional duties. Legislators must be prepared, and willing, to use the ample powers at their disposal. Too often members make careless remarks that the President "makes foreign policy," is "preeminent" in foreign affairs, and that, as Commander as Chief, he may send troops wherever he likes. During hearings in 1983 on covert operations, the chairman of the House Intelligence Committee, Edward P. Boland, remarked: "We do not meet today to dispute the President's pre-eminence in foreign affairs."[56] Such comments undermine constitutional checks and feed executive arrogance. Even the most cursory glance at the Constitution and American history demonstrates the solid base of congressional responsibilities in foreign policy and the war power.

Much of the imbalance between executive and legislative power lies in the disparate defense measures available to the President and to Congress. Presidents and their assistants are quick to react to congressional initiatives they see as invasive. The Justice Department, the White House, and other centers of the executive branch are ready to challenge and fight off legislative actions. That is as it should be. Congressional leaders, on the other hand, are often at cross-purposes: partly inclined to protect their institution, but just as disposed to defend the President's powers and interests. That is especially so when congressional leaders are of the same party as the President, but this pattern is evident even when the President is from the opposite party. Thus, the executive branch has a defense mechanism that is fairly central and unified, while Congress is decentralized and divided in purpose. This is a major institutional deficiency for Congress, and legislative leaders (as well as the rank and file) need to be sensitive about this imbalance. For all that is written about the "Imperial Congress" with its penchant for "micromanagement," there is too great a temptation on the part of Congress to let down its guard and fail to defend its prerogatives.

The post-Vietnam years offer many constructive lessons on the need for Presidents to reach an accommodation with Congress in foreign policy and national defense. Unilateral executive claims of military power are counterproductive for Congress, the President, and the country. To sustain a successful policy, the executive branch needs the support and cooperation of Congress. After championing executive power for years, in 1975 Secretary of State Henry Kissinger observed:

---

56. "Congressional Oversight of Covert Activities," hearings before the House Permanent Select Committee on Intelligence, 98th Cong., 1st Sess. 1 (1983).

Comity between the executive and legislative branches is the only possible basis for national action. The decade-long struggle in this country over executive dominance in foreign affairs is over. The recognition that the Congress is a coequal branch of government is the dominant fact of national politics today. The executive accepts that the Congress must have both the sense and the reality of participation: foreign policy must be a shared enterprise.[57]

In testimony before the Senate Foreign Relations Committee in 1988, Abraham Sofaer, legal adviser to the State Department, said that the Reagan administration recognized that Congress has "a critical role" to play in determining when the United States commits armed forces to actual or potential hostilities. No presidential policy in this area can have "any hope of success in the long term unless Congress and the American people concur in it and are willing to support its execution."[58] Robert F. Turner, who recognizes a greater latitude for presidential war power than I do, nevertheless appreciates the need for executive-legislative cooperation. In testimony before the House Foreign Affairs Committee in 1988, he expressed this position very eloquently. Although from "a purely constitutional perspective" the President possesses a great deal of independent power in the making and conduct of foreign policy, "in the long run those policies are almost guaranteed to fail if the Congress and the American people do not understand and support them." Regardless of legal analysis, Turner said it is a "political imperative" that Congress and the President cooperate in a spirit of mutual respect and comity.[59]

Members of Congress need to participate in the daily grind of overseeing administration policies, passing judgment on them, and behaving as a coequal, independent branch. When Presidents overstep constitutional barriers or threaten to do so, Congress must respond with solid statutory checks, not floor speeches and "sense of Congress" resolutions. Action by statute is needed to safeguard the legislative institution, maintain a vigorous system of checks and balances, and fulfill the role of Congress as the people's representatives. Members do more than represent districts and states; they represent popular control. Citizens entrust to Congress the safekeeping of

57. 73 Dep't of State Bull. 562 (1975).
58. "The War Power after 200 Years: Congress and the President at a Constitutional Impasse," hearings before the Senate Committee on Foreign Relations, 100th Cong., 2d Sess. 144 (1988).
59. "War Powers: Origins, Purposes, and Applications," hearings before the House Committee on Foreign Affairs, 100th Cong., 2d Sess. 56 (1988).

their powers, especially over matters of war and peace. Legislators act as custodians of the people. If they neglect that function, citizens, scholars, and interest groups must apply constant pressure on Congress to discharge the constitutional duties assigned to it.

Congress may stand against the President or stand behind him, but should not stand aside as it did year after year during the Vietnam War, looking the other way and occasionally complaining about executive usurpation. Members have to participate actively in questions of national policy, challenging Presidents and contesting their actions. Military issues need the thorough exploration and ventilation that only Congress can provide.

In going to war, members of Congress must insist that the President deliver reliable evidence, not assertions, scares, or likelihoods. Both on the Tonkin Gulf Resolution in 1964 and the Iraq Resolution in 2002, Congress let itself be swept along by executive pressures and warnings instead of independently studying the merits of going to war and putting itself in the position of making an informed judgment. Quick action in 1964 and 2002 put Congress—and their constituents—in a subordinate position. The framers valued deliberation because it strengthens the democratic process and lessens the chance of political mistakes. That fundamental value needs to govern today.

In our time, there is a tendency to dismiss what the framers said about the war power, as though contemporary conditions have eclipsed their eighteenth-century models. Yet on the willingness of Presidents to go to war for personal (or partisan) reasons rather than the national interest, the framers gave clear warning of a presidential weakness that has been in full view, particularly since World War II.

Justice Robert H. Jackson, whose entire career with the federal government lay outside the legislative branch, serving first as Attorney General and later as Associate Justice of the Supreme Court, urged us to hold fast to essentials: "With all its defects, delays and inconveniences, men have discovered no technique for long preserving free government except that the Executive be under the law, and that the law be made by parliamentary deliberations."[60]

---

60. Youngstown Co. v. Sawyer, 343 U.S. at 655.

APPENDICES

Appendix A

FRAMERS' DEBATE ON THE WAR POWER
(August 17, 1787; 2 Farrand 318–19)

"To make war"

Mr Pinkney opposed the vesting this power in the Legislature. Its proceedings were too slow. It wd. meet but once a year. The Hs. of Reps. would be too numerous for such deliberations. The Senate would be the best depositary, being more acquainted with foreign affairs, and most capable of proper resolutions. If the States are equally represented in Senate, so as to give no advantage to large States, the power will notwithstanding be safe, as the small have their all at stake in such cases as well as the large States. It would be singular for one authority to make war, and another peace.

Mr Butler. The Objections agst the Legislature lie in a great degree agst the Senate. He was for vesting the power in the President, who will have all the requisite qualities, and will not make war but when the Nation will support it.

Mr. M⟨adison⟩ and Mr Gerry moved to insert "*declare*," striking out "*make*" war; leaving to the Executive the power to repel sudden attacks.

Mr Sharman thought it stood very well. The Executive shd. be able to repel and not to commence war. "Make" better than "declare" the latter narrowing the power too much.

Mr Gerry never expected to hear in a republic a motion to empower the Executive alone to declare war.

Mr. Elseworth. there is a material difference between the cases of making *war,* and making *peace.* It shd. be more easy to get out of war, than into it. War also is a simple and overt declaration. peace attended with intricate & secret negociations.

283

Mr. Mason was agst giving the power of war to the Executive, because not ⟨safely⟩ to be trusted with it; or to the Senate, because not so constructed as to be entitled to it. He was for clogging rather than facilitating war; but for facilitating peace. He preferred "*declare*" to "*make*."

On the Motion to insert *declare*—in place of *Make*, ⟨it was agreed to.⟩

N. H. no. Mas. abst. Cont. no.* Pa ay. Del. ay. Md. ay. Va. ay. N. C. ay. S. C. ay. Geo-ay. [Ayes—7; noes—2; absent—1.]

Mr. Pinkney's motion to strike out the whole clause, disagd. to without call of States.

Mr Butler moved to give the Legislature power of peace, as they were to have that of war.

Mr Gerry 2ds. him. 8 Senators may possibly exercise the power if vested in that body, and 14 if all should be present; and may consequently give up part of the U. States. The Senate are more liable to be corrupted by an Enemy than the whole Legislature.

On the motion for adding "and peace" after "war"

N. H. no. Mas. no. Ct. no. Pa. no. Del. no. Md. no. Va. no. N. C. ⟨no⟩ S. C. no. Geo. no. [Ayes—0; noes—10.]

                              Adjourned

*On the remark by Mr. King that "*make*" war might be understood to "conduct" it which was an Executive function, Mr. Elseworth gave up his objection ⟨and the vote of Cont was changed to—ay.⟩

Appendix B

CONSTITUTIONAL ALLOCATION OF
FOREIGN AFFAIRS AND THE WAR POWER

Legislative

"All legislative Powers herein granted shall be vested in a Congress."

Power to provide for the common defense

To regulate foreign commerce

"To define and punish Piracies and Felonies committed on the high Seas, and Offenses against the Law of Nations."

"To declare War, grant Letters of Marque and Reprisal, and make rules concerning Captures on Land and Water."

Raise and support armies

Provide and maintain a navy

Make rules and regulations of the land and naval forces

"To provide for calling forth the Militia to execute the Laws of the Union, suppress Insurrections, and repel Invasions."

"To provide for organizing, arming, and disciplining, the Militia, and for governing such Part of them as may be employed in the Service of the United States."

"To make all Laws which shall be necessary and proper for carrying into Execution the foregoing Powers and all other Powers vested by this Constitution in the government of the United States, or in any Department or Officer thereof."

Power of the purse ("No money shall be drawn from the Treasury, but in Consequence of Appropriations made by Law.")

Executive

"The executive Power shall be vested in a President."

"The President shall be Commander in Chief of the Army and Navy of the United States, and of the Militia of the several States, when called into the actual Service of the United States."

"[The President] shall receive Ambassadors and other public Ministers."

Shared Powers

"[The President] shall have Power, by and with the Advice and Consent of the Senate, to make Treaties, provided two thirds of the Senators present concur; and he shall nominate, and by and with the Advice and Consent of the Senate, shall appoint Ambassadors, other public Ministers and Consuls, Judges of the supreme Court, and all other Officers of the United States, whose Appointments are not herein otherwise provided for, and which shall be established by Law: but the Congress may by Law vest the Appointment of such inferior Officers, as they think proper, in the President alone, in the Courts of Law, or in the Heads of Departments."

[The Constitution also provides that "The Privilege of the Writ of Habeas Corpus shall not be suspended, unless in Cases of Rebellion or Invasion the public Safety may require it." This provision appears in Article I, defining the powers of Congress, but the writ was suspended by President Lincoln in 1861 while Congress was adjourned. Uncertain of his legal authority, he asked Congress to sanction what he had done. Congress passed legislation retroactively authorizing his action.]

Appendix C

UN PARTICIPATION ACT OF 1945
(59 Stat. 621)

SEC. 6. The President is authorized to negotiate a special agreement or agreements with the Security Council which shall be subject to the approval of the Congress by appropriate Act or joint resolution, providing for the numbers and types of armed forces, their degree of readiness and general location, and the nature of facilities and assistance, including rights of passage, to be made available to the Security Council on its call for the purpose of maintaining international peace and security in accordance with article 43 of said Charter. The President shall not be deemed to require the authorization of the Congress to make available to the Security Council on its call in order to take action under article 42 of said Charter and pursuant to such special agreement or agreements the armed forces, facilities, or assistance provided for therein: *Provided,* That nothing herein contained shall be construed as an authorization to the President by the Congress to make available to the Security Council for such purpose armed forces, facilities, or assistance in addition to the forces, facilities, and assistance provided for in such special agreement or agreements

Appendix D

1949 AMENDMENTS TO UN PARTICIPATION ACT
(63 Stat. 735)

Sec. 5. Such Act is hereby amended by inserting after section 6 the following new section:

"Sec. 7. (a) Notwithstanding the provisions of any other law, the President, upon the request by the United Nations for cooperative action, and to the extent that he finds that it is consistent with the national interest to comply with such request, may authorize, in support of such activities of the United Nations as are specifically directed to the peaceful settlement of disputes and not involving the employment of armed forces contemplated by chapter VII of the United States Charter—

"(1) the detail to the United Nations, under such terms and conditions as the President shall determine, of personnel of the armed forces of the United States to serve as observers, guards, or in any noncombatant capacity, but in no event shall more than a total of one thousand of such personnel be so detailed at any one time: *Provided,* That while so detailed, such personnel shall be considered for all purposes as acting in the line of duty, including the receipt of pay and allowances as personnel of the armed forces of the United States, credit for longevity and retirement, and all other perquisites appertaining to such duty: *Provided further,* That upon authorization or approval by the President, such personnel may accept directly from the United Nations (a) any or all of the allowances or perquisites to which they are entitled under the first proviso hereof, and (b) extraordinary expenses and perquisites incident to such detail;

"(2) the furnishings of facilities, services, or other assistance and the loan of the agreed fair share of the United States of any supplies and equipment to the United Nations by the National Military Establishment, under such terms and conditions as the President shall determine;

"(3) the obligation, insofar as necessary to carry out the purposes of clauses (1) and (2) of this subsection, of any funds appropriated to the National Military Establishment or any department therein, the procurement of such personnel, supplies, equipment, facilities, services, or other assistance as may be made available in accordance with the request of the United Nations, and the replacement of such items, when necessary, where they are furnished from stocks.

"(b) Whenever personnel or assistance is made available pursuant to the authority contained in subsection (a) (1) and (2) of this section, the President shall require reimbursement from the United Nations for the expense thereby incurred by the United States: *Provided,* That in exceptional circumstances, or when the President finds it to be in the national interest, he may waive, in whole or in part, the requirement of such reimbursement: *Provided further,* That when any such reimbursement is made, it shall be credited, at the option of the appropriate department of the National Military Establishment, either to the appropriation, fund, or account utilized in incurring the obligation, or to an appropriate appropriation, fund, or account currently available for the purposes for which expenditures were made.

"(c) In addition to the authorization of appropriations to the Department of State contained in section 8 of this Act, there is hereby authorized to be appropriated to the National Military Establishment, or any department therein, such sums as may be necessary to reimburse such Establishment or department in the event that reimbursement from the United Nations is waived in whole or in part pursuant to authority contained in subsection (b) of this section.

"(d) Nothing in this Act shall authorize the disclosure of any information or knowledge in any case in which such disclosure is prohibited by any other law of the United States."

Appendix E

WAR POWERS RESOLUTION OF 1973
(87 Stat. 555)

JOINT RESOLUTION

Concerning the war powers of Congress and the President.

Resolved by the Senate and House of Representatives of the United States of America in Congress assembled,

Short Title

SECTION 1. This joint resolution may be cited as the "War Powers Resolution."

Purpose and Policy

SEC. 2. (a) It is the purpose of this joint resolution to fulfill the intent of the framers of the Constitution of the United States and insure that the collective judgment of both the Congress and the President will apply to the introduction of United States Armed Forces into hostilities, or into situations where imminent involvement in hostilities is clearly indicated by the circumstances, and to the continued use of such forces in hostilities or in such situations.

(b) Under article I, section 8, of the Constitution, it is specifically provided that the Congress shall have the power to make all laws necessary and proper for carrying into execution, not only its own powers but also all other powers vested by the Constitution in the Government of the United States, or in any department or officer thereof.

(c) The constitutional powers of the President as Commander-in-Chief to introduce United States Armed Forces into hostilities, or into situations where imminent involvement in hostilities is clearly indicated by the circumstances, are exercised only pursuant to (1) a declaration of war, (2) specific statutory authorization, or (3) a national emergency created by attack upon the United States, its territories or possessions, or its armed forces.

Consultation

SEC. 3. The President in every possible instance shall consult with Congress before introducing United States Armed Forces into hostilities or into situations where imminent involvement in hostilities is clearly indicated by the circumstances, and after every such introduction shall consult regularly with the Congress until United States Armed Forces are no longer engaged in hostilities or have been removed from such situations.

Reporting

SEC. 4. (a) In the absence of a declaration of war, in any case in which United States Armed Forces are introduced—

(1) into hostilities or into situations where imminent involvement in hostilities is clearly indicated by the circumstances;

(2) into the territory, airspace or waters of a foreign nation, while equipped for combat, except for deployments which relate solely to supply, replacement, repair, or training of such forces; or

(3) in numbers which substantially enlarge United States Armed Forces equipped for combat already located in a foreign nation;
the President shall submit within 48 hours to the Speaker of the House of Representatives and to the President pro tempore of the Senate a report, in writing, setting forth —

(A) the circumstances necessitating the introduction of United States Armed Forces;

(B) the constitutional and legislative authority under which such introduction took place; and

(C) the estimated scope and duration of the hostilities or involvement.

(b) The President shall provide such other information as the Congress may request in the fulfillment of its constitutional responsibilities with respect to committing the Nation to war and to the use of United States Armed Forces abroad.

(c) Whenever United States Armed Forces are introduced into hostilities or into any situation described in subsection (a) of this section, the President shall, so long as such armed forces continue to be engaged in such hostilities or situation, report to the Congress periodically on the status of such hostilities or situations as well as on the scope and duration of such hostilities or situation, but in no event shall he report to the Congress less often than once every six months.

Congressional Action

SEC. 5. (a) Each report submitted pursuant to section 4(a)(1) shall be transmitted to the Speaker of the House of Representatives and to the President pro tempore of the Senate on the same calendar day. . . .

(b) Within sixty calendar days after a report is submitted or is required to be submitted pursuant to section 4(a)(1), whichever is earlier, the President shall terminate any use of United States Armed Forces with respect to which such report was submitted (or required to be submitted), unless the Congress (1) has declared war or has enacted a specific authorization for such use of United States Armed Forces, (2) has extended by law such sixty-day period, or (3) is physically unable to meet as a result of an armed attack upon the United States. Such sixty-day period shall be extended for not more than an additional thirty days if the President determines and certifies to the Congress in writing that unavoidable military necessity respecting the safety of United States Armed Forces requires the continued use of such armed forces in the course of bringing about a prompt removal of such forces.

(c) Notwithstanding subsection (b), at any time that United States Armed Forces are engaged in hostilities outside the territory of the United States, its possessions and territories without a declaration of war or specific statutory authorization, such forces shall be removed by the President if the Congress so directs by concurrent resolution.

Congressional Priority Procedures for Joint Resolution or Bill

SEC. 6. [Provides for expedited consideration of a joint resolution or bill introduced pursuant to Section 5(b). Deadlines are established for committee and floor action, unless the House or Senate determines otherwise by yeas and nays. The objective is to complete action not later than the expiration of the 60-day period.]

Congressional Priority Procedures for
Concurrent Resolution

SEC. 7. [Provides for expedited consideration of a concurrent resolution introduced pursuant to Section 5(c). Deadlines are established for committee and floor action, unless the House or Senate determines otherwise by yeas and nays. The objective is to complete action within 48 days.]

Interpretation of Joint Resolution

SEC. 8. (a) Authority to introduce United States Armed Forces into hostilities or into situations wherein involvement in hostilities is clearly indicated by the circumstances shall not be inferred—

(1) from any provision of law (whether or not in effect before the date of the enactment of this joint resolution), including any provision contained in an appropriation Act, unless such provision specifically authorizes the introduction of United States Armed Forces into hostilities or into such situations and states that it is intended to constitute specific statutory authorization within the meaning of this joint resolution; or

(2) from any treaty heretofore or hereafter ratified unless such treaty is implemented by legislation specifically authorizing the introduction of United States Armed Forces into hostilities or into such situations and stating that it is intended to constitute specific statutory authorization within the meaning of this joint resolution.

(b) Nothing in this joint resolution shall be construed to require any further specific statutory authorization to permit members of United States Armed Forces to participate jointly with members of the armed forces of one or more foreign countries in the headquarters operations of high-level military commands which were established prior to the date of enactment of this joint resolution and pursuant to the United Nations Charter or any treaty ratified by the United States prior to such date.

(c) For purposes of this joint resolution, the term "introduction of United States Armed Forces" includes the assignment of members of such armed forces to command, coordinate, participate in the movement of, or accompany the regular or irregular military forces of any foreign country or government when such military forces are engaged, or there exists an imminent threat that such forces will become engaged, in hostilities.

(d) Nothing in this joint resolution—

(1) is intended to alter the constitutional authority of the Congress or of the President, or the provisions of existing treaties; or

(2) shall be construed as granting any authority to the President with respect to the introduction of United States Armed Forces into hostilities or into situations wherein involvement in hostilities is clearly indicated by the circumstances which authority he would not have had in the absence of this joint resolution.

Separability Clause

Sec. 9. If any provision of this joint resolution or the application thereof to any person or circumstance is held invalid, the remainder of the joint resolution and the application of such provision to any other person or circumstance shall not be affected thereby.

Effective Date

Sec. 10. This joint resolution shall take effect on the date of its enactment.

SUGGESTED READINGS

Constitutional Framework

Adler, David Gray. "The Constitution and Presidential Warmaking: The Enduring Debate," 103 Political Science Quarterly 1 (1988).

Adler, David Gray, and Larry N. George, eds. The Constitution and the Conduct of American Foreign Policy (1996).

Banks, William C., and Peter Raven-Hansen. National Security Law and the Power of the Purse (1994).

Berdahl, Clarence A. War Powers of the Executive in the United States (1921).

Caraley, Demetrios, ed. The President's War Powers (1984).

Corwin, Edward S. Total War and the Constitution (1947).

Fisher, Louis. "Historical Survey of the War Powers and the Use of Force." In Gary M. Stern and Morton H. Halperin, eds., The U.S. Constitution and the Power to Go to War 11–28 (1994).

Franck, Thomas M., ed. The Tethered Presidency: Congressional Restraints on Executive Power (1981).

Henkin, Louis. Constitutionalism, Democracy, and Foreign Affairs (1990).

———. Foreign Affairs and the United States Constitution (1996).

Javits, Jacob K. Who Makes War: The President Versus Congress (1973).

Levy, Leonard W. Original Intent and the Framers' Constitution 30–53 (1988).

Lofgren, Charles A. "War-Making under the Constitution: The Original Understanding," 81 Yale Law Journal 672 (1972).

Moore, John N. "The National Executive and the Use of Armed Forces Abroad," 21 Naval War College Review 28 (1969).

Muskie, Edmund S., Kenneth Rush, and Kenneth W. Thompson, eds. The President, the Congress, and Foreign Policy (1986).

Note. "Congress, the President, and the Power to Commit Forces to Combat," 81 Harvard Law Review 1771 (1968).

Powell, H. Jefferson. The President's Authority over Foreign Affairs: An Essay in Constitutional Interpretation (2002).

Pusey, Merlo J. The Way We Go to War (1969).

Reveley, W. Taylor III. War Powers of the President and Congress: Who Holds the Arrows and Olive Branch? (1981).

Sheffer, Martin S. The Judicial Development of Presidential War Powers (1999).

Shuman, Howard E., and Walter R. Thomas, eds. The Constitution and National Security (1990).

Silverstein, Gordon. Imbalance of Powers: Constitutional Interpretation and the Making of American Foreign Policy (1997).

Sofaer, Abraham D. War, Foreign Affairs, and Constitutional Power: The Origins (1976).

Stern, Gary M., and Morton H. Halperin, eds. The U.S. Constitution and the Power to Go to War: Historical and Current Perspectives (1994).

Thomas, Ann Van Wynen, and A. J. Thomas Jr. The War-Making Powers of the Pres-
    ident: Constitutional and International Law Aspects (1982).
Treanor, William Michael. "Fame, the Founding, and the Power to Declare War," 82
    Cornell Law Review 695 (1997).
Uyeda, Mark T. "Presidential Prerogative under the Constitution to Deploy U.S.
    Military Forces in Low-Intensity Conflict," 44 Duke Law Journal 777 (1995).
Westerfield, Donald L. War Powers: The President, the Congress, and the Question
    of War (1996).
Wormuth, Francis P., and Edwin B. Firmage. To Chain the Dog of War: The War
    Powers of Congress in History and Law (1986).
Yoo, John C. "Clio at War: The Misuse of History in the War Powers Debate," 70
    University of Colorado Law Review 1169 (1999).
———. "The Continuation of Politics by Other Means: The Original Understanding
    of War Powers," 84 California Law Review 167 (1996).

Declared and Undeclared Wars

Baldwin, Simeon E. "The Share of the President of the United States in a Declara-
    tion of War," 12 American Journal of International Law 1 (1918).
Benjamin, James. "Rhetoric and the Performance of Declaring War," 21 Presidential
    Studies Quarterly 73 (1991).
Blechman, Barry M., and Stephen S. Kaplan. Force without War: U.S. Armed Forces
    as a Political Instrument (1978).
Eagleton, Clyde. "The Form and Function of the Declaration of War," 32 American
    Journal of International Law 19 (1938).
Emerson, J. Terry. "Making War without a Declaration," 17 Journal of Legislation 23
    (1990).
Fehlings, Lt. Col. Gregory E. "America's First Limited War [the Quasi-War with
    France]," 53 Naval War College Review 102 (2000).
Fenwick, C. G. "War without a Declaration," 31 American Journal of International
    Law 694 (1937).
Hallett, Brien. The Lost Art of Declaring War (1998).
Keynes, Edward. Undeclared War: Twilight Zone of Constitutional Power (1982).
Leckie, Robert. The Wars of America (1968).
Maurice, J. F. Hostilities without Declaration of War: From 1700 to 1870 (1883).
Patch, Buel W. "The Power to Declare War," Editorial Research Reports, vol. 1, no.
    1, 1938, pp. 3–18.
Ronan, William J. "English and American Courts and the Definition of War," 31
    American Journal of International Law 642 (1937).
Sidak, J. Gregory. "To Declare War," 41 Duke Law Journal 27 (1991).
Tiefer, Charles. "War Decisions in the Late 1900s by Partial Congressional Declara-
    tion," 36 San Diego Law Review 1 (1999).
Velvel, Lawrence R. Undeclared War and Civil Disobedience: The American System
    in Crisis (1970).

Power of Commander in Chief

Carter, Clarence E. "The Office of Commander in Chief: A Phase of Imperial Unity
    on the Eve of the Revolution." In Richard B. Morris, ed., The Era of the American
    Revolution (1971).

Dawson, Joseph G., ed. Commanders in Chief: Presidential Leadership in Modern Wars (1993).

DeConde, Alexander. Presidential Machismo: Executive Authority, Military Intervention, and Foreign Relations (2000).

Deutsch, Eberhard P. "The President as Commander in Chief," 57 American Bar Association Journal 27 (1971).

Fairman, Charles. "The President as Commander-in-Chief," 11 Journal of Politics 145 (1949).

Fisher, Louis. "The Power of Commander in Chief." In Marcia Lynn Whicker et al., eds., The Presidency and the Persian Gulf War, 45–61 (1993).

Hassler, Warren W., Jr. The President as Commander in Chief (1971).

Heller, Francis H. "The President as the Commander in Chief," 42 Military Review 5 (1962).

Hess, Gary R. Presidential Decisions for War: Korea, Vietnam, and the Persian Gulf (2001).

Hollander, Bennet N. "The President and Congress—Operational Control of the Armed Forces," 27 Military Law Review 49 (1965).

Hoxie, R. Gordon. Command Decision and the Presidency: A Study in National Security and Organization (1977).

———. "The Office of Commander in Chief: An Historical and Projective View," 6 Presidential Studies Quarterly 10 (1976).

Huchthausen, Peter. America's Splendid Little Wars: A Short History of U.S. Military Engagements; 1975–2000 (2003).

May, Ernest R., ed. The Ultimate Decision: The President as Commander in Chief (1960).

Raven-Hansen, Peter, and William C. Banks. "Pulling the Purse Strings of the Commander in Chief," 80 Virginia Law Review 833 (1994).

Rossiter, Clinton. The Supreme Court and the Commander in Chief (1951).

Timbers, Edwin. "The Supreme Court and the President as Commander in Chief," 16 Presidential Studies Quarterly 224 (1986).

U.S. Congress. The Powers of the President as Commander in Chief of the Army and Navy of the United States, H. Doc. No. 443, 84th Cong., 2d Sess. (1956).

Warren, Sidney. The President as World Leader (1965).

Early Precedents (1789–1900)

Anderson, William G. "John Adams, the Navy, and the Quasi-War with France," 30 The American Neptune 117 (1970).

Baldwin, Leland D. Whiskey Rebels: The Story of a Frontier Uprising (1939).

Boot, Max. The Savage Wars of Peace: Small Wars and the Rise of American Power (2002).

Casper, Gerhard. "An Essay in Separation of Powers: Some Early Versions and Practices," 30 William and Mary Law Review 211 (1989). [Analyzes the Washington administration's handling of the Algiers problem.]

Coles, Harry L. The War of 1812 (1965).

DeConde, Alexander. "The Quasi-War." 12 American History Illustrated 4 (1977).

———. The Quasi-War: The Politics and Diplomacy of the Undeclared War with France, 1797–1801 (1966).

Dupuy, R. Ernest, and William H. Baumer. The Little Wars of the United States (1968).

Eisenhower, John. "President Polk's War," 2 Constitution 26 (1990).

Hickey, Donald R. The War of 1812 (1989).

Lynn, Brian McAllister. The Philippine War, 1899–1902 (2000).

Marshall, C. Kevin. "Putting Privateers in Their Places: The Applicability of the Marque and Reprisal Clauses to Undeclared Wars," 64 University of Chicago Law Review 953 (1997).

McClellan, Major Edwin N. "The Naval War with France," 7 The Marine Corps Gazette 339 (1922).

Mahon, John K. The War of 1812 (1972).

Millis, Walter. The Martial Spirit: A Study of Our War with Spain (1931).

Morgan, H. Wayne. William McKinley and His America (1963).

Pomeroy, William. American Neo-Colonialism: Its Emergence in the Philippines and Asia (1970).

Schroeder, John H. Mr. Polk's War: American Opposition and Dissent, 1846–1848 (1973).

Singletary, Otis A. The Mexican War (1960).

Slaughter, Thomas P. The Whiskey Rebellion: Frontier Epilogue to the American Revolution (1986).

Sofaer, Abraham D. "The Presidency, War, and Foreign Affairs: Practice under the Framers," 40 Law and Contemporary Problems 12 (1976).

———. War, Foreign Affairs, and Constitutional Power: The Origins (1976). [Focuses on the 1789–1829 period.]

Stagg, J. C. A. Mr. Madison's War: Politics, Diplomacy, and Warfare in the Early American Republic, 1783–1830 (1983).

Sword, Wiley. President Washington's Indian War: The Struggle for the Old Northwest, 1790–1795 (1985).

Tap, Bruce. Over Lincoln's Shoulder: The Committee on the Conduct of the War (1998).

Trask, David F. The War with Spain in 1898 (1981).

Ward, Townsend. "The Insurrections of the Year 1794, in the Western Counties of Pennsylvania," 6 Pennsylvania Historical Society Memoirs 117 (1858).

Welch, Richard E., Jr. Response to Imperialism: The United States and the Philippine-American War, 1899–1902 (1979).

Whiting, William. War Powers under the Constitution of the United States (1864).

Williams, T. Harry. Lincoln the Commander in Chief, Historical Bulletin no. 15 (Lincoln Fellowship of Wisconsin, 1957).

Precedents from 1900 to 1945

Calder, Bruce J. The Impact of Intervention: The Dominican Republic during the U.S. Occupation of 1916–1924 (1984).

Cleveland, Sarah H. "The Plenary Power Background of Curtiss-Wright," 70 University of Colorado Law Review 1127 (1999).

Cox, Isaac Joslin. Nicaragua and the United States, 1909–1927. World Peace Foundation Pamphlets, vol. 10, no. 7 (1927).

Denny, Harold Norman. Dollars for Bullets: The Story of American Rule in Nicaragua (1929).

DeWeerd, Harvey A. President Wilson Fights His War: World War I and the American Intervention (1968).

Dupuy, R. Ernest, and William H. Baumer. The Little Wars of the United States (1968).
Eisenhower, John S. D. Intervention! The United States and the Mexican Revolution, 1913–1917 (1993).
Garcia, Rogelio. Opposition within the Senate to the American Military Intervention in Nicaragua, 1926–1933. Ph.D. diss., Columbia University, 1973.
Koenig, Louis William. The Presidency and the Crisis: Powers of the Office from the Invasion of Poland to Pearl Harbor (1944).
Langer, William L., and S. Everett Gleason. The Challenge to Isolation: The World Crisis of 1937–1940 and American Foreign Policy (1952).
———. The Undeclared War, 1940–1941 (1953).
Larrabee, Eric. Commander in Chief: Franklin Delano Roosevelt, His Lieutenants, and Their War (1987).
Martin, Charles E. The Policy of the United States as Regards Intervention. Ph.D. diss., Columbia University, 1921.
May, Christopher N. In the Name of War: Judicial Review and the War Powers since 1918 (1989).
Munro, Dana G. Intervention and Dollar Diplomacy in the Caribbean, 1900–1921 (1964).
Offutt, Milton. The Protection of Citizens Abroad by the Armed Forces of the United States. Johns Hopkins University Studies in Historical and Political Science, ser. 46, no. 4 (1928).
Quirk, Robert E. An Affair of Honor: Woodrow Wilson and the Occupation of Veracruz (1962).
Rogers, James Grafton. World Policing and the Constitution (1945).
Schmidt, Hans. The United States Occupation of Haiti, 1915–1934 (1971).
Stuart, Graham H. Latin America and the United States (1943).
Tansill, Charles Callan. America Goes to War (1938).
———. Back Door to War: The Roosevelt Foreign Policy, 1933–1941 (1952),
Williams, William Appleman. "American Intervention in Russia: 1917–1920." In David Horowitz, ed., Containment and Revolution (1968).
Wood, Bryce. The Making of the Good Neighbor Policy (1961).

The UN Charter and Korea

"Authority of the President to Repel the Attack in Korea," 23 Department of State Bulletin 173 (July 31, 1950).
Caridi, Ronald, Jr. The Korean War and American Politics: The Republican Party as a Case Study (1968).
Devins, Neal, and Louis Fisher. "The Steel Seizure Case: One of a Kind?" 19 Constitutional Commentary 63 (2002).
Fehrenbach, T. R. This Kind of War (1963).
Fisher, Louis. "The Korean War: On What Legal Basis Did Truman Act?" 89 American Journal of International Law 21 (1995).
———. "Sidestepping Congress: Presidents Acting under the UN and NATO," 47 Case Western Reserve Law Review 1237 (1997).
George, Alexander L. "American Policy-making and the North Korean Aggression," 7 World Politics 209 (1955).
Gross, Leo. "The Charter of the United Nations and the Lodge Reservations," 41 American Journal of International Law 531 (1947).

Haynes, Richard F. The Awesome Power: Harry S. Truman as Commander in Chief (1973).

Hoopes, Townsend, and Douglas Brinkley. FDR and the Creation of the U.N. (1997).

Hoyt, Edwin C. "The United States Reaction to the Korean Attack: A Study of the Principles of the United Nations Charter as a Factor in American Policy-Making," 55 American Journal of International Law 45 (1961).

Kaufman, Burton I. The Korean War: Challenges in Crisis, Credibility, and Command (2d ed. 1997).

Kirkendall, Richard S. Harry S Truman, Korea and the Imperial Presidency (1975).

Lofgren, Charles A. "Mr. Truman's War: A Debate and Its Aftermath," 33 Review of Politics 223 (1969).

May, Ernest R. "Korea, 1950: History Overpowering Calculation." In "Lessons" of the Past: The Use and Misuse of History in American Foreign Policy 52–86 (1973).

Paige, Glenn D. The Korean Decision (1968).

Pollack, Samuel. "Self Doubts on Approaching Forty: The United Nations' Oldest and Only Collective Security Enforcement Army, The United Nations Command in Korea," 6 Dickinson Journal of International Law 1 (1987).

Pye, A. Kenneth. "The Legal Status of the Korea Hostilities," 45 Georgetown Law Journal 45 (1956).

Schick, F. B. "Videant Consules," 3 Western Political Quarterly 311 (1950).

Spanier, John W. The Truman-MacArthur Controversy and the Korea War (1965).

Turner, Robert F. "Truman, Korea, and the Constitution: Debunking the 'Imperial President' Myth," 19 Harvard Journal of Law and Public Policy 533 (1996).

Watkins, Arthur W. "War by Executive Order," 4 Western Political Quarterly 539 (1951).

Wright, Quincy. "Collective Security in the Light of the Korean Experience," In Proceedings of the American Society of International Law, April 26–28, 1951, at 165–182.

Taking Stock (1951–1964)

Abel, Elie. The Missiles of October: The Story of the Cuban Missile Crisis (1969).

Allison, Graham T. Essence of Decision: Explaining the Cuban Missile Crisis (1971).

Banks, Robert F. "Steel, Sawyer, and the Executive Power," 14 University of Pittsburgh Law Review 467 (1953).

Briggs, Philip J. "Congress and the Cold War: U.S.–China Policy 1955," 85 China Quarterly 80 (1981).

———. "Congress and the Middle East: The Eisenhower Doctrine, 1956." In Joann P. Krieg, ed., Dwight D. Eisenhower: Soldier, President, Statesman (1987).

Central Intelligence Agency. The Secret Cuban Missile Crisis Documents (1994).

Corwin, Edward S. "The Steel Seizure Case: A Judicial Brick without Straw," 53 Columbia Law Review 53 (1953).

Glennon, Michael J. "United States Mutual Security Treaties: The Commitment Myth," 24 Columbia Journal of International Law 509 (1986).

Grimmett, Richard F. The Politics of Constraint: The President, the Senate, and American Foreign Policy, 1947–1956. Ph.D. diss., Kent State University, 1973.

Heindel, Richard H. et al. "The North Atlantic Treaty in the United States Senate," 43 American Journal of International Law 633 (1949).

Kauper, Paul G. "The Steel Seizure Case: Congress, the President and the Supreme Court," 51 Michigan Law Review 141 (1952).

Kennedy, Robert F. Thirteen Days: A Memoir of the Cuban Missile Crisis (1969).

Marcus, Maeva. Truman and the Steel Seizure Case: The Limits of Presidential Power (1977; reissued in 1994).

Reichard, Gary W. "Divisions and Dissent: Democrats and Foreign Policy, 1952–1956," 93 Political Science Quarterly 51 (1978).

Richberg, Donald R. "The Steel Seizure Cases," 38 Virginia Law Review 713 (1952).

Schubert, Glendon A., Jr. "The Steel Case: Presidential Responsibility and Judicial Irresponsibility," 6 Western Political Quarterly 61 (1953).

Tanenhaus, Joseph. "The Supreme Court and Presidential Power," 307 The Annals 106 (1956).

Thompson, Robert Smith. The Missiles of October: The Declassified Story of John F. Kennedy and the Cuban Missile Crisis (1992).

Westin, Alan F. The Anatomy of a Constitutional Law Case [The Steel Seizure Case] (1958).

Williams, Phil. The Senate and US Troops in Europe (1985).

The Vietnam War

Anderson, David L., ed. Shadow on the White House: Presidents and the Vietnam War, 1945–1975 (1993).

Austin, Anthony. The President's War: The Story of the Tonkin Gulf Resolution and How the Nation Was Trapped in Vietnam (1971).

Barrett, David M. Uncertain Warriors: Lyndon Johnson and His Vietnam Advisers (1993).

Berman, Larry. Lyndon Johnson's War: The Road to Stalemate in Vietnam (1989).

———. Planning a Tragedy: The Americanization of the War in Vietnam (1982).

Beschloss, Michael. Taking Charge: The Johnson White House Tapes, 1963–64 (1997).

Burke, John P., and Fred I. Greenstein. How Presidents Test Reality: Decisions on Vietnam, 1954 and 1965 (1989).

D'Amato, Anthony A., and Robert M. O'Neil. The Judiciary and Vietnam (1972).

Eagleton, Thomas F. "The August 15 Compromise and the War Powers of Congress," 18 Saint Louis University Law Journal 1 (1973).

Fisher, Louis. "Congress Sleeps: War Powers after Vietnam," 5 The Long-Term View 118 (2000).

Friedman, Leon, and Burt Neuborne. Unquestioning Obedience to the President: The ACLU Case against the Legality of the War in Vietnam (1972).

Gibbons, William Conrad. The U.S. Government and the Vietnam War: Executive and Legislative Roles and Relationships (3 vols., 1986, 1989).

Goulden, Joseph C. Truth Is the First Casualty: The Gulf of Tonkin Affairs—Illusion and Reality (1969).

Graff, Henry F. The Tuesday Cabinet: Deliberation and Decision on Peace and War under Lyndon B. Johnson (1970).

Henkin, Louis, "Viet-Nam in the Courts of the United States: 'Political Questions,'" 63 American Journal of International Law 284 (1969).

Herring, George C. America's Longest War: The United States and Vietnam, 1950–1975 (3d ed. 1996).

Kaiser, David. American Tragedy: Kennedy, Johnson, and the Origins of the Vietnam War (2000).

Karnow, Stanley. Vietnam: A History (1991).

Kimball, Jeffrey P. To Reason Why: The Debate about the Causes of U.S. Involvement in the Vietnam War (1990).

Malawer. "The Vietnam War under the Constitution: Legal Issues Involved in the United States Military Involvement in Vietnam," 31 University of Pittsburgh Law Review 205 (1969).

Moïse, Edwin E. Tonkin Gulf and the Escalation of the Vietnam War (1996).

Newman, John M. JFK and Vietnam: Deception, Intrigue, and the Struggle for Power (1992).

Robertson, David W. "The Debate among American International Lawyers about the Vietnam War," 46 Texas Law Review 898 (1968).

Schandler, Herbert Y. The Unmaking of a President: Lyndon Johnson and Vietnam (1977).

Schwartz, Warren F., and Wayne McCormack. "The Justiciability of Legal Objections to the American Military Effort in Vietnam," 46 Texas Law Review 1033 (1968).

Siff, Ezra Y. Why the Senate Slept: The Gulf of Tonkin Resolution and the Beginning of America's Vietnam War (1999).

Velvel, Lawrence R. "The War in Viet Nam: Unconstitutional, Justiciable, and Jurisdictionally Attackable," 16 Kansas Law Review 449 (1968).

Wormuth, Francis D. "The Nixon Theory of the War Power: A Critique," 60 California Law Review 623 (1972).

The War Powers Resolution of 1973

Allison, Graham T. "Making War: The President and Congress," 40 Law and Contemporary Problems 86 (1976).

Auerswald, David P., and Peter F. Cowhey. "Ballotbox Diplomacy: The War Powers Resolution and the Use of Force," 41 International Studies Quarterly 505 (1997).

Berger, Raoul. "War-Making by the President," 121 University of Pennsylvania Law Review 29 (1972).

Boylan, Timothy S., and Glenn A. Phelps. "The War Powers Resolution; A Rationale for Congressional Inaction," 31 Parameters 109 (2001).

Clark, Robert D., Andrew M. Egeland Jr., and David B. Sanford. The War Powers Resolution (1985).

Collier, Ellen C. "Statutory Constraints: The War Powers Resolution." In Gary M. Stern and Morton H. Halperin, eds., The U.S. Constitution and the Power to Go to War 55–82 (1994).

Eagleton, Thomas F. War and Presidential Power: A Chronicle of Congressional Surrender (1974).

Fisher, Louis. "War Powers: The Need for Collective Judgment." In James A. Thurber, ed., Divided Democracy 199–217 (1990).

Fisher, Louis, and David Gray Adler. "The War Powers Resolution: Time to Say Goodbye," 113 Political Science Quarterly 1 (1998).

Ford, Christopher A. "War Powers as We Live Them: Congressional-Executive

Bargaining under the Shadow of the War Powers Resolution," 11 Journal of Law and Politics 609 (1995).

Franck, Thomas M. "After the Fall: The New Procedural Framework for Congressional Control over the War Power," 71 American Journal of International Law 605 (1977).

Gartzke, Erik. "Congress and Back Seat Driving: An Information Theory of the War Powers Resolution," 24 Policy Studies Journal 259 (1996).

Glennon, Michael J. "Too Far Apart: Repeal the War Powers Resolution," 50 University of Miami Law Review 17 (1995).

———. "The War Powers Resolution Ten Years Later: More Politics Than Law," 78 American Journal of International Law 571 (1984).

Ratner, Leonard G. "The Coordinated Warmaking Power: Legislative, Executive, and Judicial Tools," 44 Southern California Law Review 461 (1971).

Robbins, Patrick D. "The War Powers Resolution after Fifteen Years: A Reassessment," 38 American University Law Review 141 (1988).

Rostow, Eugene V. "Great Cases Make Bad Law: The War Powers Act," 50 Texas Law Review 833 (1972).

———. "'Once More unto the Breach': The War Powers Resolution Revisited," 21 Valparaiso University Law Review 1 (1986).

Rushkoff, Bennett C. "A Defense of the War Powers Resolution," 93 Yale Law Journal 1330 (1984).

Schlesinger, Arthur M., Jr. The Imperial Presidency (1973).

Spong, William B., Jr. "The War Powers Resolution Revisited: Historic Accomplishment or Surrender?" 16 William and Mary Law Review 823 (1975).

Turner, Robert F. Repealing the War Powers Resolution: Restoring the Rule of Law in U.S. Foreign Policy (1991).

Zablocki, Clement J. "War Powers Resolution: Its Past Record and Future Promise," 17 Loyola of Los Angeles Law Review 579 (1984).

Military Initiatives from Ford to Carter

Brzezinski, Zbigniew. "The Failed Mission: The Inside Account of the Attempt to Free the Hostages in Iran," New York Times Magazine, April 18, 1982, at 28–31, 61–62, 64, 69–70, 72, 78–79.

Carlile, Donald E. "The Mayaguez Incident: Crisis Management," 56 Military Review 3 (1976).

D'Angelo, John R. "Resort to Force by States to Protect Nationals: The U.S. Rescue Mission to Iran and Its Legality under International Law," 21 Virginia Journal of International Law 485 (1981).

Ford, Gerald R. "Congress, the Presidency, and National Security Policy," 16 Presidential Studies Quarterly 200 (1986).

Jeffery, Anthea. "The American Hostages in Tehran: The I.C.J. and the Legality of Rescue Missions," 30 International and Comparative Law Quarterly 717 (1981).

Kelley, Michael F. "The Constitutional Implications of the Mayaguez Incident," 3 Hastings Constitutional Law Quarterly 301 (1976).

Lamb, Chris. "Belief Systems and Decision Making in the Mayaguez Crisis," 99 Political Science Quarterly 681 (1984–1985).

Paust, Jordan J. "More Revelations about Mayaguez (and Its Secret Cargo)," 4 Boston College International and Comparative Law Review 61 (1981).

————. "The Seizure and Recovery of the *Mayaguez*," 85 Yale Law Journal 774 (1976).

Rowan, Roy. The Four Days of *Mayaguez* (1975).

Ryan, Paul B. The Iranian Rescue Mission: Why It Failed (1985).

Smith, Steve. "Policy Preferences and Bureaucratic Position: The Case of the American Hostage Rescue Mission," 61 International Affairs 9 (1984).

Stein, Ted L. "Contempt, Crisis, and the Court: The World Court and the Hostage Rescue Attempt," 76 American Journal of International Law 499 (1982).

U.S. Congress. "Seizure of the Mayaguez," hearings before the House Committee on International Relations, 94th Cong., 1st Sess. (1975).

Zutz, Robert. "The Recapture of the S.S. Mayaguez: Failure of the Consultation Clause of the War Powers Resolution," 8 New York University Journal of International Law and Politics 457 (1976).

Military Initiatives by Reagan

Beck, Robert J. "International Law and the Decision to Invade Grenada: A Ten-Year Retrospective," 33 Virginia Journal of International Law 765 (1993).

Blum, Zehuda Z. "The Gulf of Sidra Incident," 80 American Journal of International Law 668 (1986).

Bostdorff, Denise. "The Presidency and Promoted Crisis: Reagan, Grenada, and Issue Management," 21 Presidential Studies Quarterly 737 (1991).

Congressional Digest. "The War Powers Act and the Persian Gulf: Pro and Con" (December 1987).

Davis, Brian L. Quaddafi, Terrorism, and the Origins of the U.S. Attack on Libya (1990).

Haerr, Roger Cooling. "The Gulf of Sidra," 24 San Diego Law Review 751 (1987).

Kaldor, Mary, and Paul Anderson, eds. Mad Dogs: The US Raids on Libya (1986).

Rubner, Michael. "Antiterrorism and the Withering of the 1973 War Powers Resolution," 102 Political Science Quarterly 193 (1987).

————. "The Reagan Administration, the 1973 War Powers Resolution, and the Invasion of Grenada," 100 Political Science Quarterly 627 (1985–1986).

Torricelli, Robert G. "The War Powers Resolution after the Libya Crisis," 7 Pace Law Review 661 (1987).

Turndorf, David. "The U.S. Raid on Libya: A Forceful Response to Terrorism," 14 Brooklyn Journal of International Law 187 (1988).

U.S. Congress. "War Powers, Libya, and State-Sponsored Terrorism." Hearings before the House Committee on Foreign Affairs, 99th Cong., 2d Sess. (1986).

George H. W. Bush

Berger, Matthew D. "Implementing a United Nations Security Council Resolution: The President's Power to Use Force without the Authorization of Congress," 15 Hastings International and Comparative Law Review 83 (1991).

Bogus, Carl T. "The Invasion of Panama and the Rule of Law," 26 International Lawyer 781 (1992).

Burgin, Eileen. "Congress, the War Powers Resolution, and the Invasion of Panama," 25 Polity 217 (1992).

Bush, George, and Brent Scowcroft. A World Transformed (1998).

Cole, Ronald H. Operation Just Cause: The Planning and Execution of Joint Operations in Panama, February 1988–January 1990 (1995).

D'Amato, Anthony. "The Invasion of Panama Was a Lawful Response to Tyranny," 84 American Journal of International Law 516 (1990).

Donnelly, Thomas, Margaret Roth, and Caleb Baker. Operation Just Cause: The Storming of Panama (1991).

Farer, Tom J. "Panama: Beyond the Charter Paridigm," 84 American Journal of International Law 503 (1990).

Freedman, Lawrence, and Efraim Karsh. The Gulf Conflict, 1990–1991: Diplomacy and War in the New World Order (1993).

Friedman, Alan. Spider's Web: The Secret History of How the White House Illegally Armed Iraq (1993).

Gilboa, Eytan. "The Panama Invasion Revisited: Lessons for the Use of Force in the Post–Cold War Era," 110 Political Science Quarterly 539 (1995–96).

Glennon, Michael J. "The Gulf War and the Constitution," 70 Foreign Affairs 84 (1991).

Gordon, Michael R., and Gen. Bernard E. Trainer. The Generals' War: The Inside Story of the Conflict in the Gulf (1995)

Henkin, Louis. "The Invasion of Panama under International Law: A Gross Violation," 29 Columbia Journal of Transnational Law 293 (1991).

Lewis, David A., and Roger P. Rose. "The President, the Press, and the War-Making Power: An Analysis of Media Coverage Prior to the Persian Gulf War," 32 Presidential Studies Quarterly 559 (2002).

Maechling, Charles, Jr. "Washington's Illegal Invasion [Panama]," 79 Foreign Policy 113 (1990).

Nanda, Ved P. "The Validity of United States Intervention in Panama under International Law," 84 American Journal of International Law 494 (1990).

Quigley, John. "The Legality of the United States Invasion of Panama," 15 Yale Journal of International Law 276 (1990).

Schachter, Oscar. "United Nations Law in the Gulf Conflict," 85 American Journal of International Law 452 (1991).

Sifry, Michael L., and Christopher Cerf, eds. The Gulf War Reader: History, Documents, Opinions (1991).

Smith, Jean Edward. George Bush's War (1992).

Sofaer, Abraham D. "The Legality of the United States Action in Panama," 29 Columbia Journal of Transnational Law 281 (1991).

Swan, George Steven. "Presidential Undeclared Warmaking and Functionalist Theory: Dellums v. Bush and Operations Desert Shield and Desert Storm," 22 California Western International Law Journal 75 (1991).

Taw, Jennifer Morrison. Operation Just Cause: Lessons for Operations Other Than War (1996).

Tiefer, Charles. The Semi-Sovereign Presidency: The Bush Administration's Strategy for Governing without Congress (1994).

Watson, Bruce W., and Peter G. Tsouras, eds. Operation Just Cause: The U.S. Intervention in Panama (1991).

Whicker, Marcia Lynn, James P. Pfiffner, and Raymond A. Moore, eds. The Presidency and the Persian Gulf War (1993).

White, N. D., and H. McCoubrey. "International Law and the Use of Force in the Gulf," 10 International Relations 347 (1991).

Woodward, Bob. The Commanders [1991 Gulf War] (1991).

Bill Clinton

Adler, David Gray. "The Clinton Theory of the War Power," 30 Presidential Studies Quarterly 155 (2000).

Banks, William C., and Jeffrey D. Straussman, "A New Imperial Presidency? Insights from U.S. Involvement in Bosnia," 114 Political Science Quarterly 203 (1999).

Biddle, Stephen. "The New Way of War [Kosovo]?" 81 Foreign Affairs 138 (2002).

Bolton, John R. "Wrong Turn in Somalia," 73 Foreign Affairs 56 (1994).

Burk, James. "Public Support for Peacekeeping in Lebanon and Somalia: Assessing the Casualties Hypothesis," 114 Political Science Quarterly 53 (1999).

Daadler, Ivo H., and Michael E. O'Hanlon. "Unlearning the Lessons of Kosovo," 116 Foreign Policy 128 (1999).

Damrosch, Lori Fisler. "Agora: The 1994 U.S. Action in Haiti," 89 American Journal of International Law 58 (1995).

Egan, Patrick T. "The Kosovo Intervention and Collective Self-Defense," 8 International Peacekeeping 39 (2001).

Fisher, Louis. "The Bosnia Commitment: Binding the United States by Unilateral Executive Action," Legal Times, March 11, 1996, at 22–23.

———. "Litigating the War Power with Campbell v. Clinton," 30 Presidential Studies Quarterly 564 (2000).

———. "Military Action against Iraq," 28 Presidential Studies Quarterly 793 (1998).

———. "President Clinton as Commander in Chief," in James A. Thurber, ed., Rivals for Power: Presidential-Congressional Relations (1996).

Henrickson, Ryan C. "Clinton's Legal Dominion: War Powers in the Second Term," 5 National Security Studies Quarterly 49 (1999).

———. The Clinton Wars: The Constitution, Congress, and War Powers (2002).

———. "War Powers, Bosnia, and the 104th Congress," 113 Political Science Quarterly 241 (1998).

Lobel, Jules. "The Use of Force to Respond to Terrorist Attacks: The Bombing of Sudan and Afghanistan," 24 Yale Journal of International Law 537 (1999).

Lobel, Jules, and Michael Ratner. "U.S. Has No Legal Right to Bomb Iraq," Legal Times, February 16, 1998, at 25.

McCoubrey, Hilaire. "Kosovo, NATO, and International Law," 14 International Relations 29 (1999).

Mermin, Jonathan. "Television News and American Intervention in Somalia: The Myth of a Media-Driven Foreign Policy," 112 Political Science Quarterly 385 (1997).

Stevenson, Charles A. "The Evolving Clinton Doctrine on the Use of Force," 22 Armed Forces and Society 511 (1996).

"Was Intervening in Haiti a Mistake?" (articles by Robert I. Rotberg, "Clinton Was Right," and John Sweeney, "Stuck in Haiti"), 102 Foreign Policy 134–51 (1996).

Wedgwood, Ruth. "Reponding to Terrorism: The Strikes against bin Laden," 24 Yale Journal of International Law 559 (1999).

Yoo, John C. "The Dogs That Didn't Bark: Why Were International Legal Scholars MIA on Kosovo?" 1 Chicago Journal of International Law 149 (2000).

———. "Kosovo, War Powers, and the Multilateral Future," 148 University of Pennsylvania Law Review 1673 (2000).

George W. Bush

Ackerman, Spencer, and John B. Judis. "The First Casualty: The Selling of the Iraq War," The New Republic, June 30, 2003, at 14.
Bearden, Milton. "Afghanistan, Graveyard of Empires," 80 Foreign Affairs 2 (2001).
Fisher, Louis. "Deciding on War against Iraq: Institutional Failures," 118 Political Science Quarterly 389 (2003).
———. Nazi Saboteurs on Trial: A Military Tribunal and American Law (2003).
———. "The Road to Iraq: Does President Bush Have the Constitutional Authority to Commit the Country to War?" Legal Times, September 2, 2002, at 34–35.
Hanlon, Michael E. "A Flawed Masterpiece [Afghanistan]," 81 Foreign Affairs 47 (2002).
Hurrell, Andrew. "'There Are No Rules' (George W. Bush): International Order after September 11," 16 International Relations 185 (2002).
Record, Jeffrey. "The Bush Doctrine and War with Iraq," 33 Parameters 4 (2003).
Woodward, Bob. Bush at War [Afghanistan] (2002).

Covert Operations and the Iran-Contra Affair

Adler, Emanuel. "Executive Command and Control in Foreign Policy: The CIA's Covert Activities," 23 Orbis 671 (1979).
Ambrose, Stephen E. Ike's Spies: Eisenhower and the Espionage Establishment (1981).
Draper, Theodore. A Very Thin Line: The Iran-Contra Affairs (1991).
Fisher, Louis. "Congressional Access to Executive Branch Information: Lessons from the Iran-Contra Affair," 6 Government Information Quarterly 383 (1989).
———. "The Foundations of a Scandal [Iran-Contra]," 3 Corruption and Reform 157 (1988).
Gumina, Paul. "Title VI of the Intelligence Authorization Act, Fiscal Year 1991: Effective Covert Action Reform or 'Business as Usual?'" 20 Hastings Constitutional Law Quarterly 149 (1992).
Henriksen, Thomas H. "Covert Operations, Now More Than Ever," 44 Orbis 145 (2000).
Highsmith, Newell L. "Policing Executive Adventurism: Congressional Oversight of Military and Paramilitary Operations," 19 Harvard Journal on Legislation 327 (1982).
Immerman, Richard H. The CIA in Guatemala (1982).
Jeffrey-Jones, Rhodri. The CIA and American Democracy (1989).
Johnson, Loch. America's Secret Power: The CIA in a Democratic Society (1989).
Lobel, Jules. "Covert War and Congressional Authority: Hidden War and Forgotten Power," 134 University of Pennsylvania Law Review 1035 (1986).
Prados, John. President's Secret Wars: CIA and Pentagon Covert Operations since World War II (1986).
Reisman, W. Michael, and James Baker. Regulating Covert Action (1992).
Richman, Peter. "For the Want of a Nail . . . the War Was Lost: Separation of Powers and United States Counter-Terrorism Policy during the Reagan Years," 17 Hastings Constitutional Law Quarterly 609 (1990).
Silverberg, Marshall. "The Separation of Powers and Control of the CIA's Covert Operations," 68 Texas Law Review 575 (1990).

Steele, Douglas L. "Covert Action and the War Powers Resolution: Preserving the Constitutional Balance," 39 Syracuse Law Review 1139 (1988).

Stockwell, John. In Search of Enemies: A CIA Story [Angola] (1978).

Treverton, Gregory F. Covert Action: The Limits of Intervention (1987).

U.S. Court of Appeals for the District of Columbia Circuit. Final Report of the Independent Counsel for Iran/Contra Matters (3 vols. 1993).

Van Cleve, George W. "The Constitutionality of the Solicitation or Control of Third-Country Funds for Foreign Policy Purposes by United States Officials without Congressional Approval," 11 Houston Journal of International Law 69 (1988).

Whiting, Alex. "Controlling Tin Cup Diplomacy," 99 Yale Law Journal 2043 (1990).

Wyden, Peter. Bay of Pigs (1979).

Restoring Checks and Balances

Biden, Joseph R., Jr., and John B. Ritch III. "The War Power at a Constitutional Impasse: A 'Joint Decision' Solution," 77 Georgetown Law Journal 367 (1988).

Boylan, Timothy S. "War Powers, Constitutional Balance, and the *Imperial Presidency* Idea at Century's End," 29 Presidential Studies Quarterly 232 (1999).

Brands, H.W., ed. The Use of Force after the Cold War (2000).

Buchanan, G. Sidney. "In Defense of the War Powers Resolution: *Chadha* Does Not Apply," 22 Houston Law Review 1155 (1985).

Divine, Robert A. Perpetual War for Perpetual Peace (2000).

Edgar, Charles Ernest. "United States Use of Armed Force under the United Nations . . . Who's In Charge?" 10 Journal of Law and Politics 299 (1984).

Ely, John Hart. "Suppose Congress Wanted a War Powers Act That Worked," 88 Columbia Law Review 1379 (1988).

———. War and Responsibility: Constitutional Lessons of Vietnam and Its Aftermath (1993).

Fisher, Louis. Congressional Abdication on War and Spending (2000).

———. "Congressional Checks on Military Initiatives," 109 Political Science Quarterly 739 (1994–95).

———. "How Tightly Can Congress Draw the Purse Strings?" 83 American Journal of International Law 758 (1989).

———. "Presidential Independence and the Power of the Purse," 3 U.C. Davis Journal of International Law and Policy 107 (1997).

———. "Unchecked Presidential Wars," 148 University of Pennsylvania Law Review 1637 (2000).

———. "The War Power: No Checks, No Balance." In Colton C. Campbell, Nicol C. Rae, and John F. Stack Jr., eds., Congress and the Politics of Foreign Policy (2003).

Friedman, David S. "Waging War against Checks and Balances—The Claim of an Unlimited Presidential War Power," 57 St. John's Law Review 213 (1983).

Glennon, Michael J. Constitutional Diplomacy (1990).

———. "Strengthening the War Powers Resolution: The Case for Purse-Strings Restrictions," 60 Minnesota Law Review 1 (1975).

Glennon, Michael J., and Allison R. Hayward. "Collective Security and the Constitution: Can the Commander-in-Chief Power Be Delegated to the United Nations?" 82 Georgetown Law Journal 1573 (1994).

Halperin, Morton H. "Lawful Wars," 72 Foreign Policy 173 (1988).

Hamilton, Lee H., with Jordan Tama. A Creative Tension: The Foreign Policy Roles of the President and Congress (2002).

Katzmann, Robert A. "War Powers: Toward a New Accommodation." In Thomas E. Mann, ed., A Question of Balance: The President, the Congress, and Foreign Policy (1990).

Kelly, Major Michael P. "Fixing the War Powers," 141 Military Law Review 83 (1993).

Koh, Harold Hongju. The National Security Constitution: Sharing Power after the Iran-Contra Affair (1990).

May, Christopher N. In the Name of War: Judicial Review and the War Powers since 1918 (1989).

Nathan, James A. "Revising the War Powers Act," 17 Armed Forces and Society 513 (1991).

———. "Salvaging the War Powers Resolution," 23 Presidential Studies Quarterly 235 (1993).

Note. "Applying Chadha: The Fate of the War Powers Resolution," 24 Santa Clara Law Review 697 (1984).

Prober, Joshua Lee. "Congress, the War Powers Resolution, and the Secret Political Life of 'a Dead Letter,'" 7 Journal of Law and Politics 177 (1990).

Raven-Hansen, Peter, and William C. Banks. "Pulling the Purse Strings of the Commander in Chief," 80 Virginia Law Review 833 (1994).

Rosner, Jeremy D. The New Tug-of-War: Congress, the Executive Branch, and National Security (1995).

Smyrl, Marc E. Conflict or Codetermination? Congress, the President, and the Power to Make War (1988).

Stromseth, Jane E. "Rethinking War Powers: Congress, the President, and the United Nations," 81 Georgetown Law Journal (1993).

"The President's Powers as Commander-in-Chief Versus Congress' War Power and Appropriations Power," 43 University of Miami Law Review 17 (1988). [Observations by Charles Bennett, Arthur B. Culvahouse Jr., Geoffrey P. Miller, William Bradford Reynolds, and William Van Alstyne.]

Vance, Cyrus R. "Striking the Balance: Congress and the President under the War Powers Resolution," 133 University of Pennsylvania Law Review 79 (1984).

Weissman, Stephen R. A Culture of Deference: Congress's Failure of Leadership in Foreign Policy (1995).

INDEX OF CASES

SUBJECT INDEX

313